Contents

Contents

2005

COACH OF THE YEAR CLINICS
FOOTBALL MANUAL

Edited by Earl Browning

www.coacheschoice.com

ISBN: 1-58518-932-4

Library of Congress Control Number: 2005924201

Telecoach, Inc. Transcription: Kent Browning, Tom Cheaney, Bill Gierke, Larry Kindbom

Diagrams: Steve Haag

Book layout and cover design: Bean Creek Studio

Front and back cover photos of Urban Meyer: Courtesy of the University of Utah

Back cover photo of Vince Dooley: Courtesy of the University of Georgia Sports Information Department

Special thanks to the Nike clinic managers for having the lectures taped.

Coaches Choice
P.O. Box 1828
Monterey, CA 93942
www.coacheschoice.com

Mickey Andrews

...RVIEW OF THE 4-3 DEFENSE

Florida State University

...een in this area. ...Fort Lauderdale ...ama Canal. We have never been there and I am sure we will have a good time together. It is good to be here. It is encouraging to see so many coaches here tonight. I have seen times when we went to the clinics and on Saturday night, not many coaches show up. A lot of them are out on a hunting trip or doing something. It is encouraging to see those here tonight that want to learn something about football.

We are going to give you an overview of what we are doing defensively. I will cover our base defense. At the end, each member of our defensive staff will give a brief rundown of what is going on at the positions they work with. After that, we will break up into groups and go from there.

I listened to Rich Rodriquez' lecture. I have found it is a lot easier to sit in the audience and listen to his lecture on offense than it is to line up and play against them.

I am sure you have noticed I am using a cane to walk with. I had to have my hip worked on again. I just got off crutches yesterday. That was the first day I used a cane. It is hard to learn how to handle the cane. It makes you feel old. It reminds me of story of an old couple.

This old man, about 80 years old was sitting around watching TV with his wife. A commercial came on and the old man turned up the sound on the TV. After a few minutes after the old man jumped up and got dressed. As he was putting on his coat his wife asked, "Where are you going?" He said, "I am going to the doctor." She asked, "Are you sick?" He said, "No, I am going to get me some of those Viagra pills."

With that, the old woman jumped up and started putting on her coat. The husband asked her, "Where are you going?" She replied, "I am going to the doctor." The husband asked her, "Are you sick?" She said, "No! But if you are going to use that ole rusty tool of yours, I am going to go get me a tetanus shot."

We are very fortunate at Florida State to have a great staff. I want to introduce the staff members that will visit with you later.

- Kevin Steel - Linebackers
- Odell Haggins - Defensive Tackles
- Jody Allen - Defensive Ends

We have been very blessed since Coach Bobby Bowden has been at Florida State. In the last 21 years our record is 221 wins, 44 losses, and 4 ties. This record compares very favorably with any other program in the USA. One of the reasons is because we play great offense at Florida State. In addition, in this spell we have learned to play good defense.

The thing we have tried to do over the years is to get our people in position to make the play. We have had some outstanding linemen, and some good linebackers come through our teams. Our defensive backs have been very special as well. Many of our players have had an opportunity to play pro football. At the time, we have a bunch of young players that have a lot of potential. We must replace six starters on defense this year.

One thing that helps us is the fact we play a lot of people on defense. The reason we do that is because we want to be coaching next year's team this year. We make an effort to get those second team players in the game. When they go out on the field, they are not second team players anymore.

They are part of the first team because they are first team players to be. We tell our players our job is to get them on the field. It is up to the players as to how long they will stay on the field. It is always good to have players that have been in the battle and know what it takes to win when the game is on the line. We had a good recruiting year and we hope we have some of them that will be able to contribute to our team soon.

Through the years, I have been intrigued with acronyms. I cannot spell it, but I know what it is. I was working on this lecture the other day and came up with an idea I want to share with you.

Back several years ago on Mother's Day, we would take the letters and tell everyone what each letter stood for. For example, M is for the "Many" things your mother gave you. I decided to do the same thing with the word defense.

These words are important if you are going to play defense.

- D = Determination
- E = Effort
- F = Fundamentals
- E = Enthusiasm
- N = Naughty or Nasty
- S = Swarm to the ball
- E = Efficient

You can use many different words for the acronym of determination. What we are saying is this: if you are looking for players that have an abundant, desire to excel, they will not compromise. They are determined to get the job done. You may hear the word called persistent and there are several different words for it.

I will assure you if you play football at Florida State, you are going to give a good effort. We do not have loafers. The players that loaf in practice do not play on Saturday. I am sure all of you feel the same as we do on this issue. When we recruit, we are looking for players that give effort. The main thing the players must understand when they get to

Florida State is the intensity factor. I do not care how hard they learned to work in high school; it is not good enough. The reason I say that because they have never played against as many quality people as they will face during the week and on Saturday. If we are going to play at a championship level, we must have a great effort.

When I talk about fundamentals, I am talking about attacking blockers, whipping blockers, and getting to the football. I am talking about tackling. We want to be able to punish blockers, receivers, and ballcarriers. There is a bit of toughness involved with the game.

At times, people accuse us of being a little too enthusiastic. I can recall when Deion Sanders was playing for us. I love Deion as if he was my own son, and I will tell you why. I have never seen a player that enjoyed playing the game anymore than Deion. When he came to us, he was not a great player. Nevertheless, he had a great desire to become a great player. I have never had a player work any harder than he did.

Deion went on to play pro football. He was a decent baseball player in high school and college. He made himself into a great baseball player. I think a big part of the reason he was successful was because of his enthusiasm. He could get some of our players excited with all of his jumping around. Back then, I could jump, too. I was jumping about as high as he was. The thing about that is the fact they did not throw any flags on the sideline.

Coach Bowden has a way of saying the "nasty" aspect we are looking for. He tells the players, "I want you mean but clean." Our defense may say it a little different from that, but it means the same thing. I do not think you can play too tough. I do know this. The tougher you are, the better chance you have to become a dominating player if you are a disciplined player. We are going to encourage toughness. We want "mean but clean" players. We have never taught our players to play dirty. We do not teach our players to hit late and we never will teach that type of football.

We want our defense to "swarm" to the ball. When you snap that ball, we make a concentrated effort to "swarm" to the football. We tell our players that is our trademark. "Swarm to the football." We do not want only one player hitting the ballcarrier; we want eleven players to put their hats on the ballcarrier. You can see in our films that we have had as many as ten players in the pile on a tackle. I do not know why we have not had eleven players on the tackle, but that is what we want. We are going to swarm the ball and we are going to pursue the ball and get there together.

We do not care how good you are talent-wise, build-wise, how fast or how strong you are, if you cannot execute you cannot play for us. I really believe if we can get our players to adhere to those principles in the defense acronym, we will be a good defensive team again next year.

If we can reach that level with our players, we will get what we are looking for. We are trying to push our players to the point where we become a dominating defense. Our goal each year is to have the best defense in the state of Florida. If we can do that, we are a good defensive team. In addition, we want to be the best defense in the ACC. Our last goal is to be the best defense in the nation. Those are lofty goals. Our standards are set high. One thing we found out is this. If we set our standards high, we have to raise the bar with the way we work and how we prepare.

We just finished our off-season program. We still have a long way to go to become a good defensive team. However, we have some young players that can be a factor for us on defense. They are a lot better now than they were before they went through our off-season program. They know how to work now and they know how to finish a drill. When we come back to start spring practice, we will start coaching football.

In our off-season program, we have six stations that we work on. We rate the players from four to zero. A zero means they come back at 5:00 AM and go through the program again and then they have to repeat the workout again at 5:45 AM with the rest of the team. We are giving them an opportunity to make up for what they did not do. When we go through a double session, it gets into the players head. It makes the heart beat a little faster and it makes the feet move faster. It makes them want to bend the knees better. This is what you want from the beginning.

We always emphasize, "Stop the run first." This is where we start our defense. When you play a schedule like we do against Miami, Florida, and the other ACC teams, you better be able to stop the run because if you cannot stop the run you cannot stay on the field with those teams.

Our defensive front is a 4-3 look. That is our basic defense. We are primarily a man-to-man team. We do mix it up with the zone and other combinations. It does matter what scheme you use, if the players do not believe in it, and they do not work hard enough to get good at the defense, it is not going to help you. You cannot "wish" the defense to be good. When you emphasize stopping the run, you are going to get toughness. You cannot stop the run and not have toughness.

I want to go over our base 4-3 defense and then I will let the defensive staff talk about the positions they coach.

We play our defensive end a little wider than most other 4-3 teams (Diagram #1). We angle the ends inside and play what we call a "round" technique. We take the ends and attack the line of scrimmage. We are a gap-control team. We are a tight-end eagle team. Basically, we are playing a 2 technique. That may change by splits and by ability of the center or guard, and by our linemen. We are controlling the B gap with our tackle and the A gap with our nose guard.

If we get a down block by the inside linemen, we are going to try to spill and bounce it one hole wider. We want to use gap exchange.

Our Sam linebacker is in man coverage. The Mike linebacker has the first back to the strongside. The Will linebacker has the first back to the weakside or the split end side. Our corners are in man coverage on the outside receivers. Against any type of motion or against an over set our run support does not change. We simply carry our corners over with the motion.

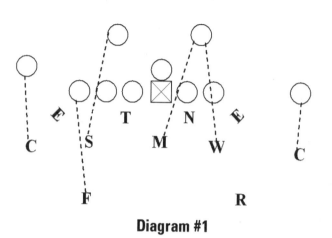

Diagram #1

Our free safety and our rover are involved in a roll-down on run support to give us an eight-man look. If we are going to attack the line of scrimmage, we must have help from one of them. You must have an extra man when you have to cover that many gaps. When the offense runs the isolation or lead play, you have an extra gap to cover. You must have an outside gap player and an inside gap player.

On the base defense, we try to roll our rover down to help with the run. We hold him as late as we can, and the free safety is the deep-hole player.

We tell our corners they do not have any help until they bring their man to an inside position on any "shallow cross route," or other type of route inside.

We tell our rover to fill the B gap when run shows to his side. If it is a pass play, he becomes the hole player. He is going to help on the inside shallow route and on an intermediate cut. The free safety helps on the bubble.

The hard part of the defense is the play of the corners. The other tough position to play is the Mike linebacker. He must be able to play the run and he has to be able to play the tight end. Again, the corners are not going to have any help until they push the receiver inside.

If we get a full flow toward the tight end and the tight end blocks outside, our Sam plays outside the

fullback, and Mike plays inside the fullback (Diagram #2). The Will linebacker has the offside A gap, and the rover has the B gap.

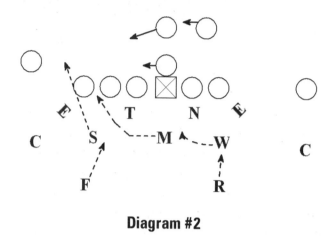

Diagram #2

The way people try to block us is with their outside receivers coming down inside on us. The thing about playing this defense is this. You had better have some corners that can run and players that can cover the wide receivers. They had better be able to tackle as well. Teams will crack on the rover and force the corner to make the tackle. We have to spend a lot of time with our corners trying to toughen them up and make them make "face" tackles. If they cannot do that, they cannot play for us.

I am not saying when we line up in that 4-3 defense we are going to play man-to-man coverage all of the time. You cannot stay on one track all of the time. Teams will take advantage of the defense if they know how you are going to play them every down. We use different stunts and different blitzes and other defensive moves to try to confuse the blocker, disrupt the timing, and then force the offense to make a mistake in their execution. If we can do that, we can generate some big plays for the defense. I will talk more about the secondary when we get into our special groups.

At this time, I want to let you hear from the position coaches. They will cover the defensive positions they coach.

John Banaszak

DEFENSIVE LINE ONE-GAP TECHNIQUES

Robert Morris University

First, I want to thank Nike for inviting me here to speak to you today. In addition, I want to thank Pete Dimperio, II, Earl Ceh, and the rest of the advisory board. My topic is "One Gap Techniques." This is an exciting subject, right? I have to talk over one hour on the 1 technique. Here is the secret: "Close on the down block and never get hooked!" Thank you! Do we have any questions?

I want to thank some other people before I get into the lecture. I want to thank Robert Morris University and head coach Joe Walton for giving me the opportunity to coach the defensive line. I also want to thank Dan Radakovich. I want to thank our other staff members for being here today. I have been a thrill for me to coach for Robert Morris University.

The first thing I talk about when I am working with the defensive linemen is expectations. I tell them this every single day. We must be better with every technique we use. I like to break things down to basics. That is how I learned to play the position. I had to do that. I had to be a technician. I was too slow, too small, and not quick enough to play the defensive line positions. I had to make sure my hand placement was where it had to be and I had to take the proper steps at the right times. I had to do that to play against the big, 280-pound offensive linemen.

I learned a great deal from George Perles. He taught me the things that have stayed with me as a football coach. I am tough, demanding, and I am intent. That is what I expect out of my players on every single rep of the football. They must improve everyday. When I walk off the football field, if I am not a better coach than I was when I walked on the field, then I did not have a good day. My players must feel the same way as I do in this regard. They have to

be better football players when they walk off that field.

I have one rule and one rule only about practice. Practice is not punishment. Practice is preparation. I have to prepare the kids for every game they play. The only way I can be sure of that is to make sure we practice hard. I will never punish a player or team on the field. That is not the place for punishment. It is for preparation. I learned this a long time ago.

I was fortunate to play with the greatest defense that ever played the game of football. I played with the greatest defensive line that ever played the game of football. From those experiences, and from the coaching staff, it is the foundation of what I believe in today. My coaching philosophy is very simple: I want to prepare the football team for every challenge it faces and I will work as hard as I can to make sure that happens. I work with as much enthusiasm as possible, because that is how I played the game. That is the way I coach the game. I coach to win the game.

There is no doubt in my mind that one of the reasons I am here today is because of my experiences and because I have won. That is irreplaceable. You learn as you go along. Again, I like to break things down to the basics. I do not want to get too technical because then I get lost. If I get lost then my players are going to get lost. I learned a great deal from George Perles. I can remember the first thing George Perles told us in training camp in Latrobe in 1975. We were watching film of games from the previous year. The only players there were the rookies and the free agents.

The first play on the film, L.C. Greenwood took on a blocker, went around the blocker, and made a defensive play. George asked the group if anyone could do what L.C. Greenwood had just demonstrated on the film. He told us there was no one in the NFL that would do that. He told us not to even think about it. That is one of my "10 Commandments of 1-Gap Play," which I will talk about later. "Don't run around a block. You have to play through the blocker's head." That stuck with me all of these years.

In the middle of the season in my rookie year, we were playing Houston at Three Rivers Stadium. Dwight White had to miss the game because of an ankle injury. Steve Furness was his replacement. I was the only remaining defensive lineman on the sideline. Midway through the second quarter, L.C. Greenwood got his leg caught in a pile and hurt his knee. As the medical staff was administering to L.C. Greenwood, George Perles was administering to me.

George got up in my face and said, "You cannot get hooked. You cannot get reached! Oh my goodness, isn't there anyone else we can put in the game?" I was stunned a little. "You cannot get double-teamed. You cannot get blocked. Damn, there has to be someone else I can put in the game." I looked around and saw that we did not have anyone left to put in the game. I started out on the field. Before I got away from George, he grabbed me, looked me right in the eye, and said, "Don't blow it!" With that motivational message echoing in my helmet, I ran on the field. By the time I got to the defensive huddle, I realized he was right. I knew I could not blow my chance. I had a chance to prove I belonged in the NFL.

I did my job in the game. I did not blow the chance I got in that game. I proved several people wrong. I got in the huddle and to the left of me was Jack Ham, to the right of me was Mean Joe Greene. Ready to bark out the signals without any teeth was Jack Lambert. To me, everyone was at ease. How bad could I blow it? Three future Hall of Fame players surrounded me. I knew if they blocked ten yards off the ball, my teammates would still be there for me. I had confidence in my teammates. I did not blow it.

I am a Polish kid from Cleveland, Ohio and I understood where the Oilers were going to run the ball. Certainly, they were not going to run the ball at Joe Greene, they were going to run it at me. I knew that. I had that going for me. It was second down and seven for the Oilers. I threw the tackle aside and made the tackle on the play. I was starting to get excited. Now it was third down and long. Joe Greene said to me, "Do you want to win the game by yourself?" I said, "No, I just want to win the game."

On third down, I shot the gap and came free in the backfield. I sacked the quarterback for my first sack in the NFL. I jumped up in the air and started waving my hand in the air. I was elated. Now, when you see the modern day NFL players celebrating on the field, just remember this. I predated all of those other heroes that celebrate in the NFL. I started all of that activity when I got my first sack in the NFL in that game. If you get sick of all of the celebrating, you can blame it on me because I started it.

Let me talk about the 1 gap. Some people do not like the term 1 gap. What we try to do is to expand the 1-gap technique all over the football field. I see high school film of players that play the 1 gap. They secure the 1 gap but they are oblivious of anything else that is going on in the game. We do not want to stay in the 1-gap technique. The point is to be successful at the point of attack. You must stay in that gap and protect it because that is your responsibility. However, we have to understand we have the responsibility to pursue to the football. Once we take care of the 1 gap, we must get to the football. We do not want to make the 1 gap a tunnel vision.

You will not be a good defense if all that your players are worried about is their gap. If your linemen and linebackers are only worried about their gap, you will not be a good defense. We want them to expand their responsibility. We want a defense that can make plays all over the field. We tell our players they have to secure their gap, then run, and hit.

Defensive linemen have to realize that their initial gap responsibility lasts for only a split second. After that split second, the expansion begins. They have to be able to find the football. We want gap control established immediately and then we want them to be on the move. They cannot hesitate. He who hesitates is lost. They are responsible for those gaps. He who hesitates is beaten and cannot recover. Just to take care of one gap is not good enough. You must expand the gap no matter of what they do from sideline to sideline.

I like to breakdown the teaching process into basic areas. I start with the "Five Critical Steps of Defensive Line Play."

First is *stance*. (Demonstrator came up to assist.) If a player does it right one time, I expect them to do it right all of the time.

We want the toe to the instep on the stance. We have the feet slightly wider than shoulder width. Then we put the elbows on the knees. Then all the defender has to do is to roll forward. When we flip-flop to the other side, what do we do? We want the hand nearest the ball to be on the ground. This is especially true when we are in a shade technique on an offensive lineman. We want to be able to get the hand of that man as quickly as possible.

The second step is to *explode* off the football. We want a great takeoff. We work on a start drill every single day. We want to explode off the football. It is the only way to play the game. We want to beat the man across the line of scrimmage.

The third step is to *engage* the blocker. Then we want to control the blocker. After we gain control of the blocker, we want to separate from him. It should happen very fast. It comes with instinct and it should happen immediately. We need to understand where the ball is going instantly. We have to combine the engage, control, and separate into a quick, distinct move. That is because it happens so fast.

The fourth step is *escape*. At times we are going to get blocked. There is no doubt about that fact. Offensive linemen are going to block you. We must learn how to escape. We must learn how to get away from that block. We have to understand what

is happening to us on that block. We have to be able to see that block, and we must feel the block, and we must have an instinct of how to escape the block.

The fifth step is to *make the play*. We have to be able to finish the play. Now comes the fun part. Get to the ball and make the play.

Looking at our stats from last year, I see that our fourth leading tackler was our defensive tackle. Our fifth leading tackler was the defensive end. Our seventh leading tackler was the other defensive tackle. We had production from our defensive linemen.

We are looking for defensive linemen. The defensive tackle can make a play on the opposite side of the field. We tell the players they had better take care of their gap and then they must be ready to run to the ball. "Go make that tackle." I love it when one of tackles makes a tackle on the opposite side of the ball on the opponent's sideline. "Where did he come from?" He is unaccountable. The offense does not have anyone assigned to block that backside tackle. We want our linemen to make tackles all over the field. Those are the five steps to great defensive line play.

I have broken down our defensive steps. Our defensive linemen only take two types of steps. First, is a *reaction step.* It is not a read step. It is a reaction step. We play with the eyes wide open. We want to be able to see the hand of the offensive lineman and his feet. When the hand moves, I know he is coming. We work on reacting to the types of blocks everyday in practice. We want our linemen to believe what they see. If the offensive lineman steps toward you, believe he is coming inside to block you. We tell our linemen to see it, believe it, and feel it. Once the defensive lineman can trust what he feels, he can make tackles all over the field.

The second type of step we take is a predetermined step. We are going to tell our linemen where to go on the play. We can call a slant, angle, loop, or anything we want to call. We are going to tell the lineman where to go. We are taking all of the guesswork out of the play. That is easy. The player better beat the offensive player in the gap. Now we have the advantage.

We teach our defensive linemen only those two steps. It is that simple. We teach them reaction and predetermined steps. We believe it is simple. That gets us to where we need to be at all times. Our linemen get excited when we let them move. For the most part, we are a four-stack, cover-2 football team. We play this alignment because our defensive linemen are very effective in this front.

This year we did not blitz as much as we did in the past. When your tackles can make the stop on first down, you do not have to blitz as much. Both of our tackles are 2-gap tackles on the guards. We have a 5 technique or a 7 technique. They offense should not be able to block them from those sets. We stack our linebackers in our 4-3 alignment.

I have had the opportunity to coach some outstanding players. My claim to fame is that I taught the great (but unfortunately, late) Reggie White the plug move. Our last year playing together was with the Memphis Showboats. Reggie White was the greatest defensive lineman I ever saw. One the first days of practice I saw him do the things he did and I said, "He is the greatest." You asked me about Joe Greene. What made Reggie White so good was his size and his speed. He was 6'5" and he could move. Not one player in the league could block him.

The first thing we do does not have anything to do with 1 gap. We feel this helps us in our defense. This is what we do. We do the 2-gap technique. We line up nose-to-nose on an offensive blocker. We play them nose-to-nose to see how tough they are. Let us see how good we are. It was how they played football when it originated. They played the game in the early days of football. They played nose-to-nose.

I tell our staff if George Perles can teach me to play 2 gap, then I can break it down and teach my players to play 2 gap. We have been able to do that over the years. We have two players here to demonstrate those steps. (Demonstration)

We work against these blocks everyday. We give each of our players an opportunity to work on these steps everyday.

We work against five basic blocks. Those five blocks are what we are going to see in the games.

- Drive block
- Double-team block
- Hook or reach block
- Seal block
- Down block

We may work on some other things during the year. I do not have the pull block listed because we do not have anyone here to demonstrate it. We need offensive linemen to show that technique. We work on the pass set depending on the type of blocking the offense uses. That is all game planning. We block on the five blocks above every single day.

We split the tackles and ends up and we work against the blocks. I take the tackles and another coach takes the ends. We want them to see the movement, feel the blocks, and know where the ball is going to be after contact. We want to engage, control, and separate. We put it all together in the drills.

We know defensive lineman get blocked at some point in the game. We must work on an escape when that happens. We have to work on this drill because we know it is going to happen in a game. Offensive line coaches do not teach blocking any more. They teach "holding." We must find some way for our defensive linemen to escape. Not only are they going to be blocked, they are going to be held. Therefore, we set up an escape drill to help them. We get into a "fit" position in a shade technique. He can be on one shoulder or the other. We want to feel the pressure, wrap the arms around the blocker, and push or pull to one side or the other and escape. We must keep the feet moving as we rip past the blocker.

Our opponents had more offensive holding penalties this year than they did the previous year.

Our linemen come to me during the games complaining about the offense holding them. I tell them there is nothing I can do about that. I tell them this: "If we can get the shoulders turned, and get underneath the 'hold,' we have a chance." One of two things happens with our move. We break the "hold" and move on, or we have a chance to escape on the illegal block and have it called.

I mentioned earlier about the "Ten Commandments of 1-Gap Play."

Ten Commandments of 1-Gap Play

- Never, ever guess

- Never stay blocked; dig it out

- Never get hooked or reached

- Close on all down blockers and take a piece of the blocker

- Keep the outside arm free all of the time

- Never go around blocks; fight through the head

- Explode off the ball and reestablish the line of scrimmage

- Never look into the backfield. Players must trust what they have been taught

- Never quit fighting for your gap

- Always attach one half of the offensive blockers body

Guessing will get you in trouble every single time. If you guess, you are done. You really have to work hard to overcome that mistake.

We want our players to dig out of any block. We assign the players a gap and tell them it is their gap and they had better fight for it. They must be willing to win every single down. We do not stay blocked.

No one offensive man should ever hook or reach our defensive lineman. If we are in a shade technique or in a 5 technique, we can never be hooked. It is simple.

We want to close on all down blocks. We want to get a piece of the lineman when he comes off the ball. We want to keep the blockers off our linebackers. Linebackers love to run and hit. Unblocked linebackers end up being All-Americans. As great as linebacker Jack Lambert was, if he was blocked it was the fault of the defensive line because we did not keep them off him.

We want the outside arm free at all times for the inside men or the 5 technique. The 7 technique should keep his inside arm free.

We never go around a block. We fight through the head of the blocker. The easy way is to go around the block. You will not get there by going around the block.

We want to explode and reestablish the line of scrimmage. When we do that, many good things happen.

We never look into the backfield. They do not need to stand up and look into the backfield. "The ball will find you."

We attack one half of the blockers body. They must understand leverage. They must be able to execute the bull rush. We said going nose-to-nose was good. They must be able to use the proper leverage. It does not happen all of the time.

I want to talk a few minutes about pass rush. We attack the blocker by going for one half of the man. From a 1 or 3 technique, we are going to force that quarterback to have happy feet. He is going to feel the pressure and he is going to be on the move. We use the "speed rush" and get upfield. We are going to get outside. We may use the spin move, and then get back inside and get depth. We do the spin moves several times in a game.

We will fit and swim, fit and rip, and do all sorts of moves. We can work on those movers in the off-season. We do not have time to work on these moves during the season. When we get into the training camp to start the season in the fall, we do not have to go over the spin, rip, swim, or other moves.

THE SIX COMMANDMENTS FOR WINNING

Florida State University

Thanks for that great introduction Larry. Coach Kindbom worked with Woody Hayes when he was at Ohio State. That fact reminded me of a story. I remember when our staff would visit Woody Hayes. We would go to Ohio State to watch them practice. Woody always emphasized not making a mistake. That point was very important to him. I remember a story he told to emphasize this point.

There was a young man who had a hundred pennies. He took his pennies to the bank to get a dollar bill. The next day he goes back to the bank, and asks to get a hundred pennies for his dollar. They gave him the pennies. The next day he came back to the bank to exchange the pennies for another dollar. This went on for weeks. Finally, the teller asked him, "Why do you keep doing this, bringing back the dollar or the hundred pennies for a dollar?" The boy answered, "Someday somebody is going to make a mistake and it isn't going to be me."

Of course, Woody was using that story to emphasize the way he was going to play football. I try to play that way now, but people get mad. People like style points, but style points will get you beat half of the time. The old-fashioned coach that I was raised on took the approach: "Don't beat yourself!" That is still the way I approach football. "You *lose* games; you don't *win* them." Every game we lost last year we did something to make us lose the game—an interception, a fumble, a jump offsides, or a penalty. This is really where football begins: not making mistakes to get you beat.

I have been coaching at Florida State for 30 years. When I went there, I did not go with the idea of failing. At that time Florida State was not doing very well—one year 0-11, next year 1-10. Of course that will get you fired every time. Ann and I went down there, and we started winning games. We decided to stay there.

I will be coaching for my 52nd year next year. When I first started coaching at Florida State, we did not draw well for our games. One year I had two tickets I could not get rid of, so I went to the Tallahassee Mall and put the tickets on my windshield. My thinking was this. At least we would have two fannies sitting in the stands. I went into the mall to get my haircut. One hour later, I came out and there were six tickets on windshield. Now, we have at least fought through that problem.

What I would like to talk about is what I call "The Six Commandments to Victory." Everything I have, I got from somebody else. The only thing is they are a lot older than you all.

Every Friday night at Florida State before a football game, we have a special meeting. I have done this for the last 30 years. Either in Tallahassee or on the road, we will have supper at 6:00. Then at 6:30, I will talk to them for about 15 minutes and give them my last little pep talk. I build those talks around six points. I do it every game.

I take six points and try to use different thoughts to motivate them for the ball game. The six points I build my talk around will win us the ball game. "Boys, if we do these things, we will win." As a football coach, there is not much you can do to control the outcome of the game. You have already done your coaching and preparation during the week. Once they have kicked off, all you can hope for is for your boys to carry out what you have practiced. I get on the crowd. They do not know what they are talking about. I call them PlayStation All-Americans. All these people know everything about football. They never played the game, but boy they know all about it. They play a game where they push buttons. They think when they push a button and pick a "six" and it comes up "six," they think they win. They hit a "seven" it comes up "seven" and they think they win again. It does not work that way in coaching. We work with human beings. We hit a six and it might come up an eight. The human factor in our part makes it work differently. Yet they think they can tell us what is wrong with our team.

The six commandments that I'm going to give you are ones that we can control as coaches. I use six commandments, but some other coaches may have more and some coaches may have less. These commandments are basic to the game of football.

NO BREAKDOWNS IN THE KICKING GAME

When everything else is equal, this is probably where you are going to win or lose your game. We have a good offense and our opponents they have a good defense. We have big kids, and they have big kids. The kicking game is where you are going to win or lose the game. You need to have the kicking game "sewed up." That is an expression from General Bob Neyland in the '30s. He used the term to have the kicking game "sewed up." At one time in football strategy when you did not know what to do, you would quick kick the football, and then play defense. You did that because all the players you had could play defense. Field position meant everything.

Be sure you have your punt team perfect, your punt rush perfect, your punt-return team perfect, your kick-off coverage and kickoff return teams perfect, and your field goals and extra points perfect. Be sure you start with that. We start out every practice with special teams at Florida State. That is the first thing we tell our kids: "We must have no breakdowns and we must win the kicking game."

NO MISSED ASSIGNMENTS

The second commandment is "no missed assignments." Now, men, these commandments I am giving you are things you can do something about. You can train, practice, and prepare your kids

to handle these things. You need to practice daily by stressing "no missed assignments."

When we put in a play, we put it on the blackboard first where we can see it. Then we explain it to the players so they can hear it. Then we have a walk-through. Next, we walk through it versus dummies. Then we try to simulate it the best we can. We do not scrimmage all the time. We cannot afford to get people hurt. Yet we need to go full speed somehow without getting people hurt.

During the season, we practice at three speeds. One is at full speed. In the early part of the season, we get a scrimmage in when we can without jeopardizing our football team. Once the season starts, we are afraid to scrimmage. We do not want to beat our players up. When we do scrimmage, we can go full speed. *Full speed* is full speed.

The next speed is "thud." That is full speed yet nobody wraps up on the tackles. We are going to hit on thud, but we are not going to get anyone hurt. When we practice, our kids will ask the coaches, "What's the speed?" We say "thud," you can hit as hard as you can hit, but you may not use your hands and arms. If you are to knock a man down, you will have to thud him down. If you are afraid of getting in bad habits by not tackling, think of this. One of the best practices for tackling is to have your defender step on the toes of the ballcarrier. Make your kids do that. I will guarantee you they will get better. One of the biggest mistakes kids make in tackling is that they throw their body before they get to the target. Make them step on his toes, and make him hit on the rise.

In our thud practice, the offense has rules too. On offense, you cannot block below the waist.

The third form of full speed is "whiz". Whiz is like thud, only you cannot hit the ballcarrier. You must whiz by the ballcarrier.

Those are three speeds used to control practices, and yet go full speed. That is better than going half speed because we do not get as many players injured.

PLAY GREAT GOAL-LINE DEFENSE AND OFFENSE

We always practice for a while at the goal line. We go full speed a lot of time because we do not get many players hurt practicing on the goal line. No one gets a long running start at anybody. By goal line, we mean from the three-yard line to the goal line. Every day in spring practice, we finish with goal line situations for five minutes.

We put the ball on the three-yard line, on the left hash, and tell them it is third and goal. They get three attempts at running the ball. They may run a play-action pass, a sweep, or another play. If they do not make it, they can still kick a field goal. After that, we put the ball on the one-yard line on the left hash mark. Now the situation is fourth and one to go for the touchdown. The offense needs to get the ball into the end zone. The defense needs to stop them. In this type of scrimmage, it is a defensive advantage. You can turn eleven people loose on defense.

Then we go to the right hash mark and repeat the drill. The kids have a lot of fun. The defense may beat them four straight series. If they do, you can bet that next day the offense will score. You need to win on the goal line.

NO FOOLISH PENALTIES

This usually occurs in the kicking game. "You would have won that game if you had not roughed the kicker. When you roughed the kicker, you gave them a 1st down, and they went on to score."

Another situation may occur when your opponent is fixing to kick a field goal. One of the defensive players lines up off sides. Now they score seven points instead of three, and you lose the ballgame. Those mistakes will get you beat. We say, "No foolish penalties."

This is the way I view penalties. We are the most penalized team we play. When we play, we always get more penalties. We try to prevent this but we have not been very successful. Here is the thing about that situation. If you want to stop penalties, cut out your aggressiveness; quit hitting people. Is that what you want? You check the conferences; the most victorious teams are the most penalized. If you are an aggressive team, you will get penalties called on your team. We tell our players, "Just don't get the foolish penalties." Foolish penalties include lining up off sides, jumping off sides, hitting the opponents in the mouth—those are the foolish penalties.

ALLOW NO LONG TOUCHDOWNS

Men, you can coach that aspect of the game. I cannot say, "Allow no short touchdowns." You ask how we can prevent the long touchdowns. Back up. Do not let anybody get behind you. The first thing I learned as a player was: if you do not know where the ball is, back up. They are probably trying to fool you, so get deeper.

I had a player named Derrick Brooks. He is an eight-time, All Pro now. Derrick was a great player, and a great student. In high school, he was at strong safety. He liked to come up, and he did not like to back up. Our safeties are supposed to go back. We decided to make him a linebacker. You cannot get beat deep. Do not give up the long ball. How deep are you playing your corners? If you are playing them at six yards, then back them up and play them at eight yards deep. You say your deep man runs a 4.8? Then play him at 10 yards deep. If he cannot run at all, play him at 12 yards deep. If I am playing defense, if you cannot get a long pass against us, and you cannot get a long run on us, how are you going to score? If I play great goal line defense, how are you going to score? You are going to have to kick to score on us.

KEEP FUMBLES AND INTERCEPTIONS TO A MINIMUM

How do you keep kids from fumbling? We do a good job on this aspect of the game. We teach them how to hold a football. The fingers go over the end of the ball. At the other end, the ball is under the arm, and the elbows are down. There should be no daylight in the cavities. We stress both hands over the ball when the runner is going down. Most fumbles occur as you are being tackled. As you are going down, the second guy comes in and knocks that thing out of the arms of the ballcarrier. We stress once you are going down, get both hands on the ball.

Something we have used to hold fumbles down is this. When we go skeletal offense, or running plays, we line up all of our extra people at 10 yards. We tell our ballcarrier the subs are going to try to knock the ball out. That way we keep their attention to let them know when they get through the line of scrimmage this "thing" is not over.

Every time we do 11-on-11 or skeleton drills, we tell the defense to knock the ball out of the arms of the ballcarrier. When they go for a touchdown, we keep trailing them until they slow down, and then knock the ball out. Invariably when we have skeleton drills, a player will catch a ball and start running for a touchdown. Before he scores, he will get the ball knocked out of his hands because he relaxes too soon. We tell him to not let up on that ball until he scores. If he does let up, we will have someone knock the ball out of his hands.

I do not talk a lot about interceptions. I am afraid I will scare off our quarterbacks and they will not throw the ball. I had a quarterback who threw an interception against Miami. I told him we could not have interceptions. The next week he kept throwing the ball one yard beyond the receiver's reach. I asked him why he was throwing the ball so far over the receivers. He said, "Because I want to keep it away from the defender." I told him not to worry about it. You can talk too much about interceptions. You just coach them to use their heads. Put the ball away from the defender.

Let me add a point or two about fumbles. When we meet in spring training, we will show our players how to hold a football. Everybody will get a ball and we will check each other. Then we will teach them how to recover a fumble. If you do not cover this aspect, you are making a mistake. There is a bad way to recover a fumble. If you do not cover it with them and they try to recover the fumble, they will not do it right. There is a right way to recover it. We roll it out there and have them recover it. We tell them not to hit the ball, but land beside it. We teach them to pull the knees up to the chin. We teach this all the first day when we are in shorts.

In closing, I want to talk about enthusiasm. When I first went to Florida State, I was high on the word *enthusiasm*. "If your team can play enthusiastically, you might win the game." If teams are equal, and your kids cannot wait to get the kickoff, you have a chance to win. We talk to our kids about enthusiasm all the time. Enthusiasm is spirit! I use a little devotion to stress the point. Spirit means full of God. That is God in you. We all have physical ability. Now we have to find something in that physical to make you explode.

I got the word enthusiasm from one of Woody Hayes' stories. He told us at a clinic the word enthusiasm comes from the Greek work *enthios*, which means full of spirit, God in you, full of God. Do not be afraid to say that, men. You are just trying to get these people to be the best they can be.

When I got to Florida State, I wanted the word enthusiasm to mean something. I have a workout room that is about 200 feet long. The walls in the room are very high. I had the word "enthusiasm" painted from the ceiling to the floor. It was just the word enthusiasm. Then over our practice field, we have a big sign that has the word enthusiasm on it. I talk about the word all of the time to my players.

The other word I use is "persistence." That probably is more important than anything else I could stress. It means, simply, a player who will not quit. He will not give up.

I see my time is up. Thanks for having me. Men, best of luck next year.

MAKING BIG PLAYS ON THE KICKOFF

University of Southern Mississippi

It is great to be here. I want to thank Larry Blackman and the Nike staff for inviting me to speak at this clinic. I have just completed my 14th year as head coach at Southern Miss. In current times, it is a little unusual for a coach in major college to hold one position that long. I feel very fortunate to be a part of this program.

It is good to be here and have the opportunity to speak to you about the kicking game. I want to talk about the kickoff return today. Most coaches do not like to talk about the kicking game. As a head football coach, I love to talk about it.

When I became the head coach at Southern Miss, the first couple of years I coordinated the offense. However, I began to realize the importance of the kicking game. I dropped the offensive coordinator's job and became a receivers coach so I could hire a full-time kicking game coordinator. In the organization of a staff, you generally have five offensive coaches and four defensive coaches. By hiring a special teams coordinator, it eliminated a coach on the offensive side of the ball. That is the reason I started coaching the wide receivers.

After a few years of coaching the wide receivers, I felt I needed to get more involved with the entire program. I think a lot of coaches pay lip service to the importance of special teams. They tell you how important it is, but never spend the time working on that part of the game. We believe in the importance of the kicking game and devote the time to accomplish our goals.

We feel the kicking game is as important as the offensive and defensive phases of the game. We have an award system within our football team. We give helmet awards every week for performance on offense, defense, and the kicking game. The offensive players have an opportunity to get two helmet decals each week. They can get them for winning the game or grading out with a high percentage on performance. On special teams, the players have the opportunity to receive five awards for each special team.

We spend a lot of time selling our players on the importance of special teams. We talk about that more than any other phase of the game. Over the years, we have been good in our special team play.

I played quarterback and coached the offensive side of the ball my entire career. I never played defense or coached on that side of the ball, but I believe you win with great defense and having a sound kicking game.

Special teams can do so many things for you in relationship to field position and making big plays. The kicking game leads to so many things that can make the difference in a football game.

We have been fortunate to win a lot of games and some championships at Southern Miss. I attribute those championships to the type of defense we play. If you know anything about Southern Miss, you know we play strong defense. We have a tradition of being good on defense.

Since 1999, we have allowed the fewest number of touchdowns by any Division I football team. The Miami Hurricanes are second, Oklahoma is third, and Kansas State is fourth. We have been good on defense, but our special teams have been responsible for just as many wins. I cannot tell you the number of games that have been turned around because of the play of the special teams.

Those types of plays do not have to be touchdown plays. They are plays that have turned the momentum of a football game. I feel that big plays in the kicking game and forcing turnovers are the biggest momentum changers in college football. That is why we spend so much time working on the game and trying to sell it to our players.

We lost our special teams coordinator and did not replace him with a full-time coordinator. Our outside linebacker coach has put together everything related to our kicking game. He has done an outstanding job of coordinating all aspects in each phase of the game. He oversees all the special teams. We have a coach who is the head coach of each phase of the game. The head coach for each phase has designated coaches to assist him.

We have more coaches and players than the high school coach has available to him. We break our staff up so that the majority of coaches that have players on a particular special team will be involved as assistant coaches in that phase. We free up as many coaches as possible to assist with special teams during that part of practice. The position coaches are still working with their players during special teams practice. They can continue to work with the players on individual and fundamental skills during the special teams period.

We try not to involve any coach in more than two special teams. We know there are certain positions that put more players on certain special teams than others. Tight ends, linebackers, and safeties are the types of players that will end up on special teams. They are the athletes with the bigger bodies and speed that most special teams need.

We get our graduate assistant coaches heavily involved with our special teams work. The NCAA only allows two GAs on the field and they are important to our program. They coach specific positions in our special team phase.

We are strapped for time because of NCAA rules governing practice. We have a difficult time getting meeting, practice, and video time for our players. We get our afternoon practices under way around 2:00 PM and our study halls begin at 6:00 PM. That gives us a limited amount of time to practice and allow the players to eat before they report to nightly study hall. That challenges us to get quality meeting time, practice time, and meaningful video time for our players.

We encourage our players to come by in their free time to watch video. I do not think you can get enough of that aspect of football. With the technology available, it is easy to get a great deal of teaching done through video. That gives your players something extra to get ready to compete on Saturdays.

According to NCAA rules, you have to take one day off during the week. Sunday is our mandatory day off. Our game plan for the following football game is done by Monday afternoon. We will meet and practice all phases of the special teams game plan Monday afternoon. It is a basic introduction and scouting report of how we want to attack each phase of the kicking game.

On Tuesday, we emphasize our punt protection and punt coverage team. We have a team meeting before practice with those teams. We emphasize the points covered in that meeting in special teams practice that day. We also meet with our punt block and return teams on Tuesday.

On Wednesday, we meet with our punt protection team again and our kickoff return team. On Thursday, we meet with all four of those phases before practice.

Our field goal and field-goal block teams practice for five minutes each day after our stretching period. The skills involved in field-goal blocking do not change from game to game and require less teaching time. We work both phases at the same time. We have our first field-goal team going against our first field-goal block team on one hash mark and the two's going against the two's on the other hash. We alternate between the two teams and go rapid fire with their repetitions at varied distances. After we get into the season, we limit the repetitions to about four kicks in that period.

We feel like we slight our kickoff coverage team. However, we get quality reps in spring and pre-season practices to keep us sharp. Kickoff coverage does not change from week to week.

Kickoff coverage is the phase of the game that has landmarks on the field and teaches assignments that do not change. We kick the ball from the left hash mark and our coverage remains constant. We get good work on the kickoff coverage on Monday and Thursday. If we feel we need additional work in this phase, we do it during conditioning period on Tuesday and Wednesday.

Unless you show your players the commitment and importance of the kicking game, you will not get results from this area. Whenever we have a special team meeting, the head special teams coach is not the only one who attends the session. Every coach assisting in that phase is at the meeting.

In our kickoff return meeting, in addition to the head coach, we had a coach with the return personnel. We had one coach assigned to the wedge personnel. We had two coaches assigned to our front five players. Each coach has his players surrounding him and goes over each assignment and adjustment they need to execute the return.

We make teaching tapes for these teams. We have about 25 players in these meetings. We want our players to know this meeting is as important as any offensive or defensive team meeting.

We have a pecking order as to what starter we want on certain special teams. We put our best players on our punt protection and coverage. We want starters on our special teams. If you only involve back-up personnel on your special teams, it de-emphasizes the importance of that phase of the game. We have a rule that a starter on offense or defense cannot be involved on more than two special teams. However, on occasion we break that rule in certain circumstances. If you have a redshirt freshman or sophomore, you do not want to put too much on his plate. If he is learning an offensive or defensive position, more than two special teams will affect his level of play.

The more experienced player can play more special teams for you. However, you do not want a guy on the field who is fatigued. At the same time, you have to consider how many plays the player is playing and whether he has a competent back-up at his position. However, we are like you in that we want to play as many players as we can to help us win a football game. If we play two sets of linebackers, we can involve the starting linebacker in more than two special teams.

Punt protection and coverage is our number one priority in our kicking game. The kickoff return is the next most important phase. If you can return the ball outside the 30-yard line, the kickoff return gives you the opportunity to establish field position and make first downs.

The kickoff return is an opportunity for a big play. It is a better situation than a punt return. There are too many variables in the punting game. Punters are using all kinds of methods to prevent the punt return. They angle the punt out of bounds, kick away from the return man, hang the ball high, and use the rugby punt. Returning the kickoff has a better chance of getting a big play.

The third priority to our special teams approach is punt return and block. The kickoff coverage team is next on our list of importance. In this phase of the game, all you need is a bunch of guys who are relentless in their effort to get down the field as fast as they can. There are techniques involved, but the biggest thing is effort and speed. It is the phase where you can be more repetitious in your teaching because you can control where the kick goes.

I want to talk about the kickoff return as to the X's and O's of how we run it. However, before I get to that I want to show you how we teach our players in respect to the kicking game.

As a head coach, I have to make a decision about our spring practice and game. If you go through spring practice and never work on the kicking game, that sends a bad message to your team. We need to work our young players in that phase of the game to see what they can do. In our spring game, we run every phase of the kicking game live except the punt block.

We conduct live kicking drills during preseason to help with the selection of our special teams. We try to create the best competition for our players that we can. We use our best personnel against our best personnel. We try to find out as much as we can about our personnel.

We are not involved in schemes. I am a great believer in simplicity. I know high school coaches know that as well as anyone. You are working with less time, players, and coaches on the field. You cannot confuse your players, especially in the kicking game.

In the kicking game, we want to be simple and repetitious. We want a chance to get good at what we do. The kickoff return is like an offensive play. If the defense changes, the offensive blocking scheme changes. We do not see many kickoffs down the middle of the football field. Teams are kicking into the corners and into the boundaries. If you have an excellent return game, you get squib and pooch kicks.

We want to be simple in our return but we want to devise a system to be effective when the kicking team squibs or pooch kicks the ball. If the kicking team skies or squibs the ball, we have to catch it at different points on the field. When the kicking team kicks the ball deep, it is in the air from 3.6 to 4.0 seconds. Everything on the return times up for a kick that is in the air at least 3.6 seconds.

When the kicking team skies the ball to around the 30-yard line, we find it destroyed our deep return timing. We have to develop a return that can still create good field position and give us a chance for the big play.

I want to take you through some of the basic things we do from a coaching standpoint. This material came out of the playbook from last year. Generally, there are no offensive linemen on a kickoff return team.

We have our offensive line coach coaching the front five on the return with a graduate assistant. The next level of the return team is the right and left end. The tight end coach coaches them. The next tier is the wing player. They are safety or defensive back types of players coached by the secondary coach. The wide receiver coach coaches the return players. We have an upback, who is primarily a communicator, and a deep back, who returns everything he can reach. We free all these coaches up during the special team period, which allows them to coach their positions.

When we have our kick return meeting, we include the scout kickoff team. I want the scout team aware of what they are supposed to do. I want them to give us the best possible look and make it as realistic as they can.

We had to answer a number of questions about the kickoff return. The first question deals with the kicker. We have to know from what position he is kicking the ball and how high and deep it goes. We want to know from what point he kicks the ball and the tendencies that go with those types of kicks.

We want to know who the safety is on the return. Does the coverage team twist their alignments as they cover? If they do, when does the twist occur? Do we have to change or renumber the coverage team as they come down? We want to know where the kickoff team is vulnerable in their coverage. We want to identify their best coverage men.

We look for tips as to alignment of the coverage team or kicker positioning as to where the ball is kicked. We may wait until the kicker approaches the ball to call the direction of our return.

We have established goals for our kickoff return team. Our goals are as follows:

- Win
- Score
- Ball security/great effort
- Average start after KOR = 30 yards line or greater
- Average KOR = 23 yards or greater
- Big returns/30 yards or greater

The team will be composed of players that give great effort and expect to win every opportunity that is presented to them! With the high expectations resulting in great productivity, this unit will help our football team win the field position battle. Three words this unit will live by are: *house, squeeze,* and *finish.*

There are some general rules about the kickoff return. We never want to block below the waist or in the back of the opponent. A cover man may not low block any wedge or double-team player. The defender must attack the return team above the waist.

Once the ball travels 10 yards, it is legal for the kickoff team to touch and recover the ball. After the kick, we may step into the 10-yard zone, but once we touch the ball, it is a free ball. If a kick travels out of bounds, we have three options. We may take the ball where it goes out of bounds, penalize the kicking team five yards and make them re-kick, or take possession at our 35-yard line. Anyone can fair catch a kickoff; however, if the ball hits the ground, the ball is a free ball.

The kick return man has rules that govern his play. If the catch momentum carries the return man into the end zone, he does not have to bring the ball out. If the return man muffs the ball in the field of play and it rolls into the end zone, he does not have to bring the ball out. However, he must recover the ball.

If you mutt a kick in the end zone, you must cover the ball and get down. If the return man catches the ball in the end zone and any part of his body crosses the goal line, he must bring the ball out. If he catches the ball in the field of play and retreats into the end zone, he must bring the ball out. A ball fumbled from the field of play into the end zone must be run out.

In the kickoff return game we have important principles we pass on to our team. The first thing is communication within the team. The upback is in charge of all communications. The team wants to field all kicks.

We have blocking principles we teach our return personnel. We want them to square up on the opponent whenever possible. Keeping the eyes below the defender's eyes allows for a great fit. We want to get a standoff in the block and let the return man go by.

The return team needs to have awareness of what the kickoff team is doing. A change in the direction of the kick can many times be detected at pre-snap. During pre-game warm-up, we answer many of the questions we have about the kickoff.

The scheme has to be simple but good. We use a system that will allow us to have two double-team blocks with a trap block. We use a call system that will allow us to change the players we double-team.

On our returns, we have to ID the coverage personnel. We will always ID five right defenders and five left defenders. The kicker will never be identified. We designate the five right defenders as R1-R5. The R1 will be the widest defender on the right side. We number the defenders on the left side the same way with the L1 defender being the widest to the left side. We still ID 5R's and 5L's even if the kicking team is a 6-4 look in their alignment to the ball. If they have six defenders on one side of the ball and four defenders on the other side, both 5R and 5L would be on the same side of the ball. If the coverage team uses a stack front, we ID the coverage personnel according to how they fill their lanes as they cover the kick.

This is an example of how we scout the kickoff. This comes from our last ball game against California. We had 68 total kicks to scout. They had no squib kicks, eight skied kicks, and no on-sides kicks. They were 50-50 on placement of the ball. They kicked to the right middle or left middle. The kicker kicked the ball to an average of the 1.5-yard line. If the ball was sky kicked the average was to the 28-yard line.

If the ball is sky-kicked inside the 35-yard line, there is an opportunity to get a good return. Of course, that depends upon the height of the kick. The hang time of their kickoff was between 3.6 and 3.95 seconds. We want to know that because of the trap return we use in our scheme. The widest two defenders away from the trap-blocking scheme are not blocked. That means the more hang time the kicker has on the ball, the more of a factor the outside defenders have on the return.

They varied their alignment from a 5-5 to a 6-4 in defenders-to-the-ball relationship. They used the stack techniques and twist techniques, usually between the number two and three defenders. From these tendencies, we draw up our return schemes.

We found that the kicker aligned five yards deep when he sky-kicked the ball. When he approached from eight yards, he kicked the ball deep. We adjusted our return from the sideline on the kicker's depth. We had the team watch us for the signal and they adjusted their depths and angles on their blocks according to the type of kick.

The position of the return man and upback depends on the kicker. If they kick the ball from the left middle position on the field, the return man is four to five yards inside the right hash mark on the goal line. The upback aligns four to five yards inside the left hash mark on the 10-yard line.

If you have a lot of success returning the football, teams will give you something else. That is why we believe in simplicity in the return game. If the defense will not kick the ball to you, it is a credit to what you have done in the return game.

Before I get into the return, let me show you the types of personnel we plug into our kickoff return team. Our left tackle is a back-up cornerback. He has good speed and he is a bit bigger than the other corners. The tackles on the kickoff team have to be able to run. If the return is set away from them, they have a longer run to get to their position. These players have to be fast but they do not have to be the most physical players on the team. They have to use leverage and run the defender by the return man.

The left guard is the starting middle linebacker. He is more physical because he usually takes on another linebacker on the coverage team. His back-up is also a linebacker.

The center on the return is our weakside, all-American linebacker. He has probably the toughest job on the return unit. Backing him up is a 230-pound fullback who is very athletic.

The right guard is a back-up running back. He is very athletic and what we call a special team guru. He plays many of our special teams. He was an outside linebacker before we moved him to running back.

The right tackle is another cornerback. He has to have more speed and probably is less physical than the guards and center.

Our left end is our starting wide receiver. In fact, the ends and wing players are all receivers, tight ends, or running backs. They are more skilled people with good hands. We have a linebacker or two mixed into this group of athletes. The return man is our starting corner.

In the spring and fall, we use the first five minutes after stretching period to work on our individual special team drills. We have two Jugs machines we use as kicking devices. We have the punt receivers in one area of the field and kickoff receiver in another. We can use a punter but the Jugs machine is more consistent and we can get more reps. On another area of the field we have our snappers and holders working on their individual skills. We also work on the squib and sky kicks during this period. In five minutes, we can get a tremendous amount of reps. It is amazing how many players you can develop in the return game. When our freshmen come in, we try everyone out to see what they can do.

The first kickoff return is what we refer to as Right-43 (Diagram #1). The right and left returns are exactly alike in their rules. The defender double-teamed by the front five is R4. The RT and RG will carry out the double-team. The front five not involved in the double-team will block L5, L4, and L3.

The defender double-teamed by the end and wing player is R3. The double-team on R3 will be carried out by the backside end and wing. The LE and LW double-team R3. The number 43 tells us the right 3 and 4 coverage man will be double-teamed.

The playside end will execute the trap block. The RE will trap block R5 as he comes down the field. The playside wing will execute the kick-outblock. He will kick out R2. The upback secures the fielding of the ball by the return man. He fits the return man into the seam of the return and blocks the most dangerous man.

The 43-Left is the same return to the left side. We can adjust the double-teams, trap, and kick-out blocks by changing the numbers of the return. If we call Right–32, we double-team R3 and R2 and trap

R4. In the Right-32, the playside wing will kick out the R1 man.

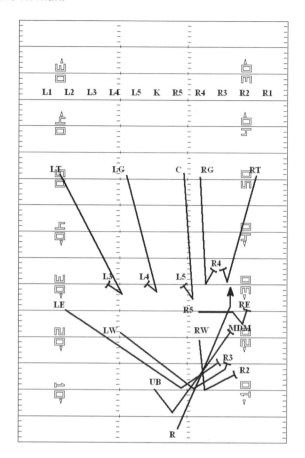

Diagram #1. Right-43

Our alignment and stance for the kickoff return will remain consistent. With the ball in the middle of the field, the tackles align at the top of the numbers. The guards line up on the hash marks. The center is two yards to either side of the kicker. In their stance, their front foot is on the 48-yard line and the back foot is on the 49-yard line. They tilt at a 45-degree angle facing the ball. The center lines up square with his heels on the 49-yard line.

The ends align at the 25-yard line at the top of the numbers. The wings line up on the 20-yard line on the hash marks. The upback aligns at the 10-yard line in the middle of the field or aligns by the game plan. The return back aligns on the goal line or according to the game plan. If they kick the ball from the hash mark, the team moves two to three yards accordingly.

We have particular mechanics for blocking. At the kick of the ball, the front five men involved with man blocking techniques turn to the inside. They drop to the 27-yard line. At the 35-yard line, they make a half-turn to check their count on the men they are blocking. They are blocking L5, L4, and L3. They plant their foot at the 27-yard line and engage the defenders while traveling uphill. They fit their blocks on the defenders and work their leverage for the return.

The front five, who are involved in the double-team, turn inside as the ball is kicked. They retreat to the 30-yard line and get hip to hip. The guard is the post man on the double-team and sets square on the R4 defender. He calls either "in" or "out" to use the leverage of the defender to their advantage. The tackle is the drive man and drives the near pec of the defender with his hands and shoulder.

The playside end performs the trap block. He takes a subtle drop and traps the defender at the 25-yard line. He has to be patient and hide as the defender comes down. This is probably the hardest block. He is coming from the outside and blocking the R5 coverage man as he comes down the field. However, this is an opportunity to really light someone up if the defender does not see him coming.

We refer to the next block as the "train." The train includes the kick-out block by the playside wing and the double-team block by the backside end and wing. The playside wing will set the train 10 to 12 yards in front of the return man. He is blocking R2 out. If the ball is kicked to the sideline, he sets the train at the top of the numbers.

The backside wing and end go to the train. The playside wing kicks out the appropriate defender and the backside end and wing execute the double-team block on R3. They use the proper mechanics for double-team.

The upback is the communicator. He calls "you" or "me" and points to the return man. He sets eight yards over the return man and verifies that he has caught the ball. He leads the return man into the fit of the double-team and kick-out block. If there is a defender coming from outside the return, he has to block him to ensure the return man gets into the seam. If there is no one behind the return, he blocks the most dangerous man.

The return man catches the ball in the soft spot between the bottom of his shoulder pads and the waist. He wants to catch the ball moving downhill with his hips and shoulders square. He wants to catch the ball off-center, not in the chest. We want him to keep the leg to the side of the return back as he catches the ball. We never want him to go any further than the top of the boundary ticks on a sideline kick.

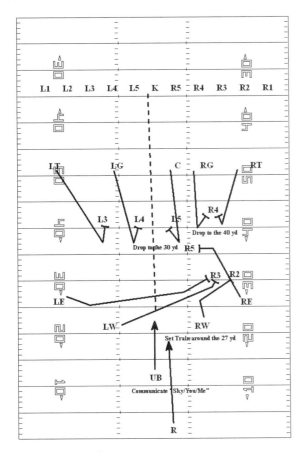

Diagram #2. Short return

If the ball is kicked short, the upback will call "short" (Diagram #2). We define a short kick as a ball that does not travel past the 15-yard line and stays between the hash marks. The front five drop to the 37-yard line instead of the 27-yard line. All other blocks in the return move up 10 yards. The train is set eight to ten yards in front of the return man.

If we have called our Right-43 and the ball is skied to the right or left, we call "sky" and we go to our sky return. We define the sky kick as a short kick greater than or equal to the 20-yard line (Diagram #3). When the ball is skied, the playside

tackle, guard, and center whip their heads toward the sideline and run outside. They block the playside one, two, and four coverage men respectively.

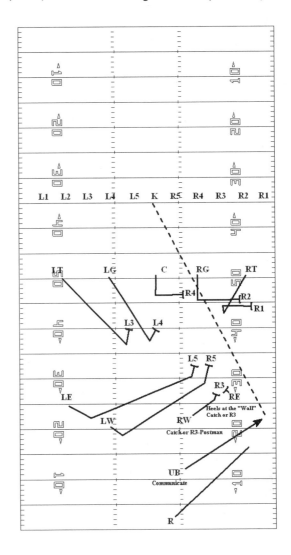

Diagram #3. Sky return

We assign the backside wing to the playside number-five coverage defender. The backside end has the backside number-five coverage defender. The backside guard and tackle block the backside four and three defenders. If the playside wing does not catch the ball, he double-teams the playside number-three defender with the playside end. The upback catches the ball if he can and returns up the sideline.

When we get the sky kick, we want to get a hat on a hat and get upfield with the ball. We want something positive to come from the return.

Another special situation occurs on the squib kick. The squib kick by definition is a kick that hits the ground quickly or is kicked on the ground. If the ball is a line drive kick that carries deep, we run our regular return. On the squib kick, we call "wedge" (Diagram #4).

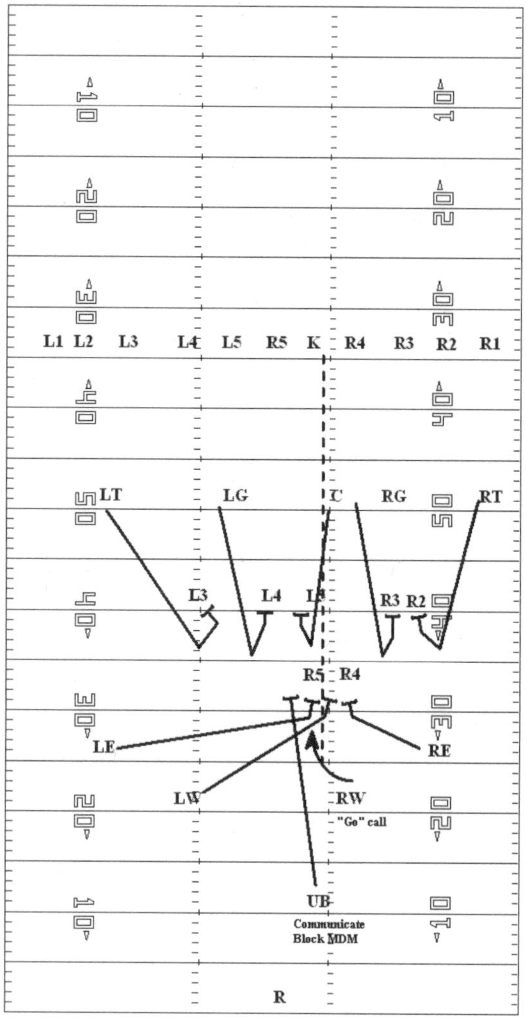

rules remain the same (Diagram #5). The players forming the wedge have to hurry to get into formation, but the return is the same.

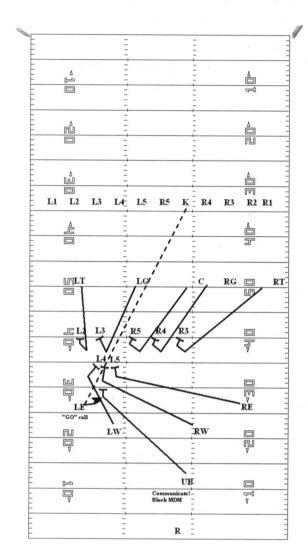

Diagram #4. Wedge

Diagram #5. Sideline wedge

When we make the wedge call, the playside tackle and guard block the playside two and three defenders. The center, backside guard, and tackle block the backside five, four, and three defenders. They drop 12 yards and try to ID their blocking assignments. If they cannot ID their blocks, they block area.

The closest non-return man sets the wedge with the remaining ends and wing players. They set the wedge and get hip-to-hip eight yards in front of the return man. The return man fields the kick cleanly and keeps his knees off the ground. He makes a "go" call for the wedge as he approaches it.

If the squib kick angles toward the sideline, the

If we have to make a fair catch, we have a simple rule for the fair catch. If the defenders are within five yards, we give a "Peter" call, make the signal, and catch the ball. If the defenders are not within five yards, we field, squeeze, and return.

We call the last return "Fisher Left." We use this return as a last-second attempt or as a gadget (Diagram #6). The front five influence the drop and set a wall down the left sideline. The left tackle starts the wall and sets it at the top of the numbers. The ends move their alignment up to the 33- or 35-yard line. The left end influences in his drop and peels down the sideline to receive the lateral. The right end influence drops and goes to block the safety. The wings set a wedge eight yards over the ball and protect. If the kickoff team kicks the ball to the upback, he gets it to the return man and fits into the wedge. If the ball goes to the return man, the upback sets the wedge over the ball at eight yards. The return man sells the return to the right and throws the ball back left to the left end. He has to make sure it is a lateral or backward pass.

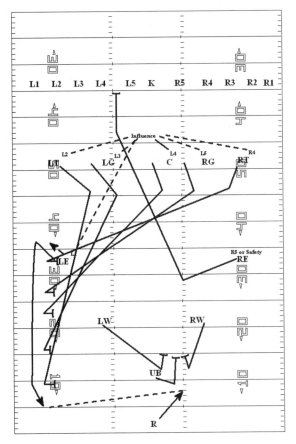

Diagram #6. Fisher left

That is all the time I have. I see a bunch of high school coaches out there today. I hope you got something out of this. I want to take two minutes to harp on something that has just come up in high school football. We have just finished recruiting and I have seen something take place in the state that I have never seen before. There were fewer qualifiers for athletic scholarships in the state of Mississippi than ever before. To qualify for an athletic scholarship the athlete must have 14 core credits and a 2.5 GPA with test scores. If you have a freshman, by the time he is a senior he must have 16 core classes in addition to the GPA and test scores.

That has become a major problem not just in Mississippi but all over the southeastern section of the country. Mississippi has the lowest average A.C.T. test scores in the country and has the lowest percentage of students taking college prep classes.

This is something we all have to work on to correct. It takes mom and dad, counselors, teachers, coaches, and the NCAA to start to get the kids a better education. Mississippi is a great state for high school football. I have seen more quality athletes in this state this year than I have ever seen before. We want to recruit the state of Mississippi because it is in our backyard. We want Mississippi to continue to put out quality student-athletes.

I want to talk about Southern Miss for just a second. We have done many good things here. We have just completed our eleventh straight winning season. We are one of eight schools out of 117 that have had 11 straight winning seasons. We just finished playing our seventh bowl game in the last eight years. We have won four championships in the nine years Conference U.S.A. has been in existence. There are only three schools in the last nine years that have won four or more championships. Those schools are Miami of Florida, Florida State, and Marshall.

We have done a lot of good things, but the thing I am most proud of is our graduation rate. Southern Miss has the highest graduation rate in our conference. We are enjoying success on the field but more importantly, we are graduating our student-athletes. They are getting an education. That really makes me feel good. Next year we will have 50 percent of our seniors either going to graduate school or getting a double major.

I appreciate you being here and listening to my lecture. If we can do anything for you, please call on us. I wish you the best for next year and please do everything you possibly can to help your athletes in the classroom. Thank you very much. It is a pleasure to be here.

THREE-STEP DROP PASSING GAME

University of Louisville

It is great to be here. I want to give you a few things about my background. I played quarterback for the University of Louisville under Coach Howard Schnellenberger. I was fortunate enough to be able to squeeze out seven years at the NFL level. I really played for some great coaches, and I played with a lot of great players and with a lot of great teams. One year I was with the Chargers in the Super Bowl. I played for the 49ers with Steve Young and Coach Steve Mariucci. I was at Tampa Bay with Coach Tony Dungy and Coach Mike Shula. I was at Denver with Coach Mike Shanahan. I was fortunate to learn a lot of football along the way in my career. It has really been valuable to me in my coaching experience.

I am working with Coach Bobby Petrino at the University of Louisville. He is a great offensive coach. One of his strengths is that he is a great leader, and he is a disciplined coach, and he makes the players work hard. He makes no exceptions from the team stand point. He sets the standards and makes the players accountable for their actions, both on the field and off the field. Our discipline over the last two years has been very good. He is very innovative, more so in the running game than in the passing game. We like to throw the ball because we have great receivers and quarterbacks. But we really like to run the football and wear teams down so we can run the ball straight at the defense and throw when we have to in the fourth quarter.

If you look at the best teams in the country, you see that they are in a "two backs set offense." They are able to pound the football on offense. They can do more than just spread the offense out to move the ball. They face a lot of different blitz packages and they must be balanced to adjust their offense to control the defense. When we go with "two backs," we are going to get a lot of single high safeties and a lot of "eight men in the box" looks. We have a lot of schemes to attack that defense with our "two backs offense" on both the run and the pass. We can use our dropback and play-action passes and we can throw the ball down the field.

This year we were very successful. We finished the season 11-1. Our offense was number one in the country in total offense, points scored, and passing efficiency. We really felt good about our offense. Next year we have a lot of players coming back on offense. Our standards are set high for our players. We will be playing in the Big East Conference for the first time. Our schedule will be tougher. Our non-Conference games will be against the University of Kentucky, Oregon State, and North Carolina. Also, Florida Atlantic is coming up to play us in Papa John's Stadium. We feel good where we are, but we know we have a long way to go.

We continue to work to improve our offense. We will visit with other colleges and pro teams before the spring practice. We are always trying to get better at what we do. We know football is not an exact science, but we feel good about the way we do things. I am not going to spend a lot of time on philosophy. I will get into some X's and O's as I get into the lecture.

We categorize our passing game. The quick passing game is our three-step drop passing game. Our drop back package is our five-step drop passing game. We do run a few seven-step drop plays. Then we have our play-action passing game. Also, we have our movement and naked plays. We have some plays where we use maximum protection and throw the ball downfield and go for the big plays.

I am going to start out talking about our quick game, or the three-step drop game. The routes we are going to run especially on the outside include the hitch, quick out, and the slant routes. On the hitch route, we always like for our receiver to have the inside foot up. We do a lot of our routes on depth and on steps. On the hitch, it is a six-yard deep route. The receiver takes big three and a little two steps and turns around. The quarterback is going to take three quick steps and get the ball out to the receiver.

Again, we want the receiver to run the five-step hitch route. It is three big and two little steps. He must burst off the line of scrimmage to create separation against the defensive back.

Let me cover the play from our two-by-two set, or our doubles left set with 90 protection (Diagram #1). We use two different types of protection with our three-step drop. We use a full slide protection anytime we are getting a zone blitz from the field, or when we are getting gap pressure. We slide the line and the back has the first back off the outside of the tackle.

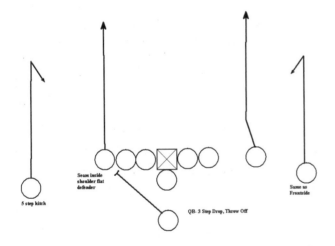

Diagram #1

The two wide receivers run the hitch route. The inside receivers run through the inside shoulder of the flat defender. We do not want to run them through the outside shoulder because they can get too wide and get in the path of the hitch route. We are really trying to throw the hitch on the play.

The quarterback takes a three-step drop and throws the football on that third step. We use to use that protection all the time, but now we use a turn protection where we bring the center turns to the first linebacker to the weakside. The back takes either one or two on the strongside. Those are the two protections we use on the three-step drop.

We can call doubles left rip, or rose – 90 Y. We have the simple hitch routes on the outside. The inside receiver is running through the inside shoulder of the flat defender. We do not want them to widen outside because we are just trying to throw the hitch route. We can throw to the inside man but it may happen only one time out of two hundred passes. We are going "one, two, three" and we are throwing the hitch route.

The coaching point for the quarterbacks is to locate the safeties—especially the strong safety or the safety to the field. We want to know exactly what the safeties are doing. A lot of teams in college disguise the coverages very well. We teach the quarterback to get a pre-snap read on the defense. We get a pre-snap read, but we are not going to predetermine what we are going to do before the ball is snapped. We are going to think we know what is going on, but we are going to wait until the ball is snapped to see what the safeties are doing and to see which linebackers are blitzing. We want to see what is actually happening on defense. We want to see if the defense is going to stay as a one- or two-high safeties defense. We get a pre-snap read and we get a post-snap read.

If we cannot get a good read on the safeties because the defense is doing a good job of disguising their defense with their safeties, then the next thing we want to know is how is the corner into the boundary playing? What is that corner on the boundary playing? We categorize how the corners play three ways. To keep it simple, we have an off corner, a press corner, and a cloud corner. This determines what routes we run. If we get pressed on the hitch route, we are going to run a fade route and run by the defender. If we get a rolled-up corner, the receiver is going to use an outside release in the fade hole. If we get an off corner, the receiver runs a six-yard deep hitch route.

Unless we have a mismatch on the wideside of the field, we would prefer to throw the hitch into the boundary. When teams start to roll the coverage into the boundary, we will throw to the wideside of the field.

If we are on the left hash mark and the play is a doubles left – 90, we would like to throw the hitch into the boundary because it is the shortest route to throw. If we have a complete mismatch on the boundary side we will throw to that side but we would prefer to throw the ball into the boundary. If the defense rolls up into the boundary, we will throw to the field side.

If we get a rolled-up corner on the hitch, we look at the opposite side on the play. This is what we do instead of just running the hitch route across the board.

If we get a press corner, we are not going to take the three-step drop and throw the fade route. We want to at least control the free safety and keep him in the middle of the field. We want to look the safety off and then throw the fade route.

Sometimes we get a quarterback that looks at the fade route and does not see the safety. As soon as the quarterback sees the rolled-up corner, he wants to look at the safety. We want to know what the corner is doing on the side to which we are throwing the ball *before* we throw the ball. If it is a press cover by the corner, the quarterback wants to control the safety with his eyes. He does not want to look at the safety until he gets a step-and-a-half on the play.

After the step-and-a-half, the quarterback gets his eyes on the safety to see what he is doing. If the receiver does not get by the safety, we teach our quarterback to throw to the back shoulder. I like to say throw at the receiver's helmet. There are different things that can happen on the hitch route.

If we are running a five-step drop, the corner can turn his head and get back to the football. On the three-step drop that corner does not turn his head to get back to the ball as quickly as he does on the five-step drop. That is our doubles left – 90. If we

have a rolled-up corner to the boundary, we are going to throw the ball to the field.

If we face a corner that is reading the quarterback on the three-step drop, we mix the plays up so he cannot key us all of the time. We can run a slot right set and run a quick play-action fake and then throw the hitch route. This prevents the corner from sitting there reading the eyes of the quarterback. We can call slot right – "quick 142 hitch." The inside receiver runs his route through the inside shoulder of the flat defender. The quarterback takes his three-step drop and throws the ball after that third step. A successful hitch route for us is a completion for nine to ten yards on the play.

The next play I want to cover is not one that a lot of teams use. From my experience in the NFL, we did not run this type of play. When I first started coaching at Louisville, I was not really sold on the play. It is an option route off the three-step drop. The receiver has a lot of different options. When you first look at the play, you wonder how you can teach all of the different options. It is a different type of play but we drill the play so much we are actually good at running this play. I am sold on the play now.

We call the play "90 – gray." Regardless of the formations, we are in we are going to have a hitch route on one side and an option route on the other side of the formation. The option route is a six-yard route. It can be run by the number-three receiver inside, or it can be the second receiver, depending on what we have called.

If we call "90 – Y – gray," it means the Y receiver is going to run a route on the play. We are going to run a hitch on one side and an option route on the other side (Diagram #2).

Our rules on the option route for our receivers are simple. The wide receiver runs the fade route using the outside release technique. The inside man runs the six-yard option route. On the fieldside, the inside receiver runs the fade route deep. The wide receiver runs the five-step hitch or fade route.

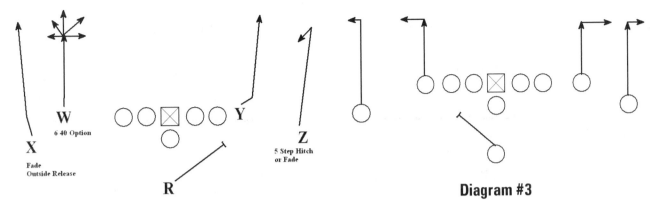

Diagram #2

Diagram #3

The receiver running the hitch route is going to push off at six yards. He can continue over the top on the route, he can snap off a skinny slant, or he can break inside or outside or he can hook up. If we are going against cover zero, he can take the route over the top or he can cut a slant route.

If the defender is sitting off the receiver, he is going to run the six-yard route and break outside, inside, or hook up. If one or two safeties are in the middle, the over-the-top route is eliminated. Now his options are simple: he can break inside, outside, or hook up.

The options the quarterback is very simple. For the X and Z receivers, they can run the out route and the Y receiver runs the double hook. The X and Y receivers run the six-yard speed-out route. They want to catch the ball and run down the sideline.

Next is another three-step pass. I have covered the hitch, and we can run the slant route. Now I want to cover the out route (Diagram #3). We are going to run the quick-out routes to the outside on both sides.

We teach our receivers to run the out route at six yards and to roll it out to eight yards. We like for them to flatten it a little, but still not too much. We can have the out route by the outside receiver and a hook route on the inside with the number-two receiver. The hook route is different every place I have played or coached. We are either going to hook inside, hook outside, or break outside. Normally we are going to hook out or break out unless there is a defender on the outside. If that happens, we are going to hook up.

We want the quarterback to read the play the same as they do on the hitch. If he sees the corner up, he is going to throw the quick out route. If we have an off corner and the safety buzzes up on the play, we are going to the hook. If we have a press corner, we are going to try to throw the fade route. We know we must control the free safety.

If we have a rolled up corner and the defense is playing cover 2, then we are going to work the second man inside on the hook route. This is determined by the linebackers. We want to work against the linebacker that is up tight and tucked inside where he cannot get outside to cover the pass route.

If we are playing against teams that want to play the corners up tight and force us to throw the ball down the field deep, we can run what we call "90 – halt." This call means we are going to run the hitch route no matter what the defense does. The corners know we are trying to run by them. We release the receiver and he pushes up to six yards and turns around. We get him the ball and the corner is still getting depth. It is an easy throw for us. Therefore, if team plays a lot of press coverage and we are running a lot of fade routes, we can call "90 – halt" and the hitch route stays on no matter what.

Three years ago, the Louisville quarterback was sacked a lot. When we looked at the tapes, we found out a lot of the problem was the way the quarterback scrambled out of the pocket. Now when we are working with the quarterbacks, and when we are designing plays, we want to make sure that ball comes out of the hands of the quarterback on that third step. We are going to do things on timing and we are going to get the ball away. If we take too many hitch steps, the quarterback will have to run the ball or throw the ball away. We do not want to hold the ball after the three-drop steps.

If it is press coverage, we may have to hold the ball a little longer to allow the receiver to work a little more. However, we do have a time limit and the ball has to come out.

We run inside option routes on both sides out of the twin sets. The inside receivers both run option routes (Diagram #4). The quarterback looks at one of the inside receivers and, if he is open, he delivers the football. If the one inside receiver is covered, the quarterback looks to the other inside receiver. If he is open, he makes the play to that receiver.

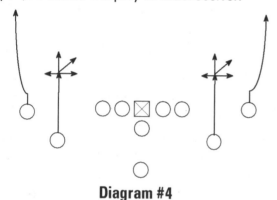

Diagram #4

The next concept we run is our hook package (Diagram #5). To the hook side, which is normally the wideside of the field, the third inside receiver is going to run a six-yard hook route. Our hook route is a hook in or out or a breakout. The second receiver runs an arrow to the flat, which is similar to what we run. We run a six-yard out route by the second receiver. The outside man on the fieldside runs his fade route. He uses an outside release.

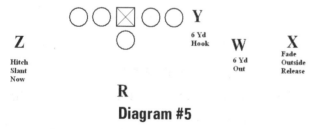

Diagram #5

The man on the outside to the backside runs individual routes. He can run a hitch, slant, or quick-out Route. We do not run these routes a great deal of the time, but we can run the individual routes if the defense is playing deep off the backside receiver. We try to make it as simple as we can for the quarterback. Unless the defense rolls up on the single receiver, we are going to throw him the hitch route.

I said we do move the pocket on our pass protection. We can move the pocket with our bootleg series and our naked series. In addition, we run the sprint-out series (Diagram #6). On our sprint-out passes, we want to get the ball out of the quarterback's hand so we can get the ball down the field and make the big play. At times we will roll out with an extra blocker and try to get the ball deep with a double move by the receiver. I will cover the sprint left slide play. We run this play against teams that are starting to jump on our corner routes.

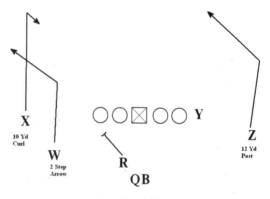

Diagram #6

The play is sprint left slide. It is a West Coast slide route. We have a receiver into the flat and we have a curl route. The progression for the quarterback is this. First, we are going to throw the ball to the flat. We make them cover the play. If the defense does not cover the flat, we are going to throw the ball to the flat. If the defense covers the flat, we are going to throw the hook route. We would like the quarterback to throw the ball on his fifth step. If the flat is not open, we want him to look for the hook route. If the hook is not open, the quarterback must stay on his path and run the play full speed. If defense has the run covered, the quarterback must throw the ball away. That is our sprint slide with the quarterback under the center.

If we run the play out of the gun, we want to throw the ball on the third step; but normally, it still takes the fifth step because it happens so quickly.

The key to the play is how quickly we can get the ball to the flat. If you get the ball to the receiver late, you cannot do much with the ball. The back is going to block the edge, and it is sprint slide blocking across the line.

The other play we run is the sprint right snag. The snag route to us is this. The outside receiver goes to angle inside, pivots at six yards, and then he sits down. If he does not get the ball inside, he comes back to the outside (Diagram #7). We always have a corner route and we have a back in the flat. Here we want to throw in the flat first. If the defense buzzes out of the area, we are going to throw the snag route.

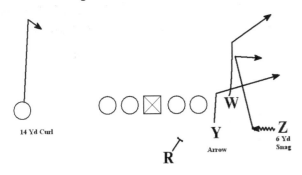

Diagram #7

Normally we do not throw the corner route at all unless it is press coverage on the corner. Really, he is just a control mechanism to clear the area for the other receivers.

The last point I want to cover is our five-step curl route (Diagram #8). This is our curl principle. We run our curl routes at fourteen yards. We have different stems. Sometimes we will stem inside, push up, and comeback up the field. Sometimes we get vertical, run to the post and then comeback. Other times we will go point-to-point. We will have someone running the curl, someone running the flat route, and we will have a receiver working in the middle of the field. Here we have curl routes by the outside receivers. The Y Receiver runs the six-yard look route. If we call "look," the quarterback is going to look for the Y Receiver first. Then the progression is to the curl route to the flat route. On all of our routes, we always have double moves off the calls.

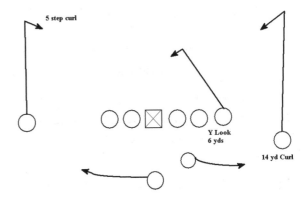

Diagram #8

I want to cover one last play. I will give it to you out of a trips set. To the tight end, we are going to run a ten-yard out route. The third receiver inside is going to run the drag route to clear out the linebacker. The number-two receiver is going to run an eight- to ten-yard inside option route. He is going to break inside or he is going to hook inside.

We run the post route on the backside and we run the stretch route with the one back (Diagram #9). We like to throw the ball to the number-two receiver. If the linebacker goes with the tight end on the drag, the second man inside on the hook or break is open. If the linebacker does not go for the man on the drag route and covers the second receiver on the hook route, we look for the tight end on the drag route.

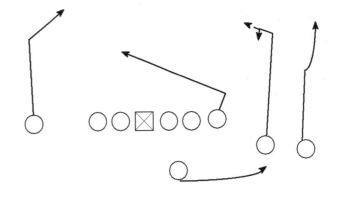

Diagram #9

The play is a quick five steps, plant, and then throw the ball. If the option route is not open, we throw the stretch route.

I will be around if anyone has questions. Thanks for your time.

DEFENSIVE PRESSURE AND BLITZ PACKAGE

University of Louisville

Thank you very much. It is a pleasure to be here. I am excited to be here tonight. I speak at five or six clinics each year and have done the same thing this year. However, I have looked forward to coming up here and sharing some ideas with you for some time.

I was a high school coach for the first three years of my career. What I am going to tell you tonight I used while I was coaching in high school. After my high school coaching, I have been at 12 universities. I have coached in the ACC, SEC, two Big 12 schools, two Big Ten schools, and two Big East schools. Since I do not have a surfboard, I probably will not make it to the West Coast. At nine of the twelve schools I have been a defensive coordinator using the same package I used in high school. My entire background has been a "Shade Fifty Defense," which is called a bend-but-do-not-break defense.

Nine years ago, I began to think that pressure defense was the trend of the future. The pressure package starts with an aggressive mentality. That mentality has to start with your head coach. When you are a pressure-type of defense, on occasion, you will give up some big plays. Coach Patrino wants the ball back because our offense is prolific.

The pressure package is disruptive for the opponent's offense. To get things going, the coaches and players have to buy into the ideas and system. When you play pressure defense, you have to get to the quarterback and when he does throw the ball, you have to have coverage.

The pressure package is a great way to jump-start your defense. This type of defensive play is a fast-break style and extremely high in tempo. When players come to Louisville, they know they will play a pressure style of defense. We are not a scheme team, but we are good at what we do. We have two blitzes every week and we add a third one, which we call a wrinkle.

When you start talking about pressure defense, players (and even the fans) get excited. When we run some blitzes, I tell our defense that one team's band is going to be playing after this play. I am just hoping it is ours. The blitzes we run are very sound. I call them sugar tablets. You give the players something and sell them. That idea will be one of the keys to success in this week's game. Our players believe that and most of the time it is true. To be successful everyone must learn his assignments and adjustments.

If you name a blitz after one of your players, it is a big deal. As simple as it sounds, there is something to that. I tell my players that the defense must be simple if I can coach it. Players make plays, not coaches. It does not matter how much you know as a coach, it only matter what your players can learn and what they can execute.

The coach has to work for carryover in his teaching. An example of this is the outside blitz man. He comes off the edge and is a containment blitz man. When we teach the outside blitz man, we teach him the hips technique. In the hips technique, we want the foot of the blitz man pointed in the direction he is going. His aiming point is the near back. The elbow is over his knee and his arm is back like a sprinter.

The blitz man sees the hips. If the hips are down and inside, he hits the tailback. If the hips go away, he hits the quarterback. If the hips come at him, he plays with his hands and leverages either the toss sweep or option. We coach that every day to our corners, safeties, Sam linebackers, and defensive ends.

A pressure package disrupts the offensive rhythm of a team. When a team plays Louisville, I do not want their quarterback to feel comfortable. I want their fans, trainers, players, and coaches to worry about protecting their quarterback. We want relentless effort from our team to get to the quarterback. We want penetration into the backfield by our defense.

The opponent has only four days to prepare for us. We want to give the opponent a number of fronts. We want to stem up and down the line of scrimmage. We want to use as many different personnel groups as we can in a game. We may align in an under defensive front and before the ball is snapped, we move to an over defense. That creates problems in the offensive line schemes. That also gives them problems in their protection schemes.

We time our stem on the quarterback. We want to break our huddle before the offense gets to the line of scrimmage. When the quarterback gets under the center, he looks right and then he looks left. When the quarterback centers his head and looks downfield, we move the defense. If they are walking to the line of scrimmage from the huddle, the quarterback is not going to snap the ball quickly. We want to give the offense problems, have fun, and make plays.

The pressure package scheme can create turnovers. We forced 27 turnovers this year. We also had 37 sacks this year. On two out of three snaps this year, we brought four, five, six, seven, or eight players on some kind of stunt or blitz. We hit the opposing quarterback 131 times last year. We want to give the offense the illusion that they have a lot to prepare for. As we get into the diagrams, I will show you several ways to cause problems for the offense, but keep it simple for the defense.

We want to make the quarterback hold the football and not throw on time. We want to use max blitzes against teams. We want to show the max blitz and drop off in coverage. We must put doubt in the minds of the offensive linemen.

We teach gap control in our defensive scheme. Coach Patrino gives us a lot of freedom. The only thing he wants is to make sure we are sound in what we are doing.

We run zone pressures as part of our overall scheme. What we like to do is run a zone pressure and come back with a maximum blitz. We compliment the maximum blitz with zone pressure, and then follow that with a maximum coverage. If you look at an offense, they have tendencies. You must know where they throw the ball and who their hot receivers are when they read blitz

Educate your players. We never say the hay is in the barn. We coach them all the way up to game time to gain an edge. We have a walk-through every Saturday morning when we play on Saturday afternoon.

I want to get into the types of pressures we run. We play with a four-man front and most of our pressure comes from that type of front. We play with a nose, tackle, end, and a rush end. We are in a zone, man-free, or man coverage with a four-man rush most of the time. If we play man coverage in the secondary, we use nine defenders to stop the run.

To be a successful defense, you must stop something. At Louisville, we want to stop the run. If we are in five-man pressure, we play man-free or fire zone in the secondary. With the six-man pressure scheme, we play a fire zone in the secondary. In the seven-man pressure and eight maximum blitzes, we are in man coverage.

Our base front is an "over defense." In the over defense, the nose, end, Sam, and Mike linebackers travel together in our front. If we call "over," we shade away from the tight end. In the "under" front, we shade toward the tight end. If we are in a straight line "over" defense (Diagram #1), the rush end aligns in a 6 technique, head up on the tight end, and contains from the outside. The tackle aligns in a 3 technique and has a two-way-go inside or outside the guard. The nose aligns on the backside shade of the center and has the A gap to that side. The end aligns in a 5 technique and comes off the edge.

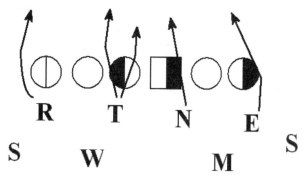

Diagram #1. Straight line

From this front, we run two-man twist games. The first on is called "tan" (Diagram #2). That twist involves the tackle and nose. The word tan stands for tackle and nose. The T comes first, therefore the tackle goes first in the twist and is the penetrator. The nose goes second and is the flasher or looper. The tackle slants hard into the strongside A gap and goes for penetration. The nose loops into the strongside B gap. The end and rush are the containment rushers from the outside. The tan is good against the running game. It distorts the gaps and makes it hard on the offensive line

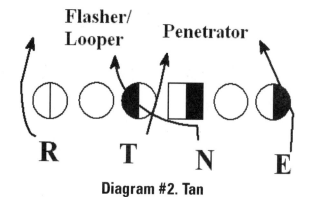

Diagram #2. Tan

The companion movement is the "nat" (Diagram #3). This movement is the opposite stunt. The nose goes first and is the penetrator. The tackle comes second and is the looper. The nose goes across the center's face aiming for the inside hip of the strongside guard. If the guard comes at the nose, he tries to cross-face the guard. If the guard blocks down on the nose, the linebacker fits into that scheme. We try to get the center to chase the nose to free the tackle as he loops around. We rip across the center, by dropping the outside shoulder, shooting the pad, and stepping through to the gap. The tackle as he comes around is in the backside A gap.

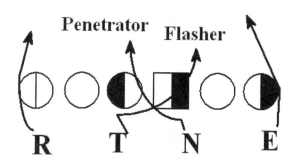

Diagram #3. Nat

The tackle steps up the field, engages the guard, and loops into the A gap. If he does not step upfield, the stunt happens to fast and the offensive line will pass off the defenders. We want to slow the tackle's loop and bring him on a delayed charge.

When we stem our fronts, most of the time we stem from an over to an under front, or an under to an over front. We can stem from the under front to the 46-Bear defense. If we call over defense, that is the defense we play. If we call under defense, that is the defense we play. If we call "stem under" we align in the over defense and stem to the under front. Some teams wait for us to call "move" before they snap the ball. They snap the ball on the move call. If that happens, we rip on the move and play football. If we face a team that does that, we do not twist much.

If we are in an under front and the tight end trades to the other side, we move the linebackers and adjust the secondary. We do not flip our line. If we call an over and that happens, we recall the front by saying "check opposite." On the call, the nose goes to the 3 technique and the tackle comes to the shade on the center. The rush comes to a 5 technique and the end moves to the 6 technique.

The "con" movement (Diagram #4) involves the contain end and the nose. The end goes first and is the penetrator. The nose goes second and becomes the looper. The end aims for the outside hip of the backside guard and goes for penetration. The nose charges upfield, makes contact with the center, and loops around through the inside shoulder of the backside tackle. We have not changed anything for the secondary. The only thing we have done is make the offensive linemen's job more difficult by giving them a different look.

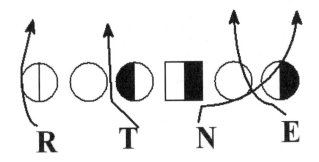

Diagram #4. Con

The companion stunt is "noc" (Diagram #5). It is the opposite stunt with the nose coming first and the contain end charging second. The nose slants hard through the B gap and is the penetrator. He is aiming for the inside hip of the offensive tackle and works for containment in his angle. The contain end, starts upfield and loops to the inside aiming at the inside hip of the guard.

We run the same line stunts to the other side. The only difference is they are one gap wider because of the alignment of the tight end. On the "tar" (Diagram #6), the tackle goes first working. He goes wide for containment off the inside hip of the strongside offensive tackle. The rush end comes second on the loop into the B gap.

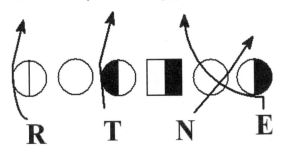

Diagram #5. Noc

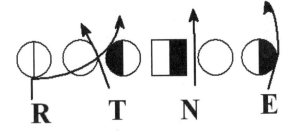

Diagram #6. Tar

The opposite of Tar is "rat" (Diagram #7). The rush end comes down over the offensive tackle into the B gap. The tackle comes upfield and loops to the outside. He works for contain on this movement.

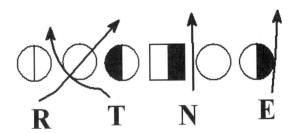

Diagram #7. Rat

The next two stunts you can emphasize as a run and pass stopper. We call "over con-rat" (Diagram #8), which is a combination stunt. We combine the con and rat stunt and twist from both sides of the line. In pass situations, I really like this stunt. People think you must have a fast noseguard to run this stunt. That is not true. The contain end tries to draw the tackle's block and the nose's path is tighter than it shows in the diagram.

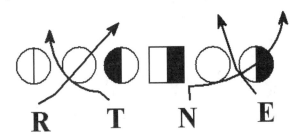

Diagram #8. Con-Rat

We want the nose to contain the quarterback, but we have a secondary contain man built into our scheme. If we play cover 2, the cornerback does not come up if containment is broken. We designate a linebacker on every play as the secondary contain man. Most of the time in cover 2, the Mike linebacker is the secondary contain man with the Will linebacker pushing to replace the Mike. Our head coach is more concerned about a second contain man than a total blitz.

The "noc-tar" is good as a run stopper (Diagram #9). This is another combination stunt with all four defender moving and we have not affected the coverage what so ever.

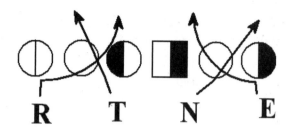

Diagram #9. Noc-Tar

We like a twist game against the draw. When teams get into the red zone, they like to split receivers and use motion to get the defense to bump the linebacker outside on motion. They want to run the draw or quarterback draw. We think the twist game is great against that thinking because it distorts the rush lanes.

We tell our defensive front to get into position to do the job. That means they may have to cheat some to get to the point they must go. At Louisville, we have built our reputation with man-free coverage and five-man pressure schemes. The first thing I want to show you is how we determine our matches in man coverage, which is our cover 1. In our over front, we align the Sam linebacker on the line of scrimmage outside the end with his toe pointed like he is coming on a blitz (Diagram #10). The Mike linebacker is in a 20 alignment over the backside guard. The Will linebacker is in a 40 alignment head up the strongside tackle. The strong safety lines up outside the tight end four yards off the line of scrimmage. The corners are over the wide receivers. The free safety splits the wide receivers at a depth of 10 yards with two-backs set in the backfield, and 12 yards with one back in the backfield.

The free safety's job on the snap is to shuffle-shuffle and read what is happening. He does not run backward because he is involved in the run game. He is the deep-hole player and helps the corners on the deep post route. If the running back goes to the flat, the Sam linebacker takes him. The strong safety and Will linebacker run a combo against the tight end and third receiver to the strongside. If the tight end releases inside, the Will linebacker takes him and the strong safety takes the back if he releases. In that situation, the Mike linebacker is the short-hole player in the middle of the field. The call for this defense is "over-single." This is a great run defense.

In our secondary, we play press man-free or off man-free with a deep-hole player. If we do not send anyone, we have a short-hole linebacker. If we tag a linebacker for blitz, we lose the short-hole player. We designate the linebacker to blitz by calling his name. If we call "over-Sam," the Sam linebacker is on the blitz.

We teach our blitz package as a concept. If we call an "inside stunt," it is an A-gap stunt. When we call "shoot", it is a B-gap stunt. If we call "plug", it is a C-gap stunt.

An example of this call would be "over-Sam-shoot" (Diagram #11). The Sam linebacker aligns on the line of scrimmage in his hips position showing an edge blitz. A second before the ball is snapped he moves off the line and cheats inside. On the snap of the ball, he blitzes the B gap and gives us five-man pressure. That stunt is a good change up in the run game as well as the pass.

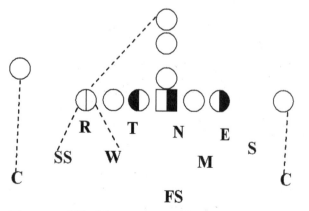

Diagram #10. Over alignment and assignment

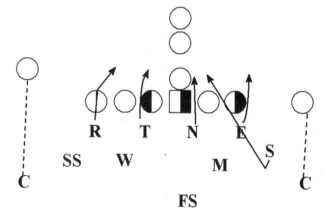

Diagram #11. Sam shoot

The plug stunt for the Sam linebacker goes by another name. If we call "over-Sam-single" (Diagram #12), the Sam linebacker knows he is running a plug stunt into the C gap. The end slants into the B gap as his rush lane. The Sam linebacker is a contain blitz man on the pass and the pitchman on the option. Teams like to run the option against pressure defensive teams.

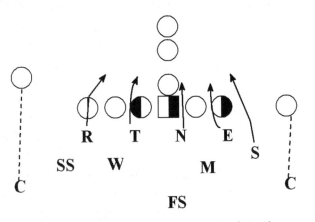

Diagram #12. Over Sam single (plug)

I will show you the blitzes I like and the ones that are most effective for us. The Will linebacker gets into the act if we call his name. The "over-Will-inside" (Diagram #13) is a stunt I really like. Offensive coaches hate A-gap penetration. If we run the "shoot" stunt for the Will linebacker, the tackle slants into the A gap. We do not run the Will linebacker on a plug stunt.

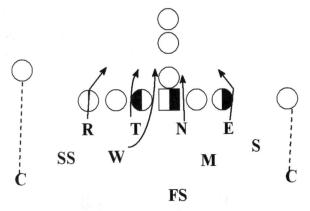

Diagram #13. Over Will inside

The combinations we can run with this type of pressure front are endless. An example of a combination stunt is "over-con-Will-shoot" (Diagram #14). The contain end and the nose run a backside twist stunt and the Will linebacker runs a

strongside blitz. The thing you do not want to do as a coach is try to run too many stunts. For each game we pick two or three stunts we think will be effective and practice the heck out of them. We do not try to use the whole package in any game preparation.

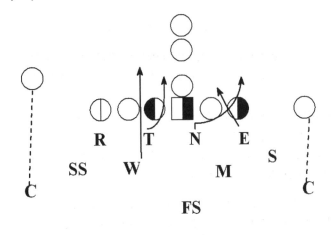

Diagram #14. Over-con-Will-shoot

The stunt we like using for the Mike linebacker is the inside stunt. We call "over-Mike-inside" (Diagram #15). On this stunt, the nose has to cross-face the center and get into the strongside A gap. The Mike linebacker times up his stunt and blitzes the weakside A gap. We tell our players that once they commit to the stunt, run it. If they have mistimed their blitz, we want them to stay at the line and come when the ball is snapped. We tell them to get their pads down and penetrate from the line of scrimmage. If they try to back out of the line and reload, at times we get caught backing up when the ball is snapped.

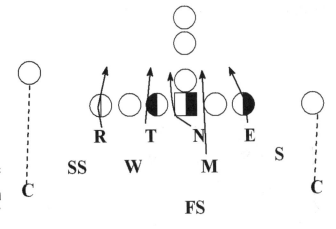

Diagram #15. Over-Mike inside

The Mike shoot is a good stunt to run with the rat or tar to the other side. That is another combo stunt involving both sides (Diagram #16).

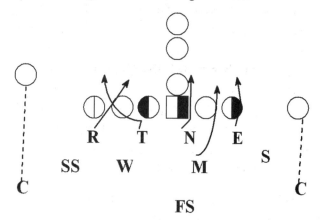

Diagram #16. Over Mike shoot rat

I want to talk about our six-man fire zones. In 1991, I was at East Carolina. We played Pittsburgh, South Carolina, North Carolina, and some other good teams. Bill Lewis was the head coach. We opened the season with the University of Illinois. The game came down to an onside kick at the end of the game. We did not get the kick and lost the game. In the game, we called three maximum blitzes and they threw three touchdowns.

After the game, we decided we did not have the personnel to play man coverage. We developed six-man fire zone and called the coverage hot. In the hot coverage, we matched up with the offense's hot receivers. This defense gives you the ability to blitz and not play man-to-man. This gives you six men blitzing instead of five. The disguise is zone coverage and, from that, you can blitz. This is good for the 4-3 defense showing cover 2 and running a fire zone. By running this defense, you take away the hot receivers from the offense. Teams we play will use maximum protection or use hot receivers.

I think I can pick the hot receiver from the opponent's formation every time. The offense on more than one occasion has thrown the football right to one of our defenders. When you use this scheme, it is like the other entire defensive scheme. It has to be simple for you players to understand. It took us two days to install the fire zone. You can run this out of every front you have. The fire zone has

the ability to adjust to all formations and keep it simple. It is a sound defense against the run.

The name of the front is "stack-G." It is an over defense with the exception of the nose and rush end. The nose aligns in a "G" position on the backside guard inside eye. The rush end goes to a 9 technique. That is an outside shoulder alignment on the tight end. We play cover 2 from this front. The coverage is hot and the blitz is hot. The coverage is a three-deep zone.

On the "hot blitz" (Diagram #17), The Sam and Will linebackers run shoot stunts. That sends them into a B-gap blitz. When the Will linebacker blitzes in the B gap, the tackle has to take the A gap. The end and rush are the contain men from the outside and the nose fires the weakside A gap.-

The nose, end, Mike, and Sam linebackers always travel together. If they go to the right of the defense, we say rip; to the left, we call Liz. The corners are aligned five yards deep and showing a good cover-2 jam technique. The safeties line up at ten yards on the hash marks like two deep safeties. Prior to the snap, the strong safety stems down to a position of two yards inside the slot receiver and six yards deep. He calls hot right or hot left. The Mike linebacker hears the direction of the strong safety, and moves to the opposite side and plays the tight end for the hot ball. In this set, the strong safety is playing the split receivers to the right. If the split receivers were to the left, he aligns on that side and the free safety moves opposite him. He sits on the quick receiver rather than the tight end.

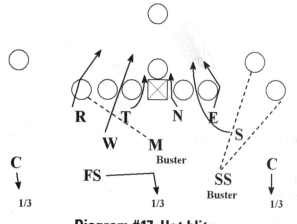

Diagram #17. Hot blitz

If the set is a balanced double slot set, the strong safety goes to the wide field. If the ball is in the middle of the field, he aligns to the defensive left.

The defense should look like a cover 2 prior to the snap of the ball. The strong safety stems down to a position of two yards inside and six yards deep on the number-two receiver and plays a "buster" technique. If the number-two receiver runs across the field, the strong safety has to get his head inside the receiver and play the coverage like man coverage. The corners retreat into the deep thirds and the free safety rolls to the middle third.

The buster technique is man coverage within an area of the field. The twin receivers could run a number of combination patterns. The twin receivers can run an out cut by the inside receiver and a fade by the outside receiver. The strong safety covers the out cut by the inside receiver. When he sees the flat pattern, his eyes go from the number-two receiver to the number-one receiver. When he sees the number-one receiver going vertical, he stays with the out cut by the inside receiver. If the inside receiver runs an out and the outside receiver runs a slant, the strong safety plays the out cut until he picks up the slant.

Another situation we have to play is the hitch by the number-one receiver and a flag route by the number-two receiver. When the corner sees the hitch, he calls "in" to the strong safety. He stays deep on the number-two receiver and the strong safety breaks on the hitch route.

The next combination we defend all the time is four verticals. The number-two receiver runs a vertical and the strong safety collisions him and settles. If the opponent likes to run the dig route to this receiver, the strong safety snaps off that route.

The last situation we get from this set is the curl by number one and the wheel route by number two. We tell the safety on a flat route by the number-two receiver to break under the number-one receiver and play the curl. We want the safety to play the curl and the corner to play the wheel.

If the set is a three-by-one set with a tight end to the trips side, we have a different adjustment (Diagram #18). The corners always start out showing a good cover-2 alignment. Prior to the snap, I want the corners back to a one yard inside by eight-yard alignment on the wide receivers. The strong safety has to tell the Mike linebacker he is hot left. The problem with that call is it sends the Mike linebacker right. Since the tight end is also left, the strong safety has to tell the Mike linebacker "trips hot left." Now the Mike linebacker can find the tight end and break on him.

The Will linebacker has to walk out into coverage on the number-two receiver in the trips set. Prior to the snap, he has to stem back inside and blitz into the B gap. The strong safety stems down and plays buster on the wide receivers in the trips set. The backside corner takes his adjustment a yard-and-a-half inside the wide receiver. He has to play the slant by the wide receiver. The good thing about this is the corners do not have to move in until the snap. If the one-back flares, the rush and end have a blitz pick-up call for them on the remaining back and one of them will cover him.

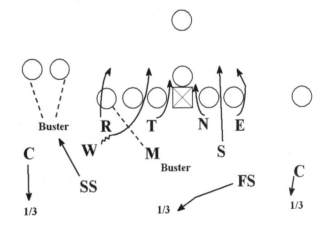

Diagram #18. Trips hot left

If the offense gave us a double slot set and motioned to a trips set, we exchange our safeties. At East Carolina, I used to run the strong safety with the motion and we can still do that. However, it is better for disguise if you swap your safeties. The stunt is the same and the Mike linebacker has his same hot coverage. The difference is the free safety stems down and the strong safety goes to the middle third. Everything would remain the same if the offense aligned in a trips set and motioned to a double slot (Diagram #19). The original call would be "trips hot left." As the motion came, nothing would change except the safeties.

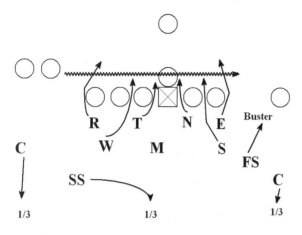

Diagram #19. Trips hot left motion

If you feel your strong safety cannot play in the middle third, run him across with the motion.

If the offense uses an I-formation and pro set, we have a flow call. The strong safety stems down and gives his hot call. If the flow is toward his call, we treat the formation as a trips formation. The Mike linebacker and strong safety are always the buster technique players. If they flow away from the hot call, the Mike linebacker works opposite the strong safety.

Before I go on, let me show you how to alter the fire zone slightly. We call this one "cardinal hot" (Diagram #20). On this defense, we left everything the same with the exception of the linebackers. We brought the Sam and Will linebackers on the outside off the edge, and brought the ends into the B gaps. Everything else stayed the same.

One of the things we found out about the pressure front was we had trouble defending the option game. We spent a lot of time trying to figure what option teams wanted to accomplish against us when we ran the pressure game. To defend the option you have to understand option principles. Option teams think the defense will continue to play the ball instead of their assignments.

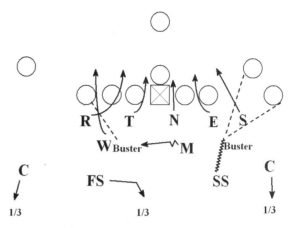

Diagram #20. Cardinal hot

In the three phase of the option game, we assign responsibility for each phase of that game. In our defense, the contain man will have the responsibility for the pitchman on the option. The alley runner has the quarterback and the dive goes to the player we designate as the dive player.

Option teams try to outnumber the defense at the point of attack. The option team tries to outnumber the defense by adding the quarterback as the third running back. They feel you cannot stop an option attack as long as the defense plays with a middle safety 12 yards deep. The option team wants to force the free safety to be a run support player.

Option teams force the defense to defend the field. I-formation teams force you to defend the vertical field with the throwing game. One-back teams force you to defend to the numbers. Option teams make the defense defend the tackle boxes. They make the defense defend outside the tackle box to the wide receiver position in the alleys. The third thing you have to defend is outside the number to the sideline. If the defense is unsound in any of those three areas, it will be a long Saturday.

Option teams will make the defense involve their defensive back in run support. If the defense does not involve their defensive back, they cannot stop the option teams. The quicker the defensive back become involved with run support, the quicker you will see the play action pass.

In my opinion, the hardest pass to defend from the option attack is the crack and go. The quarterback comes down the line of scrimmage and retreats to his set up point. The split end comes down on the inside safety as if he is going to crack back block on him. Instead of blocking him, he runs the go pattern.

The way the safeties beat the crack block is to get to the line of scrimmage in a hurry. You have to make the blocker come east and west to make the block. If he does that, it is easy for the corner to tell the difference between the block and the pass pattern.

The backside post pattern by the tight end is the next pass they run from the play-action off the option. The safety has to react up because the option has forced him to get into the running game. The backside corner must squeeze the tight end over the top to stop that route.

The last pass they throw is the throw back to the post-corner route. Let them throw that if they want. At our level, that is a tough throw for the quarterback. That is the hardest pass to complete.

Option teams believe they can take lesser athletes and beat you because of assignment football. The service academies are example of those types of teams. Army, Navy, and the Air Force Academy are going to be a hair slower and shorter on talent than most of the teams they beat.

All year long, the defensive coaches are after their teams to pursue the ball and run to the ball as hard as they can. The option teams depend on those types of teams losing their assignments in the pursuit to the ball.

The quarterback who runs the option attack does not have to be as skilled as the typical college quarterback is. Quarterbacks in the option attacks are runners and throwers. They are not passers in the sense we think of the passing game.

Option teams think they can dominate the game by controlling the time of possession. If you look at the stats sheets in today's football, the team that has the ball the most usually wins the game. That holds true if turnovers are not a factor.

If you are spending all your time as a defensive coach working on goal-line defense, you are not winning very many games. The option teams do not have a goal-line offense. What they run coming out and going in is the same offense. When they get to the goal line, their offense does not change. That is an advantage for them and they are right about that point.

The spread formation and the option are becoming the tread in college football. That is the option of the future. They want to create one-on-one tackles in the secondary. They force the linebackers to bump out in coverage. If the defense does not adjust, they stand up, hit an open receiver, and make a secondary back make a tackle in space. You have to displace the linebacker, which is what the option teams want you to do.

It is hard to duplicate the speed in practice at which these teams play. Your team has to prepare for the load, crack, and arc block in a short period. We work on option football every single day without our players realizing it.

You have four days to prepare for something the option teams do all year long. If you have not prepared for the option and you think you can do it in four days, it will be a long Saturday for you.

On the option, most people are locked into the way they play it. I want to talk out of both sides of my mouth right now. Talking out of one side of my mouth, your defense has to be sound and you must know your responsibilities. Talking out of the other side of my mouth, you had better have another way to defend the option. Out of one side, do not scheme an option football team. Out of the other side, the change ups can be simple.

Let me talk about the principles that hurt the option game. You must understand what kind of option you are facing. There is the speed option that pitches the ball off the last man on the line of scrimmage. The zone option is pitching off the safety. The G option is pulling a guard and trapping a lineman. Midline option runs are up the middle with a blocker on the quarterback defender. The spread option is the toughest one to play. There are two kinds of spread options. One option is run out of the two-by-two set or the three-by-one set with one back. They run the speed option from those sets. The second option is with three wide receivers in the game with a split back shotgun set in the backfield. They can run a dive option from this set. That is extremely hard to defend.

If you play against a team that sprinkles the option in their offense as an equalizer, they will run one of those five option schemes. A true option football team will run two or three of those different options. It is important that you define to your coaches and players what type of option you have to defend.

When playing an option team, you must disrupt the timing of the play. We do that two ways. The first way is to slow play the quarterback. The second way is a hard technique on the quarterback.

What we use at Louisville, you can get at Wal-Mart. It is a 38-gallon trashcan. They are generally gray and you can turn them upside down. We buy ten of them. I place them along a line and they represent offensive linemen. I like them better than bodies because they are good dummies. They just sit there. They do not mess around, talk to their buddies, or fool around. They sit there and represent good linemen.

I place one trashcan at either end of the tackle box. I place a manager five yards from the trashcan as a pitchman. All the Sam linebackers, strong safeties, free safeties, and corners participate in this drill. I play the quarterback and run the option at them. I want them to see the quarterback, get their outside foot back, their inside hand out, and feather the quarterback. They slow play the quarterback. They do not attack him; they play cat and mouse with him. The hard part of the drill is after they pitch the ball (Diagram #21). The first time I give them no instruction at all about angles. In 100 percent of the cases, they end up chasing the ballcarrier instead of tackling him. They have to turn and run as hard as they can down the line all the way to the sideline. When we do the drill, I do not care if they look at the ballcarrier. We do not have to use a ball, but we must give him a signal to turn and run.

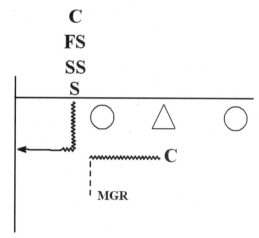

Diagram #21. Option pitch drill

We do this drill with every position on the team with the exception of the nose and tackle. We do the drill as a rapid fire drill with lots of reps. We teach the defender that he can take the quarterback and also leverage the pitch player if he takes the proper angle and sprints.

The hard technique is one of their favorite plays. They see the quarterback and attack him. I tell them to put stitches in his chin and force the training staff to break that little white capsule under his nose. The coaching point is the use of the outside arm. As the defender makes contact on the quarterback, he shoots his outside arm out and tries to hit the ball when it the man pitches it. We knocked down two balls on the pitch this year. The only time we get a big hit on the quarterback is a counter option. Teams do not run that option against us.

Most teams teach their quarterbacks to face the pitch key, and deliver the ball and fall back. When you play an option football team, take the star player away. Make the player you want to carry the ball carry it. If the quarterback is the star, make him pitch the ball. If the running back is the star, make the quarterback keep the ball. Do not let him pitch the ball to the star unless you are all over the pitch. Change up the techniques on the quarterback to slow him down and confuse him. Change the line stems, alignments, and coverage stems. Changing techniques on the quarterback puts indecision in the quarterback and makes him tentative in his play.

When we work our option responsibility drill, we do not use a ball. I do not want the entire defense swarming the ball. I want them playing responsibility. We do this drill in half line.

The next thing is the responsibilities in the pressure scheme. It is important that the player responsible for the quarterbacks in every defense knows his job. The pitch player is a single defender. The key to the defense is the half-half player. Usually the half-half player is a linebacker or backside safety. These players play the quarterback to the pitchman.

In our cover 3, or three-deep coverage, the quarterback is played by the end. The pitch player is the strong safety's responsibility (Diagram #22). The half-half player is the free safety and the pitch-and-pass player is the cornerback. The free safety reads the option in his shuffle-shuffle movement. He stays flat to the line of scrimmage and works flat behind the hip of the quarterback. We never want him in front of the quarterback. After the quarterback leaves the tackle box, the free safety attacks the quarterback from the inside out on a bowed angle. He wants to be able to attack the quarterback, but if the ball is pitched, he continues on to the pitchman.

In our cover 4, or quarter coverage, the quarterback player is the Sam linebacker. The safety is our pitch player. The half-half player is the linebacker and the pitch-and-pass player is the cornerback.

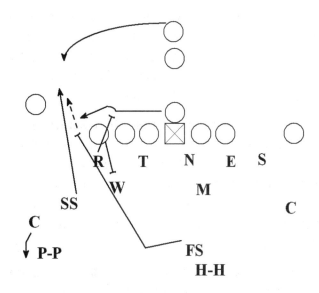

Diagram #22. Option versus cover 3

If the defense can create penetration in the B or C gap, it distorts the quarterback's pitch relationship. Penetration in those gaps forces the quarterback to pitch the ball quickly. That gives you extra players on the perimeter. If the quarterback does not get to the pitch key before he pitches the ball, the pitch key is unblocked and in the pursuit pattern. As a defense, you want to create lost yardage plays and turnovers. A lost yardage play to an option team is hard to overcome in that series of downs.

Thank you for your attention. I am sorry I did not get to the drill tape. If you would like a copy of the tape, send me a blank tape and I will see you get a tape. There are 42 drills on this tape. Again thank you for the opportunity to speak here today.

LOGISTICS OF THE NO-HUDDLE OFFENSE

San Diego State University

I am a little under the weather today, but I want to give you some ideas that may help you in your program. I am going to talk about the no-huddle offense. We have been running this offense a long time, perhaps too long. We started running this offense in 1979. I will give you a short prelude to why we went to this offense and how far we have come with the system over the years.

I served as an assistant coach at Palomar Community College from 1977 to 1982. We were the worst football team in the country. With the school openly questioning its commitment to football, I suggested to our head coach to let us run the no huddle offense. After questioning me why we should use the offense, I finally convinced the head coach to let us try it in a game. He told me we could run the offense as long as we scored on each series.

We were able to score three straight times in the first game we used the offense. On the fourth series, the other team scored a touchdown and the head coach canned the no huddle offense. We ended up getting beat 38 to 36 in that game.

That experience really had an impact on me as a coach. I took over the head coaching duties in 1983 at Palomar. I was a young coach and I was not wet behind the years so I took the job as head coach at Palomar College. After a pair of 4-6 seasons, we began to improve. By the time I left the San Marcos school for the Aztec coordinator's job, Palomar was coming off a three-year stretch of 31-2 record. We had an offense ranked among the nations top five for five consecutive years and were sporting two national championships.

After three years at San Diego State, I returned to Palomar and spent five more seasons at the school, producing another eight-win, 10-win, 11-win season, and another national title.

At Palomar College, my record was 115-56-1. Five of our teams won at least 10 games and we won three national championships and three California community college state championships. I was the State Coach of the Year five times and the Mission Conference coach of the year nine times. We posted a 9-3 record in bowl games.

I took the offense and finally figured out a way to practice with the system and we became very effective using the no huddle offense.

If you are going to be a no huddle offense, you must be committed to practicing the offense all of the time. You cannot use the offense the last two minutes of the half and at the end of the game. You must be committed to the offense to make it work.

I went to San Diego State as an assistant in 1994. I put the offense in and had great success. Ted Tollner was the head coach. In 1995, we had a 1,500 plus yards rusher, a 2,000 plus yards receiver, and a 3,000 plus yards passer. I was shocked to learn this was he first time this was done in the history of college football.

I went to San Diego State three years ago and we have the offense in the working. The thing we are excited about is the fact we are developing an offensive style and a defensive system where we can attract good players to come to our school.

I can tell you some of the advantages and some of the disadvantages of our system. There are things I am not going to tell you about our system because I just will not tell you everything we do. I can tell you as far as our calls that we use "words," we use "numbers," and we use "symbols." We use a variety of things in our offense.

When we are on offense, the first thing the quarterback does is to look to the sideline at me. I signal the formation in to the quarterback. He will call out the formation to both sides of the offense. We try to get our receivers to watch the signals as I give the formation to the quarterback. Most of the time the receivers on the side of the field where we are located can see us and pick up the signals. The quarterback wants to make sure he gets the signal to the players on the sideline away from us. That is the first thing we do from a procedure standpoint.

The next thing we do is to signal in the play to the quarterback. From there the quarterback sets the play to both sides of the formation. We control the snap count as well as the play.

It does not really matter how fast you go in running the plays. The bottom line, after the ball is snapped, is how good you are. Are you good at the football fundamentals, and are you good as football players? Teams get caught up in schemes and try to confuse the defense. It does not matter what scheme you use unless you can execute the plays.

Let me talk about the advantages and disadvantage of the no huddle offense. I have some points of reference that I will take you through. I have talked about this before but I have some different thoughts about this now. By using the no-huddle offense, we gain certain advantages.

First, our offense can create a state of anxiety for our offensive coordinator and the head coach. It can be a state of anxiety trying to run the offense if you do not make a commitment to the offense. You must make the commitment. That means you can do a variety of things. I will go over our schedule and show you how we go about our practices covering the fine details of the offense.

By creating a state of anxiety, I mean the offense is going to dictate to the defense what they can do and what they cannot do. We do not want them to be able to do things they like to do during a game. We want to force them to do things they are not use to doing in a game.

We designed our offense with the players in mind. With today's age of specialization, the kids strive in this type of offense. This is one of the factors makes football fun.

Second, it simplifies the defense. It goes back to what I just said. Some teams try to play you with certain personnel on certain downs. This offense makes it difficult for the defense to specialize with their personnel on certain downs. We may favor playing against a certain defensive personnel grouping. We can dictate to the defense as far as the personnel types they play against us.

We used to be able to establish the tempo of the games. Now that our league is going to instant replay review, we will be having too many timeouts to establish the tempo as we use to do. That is something we will have to work on.

Establishing the tempo is one of the four areas that are important in establishing the game plan. We have our first down plays. We have our third down and long, third down and short, and we have our red area. Now we can call the plays regardless of the situations in the game. You can make it all a part of your game plan.

Fourth, it gets your quarterback more involved in the game. The concentration factor goes up tremendously. It keeps the quarterback more interested. He makes decisions quicker.

In many cases, the defenses do a good job in preparing for the offense. They do a good job of disguising what they are doing on defense. We have different fronts; they stem the defense, and the string out the defense. Then we change things and go to a huddle. Now the defense comes out and plays it straight. They do not disguise what they are doing and it is what we want on offense. It is amazing to go back and change things to get the defensive look we want.

Fifth, it creates more repetitions on offense. A normal offense can get six plays in five minutes. If you are a huddle team and you have a ten-minute period, it means you can run 12 plays in that time period. If you have a fifteen-minute period, you may get in 18 plays. With the no-huddle offense, we can almost double the number of plays we can run in the same amount of time.

We have started spring practice and we have a scrimmage tomorrow. We have installed everything we need to run the no-huddle offense in three days. We start out running 12 plays per team in a series. Then we game-plan six plays in the next series and six in the third series. We picked all of the offense up by starting with three plays, then six plays, and then eight plays. We end up running about 25 plays with the no huddle and about 35 using the standard huddle. We want to push the envelope with them, but the main thing is to introduce the offense first and then do a portion of the offense at the line of scrimmage. Gradually, we build on the script and eventually we can run all of our offense in the no huddle.

Sixth, we become better practice players by using this system. It becomes a mental thing for the players and they have to concentrate on what we are doing. The mental aspects of the players are stimulated with the offense. We try to do things quicker and faster and the players are not bored. It can get boring if the players are standing around in practice.

Seventh, the team is in better condition. There is no question about this point. We struggle somewhat early in the season to stay in the huddle for the entire game. By the time we get to mid-season, we are a different football team. In our first game two years ago, we played Ohio State and they were coming off their National Championship year. We played them tough and should have beaten them but we lot to them by three points. This year against Michigan, we lost again by three points to start the season. Our offense is a style of football that allows us to be creative on offense. Our offense is an offense that can put your team into a competitive situation when you are outmatched.

Eighth, the type of offense we run allows our offense to be well organized. I will give you a couple of sequences during practice that we use that helps us to be better prepared. Our coaches know they must coach on the run.

We had a specialist come in and work with our staff and our players. He was the same doctor that worked with Ryan Leaf. He worked with our players and staff. We learned a great deal from the time spent with him.

The doctor was a "big picture" psychologist. He said if the assistant coaches are the "big picture"-type position coaches, they will pay more attention to the total game and leave out some of the small details related to the specific position they are coaching. He said if assistant coaches have aspirations of becoming head coaches and coordinators, they do the same thing in that they become big picture coaches. They leave out some of the fine details and do not stress the fundamentals as much as they would if they were not looking at the big picture.

My job was to get the position coaches from one position to the other position where they did not concentrate on the big picture as much. The head coach must be a "big picture" and a fundamentalist at the same time. This is an interesting way to view the game. The thing I got out of the procedure was to pay more attention to detail and coaching on the run. The other thing I got from the study was the way we structured our practice sessions.

Ninth, it made it difficult to scout tendencies within our offense. This may or may not be a big advantage because it all depends on how you put our game plan together. All this is for our offense is a conditioning process that we do in practice every day. Our players are used to the quick practices. Our coaches work them at a faster pace as well. When we play a team that has only been working for three days against this type of offense, it makes it difficult for them. It can overwhelm them.

I have been running this system for 27 years. In the middle of the second quarter, you can really start to see the difference in the teams. We are really a good football team right before the end of the first half. In the last part of the third quarter and into the fourth quarter, there is a big difference in the efficiency of the teams.

Let me cover some of the disadvantages of the no-huddle offense. First, it puts more pressure on our defense. This is how we approach that situation. We take the pressure off our defense by scoring. We want to have a fast breaking type of offense. By putting the pressure on the other team, it takes pressure off our defense. I have heard this from the media. The statements came from the media even though we were having a good season: "Well, you are good on offense, but you cannot have a good defense if you run the no-huddle offense. Your defense will be on the field too long." I tell them our defense is not on the field too long. We are on the field quicker at times but no more than we normally would be in a game.

Another factor to consider is this. In 2003, we had the best defensive football team in the history of San Diego State. We ranked eighth in the country on total defense. So do not tell me we cannot have a good defense. We sell our defense on this idea. You may have to be on the field quicker but we are going to take the pressure off the defense because we are going to score.

Young players get confused in the offense and because they are confused, they may lack confidence. This is an intimidating thing. We know our young players have to learn things at a fast pace and that can be a problem especially for those young players. We really try to take our younger players and expose the offense to them but we do not rush them because we do not want them to lose confidence and get frustrated.

I want to move to the next step in this lecture. I have listed some of the variations of the no-huddle offense based on the game. The first variation is tempo. I have a week's plan of how we go about putting together our game plan for the week so we can use a fast-paced, no-huddle offense. This relates to planning. What are we going to do on third and medium, third and long? What are you going to call in the red area? We have to huddle in the red area. We started six freshmen on offense this year. We played eight freshmen on offense. We were in the top 20 in the country on offense. I believe we can be good on offense in the future.

Tempo is an important process to us on offense. The young players learned to function in the offense and now they must learn it in detail. Tempo is very important to our offense. That is why we work on the play on the wideside, boundary plays, and red-zone plays.

The next disadvantage is it allows the defense to stall on their defensive alignment. We tell our offense to "wait and see!" It takes the guesswork out of play calling. Today, defensive teams will not show their alignment until the quarterback gets his hands under the center and starts calling the plays. Remember what I said earlier. If that is the case, then we will go back to our huddle. If the defense does a good job of disguising the coverage and their stems on defenses, we go back to our regular huddle. We go back to the huddle, then come up to the line of scrimmage and then call the play. The defense is conditioned to do one thing, and they may not be conditioned to do something else. That is the beauty of this system.

We call our fast alignment "bonsai." We come out with two tight ends and two wide-outs. We have used this to move the ball down the field. We can stay in that same formation and run our offense. You will be amazed how fast you can run the offense in this alignment. We do not flip flop our receivers in this alignment.

In the mid 1990s, we were able to do this all of the time. We were seventh and eighth in the nation on offense in 1995 and 1996, respectfully. But today as soon as you flip-flop your personnel it sets off an alert to the defense. What the defense has a hard time with is a balanced set on offense. It may not be the case with high schools, but that is the case for us at our level. It is funny how things change in this respect.

The squeeze is what we call a designed sequence of three or four plays that you can use in certain situations. We run a selection of plays packaged for our offense. You can go on the first sound and go as fast as you can line up. Here is an example. You may start out in a no-backs-set. We are going to come out and run three receivers to one side and two receivers to the other side on the play.

You do not want to have a complicated reading progression play. You may want to come out and run an isolation route to your best player that you know is going to be good. Next, you may want to line up in an unbalanced line because you know the ball is going to be in a certain area on the field and run the toss play. The third play will be a play to the wideside of the field. You would be surprised how well the kids strive to make the plays work. Our kids look forward to it every day. You would be surprised how fast they will line up for you.

Then you can back off and call a play to complement the plays you have just run. It gives the offense confidence and it creates a sense of urgency for when they are on the field.

We have used the "three plays" aspect one time in each half. We may not run these plays until we get to the opponent's 30-yard line. Then we use the "three plays" to hit the defense with a different tempo. It is two different sequences of plays.

Now I want to move to the "weekly schedule." The first thing we do is to figure out what are going to be our base running plays. Next, we list what is going to be our "specialty runs." This is the key. I want a "priority progression" of our favorite formations from the best to the least favorite formation. That is how we game-plan for the week:

- Running game
- Prioritize by formations
- Base plays
- Specialty plays
- New plays
- Blitz beaters

After going through the formation, we script the plays we were going to use. You see our favorite formation listed more than the other formations. We run a lot more plays from the favorite formation than we run from the third or fourth best formation. This really helps us adjust in the second half.

In the fall, we look at the new plays we plan to use for the upcoming game. The last things we look at are the plays we consider as "blitz beaters." These are plays we are going to take a shot on this play to burn the defense on the blitz. We can run a special play to get us out of a tough spot. We must have a plan to deal with the blitz and we must be able to do it from the first day. We want to work on three things in our weekly schedule: run game – new plays – blitz beaters.

This takes us into our Tuesday practice session. For high schools, it may be your Monday practice. We practice early in the morning. We do not practice in the afternoon. We practice at 6:30 AM. We have two dirt fields and the weather is nice. It is a lot cooler in the morning in San Diego. This is especially true in September. It works out great for us. One thing I like about the early practice is the fact that not many people get up and watch us practice.

The practice is devoted to the base run, pass, and the blitz beaters and special plays we are going to use in the game coming up. We work on the plays we are going to run on first and second downs. This is what a mixed down is to me, first and second downs. The first and second downs are ten times more important than the third down. The third down is the most overrated play in football. Third down is the play the media loves to talk about and discuss.

We only use the seven-on-seven once a week. When we go one-on-one, we use non-verbal signals. I do not want anyone yelling the route out. I want it all done by using signals. The wide receivers all stay outside in their position. This helps us when we get in a stadium where the noise level is so great.

When we use the seven-on-seven, we do the same thing. We stand at the line of scrimmage. I signal the play to the quarterback. I let the receivers see the formation and the play. The quarterback tries to signal the play instead of calling it out. We can split it up and run half of the plays with verbal commands and half with visual signals. By doing this, we get in more reps.

I do not like to run the nine-on-seven drill that much. I like 11-on-11. I want the receivers to be able work on alignment quickly. I want the linemen to see the defenders they are going to block. We may only go for 10 minutes but we get in 18 to 20 plays. We may have the first unit go two sets of eight plays and then the second unit comes in and runs their two sets of eight plays.

We script the defenses we want to use against our offense. We give them the front and the secondary coverage. The defense knows from the script what we want them to show the offense. I do not have a copy of the defense. It gives me a chance to rehearse to get ready for the game. You have to get ready to call the plays the same way you will be calling them in a game. The coach ends up being a quarterback calling the plays. You can train yourself to call the game from the sideline and not rely on someone up in the box to call the plays for you. You can still get feedback from the press box but you can get used to calling the plays from the sideline. A big thing with the media is the fact that I do not wear a headset. So, big deal!

On our practice on Wednesday, we compile the third down and medium, third and long, and third and extra long. You will find there are a lot more third down and medium plays than there are third down and long. You must convince your quarterback to stay out of third and long situations. We have a lot more plays to select from in third and medium than we do on third and long. We also work on the red zone area and we work on our blitz period. When we work on the third down plays, I want the entire team watching the offense. I want the team to hear the kind of plays we are going to use on third downs.

We like to go one's on one's for about seven minutes on Wednesday. We do not want them to get stale by not going live for a few plays.

On Thursday, we work on our red area, short yardage plays, goal-line offense, and screens and draws. We do not hit during this practice session.

One of our goals this spring is to be a better play-action team. Last year we threw for 2,700 yards and ran for 1,700 yards. We were successful on our play-action plays 39 percent of the time. We had a sack or a hit on the quarterback 14 percent of

the time. If we can just improve our play action passing game 11 percent it will get us up to the 50 percent mark. In our drop-back game, we are successful over 70 percent of the time. We must get the play-action game up to our drop-back game.

When I script the plays, this is how I set it up. The first play is first and ten, the second play is second and eight, and the third play is third and one. The very first third down that we have, we want to make sure it is third and one for the first down.

We come back and put the ball on the two-and-a-half-yard line. "It is fourth and three to go for the touchdown. It is the last play of the game." What play would you use? Then we put the ball back to the 12-yard line and tell them it is fourth and goal from the 12-yard line. We are not going to call the same play on fourth and three that you would call on fourth and three.

Next, we put the ball on the 38-yard line. It is fourth down and two to go for the first down. This makes the defense think about the play. It makes the offense think about the play. Our kids are ready to respond to these situations.

Someone asked me to review our middle screen play (Diagram #1). The screens and draws do not fit our special plays in our offense. We were not a very good screen team in the first part of the season. As the season went on, we got better. There is a timing and rhythm to the screen play. This is especially true of a middle-screen play.

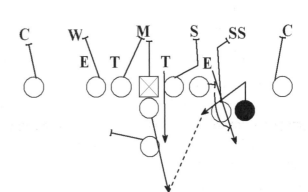

Diagram #1. Middle screen versus three linebackers

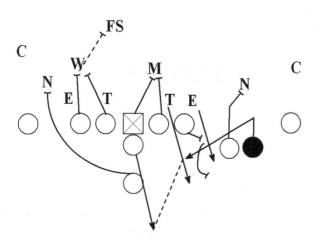

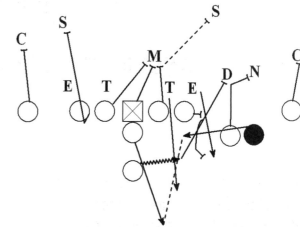

Diagram #2. Middle screen versus two linebackers

Diagram #3. Middle screen versus one linebacker

The play is designed for a three-backer rule and a one-backer rule. The first thing we do is to run this play against a three-linebacker set. We can throw the ball to any of the receivers. Our center makes a "3" call. This tells the line the defense has three linebackers. The tackle takes the defensive end back four yards deep. We throw the ball in the "tunnel" to the receiver coming back inside. We are going to double the Mike linebacker. The onside guard takes the Sam linebacker. The slot man squares out on the strong safety. The offside tackle drop steps and goes for the Will linebacker. He goes at an angle to pick up Will as he comes to the ball. The remaining back swings opposite where the pass is going.

The next set is against a nickel defense and a two linebacker set (Diagram #2). Now we are going to double the Will and Mike linebacker.

Next, we see the one linebacker set. We look for the line stunts when we see the one linebacker set (Diagram #3). We must have the linebacker call on the play so we know how we are going to block the play.

There are a lot of plays that can come off the middle screen play. We have used this play for a long time and it has been good to us.

Joe Daniels

PASSING GAME USING BASIC CONCEPTS

The Ohio State University

When we start talking about the young quarterback, there are many aspects to consider. Everyone has their base offense they believe reflects their philosophies and is what they stand for. It is like an off-tackle play as the signature run in your offense. This is the play you hang your hat on and believe in. That is good because the players are going to believe that also. You spend a tremendous amount of time doing repetitions on this play.

The quarterback gets good at running the play because he has done it so many times. In addition to the quarterback getting good at the play, so are the receivers. They get exposed to that particular route and all the situations that could occur in running the route. I am going to show you one of our base routes. You want to take the base route and incorporate it into your offense as much as possible. It is critical because it is a comfort point for the young quarterback.

Strange things happen so many times as you go through the course of the year. You get into the ninth game and your pass offense does not look anything like the offense you started with and believed in. It does not happen all the time, but it happens too many times. It happens more in the NFL than it does anywhere else. It used to drive me crazy because we would spend hours on the playbook. We had a playbook full of the things we liked and wanted to hang our hats on. We went through mini-camps, two-a-day sessions, and five weeks of pre-season and the quarterbacks really got good at what they were doing. The quarterbacks and receivers understood all the little adjustments that went with the base offense. When we got to the third or fourth game of the season, our offense had nothing that resembled what we were doing at the start of mini-camp.

I am going to show you a base route. This pattern has a dozen different names. We call the route a "fish route" because of the hook (Diagram #1). I have the play drawn up in a pro formation with a "king set" in the backfield. A king set puts the tailback behind the quarterback and the fullback in the strong halfback set toward the tight end. It is a basic seven-man protection. The fullback has the Sam linebacker and the tailback has the Will linebacker. The line has the four down linemen and the Mike linebacker.

The tight end, which we call the Y-receiver, tries to take an inside release. He takes a vertical push up the field and stops at six yards right over the football. In our terminology on that "home route," the X-end and Z-back run hard vertical pushes to 12 yards and come back into a buttonhook pattern. The fullback runs a swing or flat to his side if the Sam linebacker does not come on the blitz. The tailback checks the Will linebacker and runs a swing if he does not come.

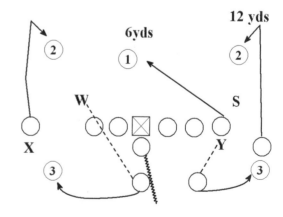

Diagram #1. Fish route

If we are in an I-formation, we run a swing route as the base. In the divide or split-backs we can get the same protection. We run the flat patterns.

The quarterback progression goes to the home route as the first read. If it is open, the quarterback throws the ball to the tight end. The drop on this play is a five-step drop. If the home route comes open, the quarterback aborts the drop and throws the ball to the tight end. It could look like a hot throw if thrown on the second or third step.

If the Mike linebacker jumps the tight end, the defense is balanced and it does not matter to which buttonhook the quarterback throws. If he chooses to throw to the strongside, the fullback becomes the third choice of the quarterback. If he looks to the weakside, the tailback is the third choice. If the Sam linebacker takes the home route away, the quarterback goes to the Z-back. If the Will linebacker takes the tight end, the quarterback throws to the X-end.

We do not convert our outside routes if the coverage is not a cover 3. If the coverage is cover 2, we live with the route and make it work. Our receivers are coached to release outside on an outside route and inside on an inside route. A hook is an inside route and the receiver takes an inside release. If the defense is cover 2, the corner will allow an inside release. The corner will jam the receiver inside, but the receiver must fight for width in his pattern.

If the defense is cover 1, which is man-to-man coverage with a free safety, the receiver has to win against that coverage. Every day we work route on air against defensive backs. A big part of that one-on-one practice is man-to-man press coverage. In this practice against man coverage, the route we want run is the hook route. Just because a defense plays press coverage, the receivers do not have to run a fade route. If the press coverage takes the inside release away, the receiver has some work to do to get back inside. He does whatever he has to do to get open.

The ball can go to the tight end or running back, but the wide receiver must get open because he is the number-two choice in the progression. Since we are not going to convert the route to something else, the receivers have to get open against any kind of situation and coverage.

We would rather not throw this route against cover 2 or cover 1 coverages, but we can. If the quarterback knows what coverage he is going to get on a particular play, he is going to have an easy game. If the quarterback knows the coverage that is coming, it will be a long day for the opponents.

Most of the time what we expect does not happen. A good team is not going to let you pick them apart with tendencies. My point is the offense has to work all their routes against all different situations so they can run them when they need them.

We number our protection schemes and have words for our pass routes. Every time I run the fish route, it is the same pattern for the outside receivers, tight end, and running backs. We can change the look by going to a different formation. However, it is the same pattern for the receivers and same read for the quarterback.

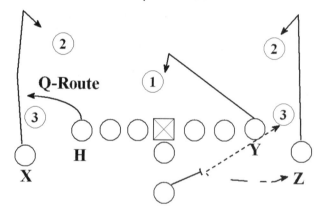

Diagram #2. Fish two tight ends/one back

The next formation is two tight ends, one running back, and two wide receivers. Instead of a fullback in the formation, we have a second tight end called an H-end. We can run the fish route (Diagram #2) from this set. We could run the home route with either the H-end or Y-receiver, but in most cases, the Y-receiver runs the home route because we shade our protection that way. If we change the protection and send the back the opposite way, the H-end runs the home route and the Y-receiver runs the flat. The wide receivers run their 12-yard hook routes. The protection is six-man protection because we have only one back. The one-back checks the Sam linebacker before he releases on the swing pattern. The H-end runs the flat route run by the fullback. We label the receiver as the Q-receiver and he becomes a quick or hot read for the quarterback. We have a six-man protection scheme and if the Will linebacker blitzes, the quarterback has to throw hot.

The quarterback's progression on the fish route is the home route as the first choice. Whoever takes the home route away, the quarterback goes opposite and throws hook to flat. It is the same read and throws for the quarterback, which builds confidence and consistency.

If we run three wide receivers, a tight end, and one-back, we still run the same patterns (Diagram #3). The tight end runs the home route. The outside receivers run the hook routes. We are in six-man protection with the running back shading the home route side. He keys the outside linebacker to that side and runs a swing or flat route. The inside receiver to the twin-receiver side becomes the Q-receiver. If a linebacker blitzes from the outside, the quarterback has to throw hot. Everything is the same in this set.

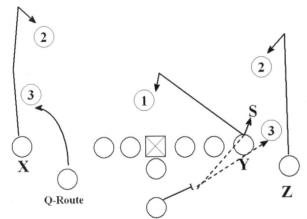

Diagram #3. Fish three wide receivers tight end

This pattern has the same five-step drop and same progression read for the quarterback. In this formation, we generally get a two-linebacker look with six in the box. If we get an inside linebacker blitz, the quarterback throws hot to the tight end.

The next set puts the tight end and flanker into the shortside of the field with the wide slot to the wideside of the field. The third receiver in the slot is the W-receiver (Diagram #4). He runs the home route and the tight end runs the flat into the shortside. The outside receivers run the hooks and the running sets to the wideside of the field and reads his linebacker. If he gets no blitz from the linebacker, he runs the swing route into the field.

The detached receiver running the home route has a basic rule. When he runs the home route, he runs it to the middle of the field. He does not necessarily run it to a position over the ball. We expect the tight end to run his pattern over the ball. The slot receiver must have a big enough split to create some space in the secondary. The home route from a split position ends up over the guard-tackle gap. This set puts a better athlete as the primary receiver.

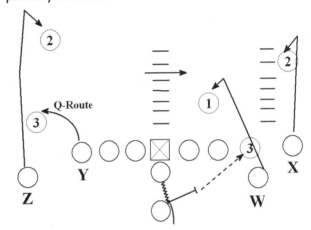

Diagram #4. Three wides/tight end shortside

If we run the fish route from four wide receivers, the W-receiver goes into the boundary (Diagram #5). The fourth wide receiver is still the Y-receiver. The slot receiver to the wideside runs the home route. It is almost identical to the last formation and pattern running. The spot of the ball tells the Y-receiver how far to come in to run his pattern. If the ball is on the hash mark, he may run the home route slightly inside the middle of the field. With four wide receivers in the game, the quarterback is probably aligned in the shotgun with the running back set to the wideside. In the shotgun set, the quarterback's drop is a three-step drop. The running back is still reading and running a swing or flat pattern. The W-receiver becomes the Q-route or hot route.

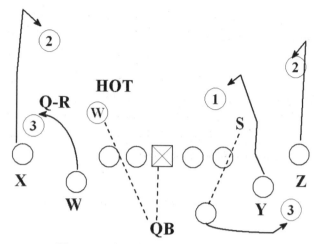

Diagram #5. Four wide receivers

The quarterback is trying to read the coverage, but he has to be aware of the blitz from the weakside and throw hot if needed. If the quarterback put the running into the weakside, the W-receiver runs the home route and the Y-receiver runs the flat or Q-route. The quarterback's hot read becomes the wideside of the field.

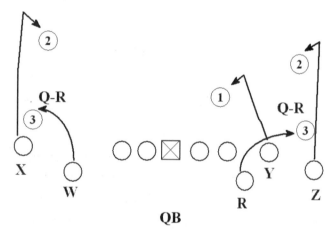

Diagram #6. No backs

I have shown a number of different looks, but the route and reads never changed for the quarterback. If we wanted to go to five wide receivers with no backs in the backfield, the play would stay the same (Diagram #6). Our formation would be a three-by-two formation with the quarterback in the shotgun. With three receivers into the wide field, the middle receiver runs the home route. The outside receiver runs a 12-yard hook and the inside receiver runs a flat. To the two-man side, the outside receiver runs the 12-hook and the inside receiver runs the flat route. The

difference in this situation is the quarterback has a Q-route to each side because we are in five-man protection. The inside receiver to each side is running a hot route for the quarterback.

The key to all these formations is that the person pulling the trigger gets to see the same thing repeatedly. He becomes confident and consistent. Every situation has an "if" to it. If the defense did a lot of stunting when we went to no backs, we would not run this type of play. Your game plan has to fit what the defense does.

If I want to run the same pattern but adjust it somewhat, I can put a tag on the route (Diagram #7). This set is a twin-receiver set to the wideside of the field and a tight-end-flanker set to the boundary. We run the fish route into the wideside of the field. The backside receivers run the 12-yard hook and the Q-route or flat route. I can call a special route for the X-receiver by adding a tag to the play call. The call would be "54-fish, W-home, X-stutter." The number 54 in the call is the protection. The W-receiver runs the home route and the X-receiver runs a stutter and go pattern.

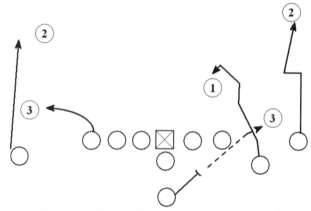

Diagram #7. 54 Fish W-home X-stutter

If I feel the defender is sitting on the hook route, I tag one of the wide receivers with the stutter call and try to get deep. You can tag receivers from all your formations. On this pattern, you want more protection because the pattern takes more time to run. We probably would go to a seven-man protection for this play. When you want to try and hit the home run, protect the quarterback and give him a chance to throw.

When we tag one of our receivers, we do not tell the quarterback to throw to that receiver. The coach in the press box watching the play develop may see the opportunity to go deep by the way the defender covered our receiver. He calls for the deep pattern again and this time the defender aligns 18 yards off the receiver. We coach the quarterback to run the play and not go to the tagged receiver. We want the quarterback to look at the receiver and if the defender is over-playing the hook, he takes a shot at the deep pass.

If we find a team playing cover 4 in the secondary, a good pattern to run is another tag route. In a cover 4, the defensive backs are keying receivers to cue their coverage. We know the inside safeties are keying the number-two receivers to their side to tell them how to react. If we run this from a three-wide receivers' look, it should play out well for us. From the middle of the field, we put the twin set to the left side of the field and the tight-end-flanker set to the right. We call "54-fish-Y-go" (Diagram #8). The safety is keying the tight end's movement.

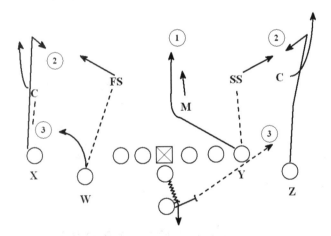

Diagram #8. 54 Fish Y-go

If the tight end runs a crossing route, the safety releases him to the linebackers. He goes to double-team on the wide receiver with the corner. If the tight end can make the home route look like a shallow cross, the safety will release him and go to double on the wide receiver. That puts the tight end turning up the field with at best a linebacker covering him deep. It is a better match if we can get a wide receiver matched up on the linebacker.

I want to show you another example of a base read. I will use the universal routes that everyone in the United States runs. We want to run this play out of an I-formation set. This pattern is a "Y-shallow" (Diagram #9). We run a sprint-draw fake with this play. We front out but you can reverse pivot with the quarterback. For the most part, the protection is slide protection. The tight end runs a shallow-cross pattern and ends up at a depth of six to seven yards. The X-receiver runs a 14-yard dig route.

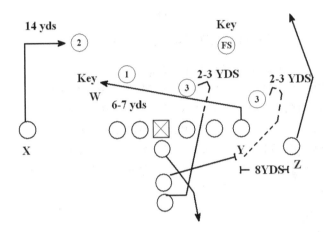

Diagram #9. Y-shallow

The Z-back runs a post pattern. He wants to cut his split down to about eight yards. The reason we cut the split down is to affect the safety quicker. The quarterback understands the post route is not in the progression of throws, but he has to know it is there. The tight end is the first choice in the progression. The dig route is the second choice and the fullback and running back are the third choices.

The reason the quarterback has to be aware of the post is the play of the safety. If the safety plays the shallow cross and does not get depth inside the post route, we have to be able to throw that pass. The post does not have a number of choices by the quarterback, but he must be aware of the possibility. When we cut the flanker's split down to no more than eight yards, the read happens quicker for the quarterback and it puts more pressure on the free safety.

We put the flanker wide and motioned him inside to the width of eight yards as one variation. If we lined up in the formation, we designated the flanker's position as a squeezed formation.

As we snap the ball, the quarterback reads the free safety. That gives us an indication of what the coverage is going to be. However, reading the coverage is not as critical as knowing the progression. The tailback is at a depth of eight yards. The fake from the quarterback to the tailback does not have to be a great fake. The linebackers cannot drop until the quarterback passes the tailback. Therefore, they hold and do not drop until that happens.

The quarterback has a high-low route working with the tight end on the shallow cross and the X-receiver running the dig pattern. We do not want to run the dig off the post-pattern cut because the receiver gets there too quickly. The farther the dig came across the field, the more he became involved with underneath coverage. We run it from a square in. The tailback is taking the fake, goes inside, and checks up at a depth of two to three yards. The fullback is faking a kick-out block on the edge and releasing to the outside at a depth of two to three yards.

We can take the same play with the same reads and give it a tag call. On this pattern we simply call "Y-shallow, X-comeback" (Diagram #10). The reads and progression are the same for the quarterback. He looks briefly at the free safety because he always has post by the Z-back in mind. His progression is the Y-receiver, X-receiver, to the backs coming out of the backfield.

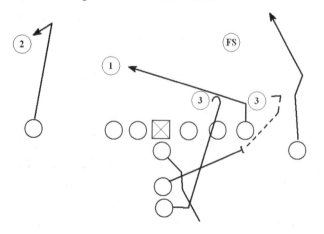

Diagram #10. Y-shallow, X-comeback

Coaches teach the defensive backs to recognize pass routes. They play routes and see the Y-shallow coming across the field. The linebacker gets into the big area on the backside of the pattern anticipating the cross pattern coming to them. The X-receiver breaks his pattern back to the sideline and we high-low the backside coverage. If the tight end clears all the coverage, he gets the football. If they find the tight end, we have the comeback into the sidelines. When we run this pattern, we drive the corner off for 17 yards.

The X-receiver sets his comeback with a go route or a very skinny post route. If the corner sets on the receiver's outside, the receiver runs a skinny post and gets the corner to run with him. If he can do that, the comeback is a sure thing for him. The young receiver has a tendency to get too flat with his post route. If he gets too flat, his comeback cut is harder than the cut of the defensive back. That spells interception for the quarterback. He has to run at the inside shoulder of the corner to get him to turn his hips inside.

We can take the same play one more step. We run the Y-shallow and swap the X-receiver and Z-back's pattern (Diagram #11). The X-receiver runs the post and the Z-back runs the 14-yard dig route. The backs do the same thing.

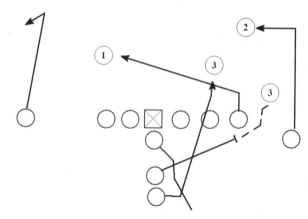

Diagram #11. Y-shallow, X-Z swap

That gives us another variation from the same play. We are involved with this play and we have taken it another step. We have taken it to the bunch set (Diagram #12). The receivers in the bunch could be the flanker, tight end, and fullback. From that set, the patterns are the same. The tight end does his Y-shallow pattern. The Z-back runs the 14-yard dig route and the fullback runs his check down route.

All these variations are off the same pattern. The key is the amount of repetitions you do with the quarterback. He is throwing the same pattern repeatedly and becoming more confident and consist with his reads and throws.

From the three-wide receiver set, we can run the same set of patterns (Diagram #13). Because we have run this route over the years, we have found out a few things. In the spread formation, we would prefer to put the twin set into the wideside of the field, with the tight crossing into the wide field. On this pattern, we tag the X-receiver to give his a different route and give the tight end space to run his shallow route. We tag the X-receiver to run the comeback route.

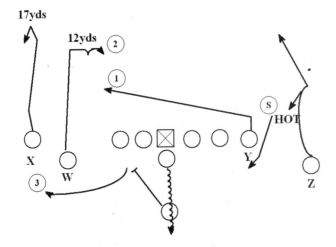

Diagram #12. Bunched set Y-shallow

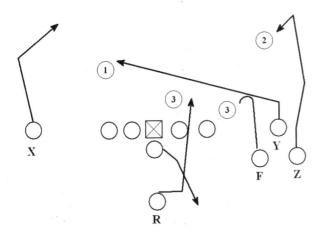

Diagram #13. Y-shallow/three wides

The W-receiver instead of running a dig runs a pattern, looking for a hole to settle into. He takes an outside release and gets up the field. The linebacker aligned on him wants to force him outside and out of the middle of the field. He has no trouble releasing outside. He is running his pattern at 12 to 13 yards and looking for a hole in the zone to settle.

In our protection, we would rather set the back into the tight-end side. However, we get wide field blitzes more than anything else. Because of that, we send the back protection to the field side of the set. That has evolved into a rule for us. Unless we have specially game-planned, the back protection always goes to the wideside of the field in this formation. There is a statement with always and never. "Always and never are two things you should always remember and never say."

In reality, putting the back to the wideside helped us. It gave us a swing to that side after the back checked his protection key. That helped to loosen the underneath coverage because it gave the defense one more thing to look at. The linebacker playing the slot receiver has a choice to make. He walls off the number-two receiver and carries him to the deep coverage. If he does that, the shallow cross is open. If he releases the number-two receiver and drops back on the shallow cross, the slot receiver can find a hole. The progression is tight end, slot receiver, and running back.

The problem with this protection scheme is the boundary-side protection. If the Sam linebacker blitzed from the tight-end side, the hot read would have to be the tight end or we had to get into sight adjustment by the flanker. We did not want to sight adjust but we could not avoid it. The flanker keyed the Sam linebacker or the corner for any kind of backside blitz. If he saw it coming, he ran a hitch route as his Q-route.

We have many things we can do with the Y-shallow route, with a two-man pattern run by the X- and W-receivers (Diagram #14). We can run a two-man pattern and utilize the shallow route at the same time. In our protection, we put the back to the field. On this example, we send the W-receiver on a go pattern and dig the X-receiver. We still have the tight end running the shallow cross. We still have the high-low with the W-receiver and Y-shallow and the quarterback is reading tight end, W-receiver, and running back.

The flanker to the backside has a Q-route, which turns into a post if there is no blitz. This was his primary pattern for all combination routes to the two-man side.

The two other patterns that we ran with the two-man game were a double-dig route and sail pattern. The double-dig pattern (Diagram #15) is always effective and is similar to a double post. The outside pattern trailing the inside route is generally the one that is open. The inside dig clears the defenders and the outside dig has body position on the corner.

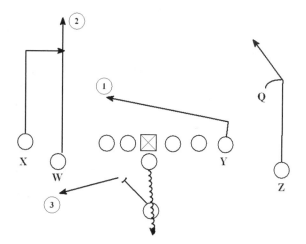

Diagram #14. Y-shallow two-man game

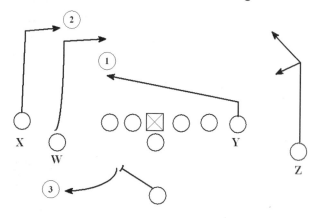

Diagram #15. Double dig

With the sail pattern (Diagram #16), the X-receiver cleared out for the inside receiver. The W-

receiver ran a shallow corner under the drop of the corner and over the drop of the underneath coverage. If you wanted to take the tight end out of the game and replace him with a wide receiver, he could run the shallow game. Everything else on the pattern is the same.

The original premise was to give the young quarterback things he could understand and become good at executing. He became good at the passing game because of the repetition of the patterns. As long as the quarterback understood the base play and could utilize them in all the different formation, he could succeed.

We color code all our personnel groupings and formations. Our four-wide receiver set is red. The three-wide receiver, tight end and one-back is a gray call. If we wanted a fullback in the game instead of the tailback, we call jumbo-gray.

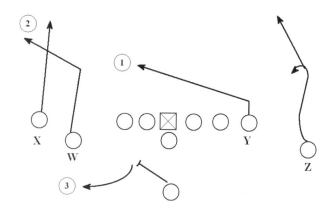

Diagram #16. Sail

If we want to move the running back in the protection scheme, we use the term "dart." That generally happens from the shotgun set. That allows the back to align on one side of the quarterback and have blocking keys to the other side. The direct snap comes to the quarterback and he fakes a run to the running back as he changes his position from one side to the other. That keeps people from keying your tailback for protection strengths.

Thank you very much.

LINEBACKER DRILLS AND PASS COVERAGE

Washington State University

Today I will talk about linebacker play, how our defense is structured, and our blitz package. I am not going to talk a lot about Washington State. It is a long way from here. We recruit primarily in the states of Washington and California.

When we arrived at Washington State, we struggled with the program. In 1994, I became the defensive coordinator and, just by chance, we started a drill called "double huddle." If you have enough players to do it, I think it builds pride within your players. They huddle to start the play and then huddle after the pursuit drill.

The type of offense you run just about determines the type of defense you can play. If you are a "three yards and a cloud of dust" type of offense, you can afford to be a "bend but not break" style of defense. If you are a high-risk offense, you cannot be a "bend but don't break" defense. If your offense turns the ball over and the defense takes twelve plays to stop the opponent, the defense will play a lot of football. By the middle of the second quarter, the defense is worn out.

We were a high-risk offense, so we became a high-risk defense. We really stressed "three and out" for the defense. We blitz, play man-to-man coverage in the secondary, and try to make the big play on defense. To play that defense, we started the "double huddle." In the huddle, we tell our players no matter where the ball goes, the entire team sprints to the ball. Once everyone gets to the ball, the players get their hands together and say "break, defense." They break and jog back to the ball. They sprint to the ball and jog back to the huddle.

When the first defense runs to the ball, I always find someone who is not running hard. They leave the field and do five up-downs. The next unit comes on the field and works a little harder. They may get two reps before I find someone not running hard. They go off the field and do five up-downs. The third unit comes on the field. This group is generally your young kids who are fired up. They get three reps before I kick them off the field.

All this time, the starters are watching this happen. They only got one rep while the second and third teams got four and six reps. The drill creates peer pressure among your players. We try to instill in our players that it is a privilege to practice. If they do not bust their butts, they are not going to practice. We are not going to let them go repeatedly just because they are loafing. If it is continually the same player that finishes last, we replace him.

We practice for an hour-and-a-half. We emphasize going hard in practice so we do not have to go through conditioning after practice. We run to the huddle, from the huddle, and to the next drill. One point I had to get over to my coaches was to stay behind their players as they went to and from drills. I do not want them in front leading and half the group loafing behind them. The coach stays behind the players and tells them if he beats any of them to the next drill, they are all running.

Our strength coach talked to our players and convinced them the only way we were going to get better was to be bigger and faster. We do not get the Parade All-Americans. To win games, we had to get an edge; to get the edge, we had to be bigger, stronger, and faster.

The first thing we did was to improve their eating habits. We have a training table for our players. For the guys who live off campus, the strength coach had five meals they were required to eat each week. If they lived in the dorms on campus, they had ten meals they were required to eat. They had to eat four of the five or eight of the ten meals in a week's time.

If one member of a group missed one meal during the week, the entire group ran a gasser. If it happened the second time, the entire group ran another gasser and the individual ran an additional one. If it happened the third time, the player is sent to see the head coach. In the four years that we have been working on the eating regimen, it has never happened three times.

This is working for ownership in the program. If a player misses a class or academic appointment, they have a 5:30 AM Wednesday morning scheduled meeting with me. At the meeting, we do some conditioning to remind them of their responsibilities. Many kids would rather condition than go to class. If he has a 9:00 AM class, the player is there from 6:30 to 9:00 making up his class work.

Big plays go hand-in-hand with turnovers. We were last in our league in turnover margin when we came to Washington State. People talk about turnovers, but spend very little time teaching them. We condition our players all summer. We had 73 players stay all summer and only six of them missed more than one workout.

During spring practice, we told our team we were going to run one sprint for every team we played. We also told them that for every big play they made in practice, we would reduce the number of sprints by one. The big play can come in any type of drill. It could be individual, group, or team drills. The coaches award the big plays, but the players are constantly lobbying for them. It keeps all the players involved in practice. It keeps the theme of the big play in focus for our players

We went from last in the PAC Ten to first in the nation in turnover margin. We had good players, but we emphasized the big play and made it important for everyone on our team. The players bought into the idea.

Pride building, better nutrition, strength, and the focus on big plays helped us tremendously. It turned our program around. We went from an average football team the year before to a team that had three consecutive ten-win seasons. We were the first team in the PAC Ten to do that since 1937.

What I want to do next is talk about linebacker play. I used to coach the linebackers, but I do not coach much any more. When I do coach, I get involved with our linebackers.

We always start with the stance. What you teach as a coach, you have to sell to your players to be successful. We do not want a wide stance. A player in a wide stance cannot cover any ground in his first step. We want his feet under his body with his feet at shoulders width. We have one linebacker we let take a wider stance. We allow him to play with a wider stance to slow him down. He is super-quick and taking a wider stance slows him down and keeps him from over-running the play. The linebackers do not have to be in a hurry. They are five yards off the line of scrimmage. We want them to make sure they know where the ball goes before they get downhill in their attack.

We want our linebackers standing tall so they can see. If the linebacker is a 6'3", his forward lean and knee bend is greater than a linebacker that is 6'0". These linebackers are not going to hit anyone for at least three yards. By the time they make contact they are back into a low posture.

We want the linebacker to put his hand on his knees with his thumbs inside of the knee. We want his back arched, stomach out, and head up. He takes his hands off his knees and he is ready to play football. He gets his hands up because we play exclusively with the hands. The weight in the stance should be inside. The stance should be a little knock-kneed so directional movement becomes easier and faster.

The second thing we teach in the fundamentals for a linebacker is first step. In a simple drill, the coach faces three linebackers. They get into a good stance and on movement of the coach they take a short first step. The first mistake the young player will make is to leave the trail leg and foot where it was. When the linebacker takes the first step, he has to bring the back foot back under his body.

We do a simple key drill (Diagram #1) in teaching directional stepping. I align three linebackers in their positions and I stand behind them. I use a manager five yards in front of the linebackers. I direct the manager where to go and the linebackers react to what he does. We do this in pre-practice and it is intense. We key linebackers to backs. The mistake that is most commonly made is to step forward instead of laterally before getting downhill. The lateral step gains ground slightly toward the line of scrimmage. By stepping laterally, he stays out of all the trash and keeps his body out front. We want the step short so the linebacker slows and has a chance to change direction on a counter play.

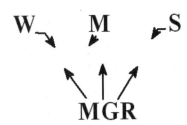

Diagram #1. Key drill

The next fundamental for the linebacker is his eyes. The linebacker must see the direction of the offensive lineman. That gives him his first step. The next thing he sees is the direction of the backs. If he reads counter, he has to find the player assigned to block him. If he keeps his eyes riveted on the back, an offensive lineman will ear-hole him. We teach the counter steps in the key drill. It is a simple drill done before practice begins and very effective in teaching first step and reaction.

When we coach defenders to key the ball for take-off, we go a step further. Before they snap the football, the centers move it all over the place. We tell our players to key the back tip of the football. That makes them focus on one thing and keeps

them from jumping off sides. In drills, we give them all kinds of cadences and inflections to try to influence them to jump. They are watching the back tip of the ball and waiting for it to move.

With foot movement, we do not worry about false steps. I listened to a receiver coach talk about releases. He timed his receiver's release. When he took a false step, rather than coming straight off the ball, he was quicker in his release. I am not telling you to take two steps to come forward, but we false step, rock our shoulders, and react.

We are a blitzing defense. We generally do three things in our blitz game. We "show blitz" and come on the blitz. We "blitz" from our linebacker depth, or we "show blitz" and bail out into coverage. Linebackers have a tendency to over do their acting when they fake the blitz. They jump all over the place by moving in and out of gaps. Quarterbacks generally ignore all that kind of movement. What they are looking for is the subtle movement of the linebackers toward the line of scrimmage. That is why we like to blitz from depth.

Linebackers do not backpedal as much as defensive backs. We do not backpedal much in our drops. When we do, I tell our linebackers to keep their heads down and look through their eyebrows. When a linebacker lifts his head, his butt goes down and he falls on his tail when he tries to backpedal. When we teach our drops to our linebackers we go to a slight backpedal before we go to our angle drops. The angle drop drill is a good drill. We do not do it for conditioning; we are trying to teach them something (Diagram #2). We teach the linebackers to watch the front shoulder. If the shoulder tilts back, they break deep; if it flattens, they break parallel to the line of scrimmage.

The coach faces the three linebackers. They are five yards from him in a good linebacker stance. He raises the ball and they start a short backpedal. He raises the ball and tilts the shoulders to give the linebackers direction. The linebackers retreat in a 45-degree angle drop. When the coach starts the throwing motion, the linebackers flatten and sprint outside parallel with the line of scrimmage.

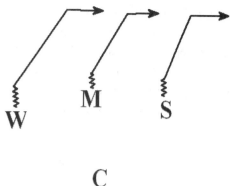

Diagram #2. Angle drop drill

If I am a Will linebacker on the X-receiver side, I false step and become a run defender first. As soon as I recognize pass, I want to open my hips to the X-receiver and snap my eyes out to see what he is doing. By the time, I do that, the receiver is four or five yards off the line of scrimmage. I do not need to watch the quarterback drop back. By the time I recognize the three-step drop, the quarterback already has his feet set. The Will linebacker reads from the second receiver to the first receiver to his side.

He must stay under control. He is five yards deep in his alignment. As he opens up, crosses over, and scuffles, he is at a depth of eight yards. The linebacker does not need depth as much as he needs to be under control. If he is under control, he can break on the ball. He must collision the number two receiver if he comes into his area. If there is no receiver, he looks to the X-receiver to see what he is doing.

He wants to know if the receiver is running a stop, curl, or dig route. After he identifies the pattern, he snaps his eyes back to the quarterback. If the quarterback sets up to throw in his direction, he is ready to react and break on the ball because he knows where the receiver is going.

The next drill we teach is the shuffle drill (Diagram #3). This keeps the linebacker's shoulders square to the line of scrimmage. We simply give them direction on movement of the ball and watch their feet. If the ball comes at the linebacker, he shuffles and fills downhill at the ballcarrier. If it is a toss sweep, the linebacker goes into a crossover run. The thing we want them to concentrate on is keeping their shoulders square to the line. If the

toes turn during the run, the shoulders will also. After the crossover run, they attack downhill to the line of scrimmage.

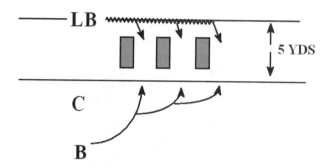

Diagram #3. Shuffle drill

We do a fumble recovery drill. I have two linebackers facing me. At the movement of the ball, they buzz their feet. I say "down," and they do a belly drop and get up. I call "pass," and they raise their hands in the air. They do not jump on this command. I drop two balls on the ground and they have to recover them. They want to get their bodies between the ball and the offense. The linebacker drops on his inside shoulder past the ball, curls up in a fetal position, and squeezes the ball. When both linebackers drop, they should be butt-to-butt and back-to-back on the ground.

We do a sled drill next. We have a "hit-and-lift" sled, which is remarkable to teach this skill. It is called the LEV Sled made by Rogers Sports. This sled has a small plunger in the mechanism that will not allow the player to lift the dummy unless the pad becomes depressed. I am not selling this sled, but I think it is one of the best they make. We work all kinds of drills on this sled. To stop an offensive lineman, the linebacker has to hit him hard before he can lift. If you do not have one of these sleds, you can do the drill on a one-man sled.

The next thing we do is a shed drill (Diagram #4). We start the linebackers on their knees.

The first thing we do is work on hand placement. We shoot the hands making sure they are above their eyes. We used to teach flippers, but the offenses of today grab the forearm and hold. We have to use hands to keep the offensive lineman from holding us. By shooting the hands above the eyes, it makes the linebacker get down and keeps his feet back. We are shooting the hands and locking out for separation from the offensive blocker.

Diagram #4. Shed drill

We hit with the hands and throw the blocker right or left on my command. Our kids do not know right from left so I tell them to throw them to the library or to the stadium. That keeps us from making a mistake in direction. When they throw the blocker, they get their shoulders past the defender. The next step is to throw the lineman, get the shoulder past the blocker, and step through with the foot. We do this from a kneeling position.

From the kneeling position, we stand up and do the same thing. The important thing in this phase is the lead foot. As the hands move up for the punch, the lead foot plants firmly into the ground. The foot hits first to give the anchor in the ground and then the punch. As we make solid contact, we want to drive the offensive blocker back. Most of our linebackers are not strong enough to throw 300 pound offensive linemen around. We tell the linebacker to let the linemen throw himself off. The linebacker punches and drives on the offensive lineman. As soon as he feels the offensive lineman start to resist and push back, he uses the momentum of the offensive lineman to throw him.

There are numerous ways to teach the same skill. Some coaches teach the same skill ten different ways and one of them may sink into their players. We teach hand above the eyes to keep the linebacker low. There are other catch phrases to teach the same technique. Use what works for you.

In college football, it is legal to post and chop block. It is illegal for a 190-pound wide receiver to crack block on a linebacker. The fact that a 300-pound guard can block down on the ankle of a nose tackle is a mystery to me. We use a cut drill to fight those kinds of blocks (Diagram #5).

Diagram #5. Cut drill

We do this drill on one foot. We have three blockers in a six-point stance. The linebacker starts on the first blocker. The blocker lunges forward at his inside knee. The defender punches down on the blocker with his hands and punches his facemask into the helmet of the blocker. He hops to the second and third man and repeats the same skill. We use this drill in pre-season while we are in shorts.

Let me go through some of the tackling drills we use. The linebackers line up facing each other. My old high school coach used to say, "Let's pair up in groups of three." We pair up in groups of two. They get at an angle to one another one yard apart. The ballcarrier has the ball in his outside arm. We use a term called "holster the hands." That is a movement as if you were going to draw your guns from the holsters on the hips.

The drill is a three-command drill. The first thing we do is to step and holster the hands. The first command is "fit." On this command, the face goes into the body with the chin over the ball and contact made with the inside shoulder. The hips are low on contact. The next command is "wrap." On this command, the hands are unholstered and shot as high as the linebacker can get them. The hand going to the ballside should go across the back tip of the ball to the triceps of the ballcarrier. We want to squeeze our elbows inside and grab cloth. The next command is "drive." On the third command, the linebacker works his hips back to a square position on the ballcarrier and works the feet.

I tell the linebackers to pretend they have no hands and they have to tackle the ballcarrier with their elbows. If you tackle with the elbows, the head is up and every other phase will be correct. Always emphasize getting the hands high and squeezing with the elbows.

The next drill is an open-field tackling drill (Diagram #6). We do not hit much. If I have to teach them to hit, we are in trouble. We do not need to try to kill one another in tackling drills. That is a good lesson for youth league coaches. Do not force your players into full-speed tackling drills. Teach the fundamentals and form tackling. When they are ready, they will increase the intensity on their own. If you force them to go full-speed before they are ready, you may ruin their approach to the game. When young kids are ready to hit, they will hit. If you force them into it, you can chill them on the game.

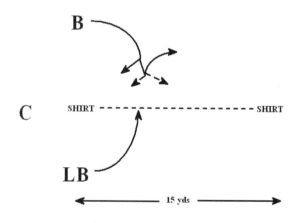

Diagram #6. Open-field tackling

The coach stands in the middle with the ballcarrier five yards from him on one side and the linebacker five yards from the coach on the other side. Fifteen yards in front of the coach is a scrimmage shirt. The ballcarrier has the area between the coach and the shirt to get away. I tell the ballcarrier to use every move he has to elude the tackle. I do not want him to try to run over the tackler.

The tackler approaches the ballcarrier and "comes to balance." We do not say, "buzz your feet." When they buzzed their feet, they stayed in the one place. We never want the tackler to stop as he approaches the ballcarrier. We want him to continue to move forward but in control. Most good tacklers tackle off one foot. They tackle off one foot, bring the trail leg, and run right through the ballcarrier.

The biggest mistake the tackler makes is on the outside move of the ballcarrier. If the tackler's reaction to the outside move is to step at the ballcarrier, he will end up behind him. He has to step at an angle in front of the ballcarrier so he makes contact with the correct shoulder and head position.

I call the last drill "power tackling." I guess I am lucky because I have not gotten too many players hurt in this drill. This is the only tackling drill we teach where the ballcarrier is put on the ground. This teaches the tackler to wrap up and get the ballcarrier on the ground. We line the tackler and ballcarrier four yards apart. The only rule governing the ballcarrier is he has to make contact before he can do anything else. He cannot simply run away from the tackler. The ballcarrier will blast hard into the tackler and try to spin free or simply run over him. The tackler has to wrap up and do everything he can to get the ballcarrier on the ground.

We run a 4-3 front with cover 4 on defense (Diagram #7). We used to be a 4-2 front with cover 3 behind it. We tried to hit and read the head of the offensive blocker. When we played that way, the defensive lineman made one and two tackles a game. We went to a gap control and read on the run type of defense. We put our facemask into the V of the offensive lineman's neck and get upfield. I tell our 3-technique tackle not to worry about the linebacker getting blocked if he makes the tackle. If the defensive lineman gets double-teamed, he has to make the play if one of the blockers slips off to block our linebacker. I want him attacking upfield. At first, they trapped him, but he figured out how to play the trap.

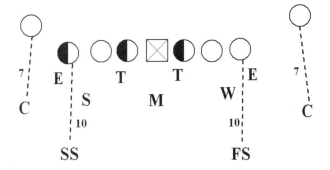

Diagram #7. Base 4-3 defense

That is why we play with hands. If the offensive blocker goes inside and the defender shoots his hands, he is automatically coming inside to bubble the trap. We are not blowing gaps and getting upfield. We are getting hands on the offensive blockers and getting upfield.

In the PAC 10, we see so many one-back offenses. That is why we went to cover 4 in the secondary. The tackle to the strongside is in an outside shade on the guard and the weakside tackle is in an inside shade on the guard. The defensive ends are in 9 techniques. We have three linebackers: Sam, Mack, and Willie. We base the linebacker's alignment on the offense. If the Willie linebacker has the tight end to his side, he wants to collision him at eight to ten yards on a vertical release. If the tight end is slow, he can play inside more. If it is a fast tight end, he has to get outside more. He is a C-gap player.

The Mack linebacker is the same way. He has to beat the block of the center. If the Mack linebacker is fast and the center is not too good, he can cheat to the weakside. If the center is very good, the Mack linebacker has to cheat to the strongside. If the center is an all-American, we can shade him with the nose guard and drill him coming off the ball. The Mack linebacker has the A gap strong and the B gap weak. He lines up and splits the difference between the two gaps.

The Sam linebacker plays an alignment that allowed him to do what he is supposed to do. He originally aligns in the strong C gap. The corners are seven to eight yards deep. The free safety is just off the hash marks over an imaginary tight end if there is a split end to his side ten yards deep. We determine his alignment by the scouting report as far as depth and adjustments. The strong safety is over the tight end and has the same alignment adjustments by scouting report.

The thing I like about cover 4 is that it allows us to get nine men in the box on run support (Diagram #8). Our safeties are 10 yards deep and are flat-footed keying the number-two receiver to their side. Playing flat-footed means they are not making a drop on the snap of the ball. They play run support on all runs. If the ball goes away from the free safety, he is shuffling and coming downhill for run support on the cutback run in the B gap. The strong safety is reacting and playing over the top to the strongside. That allows the defensive end to be aggressive. The strong safety plays opposite the defensive end. If the end goes out, he is inside; if he goes inside, he is outside. If the ball comes toward the free safety, he is playing opposite the Willie linebacker.

The corners are playing loose man coverage from the time they step on the field until the time they leave the field. The last couple of years, we have played some cover 2 with the corners, but our base coverage is cover 4.

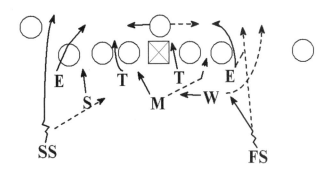

Diagram #8. Safety run support

From our defensive front, we can play shade, over, and under with our defensive line. However, the base front we teach first is the straight 4-3 defense. If the offense comes out in a two tight end set, we check to a "heads call." This is an even technique for the defensive tackles (Diagram #9). The strongside tackle aligns in a 2 technique and has B gap responsibility. The weakside tackle aligns in a 2 technique and has A-gap responsibility weak.

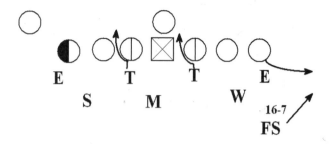

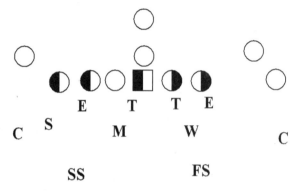

Diagram #9. Heads call

The coverage behind the heads call is "cover-4 sky." The strong safety and corner play cover 4 as they normally play the coverage. The strong safety is ten yards deep and the corner is seven yards deep with an inside alignment. The free safety gives a "sky call" and calls "down." The "down" call means he is coming into the box with his alignment, which becomes six to seven yards deep. The Willie linebacker moves slightly to the strongside and the free safety plays over the Willie on run support. On a pass to his side, he keys the number-two receiver and has him if he runs into the flat. That gives us the extra run defender and eight players in the box.

The reason we went to 9 techniques for our defensive ends was the size of our defenders. We had great athletes at the defensive end and were getting them blocked by our alignment. They were a bit undersized and we did not want to put them in a 7 technique on big tight ends. We widen the defensive end and let them have the freedom to be aggressive.

We also can go to an "Eagle front." We slide the front toward the weakside and step the Sam linebacker up to the outside in a 9 technique. That gives us a defensive end in what we call a 6 technique. We number our techniques differently from everyone else (Diagram #10). Instead of using number 1, 3, 5, 7, and 9 techniques as shoulder alignments, we number in sequence from the inside out. The techniques on the guard are the same; however, the offensive tackle's inside shoulder is a 4 technique. Head up the offensive tackle is a 5 technique and his outside shoulder is a 6 technique. The techniques on the tight end are 7, 8, and 9 technique from inside to outside.

Diagram #10. Technique numbering

The Eagle front puts the strongside tackle in a strongside shade on the center. The strongside defensive end is in the 6 technique and the Sam linebacker is in a 90 technique (Diagram #11). Toward the weakside, the tackle is in a 3 technique and the defensive end aligns in a 9 technique. The Mack linebacker slides to the strongside and aligns in a 30 technique. The Willie linebacker moves into a 60 alignment in the backside C gap.

Diagram #11. Eagle front

We installed this defense in 1994. We ran cover 2 twice the entire season. We practiced the hell out of it, but played cover 4 and blitzed the entire year. We were a hell of a defense in 1994. We ranked number one in the nation in scoring defense and were second in pass and rush defense. In our first four games that year, we played Illinois at Soldier Field, Fresno State at home, at UCLA, and at Tennessee. In those four games we gave up one touchdown and lead the nation in every defensive category. On that defense, we had nine players go pro. It ain't all coaching.

Let me explain our cover-4 coverage (Diagram #12). The receivers are numbered from the outside going inside on both sides. The safeties and corners play the same regardless of which side they align. The corners key the number-one receiver and play man-to-man coverage on them. The safeties key the number-two receiver going to number one. The outside linebacker also keys the number-two receiver. If the offense sends four vertical patterns, the corners and safeties are man to man on those receivers.

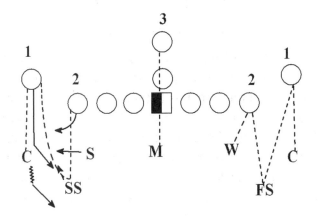

Diagram #12. Cover 4

If the number-two receiver runs to the flat, the outside linebacker takes him even if he continues his pattern up to the wheel route. The safety reads number two into the flat and turns him over to the linebacker. He directs his attention to the number-one receiver. He plays number one, looks to help on the post route, and gets under the curl route.

The Mack linebacker has the number-three receiver and looks to get under him wherever he goes. There are other adjustments but that is what the coverage does.

When we get a trips set to the tight side, we call that "Trey" and play cover 4 (Diagram #13). The corner, strong safety, and Sam linebacker are playing cover 4 on the two outside receivers. The Sam linebacker drops over the number-two receiver. The Mack linebacker drops over number three, which is the tight end. The free safety keys the tight end.

If the tight end goes to the flat, the free safety turns him over to the Sam linebacker and helps the backside corner on the split end. If the tight end goes vertical, the free safety has him. If the tight end runs a drag pattern, the free safety does, what we call "zones the quarter." If the free safety turned the tight end loose as he started to drag, the tight end could run deep off the drag and no one would pick him up. We "zone the quarter" until the tight end passes the middle of the field. To get that

adjustment, we tag the term "stay" onto the coverage and that keeps the free safety in the middle of the field.

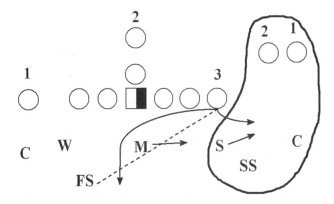

Diagram #13. Cover 4 versus Trey

If the set was a trips set with the tight end on the backside and three wide receivers to the other, we call that "trips" (Diagram #14). The corner, strong safety, and Willie linebacker are into the coverage on the three-receiver side. The free safety cheats to the middle of the field and keys the inside slot receiver, or the number-three man. He takes him man-to-man if he comes vertical. The Willie linebacker widens his alignment and covers over the number-two receiver. The number-three receiver cannot cut him off. We play the coverage the same way with the strong safety and corner playing the two outside receivers.

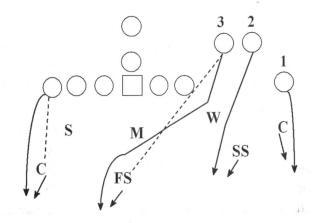

Diagram #14. Cover 4 versus trips

It may appear that the free safety is too far away to cover the number-three receiver deep. However, when offenses run four vertical routes, they want the receivers to split the field to prevent coverage by one man. That means in order to get the proper spacing, the number-three receiver has to come toward the free safety. The outside receiver runs the sideline, the outside slot runs the hash mark, and the inside slot comes right to the free safety. He does not have to cheat that much to cover the number-three receiver vertical and he can still give run support to the backside.

The way to beat cover-4 deep is from a two-by-two set. The outside receivers run hitch patterns. That draws the outside linebackers to the flat area. The inside receivers run corner routes to pull the safeties out of the middle of the field. The offense brings the number-three receiver through the line of scrimmage deep down the middle of the field. That leaves the Mack linebacker covering a running back on a deep vertical route. To stop that from happening we call "cover-4 stay," and that keeps the free safety in the middle of the field.

If a receiver runs a shallow drag route, we carry him to the next defender. We switch the coverage as the drag pattern goes across the field. We switch from linebacker to linebacker or corner. Our corners never chase a shallow drag, even in man coverage. They carry them to the next defender in the coverage. We do this drill as often as we can. I line up the three linebackers in their position (Diagram #15). I have a tight end, running back, and slotback with two cones representing the wide outs to each side. It is a one-back set.

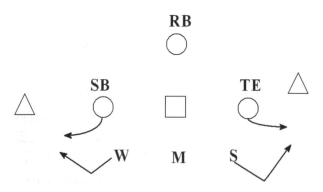

Diagram #15. Shallow drag drill

I have two or three groups going against the defense. That way we can get multiple reps in a short time. The first pattern we run is flat routes for both receivers. The Sam and Willie linebackers

get on top of the flat receivers and play football. They open and key the number-two receiver to the number-one receiver. The primary thing the linebackers do wrong is get too flat and end up chasing the receiver into the flat. We want to carry him and stay on top of him in the coverage.

The next situation I give the linebackers is a drag by the tight end, a flat by the one back toward the tight end, and the slot receiver in the flat (Diagram #16). The Sam linebacker drops over the number-two receiver, which is the tight end. He reads the tight end's drag route and calls "drag" to the Mack linebacker. He jams the tight end and takes the third receiver going to the flat.

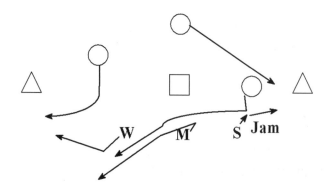

Diagram #16. Carry-and-switch mack drill

Since the number-three receiver is releasing to his side and the number-two receiver is dragging, the number-three receiver becomes number two to the Sam linebacker. The Mack sees the number-three receiver releasing toward the tight end. He reads three to two, sees the drag, and hears the drag call. He picks up the tight end and carries him across the field, staying on top of him. He does not jump him. He looks ahead for the Willie linebacker. If he sees the numbers of the Willie linebacker, he carries the drag route across the field. He sees Willie's numbers and knows he is in coverage with his back to him.

The next situation is the tight end on the drag. The running back runs a flat to the tight end, and the slot receiver goes vertical. If the slot receiver runs vertical, the Willie linebacker reads the slot coming up the field (Diagram #17). He jams the slot, widens to the curl area, and turns the slot over to the free safety. The Mack linebacker carries the drag to the

Willie linebacker, calls "drag," and drops into the curl area. The Willie linebacker picks up the drag and releases the curl to the Mack linebacker. We know if the inside slot is going vertical and the tight end is dragging, the wide receiver is running a dig, deep comeback, or something coming inside. We release the Mack linebacker. He turns his back to the quarterback and begins to look for the inside pattern coming from the wide receiver.

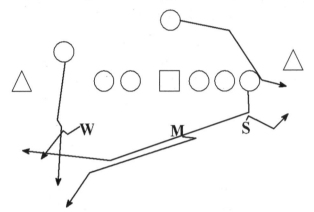

Diagram #17. Switch-and-cover Willie

We run the same patterns the other way. It becomes tougher on the Mack linebacker because the drag pattern comes from the slot, which is a wide receiver. If the Sam linebacker is in coverage in the flat area, the Mack linebacker has to carry him across the field. The thing that helps him is the distance the slot has to come. He is further away from the Mack linebacker than the tight end. The Mack really has to get on his horse to stay with the receiver. However, the coverage is the same.

This is also the way we play our man coverage. What I just talked about is our "cover −1 and cover3" coverage. The only difference is if the slot receiver goes vertical on the Willie linebacker. Will runs with him in cover 1. If we are in man coverage, and the wide receiver starts the shallow cross, the corner carries him to the next defender in coverage and releases him to that next defender.

We number our zone coverages and color code our man coverages. The defensive end does not know what happens in cover 2 or cover 4. However, he should know the difference between colors, words, and numbers. If a defensive end hears a number, he

knows he can attack and not worry because he has a safety behind him. If he hears a color, he has to be more cautious because his safety may be gone in coverage. He has to play more conservatively and make sure to keep everything inside of him.

I want to get into our blitzes and how we call them. Offensives use two wide receivers to the same side to get your Willie linebacker out of the box. If they can get the Willie out of the box, they run the bend play and make it tough on your Mack linebacker. When people start to split us we call "cover-4 alert"(Diagram #18). The alert call means we check to red coverage, which is man-to-man coverage. Red tells the Sam linebacker he has the tight end man-to-man. The corners take the wide receivers in man coverage. The free safety stems over and takes the slot receiver. The Mack and Willie linebacker key the one back. The Mack linebacker aligns over the strongside guard and fills the weakside A gap. The strong safety is free and fills the strongside B gap on run away from him. The Willie linebacker keys the one back and comes from the outside on run his way.

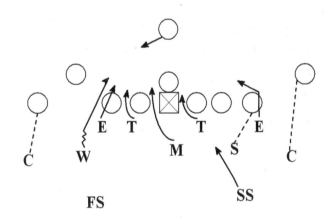

Diagram #18. Cover-4 alert

In this coverage, if we get a pass play and drag patterns from the split receivers, we handle it like the drag rules in cover 4 (Diagram #19). The defenders carry the drags to the next defender. In red coverage, we end up with a low-hole player and a high-hole player. The defender that passes the drag route becomes the low-hole player in the middle. The strong safety is free and is the high-hole player deep.

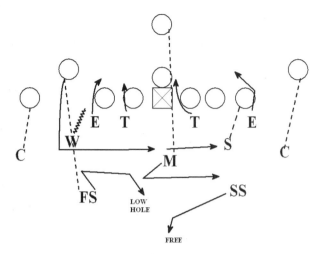

Diagram #19. Red coverage

If we want to blitz a linebacker from this defense, we change the color from red to "crimson." That tells the defensive backs there is no low-hole player and they cannot pass off the drag patterns.

I will go through the blitz game very quickly for you. We color-code our blitz coverages. We call the first one we teach "blue" (Diagram #20). On a blue call, we send all the linebackers on a blitz. The corners have the wide receivers and the safeties have the inside receivers man-to-man. The strong safety has the tight end or he has the number-two receiver his way. The free safety has the number-two receiver to his side. The linebacker away from the formation call is free to blitz anywhere he wants to go. The linebacker to the call side has a blitz pick-up of the remaining back his way. In diagram 20, the call side is left. The Sam linebacker has the blitz pick-up his way and the Willie linebacker is a free blitz linebacker.

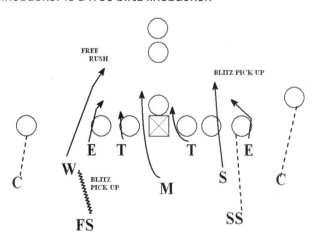

Diagram #20. Blue coverage

If the back sets to the strongside of the set, we call "purple." The free safety picks him up and Sam linebacker has no blitz pick-up. The outside Willie linebacker to the weakside has the blitz pick-up on the back coming his way. If there is a one-back set, we call "black." That means both outside blitzers have blitz pick-up on the back his way. If we added a carpenter's tool to the call, the Mack linebacker takes the remaining back and both the outside blitzers were free. A "blue hammer" brought the Sam and Willie on stunts with the Mack linebacker taking the remaining back.

Let me show you our "city-blitz-blue." How many times have you called a blitz and then wished you had called it from the other side when you see the set? Some people call it "formation-blitz-blue." We blitz according to what the formation tells us to do. When we design our blitz package, we look at the way teams protect the quarterback. If the offense is a one-back offense, we want to blitz from the backside. The back blocks opposite the slide of the offensive line. We want to get the back blocking on our defensive end or linebacker. If we come from the open side of the formation, we call it "Omaha." If we come from the closed or tight side, we call it "Tacoma."

The set is a shotgun one-back set with twin wide receivers right and tight end and wide receiver left. The one-back sets to the tight end side. The coverage for the one-back set checks to "black" (Diagram #21). Both tackles slant into the A gaps. The Mack linebacker blitzes the B gap to the open side of the set. The Sam linebacker blitzes the B gap to the tight side of the set. The strong safety has man coverage on the tight end and has the C gap on run his way. The end to the tight end side stays outside. The defensive end to the openside comes hard on the offensive tackle. The Willie cheats up and comes outside.

Teams began to see what we were doing and moved the back across to the openside to block the free blitz man. To counter that move, we put in "slide-blitz-blue" (Diagram #22). From the same set, we shade the center with the openside tackle. We twisted the tackles with the shade tackle going to the strong A gap and the tight tackle coming to the open A gap. The Willie and Sam linebackers blitzed the B gaps to their side. The defensive ends stay outside on their charge. The Mack linebacker keyed the movement of the blocking back and blitzed through the B gap opposite the move. That put two blitzers through the same gap. That is really a good run blitz.

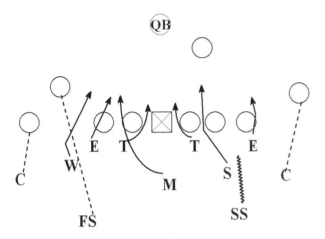

Diagram #21. City blitz Omaha

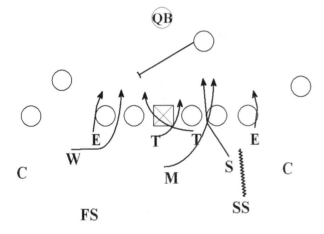

Diagram #22. Slide-blitz-blue

Another blitz that gives offenses fits is called "eagle-spear-orange" (Diagram 23). I saved the best blitz to last for the guys that stuck around to hear the end of the lecture. If the offense is in a one-back set, they cannot block this one. The spear call means the strong safety blitzes. We align in the eagle front. We stem the Willie linebacker outside early to show the offense he is coming. The tackles and ends blitz their gaps and the Mack linebacker comes through the weakside A gap. The Sam linebacker aligns outside as if he is going to blitz. At

the last second, he grabs the tight end in man coverage. The free safety cheats over and takes the slot receiver. The strong safety cheats and blows the weakside B gap.

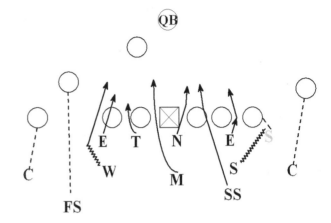

Diagram #23. Eagle-spear-orange

The weakness of the blitz is when the Willie linebacker has a blitz pick-up on the running back. In our terminology in the one-back set, if the back is behind the quarterback, we call that "Ace." If he is set to the strongside, we call that "Jack." If he is set to the open side, we call that "Jill." In the two-back set, an off set to the strongside is "King" and the weakside is "Queen."

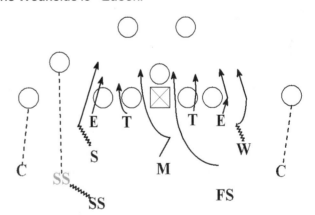

Diagram #24. Snake-blitz-blue

Another blitz which is good against a three-wide receiver set is called "snake-blitz-blue" (Diagram #24). The snake tells the free safety to blitz. The corners and strong safety play man-to-man coverage on the two wide receivers and the slotback. The ends have an outside charge. The tackles rush though the B gaps. The Mack linebacker fakes to the weakside A gap and blitzes the strongside A gap. The Sam and Willie linebackers come outside and have blitz pick-up on the remaining backs to their side. The free safety blitzes though the weakside A gap.

We run another front we call "Mace," (Diagram #25) which means "Mack in your face." We walk the Mack linebacker up into a 2 technique over the openside guard. The tackle moves over the center and is responsible for the A gap toward the tight end. We tell him to block the center and come off into the backside gap. We do not tell him to play two gaps. We play 39 with our tackle and end to the tight end. The Sam linebacker plays a 60 technique. The Willie linebacker is stacked behind the Mack linebacker. We want the Mack's alignment with his toes inside the defensive linemen's feet. That way the offensive has to count him as a lineman rather than a linebacker. This is good against a two-back set. We call the defense "shade-Mace-crimson." We have to go to crimson because we lose our low-hole player. The corners have the wide receivers and the strong safety has the tight end. The free safety is free in the middle.

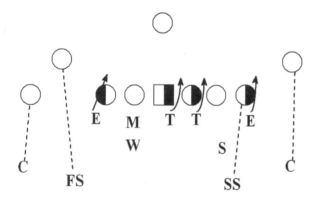

Diagram #25. Shade-Mace-crimson

This defense stops the trap because there is no one to block the linebacker if the guard pulls. If the guard down blocks and the offense tries to isolate the linebacker, he will blow the play up in the backfield. This is our heavy defense if we replace the linebacker with another defensive tackle. We can play this on the goal line or short yardage and still be sound against a one-back set because we still have four defensive backs in the game. We can play this defense in the middle of the field with the front four looking for run and the four defensive backs looking for play-action pass. I like to have someone head up the center in goal line because of the quarterback sneak.

I have run out of time but, before I finish, I want to tell you one more thing. Remember to be proud of what you are doing. You have no idea of the influence you have on your players. I have been doing this for 42 years and I still get letters from my former players. They remember everything you say and the things you have done. I know a guy that owns two factories and he told me he got his work ethics from me. When you are in the office and the cars are still parked out front at midnight, they know you are still working.

I will leave you with one more thing. Our strength coach talks a lot about motivation and he simplified it for me. I think he is right. He said in order to motivate kids, you have to do two things. The first thing is the players have to know you care. The second thing is they have to be getting better at what they are doing. If you do not care about them, they will not play for you. If you care about them but they cannot see any improvement in what they are doing, they will not play hard.

That helps us because we have great rapport with our kids. Football is the best taught subject at any school. You work at it harder than anybody does. Guys, remember, what you say and what you do is more important than anyone else in the entire school. Take pride in your profession because it can change lives of young people. Thank you very much. It has been a pleasure.

TECHNIQUES IN DEVELOPING LEADERSHIP

Sports Psychologist

It was not long ago when I was a coach and I was sitting in the seats where you are today. I see several of my friends here today. Coach Bobby April of the Bills called me earlier to let me know he was coming down to listen to my lecture. I am a former football coach. I actually coached in Pittsburgh. I coached at West Allegany and I coached at Duquesne. In addition, I coached in New Jersey. I went back to West Virginia University to get my Masters and Doctorate. I picked up this "twang" in my accent in Morgantown.

I left this area and went with the United States Olympic Committee. I went with the International Olympic Committee and then came back to work on my Doctorate. I worked with one of my best friends, Tom Donahoe, for a short time and worked on my Doctorate.

I worked with several pro teams in the last several years. I worked with the Miami Dolphins for the last ten years. I went into LSU and worked with them the year before they won the National Championship. The program we put into place at LSU was a five-step program. Coach Nick Saban was fabulous in the way he kept the program going and how he went about administering the program. The autobiography of Nick Saban came off this system. His autobiography is entitled: *No Mental Clutter*. He used this motto when he went to the Sugar Bowl to play Oklahoma in the National Championship. I will go over the way we covered the material before the game.

I have been doing the same things with other football teams recently. Last week I was at LSU with Les Miles. Yesterday I was at Nebraska putting this system in for them.

The coaches that I have worked with include four individuals that really talk the mental game. One of the best jobs I have seen in this area was the job done by Nick Saban two years ago. These coaches talk the mental game and they talked about how to get a vision. I will not talk about X's and O's. Some coaches expect you to talk about X's and O's when you come in to talk with them about improving their program.

Let me give you a story to give you an idea where we are going. This older man went to see his doctor. His wife went with him and she went in the office for the examination. After the doctor spent some time with the couple, the doctor asked the wife if he could see her alone. The husband stepped out of the room and the doctor started talking to the wife. "Mary, your husband is in bad shape. There are three things you must do to help keep him alive. First, you have to cook him three healthy meals a day. Second, you must provide him with a stress free environment. You must passionately make love to him daily."

On their way home not one word was said for several minutes. Finally, the husband said, "Mary, what did the doctor tell you?" Mary replied, "He said you were not going to make it and that you were going to die."

Let us talk about making it. Listen to this phrase, "First the ear hears the word and the word becomes flesh." This is where you start. You must get the picture.

When I was at LSU the day after the National Championship, Skyler Green came out in the paper and said, "We won the National Championship in February."

I just told Nebraska about their Texas Tech game. "Do you know when Texas Tech beat you? They beat you in March and they beat you in April. They are sitting home right now thinking about you." You have to have a picture when it started. You must have clear-cut goals of where you want to go. You must know where you going. You have to talk, and talk, and then you must move to the picture.

Let me give you another example of seeing the picture. This divorced woman ran an ad in the paper. "Wanted: A man who will not beat me, and a man who will not run around on me." The next day the doorbell rang and the lady came to the door. She looked at the man and asked him what he wanted. He said, "I am here inquiring about the ad you ran in the paper yesterday." She looked at him and said, "You have no arms." The man replied, "You said you wanted someone that would not beat you. I do not have arms so I could not beat you." The woman said, "You do not have any legs." The man said, "You said you did not want someone that would run around on you. I have no legs so I could not run around on you." She said, "Let me ask you one more question. How good are you at sex?" The man replied, "I rang that doorbell, didn't I?" He had a vision.

You must start with a vision and you have to go after it. When I was 19 years old and I went to the library, it was on a Friday night. I was studying to be a biology teacher and a football coach. I saw a book and I started reading it. The title was *The Psychology of Coaching*. I picked the book up at 3:00 PM and I was still reading it at 9:00 PM.

I went home and my father was coming home from the fire hall. We walked into the house together. I said, "Dad, I know what I want to be when I get out of school." At that time, the big deal was the Pittsburgh Steelers and the Dallas Cowboys. I said, "Dad, I want to be a sports psychologist for the Pittsburgh Steelers and the Dallas Cowboys, and I want to be on the United States Olympic Committee." My dad did not graduate from high school. He said, "What is a sports psychologist?" I replied, "I do not know!" He told me to shut up and eat my supper. Let me assure

you, I never lost that picture. Those thoughts never escaped me.

I was at West Virginia University and I was presenting a paper that I had prepared. There were only six people in the room. I gave the report and then we all left the room. That was in April.

In November, I went into the Steelers Office and one of the secretaries told me I had a phone call from the United States Olympic Committee. "How do they know me? How did they get my phone number?" She replied, "It was about that paper you presented in April. The President of the Olympic Committee was one of those six people in the back of the room. They want you to come to work for them." I could not believe it.

I went to the Olympic Committee and later worked for the International Olympic Committee. While working for them in Greece, this is what I figured out: "I love America. I am coming home."

I came back and worked in Pittsburgh for a short while. I had a vision and I never lost it. Working for the Steelers on draft day is boring. It is like watching paint dry. It is a long day. I was at Three Rivers and I was in the back of the room talking with some kid. I did not know this kid at all. His name was Andy Gailey and his dad is Chan Gailey who was with the Cowboys at the time.

Can I give you an interesting statistic? Do you know we have immigrants come to this country that do not have a penny to their name and they are without an education? They are four times more likely to become a millionaire than any U.S. citizen is. I thought education was the answer. It is all about money. They have you beat. They have four times better chance of becoming a millionaire than we do. Do you know why this is true? They do not come to this country to get on welfare. They are coming with a dream of making it big in a new world. They have a dream they are going to make it big.

I know most of you have heard of the former baseball pitcher Tug McGraw. He was pitching for the Philadelphia Phillies. A sports writer asked him which he liked better, "AstroTurf or grass?" He replied, "I do not know. I have never smoked AstroTurf."

Tug McGraw's son is a country and western singer. He is married to Faith Hill, the country singer. Tug McGraw passed away last year of cancer of the brain. In March of last year, a song came across the desk of Tim McGraw. He looked at the words of the song and said, "That is my dad. That is my dad." Tim McGraw made his recording of the song.

The song is about a man that got a bad report of an X-Ray he had taken at the hospital. He went to one of his friends and told him, "This may be it for me." The friend asked him, "What did you do when you realized your life was near the end?"

Tug McGraw replied, "I went sky diving, Rocky Mountain climbing. I went 2.7 seconds on a bull named Fu-Man-Chu. My life was sweeter and I loved deeper, and I gave forgiveness to someone I was denying." The next line is from Shakespeare. It really gets me. He said, "Someday I hope you get the chance to *live like you are dying*."

I sat down with the Nebraska people and asked them this question: "How many times do you think you are going to get a shot at beating someone?" How many times do you think you will get to walk on the playing field? How many times will I get a chance to love my kids? Do you know what? Time is your wealth, not your money. You do what you love. You must get the picture.

If you watch Nick Saban on the highlight film, you will hear him calling out to the players, "Stay on the picture. Stay with what you want. Don't think about the thing you do not want." We want to keep closing in on the picture and focus on what we want. Keep on closing in on that picture.

I was speaking for Wachovia in Virginia at the Homestead. A man came up to me and told me he had heard me talk before and that he wanted to tell me his story. He said, "My son was going off to Iraq. I told my son that I wanted him to get a picture before he left for Iraq. The picture I wanted him to get was of a USA Aircraft Carrier pulling into the harbor in San Diego. I wanted to see my son walking off that Aircraft Carrier without a scratch on his body. 'Your father will be there to embrace you as you come off the carrier.' I wanted him to get that picture so he would be able complete that mission and make it home safely."

Let me talk about one of the biggest problems I see in coaching. Most of you try persuasion. It does not work. Repetition makes the difference.

Listen to this story. An official with Amway from Grand Rapids, Michigan, got a heart transplant. Shortly thereafter, he had lunch with the woman that gave him his heart. She needed a liver transplant. She got someone else's heart and liver. She gave Richard her heart. They had lunch together. You heard me right. You thought I was going to say the woman was dead. You may say there is no way this story could be true. Why do you say that? Because you hear it over and over again about heart transplants that do not make it very long.

You become hypnotized. That is how you coach. You must tell them to focus on the picture over, and over again. You must give them rep after rep. You do not want to over coach them, you want to give them rep after rep.

The man that started this was Maxwell Moss, a plastic surgeon. He did unbelievable surgery with people that had been in car accidents. He worked on one woman that was gorgeous. The woman did not think so. He said her problem was that she had visions of what she should look like.

You go ahead and coach the X's and O's. The coaches at LSU and Miami coach the picture. What is your picture?

The Australians from down under had lost every American Cup. Every year they finished in last place. They got a person and put him on a microphone and he talked to the crew each day during the race. The crew listened to him on their headphones for three times a day in pairs for four years. They heard him talking to them 5,000 times. They finally won the American Cup.

The media interviewed the Australian captain. They had shocked the world. They asked the captain if he was surprised that they had won the American

Cup. He said, "No, I am not surprised. We have already won the cup 5,000 times. What is the big deal?"

This is the key to coaching. Stay on the picture. Make sure your players are determined to stay on the picture. You must coach them up. You must do your job. You must start your picture with one answer.

Are you with me on this? It all starts with a picture. You must get the picture because that is where it all starts. You must start the picture with one answer. Several years back, the USA hockey team was picked to win the gold medal in Japan. They did not win any medal at all that year. Czechoslovakia won the gold medal. The captain of their team was Jaromir Jagr. He was a hockey player in the National Hockey League and played for Pittsburgh. He wore number 68 as his jersey number. He played on the Czechoslovakia Olympic hockey team in the 1984 Olympics Games. His team ended up in the finals playing the Russians for the gold medal. In 1968, the Russians invaded Czechoslovakia. His grandfather and many other Czechs were killed in that encounter. That is why he wore the number 68. It was a constant reminder of that fateful year. His coach came into the locker room to get the team ready before the gold medal game and asked Jaromir if he was ready to play. To which Jaromir replied, "I've been ready to play this game all my life!" He said his commitment as a hockey player was to beat the Russians in the Olympics for all the people they killed including his grandfather in 1968. That was Jaromirs commitment.

The moral of this story is this: "What is your 68?" As coaches, we need to remind our players that everyone needs to have a "68"-type commitment to a standard of excellence. They have to be willing to put in the work, to invest time into it, and to be persistent.

I have attended the Combines for years. I ask the players that win the contest this question. "What is your identity?" The players from USC and LSU respond instantly. The winners all have an answer. The players that are not winners are confused by the question. I am not trying to tell them what their identity should be. The winners know what they are about. If you go to your team and they do not know what you stand for, or they do not know what your "68" is, you are not going to win big.

Tom Donahoe of the Steelers likes to tell this story. When he first came with the Steelers, Chuck Noe was the head coach. In their first game, they lost 55 to 0 to Cleveland. They lost the second game of the year to Cincinnati 42-7. Tom was standing in the corner of the dressing room and Chuck Noe walked by. Chuck looked at Tom and said, "Tom, if those were not the two best teams in the NFL, you are in for a long year." Chuck Noe talked to the team and told them they were a great team and that they had worked hard. He went on to tell them they were going back to work and they were going to work on fundamentals. The Steelers went on to win seven straight games and only missed the Super Bowl by one game. Chuck Noe had a "68."

What is it that drives us? Arnold Palmer holds a golf tournament for blind golfers each year in Birmingham, Alabama. The media was interviewing Arnold and this blind golfer. The officials would ring a bell and the blind golfer would hit the golf ball. During the interview, he told Arnold Palmer he could beat him in a golf game. Arnold Palmer said, "I am Arnold Palmer, and you are blind. You can't beat me." The blind golfer said, "Let us make it interesting. I will bet you five thousand dollars I can beat you for 18 holes." Palmer said, "Okay. When do we play?" The blind man said, "Ten o'clock tonight."

This next story made the Make a Wish list. The doctor told the mother of a young boy that he only had two months to live. The mother took the boy home and asked him this question. "Bobby, when you grow up what do you want to be?" He was six years old and he was sick. He replied, "I want to grow up to be a fireman." The mother said, "Let me see what I can do about that."

She called the firehouse and talked to the chief. She told him her son was sick and only had a few months to live. She told the chief that her son wanted to be a firefighter. She went on to tell the chief that she did not think the son would live long enough to be a firefighter. "Could he come down and hang out at the fire station for a day?

The chief said, "I can do better than that. I am going to make him a firefighter. I will get him a hat, boots, and a complete outfit for a fireman." The young boy was able to spend the day at the fire station. When he got home that night he was so excited he could not go to sleep. "I got to be a fireman. Wow!"

A couple of months later the mother called the fire chief and told him that he had given her son the best day of his life. "That was all he talked about for two months. Could you stop by the hospital to see him because he only has a few more days to live?"

The chief said, "I will do better than that. We will come to see your son." He told the mother to tell the people at the hospital not to get alarmed when they bring the fire truck down to the hospital at 6:00 that evening.

The firefighters went to the hospital in the fire truck with the siren going full blast. They pulled the truck up under the window of the little boy and proceeded to climb up the fire ladder to the window of the little boy. He was several stories high in the hospital. They went up the ladder one at a time until all fourteen firefighters went in the window and in the room with the boy. They all gave him a big hug. He was all smiles the rest of his time.

How would you deal with that? I bet you would be very good. You have a picture and you move right to the picture. "What is your 68?" That is where it all starts. It is what is in the hearts of those brave men. This is what it is all about when you have a picture of what you want.

I want everyone to take one minute and ask the person next to you to share a few things with you. Tell him what your identity is. If you do not know, this is what we are here for today. This is what our heartbeat is. Every team I know that is good knows what their identity is immediately. Tell the person next to you, "This is *my* 68." Take one minute and then we will come back and continue.

Let me get everyone back to the subject. I have seen programs where a negative factor takes over and causes problems. I say you are going to get exactly what you see.

When LSU played Georgia in the regular season two years ago, they beat them by four points. The two teams ended up in the championship game of the SEC. The night before the game, Nick Saban called all of the players together. He had 100 white paneled autographed game balls in the room. Each of those game balls had the number "68" stamped on them.

Coach Saban called the first player up in front of the group. He asked the player if you could give that game ball to only one person, whom you would give it to. The players said, "My Grandmother because she raised me." Coach Saban called another player up before the group. He asked the same question. "Who would you give the ball to?" He said, "My son! He will be able to look at that ball for 50 years." Coach Saban gave out 100 game balls with "68" stamped on them. I think LSU beat Georgia by 28 points in that championship game. This is all what we are about.

I said we would cover five steps to the program. We have covered the first point to "get a picture when it started." We must keep moving to the picture. The people that do not win are confused. If you do not have a "68," you are confused by the question.

The second point is the players must own the picture. We all work on accountability. If we are only teaching and not working our tails off, then accountability will not get it done. The players must take ownership in their team. A good example of this was with Michael Jordan. He used to walk out on the floor and tell the other players, "Match my intensity." The players must get to a point where they take over. You must get the players to a point where they take the ownership. How? You know the Wizard of Oz story. You tell it over and over again.

I have about five people that go tell others about Kevin Elko. I traced almost all of my income back to one person. What Paul Revere wrote, another person wrote. They listened to him. Everything that he said, they responded to. You have to get two or three players to spread your story. Get your Paul Reveres. Go get the leaders and work with them. Get them to run the story over and over to the rest of the team. It has to get to a point where the players own the team. They must take ownership in the team.

I was sitting in the back of the room with Calvin Hill when I was with the Dallas Cowboys. It was a Saturday night and we had a game the next day. As we came out of the meeting, Calvin told me this story. He said Vince Lombardi went to visit Bart Starr in his new home he just had built. Coach Lombardi was getting ready to leave and Bart Starr started crying. Coach Lombardi asked Bart why he was crying. Bart Starr told him, "The year before you came to Green Bay, the fans were ready to run us out of town. Now we are winning and things are a lot better. It makes me want to cry."

Listen to this phrase. "Love the players, love the people. It is a choice. Decide to love them." I have never been with a team that won a National Championship, or the Super Bowl team I was with, where the coaches did not show that love for the players. They were not "bad-mouthing" the players. Part of the picture is caring and loving each other.

Let me bring you up-to-date. First step is to get the picture. The second step is to take ownership.

There is a man that can predict with a 95 percent accuracy if a person is going to get married within five years. I asked that person how could that be. He said when a positive and a negative interaction occur it is five to one that they will stay together.

We must build a vision. Part of that vision is telling them you love them and that you care about them. We must get the picture and we must take ownership of our actions.

Captain Charles Plumb graduated from the Naval Academy at Annapolis and went on to fly the F-4 Phantom jet on 74 successful combat missions off the carrier USS Kitty Hawk over North Vietnam.

On his 75th mission, with only five days before he was to return home, his F-4 jet was shot down, and he was captured, tortured, and imprisoned. He spent 2,103 days as a prisoner of war in a communist prison camp known as the Hanoi Hilton. During his nearly six years of captivity, Charlie Plumb distinguished himself among his fellow prisoners as a professional in underground communications, and served for two of those years as the chaplain in his camp.

Years later, he was sitting in a restaurant. He noticed a couple of people starring at him from the table next to his table. They were trying to figure out where they had seen him.

Finally, one of the men came over to him and said, "You are Captain Charlie Plumb, aren't you?" He replied, "Yes, sir!" The man said, "You were on the USS Kitty Hawk?" Again, it was, "Yes, sir!" He went on to say, "You flew 75 missions over Vietnam?" Captain Plumb said, "How do you know all of this?" The man said, "I was on the USS Kitty Hawk with you. I was the guy that packed your parachute that day you were shot down." The Captain said, "I did not know who you were. I am sorry I did not know you. Thanks for doing a great job with the parachute."

How long has it been since you have told the people around you that you know what they do for you? Have you thanked the people that pack your parachute? Coaches should tell their kids "You just did not drop out of the sky and land here at football practice. Many people have been packing your parachute. Your parents and teachers and coaches have gotten you to this point."

The other part of that message is this. Whose parachute are you packing? All of the folks you come in daily contact with, how you treat them is important.

I ask you about the smallest player on your team. When was the last time you told him you know what he does for the team? "You pack our parachute." I am going to think about one or two people that have encouraged me. I want you to think of one or two people that have encouraged you over the years.

A few years back there was this rich man in England. He got married and, in a few years, his wife went to the hospital to give birth to their child. It was a boy but the wife died in childbirth. The wealthy man hired a butler and a complete staff to help raise the boy. When the boy turned 11 years old, he became ill and died. A few years went by and the father died. He had spent all of his life collecting art. He had put all of his wealth into the art collection. So after his death, the estate had an auction. People came from all over Europe to see all of this famous art collection. The auctioneer was up front reading all about the items that were to be included in the auction that day. Finally, they started the auction. The first item auctioned was a painting of the young boy. The auctioneer said, "This painting is not worth much compared to some of the other items that are to be auctioned off here today. However, this is where we will start the auction."

A man from the back of the room was the only person to bid on the painting of the young boy. After the man paid for the painting an attorney stepped up and opened a letter. He read the letter to the auctioneer.

"As the will states, whoever bought the painting of the young boy received all of the other art that was to be auctioned off at no extra cost." The man that made the bid was elated. He told the lawyer that he was not aware of the letter. He said, "I am the butler, and I raised that young boy and I loved him."

Get the picture. Coach them hard. They must be accountable.

Every year I hear all of this talk about us having an educational problem. We do not have an educational problem. We have a parental problem. We will continue to have that problem as long as it takes the same amount of education to have a kid as it does to get a fishing license. It is not going to change. The problem is with the parents. If kids do not get it from the coaches, they do not get it.

I want every man in this room to stand up. I want you to walk over to one or two men in this room and give them a DWD. Tell them why you are giving them a Damn Well Done approval. "This is what you did for me." If you do not have anyone here that did anything for you, just walk around the room and look busy. That worked very well! Everyone please go back to your seats.

You are always going to have some challenge. Let me tell you a story to illustrate my point. This man died and went to heaven. St. Peter met him at the pearly gates. He asked the man if he ever cheated on his wife. The man said, "I was married fifty years and I never cheated on my wife." St. Peter said, "Good for you. I will give you a Cadillac and you can drive through the gates." Of course, the man went into heaven.

The next man came to St. Peter and he asked him the same question. "Did you ever cheat on your wife?" The reply was "In twenty five years I only slipped one time." St. Peter said, "I am going to give you a Chevy." The man drove off in the Chevy.

The third man came to St. Peter. Again, it was the same question. "Did you every run around on your wife?" The man replied, "Every day I cheated on my wife." St. Peter said, "I will have to give you a skateboard."

The man rode off on the skateboard and the first person he saw was the man in the Cadillac sitting on the side of the road. He was crying his eyes out. The man on the skateboard stopped and went over to the man in the Cadillac. "What is wrong with you? You got a Cadillac so you should be happy." The man replied, "I know I should be happy, but my wife just came by on a skateboard." You are always going to have some challenge.

The third point is simple. We must have a sustained steady effort. Never look at the clock. Keep punching. Do not judge the score, and do not judge the opponents. Keep punching until the game is over. Keep your effort at a steady pace.

A young boy had his left arm severed in an accident. He could not take part in many sports because of this handicap. His parents enrolled him in a Judo class. The Judo master worked very hard with the young boy and he was able to compete in the Judo meets. He went all the way to the championship. He went into the championship match and was able to win first place.

On the way back from the championship meet, the young boy asked the Judo Master why he had put him into the championship match with only one sound Judo move. The instructor told him, "I did tell you to master that one move that I taught you, right?" The young boy agreed the instructor had taught him to master the one move. Again, the boy asked him why he had only taught him only one judo move for the championship. The instructor said, "I taught you that one move and the only counter for that move was for your opponent to grab the left arm."

You have to get away from judgment. Let me tell you what the good running backs are thinking when they run the ball over and over. It is not to score a touchdown. They are thinking "water bamboo!" Do you know what you get if you water bamboo for a year? You get nothing! What if you water the bamboo for two years? Again, you get nothing! How about three years? Nothing! Do we get anything if we water bamboo the fourth year? "You get 90 feet in six weeks." What is the analogy here? Run full speed the whole game and the hole will open. I hate the phrase, "Go make a play." If you will go full speed, the play will come to you. Coach Saban told his players over and over, "You never know when a big play is going to show up until *you* show up." Learning becomes instinct. Get the best at what you are doing. Give your best and the play will come to you.

You must be careful not to over-coach your players. I have asked players what they were thinking about when they had a great athletic performance. I have asked all kinds of athletes the same question: "What were you thinking when you had that great run?" I get the same answer every time: "I was not thinking about anything when it happened. It just happened instantly."

The next point is very important. I do not believe in coaching positive. No mental clutter! Get their heads quiet. I want to keep everything in their heads

simple. I do not want to give them too much to think about. Most coaches over-coach. Many coaches forget what it is like to play the game. Get out of the way and let the players play. The head has to be quiet.

We want to teach our players to trust what the coaches teach them. Trust is a choice. If a team is having a losing season, you can ask the players if they trust the coach. Almost every hand indicated that they did not trust the coach. If you ask the teams that are having winning record if they trust the coach and again, almost every hand will indicate, yes, they trust the coach. It is a choice. We want no mental clutter. After a while, it becomes a matter of execution.

I work with tight end Chad Lewis of the Eagles. He had two great catches in the league championship game. That got them into the Super Bowl. Here is what he says on every down: "Catch the X." He has one phrase that he uses repeatedly. "Release, and catch the X." He does not say when, score, or anything else. He wants to catch the X, which is on the front of the football. It is a simple phrase but that is all he says. Get a simple phrase in their head so they can execute.

How can you beat anyone else if you have clutter? It is a choice. You make sure there is one place where there is no clutter and that is with you. I am going to choose my attitude.

Get the picture that you want that team to be and then grow into that picture. Get your Paul Reveres and talk to them. Get them to a point where you can tell them to match what you do. Talk to them constantly about sustained effort. No mental clutter!

Here is the last point. I studied the Steelers when they won all of those championships. Tom Donahoe said they had already won the championships they just had to go out and claim them. The last step is claiming what is yours. You get to the Super Bowl and you know you have already won it, but you are there to claim it.

LINE DRILLS ON ZONE AND COUNTER PLAYS

New York Giants

It is a privilege to be here. I want to thank Pete and John for inviting me. Talking to one another and exchanging ideas is why you come to clinics.

There is no off-season in football anymore. There is an out of season, but no off-season. Players continue to work and get better. To players in the NFL this is a job and there is no question about that.

I have 90 minutes today to talk football. That is not much time to accomplish a great deal. Time flies when you do a clinic lecture. I want to give you a look at some of the drill we do and talk about the inside zone, outside zone, and the counter play we run.

At the New York Giants, we are a zone-oriented team but we also run with power. When we talk to our team, they know the signature play is the power play. The power play is the play our opponents know they must stop. That is the play on which we hang our hat. We double-team on the frontside, pull a backside guard, and run the play downhill. We ran the power play this year at a three-to-one ratio to our other plays. We ran the power play from all formations and in any situation.

We were fortunate to have an outstanding running back in Tiki Barber. In 2003, we were 28th in rushing and in 2004 we went to 11th in the league. We made a jump in our league statistic, but we are still not where we need to be. We run the inside zone and the outside zone. Tiki Barber loves to run the outside zone play. We have two ways we run the play. We have an outside zone play called the "boss" and one called "sprint." We also run the counter off the inside zone play. I will talk about these four plays as I go through my lecture.

The first thing I want to do is show you some tape of some drills we do. We want to get into an explosive stance. Football is not a comfortable game, so I do not want to use the word comfortable in relationship to the stance. We want to get into an explosive stance. An explosive stance is one that allows you to come off the ball with some power. From the stance you have to move right, left, and be able to pass protect. You want to be able to go in four different directions from the same stance. In a short yardage or goal-line situation, we change the stance somewhat.

Footwork is the first thing any offensive linemen have to work on. When the offensive linemen step off the ball they must come off with leverage and balance. The must know their landmark and where to place the hands. We want good knee and hip bend to create explosion. When he comes off the line of scrimmage, he wants his shoulders low and on an angle to create power. He needs to keep his hips behind his shoulder, get his second step on the ground quickly, and explode.

Linemen block people at an angle. Very seldom does an offensive lineman take on anyone straight ahead. Defenses today are gap-control defenses. The down linemen will get into gaps and or shade when they play defense. It is important to keep your hips behind the shoulder, keep the proper footwork, get the second foot on the ground, and block them. You end up blocking at a 45-degree angle. You never want to get the hips turned to the sideline at any time during run blocking.

This first drill is a bag drill to get your linemen loose. We lay six bags down on the ground and run the linemen over them. The bags are approximately one yard apart. This loosens up the muscles, especially the groin. We go through the bags at about 75-percent speed. They step over the bag with high knees. That loosens them up in the hips and groin. The next thing we do is go over them laterally. When we do this exercise we keep the hips down and the shoulders square. We want them to look straight ahead and not turn their shoulders.

The next thing we do is step over the bag laterally. Between each bag they have to take two steps before stepping over to the next bag. That makes them pound their feet in between each bag. One of the biggest assets an offensive lineman has is his feet. He has to move his feet to block and it is important to stay on them when he is blocking.

The power in a block comes from the hips and knees. The hand placement comes later in the lecture. The next thing we do over the bags is to bring the trail knee over first. That stretches the hip flexor and groin. We want to bring the knee over the top and keep it high.

The next drill is a simple reach-blocking drill. The blocker has a defender with a shield across from him. He works three steps in the drill. He comes out of the stance and works three steps. He goes to the right and then to the left working three steps out of the stance.

We follow that drill with a demeanor drill, which requires blocking at an angle. What we check on this drill is the knee bend and weight on the insteps of the feet. We want them to bend at the knee and not the waist. It is important as they run for them to pump their arms. We want them to feel the power angles and the weight on the insteps. We go both directions on this movement also.

The variation of drills is important no matter what group you coach. We do the drill day-in and day-out. However, we do to other things as well.

We constantly have the linemen check their balance in their stance. We have them pick up the grounded hand. They should not be leaning forward on their toes or back on their heels. We want a balanced explosive stance.

This off-season I had 14 linemen working four day a week doing these drills. The next drill involves a medicine ball. We do any number of things with the medicine ball. The medicine ball we use is 19 pounds and 23 inches in diameter. In this drill, the lineman gets into a kneeling position, explodes through the medicine ball, and throws it toward his partner who is five yards away. We do not want to build bad habits while doing this drill. The elbows have to stay inside as he explodes with his hips behind his shoulders.

The offensive blocker has to get his hands inside to control a defender. If his hands are outside the defender's hands, he has no control. He wants his hands inside with the thumbs up. As the lineman explodes through the medicine ball, he throws it over his partner's head. We do this at five yards for three reps. After the third time the partner backs up to seven yards and we repeat that three more times. The third time the blocker can put his partner wherever he wants to launch the ball over his head. The emphasis is place on the hips coming through and the lineman landing on his thighs. We watch the elbows and hands to make sure they stay tight and to the inside.

We have six or seven pass protection drills we do with the medicine ball. We use this big out-of-season conditioning tool. Once the season begins, we do not have a lot of time for individual drills. We have to do the drill work in the off-season. During March, April, May, and June is the time we do these types of drills.

We use the two-man sled in our off-season work. We do a number of drills on the two-man sled. The first drill I do on the two-man sled is a fit drill. They get into the sled with a good knee bend; their neck is squeezing a strut on the side on the sled. Their head is up with their eyes looking at me.

We go two at a time on the two-man sled. We back them one-step off the sled. They both step with their inside foot and strike the sled. They explode into the sled, gather their feet, and run lifting the sled as they run. If they do not work together and keep their hips behind the sled, the sled will spin. If the sled starts to spin, the linemen have to adjust and get their hips behind their shoulders.

Following the sled drill, we use people instead of dummies. We do the same drill without the sled.

We partner-up our players. We give hand shields to the defenders. The first thing you need to do is teach the shield holder how to hold the shield. To get something out of this drill the dummy holder has to know what he is doing. He has to get low and give passive resistance to the offensive blocker. If he stands up, the blocker will be on the same plane, which is a bad habit.

In this drill, the offensive blocker does what he did on the sled. He comes off on the defender, has good knee bend, strikes with his hips through his shoulder, and drives with his feet. The dummy holder gets low in his stance. On the contact, he gives strong resistance. As the blocker begins to pump his feet, he relaxes the resistance and gives ground grudgingly.

We do the same drill blocking on a 45-degree angle. In each of these drills, we teach explosion, landmark, leverage, and finish. I watch the drill and as the offensive blocker gets to the end of the block, I yell, "Finish!" The blocker has his hands inside on the dummy holder. When he hears the "finish" call, he presses his hand upward, locks out on the defender, extends his legs hitting the ground on his thighs, and ends up on his belly.

In every drill we do, there is a finish to the drill. If we have a passing game scrimmage and the ball is passed downfield, I want the offensive linemen to show me a burst of speed for five yards chasing the ball. That gives them good habit of following the ball.

The zigzag drill is an offensive blocker and a defender locked up in the fit position. The defender reacts much like the two-man sled. He moves from side to side. The offensive blocker has to adjust to his movement and keep his hips behind his shoulders. He gets his weight on his insteps and pounds his feet. We run the drill for 15 yards. We look for good hand placement.

I stand behind the blocker. I should not be able to see his hands or his elbows. The offensive blocker cannot anticipate the movement of the shield holder. He has to adjust to the movement when it comes. He has to stay Velcro-ed to the shield and keep his hips behind his shoulders. The defender moves a couple of steps to the right and comes back left for a couple of steps. They continue to move backward for 15 yards.

We teach our pull differently than you probably do. If your lineman opens up and swivels his hips to pull, his shoulders are parallel to the sideline. We pull guards on the power play for linebackers. If the linebacker lines up four yards deep and fill outside in the C gap, he is running downhill most of the way. The guard is not ready to block the linebacker because his hips are not behind the shoulders.

We teach our guard to use a square pull. That keeps his shoulders square to the line of scrimmage and keeps his hips behind his shoulders. With his playside foot, the guard steps back for depth. He has to step deep enough to clear the player next to him. He takes his backside foot and replaces his playside with it. He moves down the line, has his hips behind his shoulder, and is ready to take on a linebacker running downhill.

As the guard turns up on the linebacker, he has a landmark he hits. The landmark is the outside armpit of the linebacker. We hit the landmark, get leverage, and finish on the linebacker. We use the square pull when the backside guard pulls around for the Mike linebacker. To become good at the square pull, you have to work hard on it with countless reps. If you coach the offensive line, you must do a lot of repetition work on each technique.

I have found if the lineman does not trust his technique, he will go back to his normal pull. We had a left guard who came to us from Tampa Bay right before the season started. He had never used the square pull. It took a couple of games before he could do it and five games before he became comfortable with the pull. However, it helps our linemen block those linebackers.

If the guard has to get out on a screen or block for a wide receiver screen. He uses his normal pull. He pivots and runs to get into the screen. We use the square pull when we block a linebacker within the tackle box. On a toss sweep, we use the square pull.

Men, it is impossible for me to go over all the techniques of each block we use on the running plays, but I will give you what I can.

When we run the inside zone play we use a "reach block," a "scoop block," and a "slip block." The reach block is a one-on-one block like the ones I showed you on the drill tape. A scoop block (Diagram #1) is a combination block between our tackles and tight end.

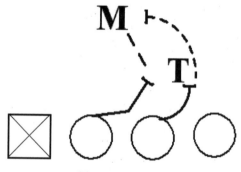

Diagram #1. Scoop

The slip block (Diagram #2) is a combination block between our guard and tackle.

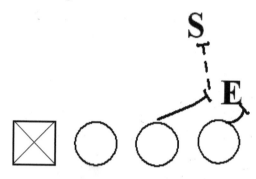

Diagram #2. Slip

On the outside zone play, we have a "Ted" block or "tag" block. The Ted block (Diagram #3) is the tight end blocking down on a 5-technique tackle and the tackle pull around for the outside linebacker.

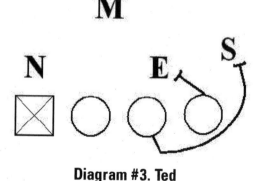

Diagram #3. Ted

A tag block (Diagram #4) is a tackle blocking down on a 3 technique with the guard pulling around for the linebacker. We can use the scoop and slip block on this play.

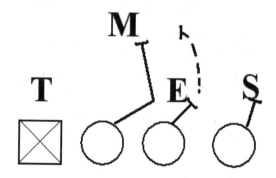

Diagram #4. Tag

We change the technique depending on what type of front we face. If we play a 3-4 front we may use the Scoop and Slip scheme, but against 4-3 front, we can use the Ted and Tag scheme.

The first play is the inside-zone play against a "4-3 under defense" with a bubble look to the tight end side (Diagram #5). On this defense, the offensive line uses a slip block between the strongside guard and tackle. The tight end reaches the Sam linebacker aligned on him. The strong side tackle reaches on the 5-technique defensive end. He does not worry about the defensive end coming inside because the guard is one-step reading.

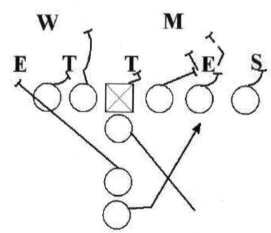

Diagram #5. Inside zone versus under

The strong guard protects the tackle from the inside. He uses a one-step slip with the tackle. He steps and keys the inside knee of the defensive end. If the knee comes toward him, he prepares to help the tackle up to the Mike linebacker. The guard watches the tackle's knee with his peripheral vision. He has to see the Mike linebacker also. It is a one-step read on the defensive end. The guard cannot afford to cross-step to the defensive end and let the linebacker run downhill into his gap. The backs aiming point is the inside leg of the front side tackle.

The center reach-blocks on the nose tackle. To the backside, the guard and tackle use a B-block on the backside 3-technique tackle up to the Will linebacker. The fullback blocks the backside defensive end.

Our on-the-line posture will change from game to game. We have two types of postures in our splits. We have a horizontal posture, which means the splits between the offensive linemen, and a vertical posture, which is the depth off the ball. In a short yardage or goal-line situation, we want to crowd the ball as much as we can. If we play a heavy stunting team, we may get off the ball as far as we can. With the guards and tackle, we are normally at two-and-a-half feet. The tight end may be wider. When we get to the goal line, we tighten our splits a little.

If we run the inside zone play into an over defense, we scoop block with the tight end and strongside tackle (Diagram #6). The tight end reaches the defensive end. The tackle takes a one-step scoop read with the tight end. He keys the inside knee of the defensive end. If the knee comes toward him, he combo blocks with the tight end up to the Sam linebacker.

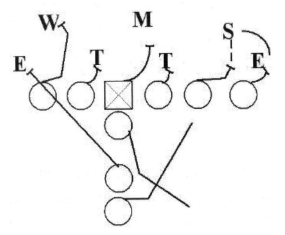

Diagram #6. Inside zone versus over

The guard reaches the 3-technique tackle. The guard takes the proper angle and covers up the tackle. His landmark is the play side breastplate of the defensive tackle. He uses landmark, leverage, and finish to make the block. The backside guard has to help the center on anything in the center's backside gap, up to the Mike linebacker. The backside tackle comes through on the Will linebacker. The fullback blocks the backside end.

I have some tape on the inside zone play. The B-block is a combination block by the backside tackle and guard. It is a backside slip block (Diagram #7). On the B-block, the tackle has to work with the guard and not against him. It is a two-on-one block. The tackle and guard want their shoulder in relationship to the running back. If the tackle comes down on the defender with his shoulders turned, he works against the guard. He has to get his shoulders square to the line of scrimmage and work with the guard.

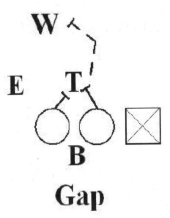

Diagram #7. B-block

If the nose tackle moves into the strongside A gap, the center calls "philly." The slip block between the guard and tackle turns into a philly call (Diagram #8) between the center and guard. The center and guard work a combination block. On the philly, the footwork by the center does not change. The center takes his proper footwork to his block like a reach block. The guard picks up his inside foot and puts it back down. He comes through the outside breastplate of the nose tackle up to the Mike linebacker.

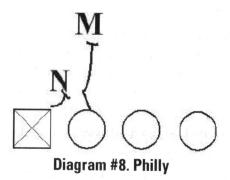

Diagram #8. Philly

On this play we get into a two-tight end set by moving the fullback up into the backside tight end position (Diagram #9). The defense balances their defense by moving the tackles into head-up positions on the guards. On the inside zone play, the center blocks with the onside guard on the playside 2 technique and block back on the Mike linebacker. The playside tackle and tight end use a scoop block on the defensive end and Sam linebacker. The backside guard and tackle B-block on the backside 2 technique up to the Will linebacker. The fullback has to cut off the backside defensive end. To cut off the defensive end the fullback must get his backside pad into the inside armpit of the defender.

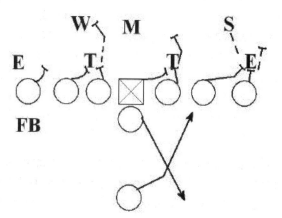

Diagram #9. Balanced defense

If the defensive end and Sam linebacker are stacked, we scoop them. If they are both on the line of scrimmage, we reach block them.

The aiming point for the running back on the outside zone play is two yards behind the tight end and two yards wide of the tight end.

[Cell phone rings in lecture hall.]

It is a fine if a cell phone rings in one of our meetings.

We run this play toward the 3-technique tackle. Against the under 4-3 defense, the tackle and tight end run a Ted block. The tight end blocks down on the defensive end. When the tight end blocks down on the defensive end, we call it edging the defense. The tackle square pulls around the tight end and attacks the Sam linebacker in the outside armpit.

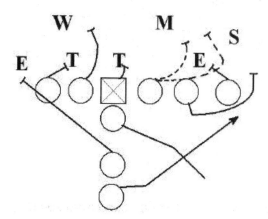

Diagram #10. Outside zone versus under 4-3

The playside guard square pulls for the Mike linebacker. The center reaches the nose tackle. On the backside, the tackle and guard run a "B-1 Block." That means the tackle comes down hard and clips the 3-technique tackle. The guard gets up on the Will linebacker. He must not be held by the 3 technique. He has to avoid the 3 technique and get up to the Will linebacker.

The philosophy of the outside zone play is to edge the defense. The philosophy of the inside zone play is to get double-team movement at the point of attack. The inside zone play can and will cut back to the backside. The outside zone play will cut up but never cut back.

Most defenses in the NFL are playing a shade technique on the inside shoulder of the tight end. The coaches tell the defensive end, if the tight end blocks him, they will look for another defensive end. We have a tight end that does not block so well, but he is a tremendous pass receiver.

On the over 4-3 defense (Diagram #11), the tight end blocks the defensive end. The playside tackle and guard use a tag block with the tackle blocking down on the 3 techinque and the guard square pulling for the Sam linebacker. On the over front, the

Mike linebacker plays in the strongside A gap. The center takes an angle through inside leg of the 3 technique to get to the Mike linebacker. If the center does not think he can cut off the Mike linebacker, he can pull around the down-block by the tackle and come up on him.

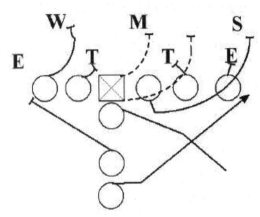

Diagram #11. Outside zone versus over 4-3

The backside guard cuts off the shade tackle to his side and the backside tackle gets up on the Will linebacker.

I have some more film on the outside zone play. The first play in the film is the outside zone play against a 3-technique tackle. The playside guard can either reach the 3 technique or tag block with the tackle. If he reaches the 3 technique, the tackle runs the scoop scheme with the end. If the guard calls for a tag block, the tackle blocks down on the 3 technique and the guard pulls for the Sam linebacker. On this play in the film, the center goes up on the Mike linebacker and does not pull.

The thing to remember about the outside zone play is that the landmark for all the playside linemen is the outside armpit of the defender.

When the tight end blocks down on a 7-technique defensive end, it is a tough block. He steps with his inside foot to stop penetration by the defender. His aiming point is the near shoulder and his landmark is the breastplate. He puts his eyes across the breastplate of the defensive end. As he comes down, he has to read if the defensive end will try to cross-face his block as he reads the pulling tackle. If he thinks the defensive end is going to cross-face him, he puts his eyes behind the near shoulder.

If the center has a nose guard aligned on him, he has some blocking adjustments to make. If he feels the nose tackle will play straight, he reaches him. If he feels the nose guard is going to the backside gap, he calls an "A-B1 block" (Diagram #12). In the B1 block, the backside tackle clipped the 3 technique aligned on the backside guard. On the A-B1 block, the backside guard chops down the nose guard coming to the backside A gap. The center steps into the strongside A gap and gets up on the backside linebacker.

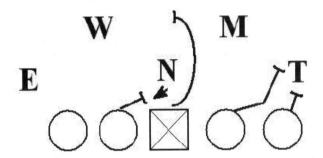

Diagram #12. A-B1 block

Our running back loves to run the outside zone play. Any time you can edge the defense on an outside running play, that is an advantage. Edging the defense means blocking down on the outside defensive lineman on the line of scrimmage. The best way to edge the defense is with the man-to-man scheme. However, if you are playing a defensive front that is stunting a great deal, you are better off zoning the play. With the linemen's square pull, the block becomes a stalk block by the linemen.

If the tackle and guard run a slip scheme for the 5 technique and Mike linebacker, the tight end reaches the Sam linebacker. On the outside zone play, you get push off the line of scrimmage, but you never get the outside. The play ends up running laterally and we never get to the outside.

If the center has a nose guard that he cannot reach, he calls a "playboy block" (Diagram #13). The playside guard blocks down on the nose guard and the center pulls around the guard's block and up on the linebacker. The reason we call it a playboy block is the technique used by the center is a center-fold block.

The offensive line has to work their techniques repeatedly. When they play, they have to trust their technique and run the scheme. The linemen cannot let the defenders throw them out of sync with their technique.

We have an outside zone play with a lead back. We call this our "boss play" (Diagram #14). On the outside zone play, the running back's aiming point is two-by-two yards outside the tight end. On the boss play, the aiming point is the playside tackle area. When the running back gets into that area, he bounces the ball outside. The fullback gets to the outside and blocks the strong safety.

Diagram #13. Playboy block

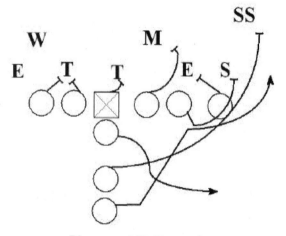

Diagram #14. Boss play

In the offensive line, we block the front like the outside zone play. The tight end and tackle run a Ted block, with the tight end blocking down the defensive end and the tackle pulling for the Sam linebacker. The playside guard reaches, pulls for the Mike linebacker, or has a playboy block with the center. The center reaches or blocks the Mike linebacker. On the backside, we have a B-block between the backside guard and tackle. They could use a B1 block with the guard escaping for the Will linebacker.

If we have a 3 technique on the playside guard, we tag block and pull the guard for the playside linebacker (Diagram #15). The center goes through or pulls for the Mike linebacker. The backside guard and tackle cut off their defenders. The tight end reaches the defensive end. The running back and fullback do the same thing.

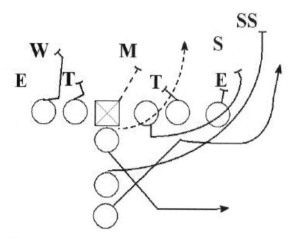

Diagram #15. Boss play versus 3 technique

The last play I have to put up is the "counter play" (Diagram #16). The counter game is one that we could talk about for a long time in detail. On this play, we fake the inside zone play. The inside zone play aims at the inside leg of the frontside tackle. The rules for the offensive line are the inside zone play to the right. On the zone play right, the fullback blocks the backside defensive end. He does the same thing on the counter play. The quarterback and running back fake the zone play to the right, counter back, and read the fullback's block.

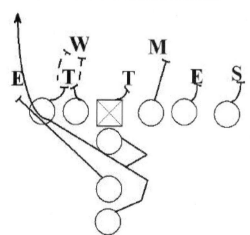

Diagram #16. Counter play

If the defensive end cross-faces the block of the fullback, the fullback logs him in and, running, bounces the play outside. If the defensive end jumps outside, the fullback kicks him out and the running back runs inside the fullback's block.

If we run the counter play toward a tight end set on the line of scrimmage, it is much cleaner than bringing the tight end in motion (Diagram #17). We fake the inside zone to the right again. To the left side, the tackle blocks down on the 3 technique. The tight end releases the defensive end and comes down on the Will linebacker. The guard comes through and up on the Mike linebacker. The center reaches on the nose guard. The backside guard and tackle run a slip scheme on the defensive end and Sam linebacker. The backs do the same things.

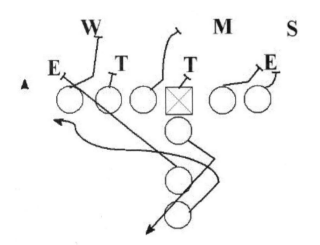

Diagram #17. Counter to the tight end

I hope you understand that techniques on all the blocks are a separate clinic in itself. I wanted to talk more about the blocks, but did not do them justice. I hope you got something that you can use. I will be here if you want to talk additionally about anything in the lecture. As I pointed out at the beginning, you are a special group. You stayed at the clinic to listen to a boring coach like me to learn more football. I hope it was worth it and you picked up one or two things to take back to your players. You are coaching a great sport and there is nothing like the game of football.

Continue to do the great work you do in teaching the youngsters the fundamentals of this great game. Men, do not stop teaching the players. They need to learn the basic skills and fundamentals. When the players get to our level they still need to review the fundamentals. The first thing I talk to my players about is their neck. I talk about keeping their head up. I talk about keeping their chin up and their eyes open when they block. The neck is so important because it connect the spinal cord. I give my players a long dissertation on the anatomy of the neck. If you turn the neck to the side, they strain the muscles because they are not in a supporting position. The same thing happens when you put your head down.

Talk to your players repeatedly to get them to keep their chin up and eyes open when they block or tackle. This is a collision sport. Players should not be intimidated by the collision as long as the coaches teach them proper techniques of the game. Fundamentals are so important to the game of football.

I love watching high school football games. As high school coaches, you have a chance to build the foundation of players throughout the country and my hat is off to you. I appreciate your time and your effort. Best of luck.

ADJUSTMENTS IN THE VERTICAL PASSING GAME

Texas A&M University

When people talk about big-name coaches, I fit into that category. When I applied for a job at a particular school, they told me they were looking for a big-name coach. I told them they could not get a bigger named coach than me because my name had 10 letters in it. It is nice to be here today. There are so many familiar faces and that makes it fun to be here.

I earned my spurs in the Western Athletic Conference. I guess it is the Mountain West Conference now, but it will always be the W.A.C. to me.

I am going to talk about a series of passes from our four-receiver package. This pass does not have to come from the four-wide receiver set. It can come from the two-by-two sets. It does not matter what set you use because the principles are the same. We run primarily the same patterns from any two-by-two set. We call our passing series with boys and girls names. The plays have numbers that go with them but we very seldom use the numbers. The series I will talk about in our passing game is "Vickie" (Diagram #1). Since Vickie is a girl's name, it defines which way the offensive line slides in their pass protection.

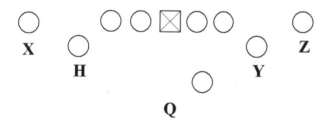

Diagram #1. Vickie

Vickie essentially starts out as a four vertical pass route. There is nothing earth shattering about these patterns. In our four-wide alignment we have

an X-receiver, Y-receiver, Z-receiver, and an H-receiver. In the doublewide slot set, the H- and Y-receivers are in the slots. Against two-deep coverage, we used to run H or Y on an arrow routes. We very seldom throw that pattern any more.

Now we read the coverage with our receivers. Every defense we face these days is generally a two-deep or one-deep concept. On the four verticals pattern, the inside receivers have an option route based on their reads. All our receivers have a mandatory outside release against a two-deep secondary.

In a two-deep coverage, the corners roll up to the flat area. We talk to our outside receivers about a five-yard highway. The five-yard highway means the outside receivers stay five yards from the sideline until the ball leaves the quarterback's hand. That gives the quarterback a place to throw the ball. By throwing the ball into the five-yard area, the quarterback can avoid throwing an interception. If he can drop the ball over the receiver's outside shoulder, the receiver has an opportunity to catch the ball and not be out of bounds.

The pass is either complete or incomplete. The bottom line to that thinking is no turnovers. We were very good with turnovers last year. In seven games, we did not turn the ball over. We had eight turnovers in 11 games. We were one of the leaders in the nation in that category.

Every pass we have in our offense has some concepts on where the quarterback should throw the ball. Our best running play from this series is the quarterback scramble. Our quarterback was very good at doing that. It frustrated the defense when he escaped the rush and ran for big yardage.

The inside slot receivers on the Vickie series run 10- to 12- yard option routes (Diagram #2). If the receivers face a two-deep safety look, they cannot go any deeper than 10 to 12 yards. They have the option to hook inside or outside the linebackers. If the linebacker is trying to wall off the receiver, the receiver probably will run the pattern outside. However, he could get inside the linebacker on an inside hook. If the linebacker is hanging inside, the receiver definitely wants to take the pattern outside. We are not going to force four vertical routes with four defensive backs sinking and the safeties in position to play the ball.

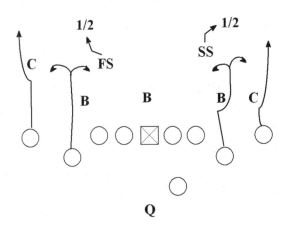

Diagram #2. Slot option

However, if the secondary spins one of the two-deep safeties into underneath coverage or into the box area, the coverage is no longer two deep (Diagram #3). When the safety spins down, the secondary goes to cover-3-type coverage. The slot receivers read the safety dropping down as they run their routes. They stay vertical and we have a three-deep secondary to throw the four vertical routes against. That is the best of all worlds for the receivers because we have four receivers on three defenders. The quarterback looks to the inside receivers first because they have a definite two-on-one scheme.

If the secondary has one defender in the middle of the field, it may not be a three-deep zone. It could be a man-free concept with the free safety in the middle of the field (Diagram #4). When the quarterback reads the man-to-man coverage on the four vertical routes, he works to the outside receivers. If he

throws to the inside slots, the free safety could possibly impact the inside throw. The free safety cannot get to the throw against the sideline.

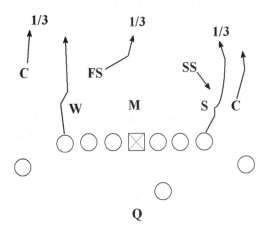

Diagram #3. Safety spin

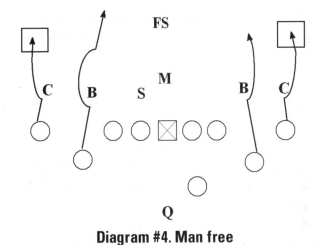

Diagram #4. Man free

That is how we run Vickie against two deep, three-deep spin, three deep, or man free. We are in the shotgun set when we run this series. The quarterback takes a three-step drop from the shotgun position. The quarterback holds the ball longer if we have to run the option route. If he has the vertical routes working against the spin safety, he throws early into the second level of coverage. That is the area between the linebackers and the deep backs.

If the defense is a two-deep man under scheme, the slot back reads the coverage as two deep (Diagram #5). They are thinking option routes. That gives the slot receivers more field to work because the corners do not roll up to the outside. They have vacated the flats chasing the verticals from the wide receivers. If the defense is using linebackers to cover the slot receivers, they are at a disadvantage. The slot receivers have too much field to run their patterns.

If you have that concept down, I will let Mark Tommerdahl come up and talk to you about protection. Mark has been with me at four different schools. I keep giving him expense checks to go out and recruit and he keeps coming back. He is still with me. He has been a very good friend and staff member. We do not have many turnovers in our coaching staff. Mark is the coach on our staff that other coaches identify with. This man will be a head coach some day. He will take about five minutes to talk about our protection scheme. Coach Mark Tommerdahl.

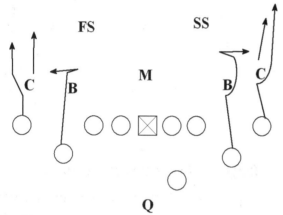

Diagram #5. Two deep man under

COACH MARK TOMMERDAHL

Before I get started let me tell you a little bit about Coach Franchione. Most of you are familiar with his reputation for turning around losing programs. He has a great system. When he takes a new job with a school, there are three things he always does. The first thing he does is draw the team together. He has a system for doing it and works hard at it. He is a 100-percenter. The second thing he does is embraces the high school football coaches in the state. The third thing he does is will a team to get bigger and stronger in the weight room. The cornerstone in our program comes from the weight room. He is stubbornly loyal to his assistants.

The pass protection scheme is simple stuff and we have done it forever. In our five-step

passing game we are a half slide team (Diagram #6). We declare a man side and a slide side. We give boy and girl names to our passing schemes. We call our protection schemes boy and girl protections. Since girls are generally physically weaker than boys are, girl protections are weakside protection schemes. Since Vickie is a girl's name, our blocking back goes to the weakside of the set. The call side is our man protection side. On the Vickie pass, the weakside is our man protection side. The strongside is the slide side.

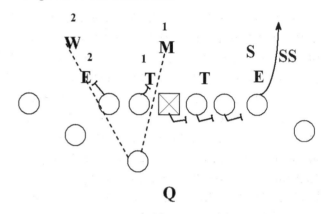

Diagram #6. Vickie protection

In boy protections, since boys are stronger than girls, the back sets to the strongside of the formation. The man protection will be to the strongside and the slide protection will be weakside. To the man side the linemen count from the inside going out to determine whom they block. The guard handles the first man and the second man belongs to the tackle. The center blocks opposite the call side.

If the center has a shaded nose tackle aligned on him, he generally sets to the shade techniques. He gives a call to the guard to let him know he is not sliding to the backside.

The back keys the two linebackers to his side. He reads inside first and outside second. His read is one to two to the call side.

If the slide side tackle has an overload to his side with a blitz runner outside of him, he makes a "bam" call for a full slide by the line (Diagram #7). With the full slide call, the back has to take first man aligned outside tackle.

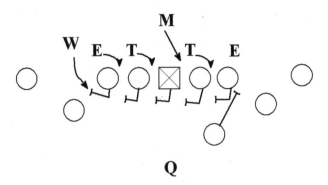

Diagram #7. Bam full slide

Against a base fifty front defense, we man-block all the way across the front (Diagram #8). This gets to be a little clinic talk because we very seldom see that kind of front. The back is responsible for the outside linebackers. He scans from one linebacker across to the second linebacker on the backside. If there is the threat of a four-man blitz off the weakside, the tackle gives a bam call and we get the four-man slide to the weakside (Diagram #9). The back in that instance takes the call side inside linebacker to outside linebacker.

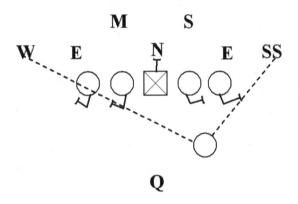

Diagram #8. Fifty front

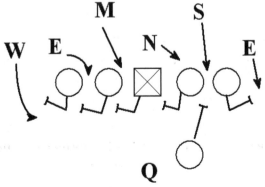

Diagram #9. Fifty front bam

This protection is very simple and this is what we do. This is not just a clinic presentation for you. This is how we protect on the field. I will turn it back to Coach Fran.

COACH FRANCHIONE

We are going to the film to see the pass series in action. You can see some variations on the patterns. If we do not know what pass to call, we go to a Vickie or Vickie switch. On the Vickie double switch (Diagram #10), the receivers crossed their patterns. The slot receivers crossed behind the wide receivers and became the sideline runners. The wide receivers came inside and ran the seams.

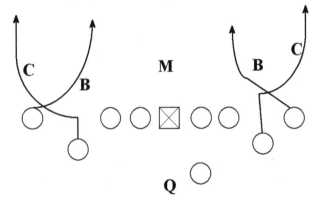

Diagram #10. Vickie double switch

In this play on the film, the defense played what looked like a man-free coverage. It was a man-to-man defense on one side and a zone concept on the other (Diagram #11). To the man side of the defense, they blitzed the inside linebacker. The quarterback knew something was up by the pre-snap read. He got excited and did not make a good throw. He went to the proper receiver but threw high. The slot receiver to the man-to-man side read the man coverage with the free safety, broke off his pattern, and worked outside on the linebacker.

The read by the slot receiver to the zone side is a two-deep look and he runs his option route. The slot receiver to the man side reads a two-deep look and breaks off his pattern. Since the corner is gone, he has more room to work his pattern outside.

I did not talk about this situation when I introduced the pattern. If the coverage brings more defenders than we can block, the inside receiver breaks his pattern and becomes the hot receiver.

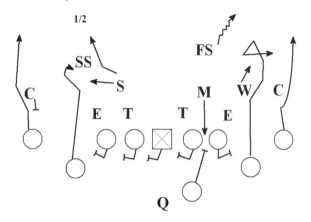

Diagram #11. Split read

In this case, we are in a tight end pro set on one side and a twin set to the other side. The tight end is the seam runner on this play and the wide receiver is the sideline runner. To the twin's side of the set the slot reads a two-deep coverage to his side. At the last second, the linebacker leaves him and blitzes off the edge (Diagram #12). He also sees the Mike linebacker coming off the man-blocking side. He knows there are four blitz men and only three blockers. He breaks his pattern and runs a hot pattern to the inside.

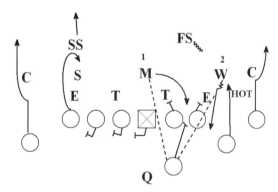

Diagram #12. Hot pattern

On this pass, we are committed to a six-man protection. For that reason, we very seldom release the back on any kind of pattern. However, people are starting to use more of the Tampa-2 coverage (Diagram #13). That coverage drops the Mike linebacker down the middle of the field. That allows the safeties to get wider in their cover-2 drops. If teams continue to play Tampa 2, we will

bring the back out of the backfield into the void created by the Mike linebacker dropping deep.

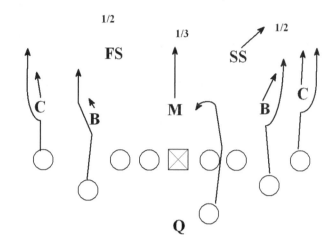

Diagram #13. Ace versus Tampa 2

This next play is a good example of why we must release outside on all Vickie passes. The receiver to the top of the screen takes the easy way out and releases inside on the hard corner. Because he released inside, he led the corner into the option route of the slot receiver. The slot receiver reads cover 2, breaks off his route, and works outside. The release by the wide receiver puts the corner in a position to make a play on the outside move of the slot receiver. If he had released outside, the corner may have pushed him out of bounds, but he can come back in bounds and still catch the ball. In addition, by making the corner ride him wide, he opens the window for the slot receiver working out.

The next play shows the secondary in quarter coverage (Diagram #14). The slot receivers read no safety in the middle of the field. They break their patterns and work on the linebackers. The linebackers are walling the receivers out of the middle and the safeties are breaking down on anything short by the slot receivers. The quarterback reads from the inside receiver to the outside receiver. He sees the double on the slot receiver and goes outside with the ball to the one-on-one pattern.

The seam runners on the four-deep patterns get some heavy contact as they try to get deep. If they get too far inside, they will get too close to one another. We tell them they can never be more than two yards inside the hash marks.

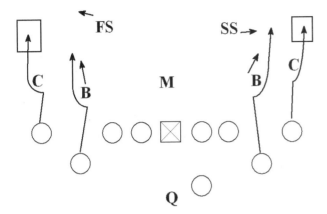

Diagram #14. Vickie versus quarters

The reason we run the switch pattern is the release of the receivers. We teach our hard corners to jam the outside receiver to the inside and the linebackers to wall off the number-two receiver and keep him outside. Some corners are very physical with their jams on the wide receivers. At times, it is too hard to get off the line of scrimmage. The switch lets the receivers do what the defenders want them to do. The outside receiver releases inside and becomes the option runner and the slot receiver releases outside and runs the vertical. This gets the receivers off the line of scrimmage and open.

The switch pattern is also good against pressed man coverage. The receiver can run the switch and get a rub or pick from the other receiver or defender. We were second in the Big Twelve Conference in passing the football. Which was not bad because the leader was Texas Tech, and they threw the ball 65 times a game.

When the receivers run their option routes, they need to get vision to the quarterback. As they turn to the quarterback, the receivers must move if he cannot see him. If he has worked in and cannot find the quarterback, he has to work further to the inside or come outside. Not all our receivers are fast but they all read coverages well. That is an asset because they get open.

If the option runners run their patterns too deep, they make the quarterback hold the ball too long. That is dangerous because it causes forced throws

or sacks. That is the reason we emphasis the depth of the pattern. We want them 10 to 12 yards in depth. We feel the defense gets into mismatches if they try to cover wide receivers with linebackers.

If we call "Vickie H-Y option", that means the inside receivers run the option route regardless of coverage. They do not read and break their patterns. They run the option route off the linebackers. We seldom do this type of pattern. However, if the press box coaches feel it is a good call, we run it.

The "Vickie shake" is an adjustment we use with this series of passes (Diagram #15). We run this pattern against quarter cover reads. With the safety reading the slot back, we show him the out route by the slot receiver. When he jumps to the outside vertical of the wide receiver, the slot receiver plants, and comes back to his vertical route. The corners squat to play the slot receiver coming to the flat and the safety goes over the top to take the vertical pattern by the outside receiver. We never want to get too wide with the slot receiver. As soon as the safety triggers on the wide receiver, he turns into the vertical pattern.

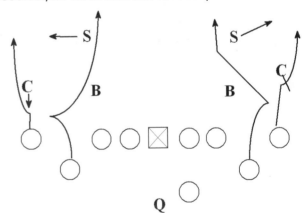

Diagram #15. Vickie shake

In the film, you see what happened. The safety saw the shake route coming back to the inside. He jumped back to take the slot receiver. The corner rolled to play the flat. When he saw the flat route go deep, he was in bad shape to get back on the vertical pattern on the boundary.

Another variation is our "X-Z hitch" (Diagram #16). We have two tight ends and two wide outs. The X- and Z-receivers run hitch patterns at seven yards on the outside unless it is a rolled up corner. If that is the case, they take the patterns deep. The tight ends run the vertical routes. If the coverage is cover 2, the X- and Z-receivers run the verticals and the tight ends run the option routes.

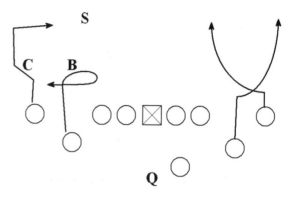

Diagram #17. Y-pivot

the four vertical using the rules of the Vickie pass. The only difference in this play is the third receiver to the trips side runs deep up the middle of the field. This makes it almost impossible for the safeties because of the threat up the middle of the hash marks. The slot receivers run their option route because of the cover-2 look, but the safeties cannot move outside because of the threat in the middle.

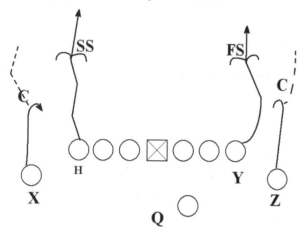

Diagram #16. X-Z hitch

We tell the quarterback to take the hitch right now if it is open. He goes to the softest coverage when he throws the hitch. If the corner presses the receiver converts to a vertical pattern. If the corner jams the receiver, the hitch is off and he runs a vertical.

We can run individual patterns off the Vickie. We can call a "Y-pivot." This is a one-on-one move by the Y-slot receiver on a linebacker. We run the switch pattern to the backside and send the Z-receiver on a dig route into the middle.

I want to show you one more pattern before I quit. We run this from the empty set. We get into a three-by-two look. We can shift into this set or line up in it. The play is "599 vice" (Diagram #18). We run

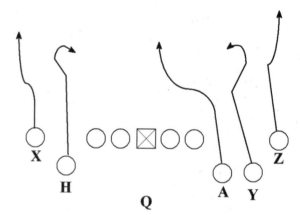

Diagram #18. 599 vice

I appreciate your time. If we can do anything for you, please call on us. Come see us.

DEFENSIVE LINE TECHNIQUES

Indiana University

I appreciate being here today. This is the warrior group here today. Being the first speaker after lunch is tough. I know some of those coaches want to take a little extra time for lunch. Some of the coaches may be taking a nap after lunch. Therefore, I appreciate you being here today.

The title of my lecture is "Defensive Techniques and Drills," but I am going to go in a different direction to get us started. To have a direction of what you want to do as far as techniques are concerned, and how you are going to play your defensive front, you have to mesh all of this with your defensive philosophy.

I am the co-defensive coordinator at Indiana. That was the same position I held at Miami, Ohio last year. First, I want to talk about our defensive philosophy. Then I will tell you how we like to do things with our defensive line. I want to cover the defensive goals we set at the beginning of the year and why they are important to us.

This is what we start with at the beginning of the season. We want to know what we want to accomplish on defense and what will it take to be the best defensive team in our conference. Each year we want to be one of the top ten defensive teams in the country. We look at our stats from the past year and then we look at the stats of the top teams in the country. From that we try to determine what it will take to get into the top ten in the country. We want to set our goals as high as we can. We want to set realistic goals, but we want to be the best we can possibly be.

Goals

- Win – Fight to win!
- Hold Opponents to 21 Points – Keep the opponents out of our end zone.
- ThreePlus Turnovers – Create! Give the ball back to our offense.
- Sixty Percent Success on First Down – Keep our opponent to three yards or less on first down.
- Win The Third Down – Stop our opponents 65 percent of the time on third down. Chart and Stress "three and outs."
- Camera Club Seven-Plus – The number of defenders we average in the camera when the whistle blows.

You do not see how many yards we give up on this chart. I do not care how many yards we give up on defense. I want the number of *points* we give up on defense. We must understand the defense cannot stop everything the offense does. We are going to give up certain things, but we need to make the offense earn their way down the field to score points. We never get upset about a 14-play drive by our opponents. If the offense is good enough to drive the ball that long, they have done a great job. The thing we have to do is to stop the one play drive. We have to stop the big play. We have to eliminate the missed tackles. That is the reason you do not see a lot of information on yardage.

To stress the point about turnovers, we did something different this year to start the season. We put a decal on every defensive player's locker. The decal or logo was this: ODB. That stands for "Our Damn Ball!" The ball does not belong to the offense. They do not own the ball. If we made an interception, or made a sack in our team drills, we gave the player a decal for his locker: ODB.

To get our players to get to the football, we use the two whistle concept. During every snap, we stress pursuit and we want them to run to the ball. We want the defensive players to sprint to get into the camera on that last frame on each play. We blow the whistle the first time and the offense stops. Then we blow the whistle again and everyone sprints to the ball and makes the defensive huddle. Then we blow the second whistle. They clap their hands and break the huddle again. They will come to the ball and chop their feet waiting for that second whistle. On Sunday, we come in and grade the film. We count the number of players that are in the camera on each play. Each player gets a grade on the percentage of time they are in the camera for the game. This is a great test to see where they are at as far as running to the ball.

We have other objectives that we want to be aware of but we did not set a specific number of times we want to achieve those objectives.

OBJECTIVES

Pressure

Pressure the passer. Sack, hurry, and harass the quarterback. Pressure the running backs with TFL's. We counted hurries when the defender caused the pass to be incomplete. If a player hits the quarterback and causes the pass to become incomplete or intercepted, we count that as a hurry. The harass was when we hit the quarterback regardless of the result of the pass. It could result in a touchdown, but if our defender knocked the quarterback down, he would get a harass on the play. We tell our defensive line that the quarterback has to be on the ground for us to count it as a Harass.

Be Great Tacklers

Record the total number of missed tackles. The only way we get better is through our improvement in tackling. Measure yards after missed tackles.

Eliminate Big Plays

No runs over 15 yards. No passes over 25 yards.

Goal-Line Success

The odds are against us from the five-yard line going in. Our level of toughness will show in this zone.

Sudden Change

If the ball is turned over inside our 40-yard line, we will allow no touchdown drives.

Big Hits (Bone Award)

Number of de-cleaters or big hits in a game by the defense.

We make a big deal out of big hits. We went to the meat market and got the butcher to give us a big cow femur bone. We cleaned it up and then boiled it and got all of the meat of the bone. Then we painted it red. We put the bone in a toolbox. The player that made the big hit in the game would take the toolbox with us to the next game. After a few games, we would cut up the film for the past game and make a big hit film. Then we would bring the team in, show them that film, and allow them to vote on the player that would get the bone for that week. The players loved that aspect of the games. It encouraged the players to make the big hits in the game.

Next is our defensive film grading system. We grade our players on every play in three areas: assignment, execution, and camera club. We keep a fourth area that we call productivity. They receive a percentage grade from each area.

GRADES = (+) CORRECT, (-) INCORRECT

Assignment

A (+) or (-) will be given based upon correct alignment, correct calls, and correct adjustments.

Execution

A (+) or (-) will be given whether the player executes the proper responsibility and/or technique.

Camera Club

A (+) or (-) will be given whether the player was in the picture when the camera turns off for the next play. On wide copy, the player must be five yards from the football and running to the ball. Walking does not count. If a scramble situation occurs followed by a sack or an incompletion, a secondary defender locked on his responsibility can earn a (+) grade for camera club. In a pass situation, pass rush defenders will be graded on effort after the ball is thrown.

Productivity

The fourth area evaluated is productivity. Is the player making plays, tackles, or assists? Missed tackles, interceptions, pass breakups, sacks, and hurries are counted.

PRODUCTION POINTS

Production Points	Value
Tackles	+2
Assist	+1
TFL	+4
Sack	+6
Hurry	+2
Harass	+1
PBU/Deflection	+3
Caused interception	+4
Interceptions	+6
Block on interception	+1
Caused fumble	+4
Recovered fumble	+6
Score	+7
Exceptional effort	+1
Big hit tackle	+3
Negative Points	**Value**
Missed Tackles	-2
Missed sack	-4
Missed Interception	-4
Missed Fumble Recovery	-4
Foolish penalty / Error	-4
Critical error	-6
Impact Percentage	
Production points/Number of plays* 100	

INDIANA DEFENSIVE LINE PHILOSOPHY

At Indiana, we crowd the football with our weight forward, attack our gap, and create a new line of scrimmage on the snap of the ball at the heels of the offensive lineman. We are successful because we completely understand our responsibilities.

Keys to Front Four Dominance

- "Put the ball down" attitude
- Explosive quickness
- Obtain penetration
- Fight pressure
- Shed blocks
- Relentless pursuit
- Make tackles

Attack!

Defensive Line Position Skills

- Ability to move on ball movement
- Ability to strike and extend with down hand
- Ability to take proper attack steps
- Ability to execute a blood move
- Ability to execute a proper tackle
- Ability to attack half of a blocker on pass rush
- Ability to use cut, hook, swim, rip, spin, and bull rush techniques
- Understanding of defensive front, movement, and blitz assignments
- Ability to recognize and attack blocking schemes with proper technique
- Ability to stay on feet and get back on feet quickly
- Ability to make a play when an opportunity presents itself
- Ability to change direction quickly
- Ability to play with leverage

- Attitude to never give up or take the easy way out on a play

- Conditioning to be able to play a long series at 100 percent

- Attitude and conditioning to run to the football on every play

- Ability to beat blocker on a pass rush in three seconds or less

- Ability to take coaching and to improve deficient skills

- Willingness to study the game of football by paying attention when you are not in a drill or in a game and when you are watching film on your own

Front Four Terminology

backside: Using the ball and the center as a reference point, we use this term to describe the area away from the run or pass action.

"ball presents itself": Ballcarrier commits to a certain gap.

blood move: Term used to describe the action of crossing an offensive lineman's face on ball movement. Technique is slide, step, and rip.

bubble: Prying upfield a block to force the ballcarrier to run laterally.

chase contain: The responsibility of a defensive end on a "go" call. The end should split the difference between the line of scrimmage and the ballcarrier and be alert for reverses.

frontside: Playside or side of the center on which the ballcarrier goes.

gaps: Relationships between offensive linemen, given letter values of A, B, C, or D.

key: Offensive lineman whose action dictates our reaction.

loosen: Term implying widening of a given alignment.

pry: Leverage term meaning under blocker and upfield.

playside: Side of center to which ballcarrier goes.

separation: Locked out elbows position on offensive lineman required for shed.

strongside: The area to the side of the center towards the formation strength.

tighten: Term implying closing down of a given alignment.

weakside: The area to the side of the center away from the formations strength.

Alerts

Free: Term used to alert the nose man that the end may use an inside rush move and the nose man should scrape to contain if he does.

Hawk: Term used to alert defense to a two TE set. Nose and weakside end should adjust alignments. Nose aligns in 2i and weakside end a 6i.

Louisiana: Term used to tell the defensive line the blitz is coming from the left side.

No: Term used by defensive lineman to communicate that the offensive lineman across from him has his weight forward (run).

Orbit: Term used to call off a line movement, usually paired with a "hawk" call.

Rhode Island: Term used to tell the defensive line that the blitz is coming from the right side.

Russian: Term used to alert boundary end that there are two receivers into the boundary and he is to rush instead of dropping into coverage.

Twins: Term used to alert boundary end that there are two receivers into the boundary and that he will drop to the hook/curl instead of the curl/flat zone.

WETSU: Alerts the whole defense that we have intercepted the ball.

Yes: Term used by defensive lineman to communicate that the offensive lineman across from him is sitting back in his stance (pull or pass).

Stance

Tackles: In a three-point stance, technique hand down, short stagger, weight forward, able to see the ball peripherally.

Ends: In a three-point stance, technique hand down, medium to long stagger, weight forward, low hat-high tail, eyes on the ball.

Front Four Responsibilities

General

- Crowd football - we want to pressure offensive line with our alignment.
- Get off on ball movement.
- Attack your gap and penetrate to the heels of the offensive line.
- First contact is with the hands.
- Achieve separation with your head out of the mix.
- Keep your feet moving.
- Locate and sprint to the ball.
- Tackle the ballcarrier.

Movement and Punch

- Get off on ball movement.
- Shoot your down hand.
- Contact point is the "V" of the neck of your key. Hands under the pads for leverage.
- One hand should be on chest of key. The other needs to be on the edge of your key on the side towards your gap.
- You must obtain separation.
- You must be in position to make a tackle if the ball presents itself.
- Locate and sprint to the ball.

Defensive Front Alignments

Techniques identification for front alignment. (Diagram #1)

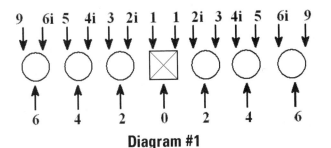

Diagram #1

Gap Identification

See Diagram #2.

Diagram #2

Note: As the offensive players move, the gaps move. The gaps are defined as the area between the facemask of the inside lineman out to the facemask of the next adjacent outside lineman.

Example (Diagram #3): At the line of scrimmage, and after the snap.

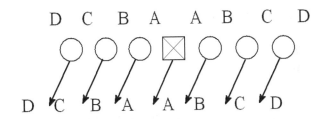

Diagram #3

DEFENSIVE POSITION NAMES

Front Four

E - Ends

T - Tackle = To call (Usually 3 Tech)

N - Nose = Away from call (Usually 1 Tech)

Linebackers

S - Sam = To TE (2 TE or no TE to the field)

M - Mike = Middle Backer

W - Will = To SE (2 TE or No TE to the boundary)

Secondary

H - Halfback = Field

A - Apache = To Tight End

F - Formation safety = Aligns to formation strength

C - Corner = Boundary

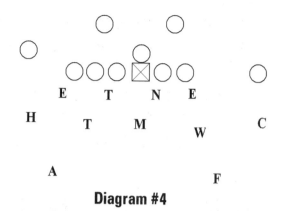

Diagram #4

We define how we want to play each block. We talk about the different types of blocks and how we want to play against those blocks. First is the hook block.

Hook Block

Reaction:

- Get off on ball movement.
- Attack visual key with down hand on near numbers.
- Gap side hand should grab near shoulder of key.
- Attack up the field while keeping our head in your gap and arm extended.
- Recognize the flow of the play and adjust your angle of pursuit accordingly.
- If the ball cuts back inside of you, fight back into the block to constrict the running lane.
- Shed the block and take a pursuit angle to the ball.

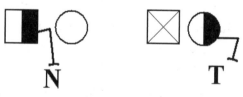

Diagram #5

Diagram #6

Back Block

Reaction:

- Get off on ball movement.
- Attack visual key with down hand on near number.
- Gap side hand should grab near shoulder of key.
- Squeeze the hole by fighting pressure.
- Rip and cross the blockers face in the direction of the puller.
- Take a pursuit angle to the ball.

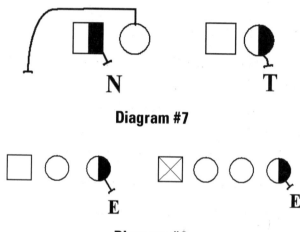

Diagram #7

Diagram #8

Down Block

Reaction:

- Get off on ball movement.
- Attack visual key with down hand on near number.
- Gap side hand should punch key's gap side hip.
- This should carry you flat down the line of scrimmage.
- Wrong arm any run block that you encounter.
- Pry the block up the field to force the ball carrier to bubble.
- Shed the block and take a pursuit angle to the ball.

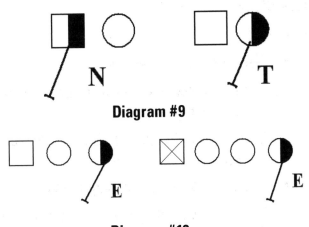

Diagram #9

Diagram #10

Cut-Off Block

Reaction:

- Get off on ball movement.
- Attack visual key with down hand on near number.
- Gap side hand should grab near shoulder of key.
- Squeeze the hole by fighting pressure.
- Rip and cross the blockers face.
- Take a pursuit angle to the ball.

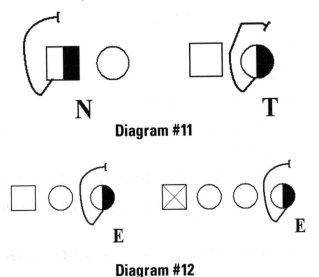

Diagram #11

Diagram #12

Double Scoop

Reaction:

- Get off on ball movement
- Attack visual key with down hand on near number.

- Gap side hand should punch key's gap side hip.
- Get penetration up the field, disruption the release of your key.
- If overtaken by the scoop, do not allow your key to release to the next level.
- Shed the block and take a pursuit angle to the ball.

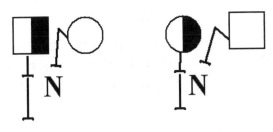

Diagram #13

Diagram #14

Double Hook

Reaction:

- Get off on ball movement.
- Attack visual key with down hand on near number.
- Gap side hand should grab near shoulder of key.
- Get penetration up the field preventing your key from crossing your face.
- When the other blockers release up the field, spring into your gap and keep your arms extended on your key.
- Shed the block and take a pursuit angle to the ball.

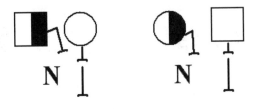

Diagram #15

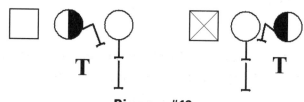

Diagram #16

Double-Team

Reaction:

- Get off on ball movement.

- Attack visual key with down hand on near number.

- Gap side hand should grab near shoulder of key.

- Get penetration up the field.

- Pull with your down hand and push with the gap side hand, turning your key's shoulders.

- Keep your base parallel with the line of scrimmage.

- If you are driven off the LOS, drop and take both blockers with you.

- Shed the block and take a pursuit angle to the ball.

Diagram #17

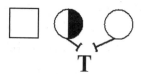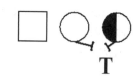

Diagram #18

Next, I have some drills and techniques that I want to cover. I will show you all of these drills at the end of the lecture. These are all on stance, start, and take-off. They are drills to help the players stay low coming out of their stance. We spend quite a bit of time working on these drills. To

me the most important thing for the defensive linemen is their "get off."

I. Take Off - (Stance, Start and Leverage)

Line Drill

- Good warm-up drill.

- Right hand stance - right foot on line

- Objective is to step straight down the line teaching proper take off steps

- Start with one step, and then two steps, the last part is a full speed take-off

- Other emphasis - leverage (low, flat back), shoot hands (D-line should always lead with the hands), stride length (varies with situations)

Arizona Drill

- Leverage drill.

- The drill starts with two steps, a forward roll, and then a sprint to finish. This teaches proper leverage at take-off (good forward lean, flat back, leading with the hands). This drill also teaches lineman to get up off the ground quickly and sprint to the ball.

- Second drill starts with two steps, hands over bag, step over bag, and then a sprint to finish. This drill teaches proper leverage at take-off (good forward lean, flat back, leading with hands). This drill also teaches lineman to keep feet moving on contact.

Chutes

- Leverage drill.

- First part of drill works on proper leverage at take-off. It also emphasizes quick take-off.

- Offensive players with bags may be held in front of defensive lineman to work on hand strike, footwork, and shedding blocks.

- Second part of drill works on leverage and quick change of direction and pursuit (emphasis on staying parallel to the line of scrimmage).

Blood Move Drill

- Line game drill.

- Objective is to teach the proper technique for executing a one-gap movement.

- Lineman should place the hand down in the direction they are moving. On the snap, they move from start cone to finish cone using blood move technique.

- Blood move technique: the blood move starts with a slide step, parallel to the line of scrimmage. The lineman then rips with the opposite arm across the face of the opponent, and then he pry's upfield to prevent being washed down the line.

- The second part of the drill is teaching lineman to move only one gap when blocking flow is going opposite their movement.

- Emphasis is on reacting to the flow by changing direction and ripping in the opposite direction order to maintain gap.

II. Agility

Bags

- Agility, change of direction, knee bend

- Drill always finished through quarterback

- Defeating chop block and tackling may also be incorporated in this drill.

III. Tackling

Roll Tackle

- Purpose: Defensive linemen are rarely in position to make a head up form tackle. This teaches a tackling technique at a sharp angle that prevents the ball carrier from gaining additional yardage.

- Technique: Tackle is made at thigh-board level, head is in front of the ballcarrier, shoots arms and roll hips up through the ballcarrier, rolls onto backside, opposite ballcarrier's momentum, bringing him down.

IV. Strike

Three-Man Sled

- Objective is to strike blocker with proper hand placement, leverage, and explosion.

- Lineman puts hand down in stance to the side of the pad he is striking. Down hand should strike outside shoulder area. Thumbs should be up and arms should reach full extension.

V. Pass Rush

Hoops

- Emphasis on being able to turn corner on blocker to get to quarterback (proper lean and speed are essential to good pass rush)

- Blockers are added to the drill to make the defenders work their hands while running the hoop

VI. Tackling Circuit

VII. Turnover Circuit

The first two items of equipment the defensive line coach needs to have available is a football on a stick and a football on a rope. The ball on the rope is used in the hoop drill. We always finish through the quarterback in every drill we do. We want to knock the ball out of the quarterback's hand. You can work on your entire pass rush techniques in the hoop drills.

I want to get the tape out to show all of these drills. (Tape)

It all goes back to using what you have that works best for you. We do not all have the big players all of the times. If we know how to play the techniques, you can survive on defense even if you are in a mismatch.

We try to combine many of these drills to include as many techniques as possible. I will be around if you want to talk more about what we do with our defensive linemen. Thank you.

ATTACKING THE WEAKSIDE 4-3 DEFENSE

Mount Union College

It is a pleasure to be here with you today. Earl Browning invited me to speak a couple of years ago, but I could not make it. I am thankful Earl gave me another opportunity to speak.

I commend you coaches for being here at the coaching clinic because I know there are other things you could be doing. Sometimes the demands on a football coach can be overwhelming. I know it is a challenge and some times costly for you to be here.

My topic is "Attacking the Weakside of the 4-3 Defense." I realize the topic is specific, but that will be my primary focus during the lecture.

At Mount Union, we are a balanced offensive team. Our offense comes from a two-back set, with a tight end and two wide receivers. I know the spread offense is the popular offense in football today. We hired a new coach, who has spent some time as a graduate assistant in a program that ran the spread offense. He has some ideas he wants to introduce to our program.

Division II installed a new ruling, which will affect our football program this year. It will be the first time Division II will allow teams to have spring practice with a football. We cannot wear pads or helmets and cannot have contact drills, but at least we can have a football on the field. We can work on our offense and special team concepts during the spring. I want to incorporate some of the things Coach Montgomery is doing.

When you have a young assistant who is interested in going to clinics and learning new ideas, you should give him a chance to experiment with those ideas. You should listen to him and evaluate what he has to say. The new coach's knowledge about offense is what he learned as a graduate assistant.

When he played for me, he was a defensive football player. He did not know much about Mount Union's offensive football scheme. I said all of that to make two points. What he learned is of interest to us as a coaching staff and may be an asset to our program. Now that we have spring practice, we can experiment with his idea to see if they fit. The second point is to show respect for what he has learned and where he has been. I need to listen to his ideas.

The older I get the more I become set in what we do on the field. However, I do not want to become intolerant to the ideas of our young coaches. These ideas are like the measles. The more you get around them, the more chances you have to catch them. The more I watch high school players in the spread scheme, the more I realize there are fun spread offensives you can run. That does not mean what we have done over the years is not fun.

What is amusing to me is the read scheme Coach Montgomery showed on his tape. We were doing that a long time ago and I forgot about it. Listen to your young coaches. I say that to the head coaches in this room. To the young coaches I would say, "Press on and explore the ideas you like." However, always keep in mind that an idea is only good if you can teach it. It can look great on video, but if your players cannot learn it, it is not a good idea.

To teach an idea to your players, you have to understand every aspect of that scheme. You have to know it well enough to teach it to your players. The first thing I write on our grease board each season is: "No learning equals no teaching."

That means no learning by the players equals no teaching by the coaches. I do not want an assistant coach telling me a certain player cannot learn how to do a particular skill. If he cannot learn the way you are teaching the skill, try to teach it in a different way.

I have some advice for any young coach who wants to learn and expand the ideas. Make sure you can go out on the field and teach what you want them to learn. Make sure the methods you use to teach kids are going to get your ideas to work.

Make sure, when you pick the offensive scheme that you know those plays thoroughly. That will be the key to how well your players learn.

I want to talk about attacking the 4-3 defense. At Mount Union, we have two running backs, one tight end, and two wide receivers as the basis for our offense. Let me talk about the types of players we want in those positions.

At the tight end, we look for a third receiver, who can occasionally line up next to an offensive tackle. The criterion for the tight end is a player who can catch the football, block on the perimeter, and block on the line of scrimmage. That is the order of importance for our tight end. We flex him quite often in our offensive sets. If we did not have a player who could do those things, we moved an offensive tackle into that position. That gives us a three-man blocking side.

In the running back, we look for an athlete who can run the ball, catch the ball, and block. If the running back can run and catch, but not block so well, we substitute a better blocking back when we need him.

In the fullback, we look for a player who is a linebacker type. Our running backs are in the 190-pound range. The techniques they use in blocking are not powerful, bone-crushing blocks with intensity. The thing that is important to us is the versatility of the running back.

We substitute in our packages to get the personality we want for each play. We wanted two versatile running backs, versatile tight ends, and two wide receivers.

There are some essential elements to attacking the backside of the 4-3 defense. The first element to attacking the backside is to be able to run the ball to the wideside of the field. That makes the Mike linebacker make plays into the wideside. That presents a challenge for him. It does not matter whether the play is a toss or an outside zone play, you have to make the defense respect your ability to get into the wide field. An option play is an excellent way to get the ball to the outside. Stretching the defensive to the wideside sets the offense up to attack the backside of the defense. In the passing game, you can attack the wideside of the field with a sprint-out pass or bootleg.

In the 4-3 defense, the defensive coordinators try to get the athletic defensive ends to give an edge to their perimeter defense. The defensive coordinator selects the defensive ends and particularly the backside defensive end carefully to play those positions. They want fast defensive ends to come off the edge and put pressure on the quarterback.

If that is the case, the defensive end comes up the field hard. In our offensive scheme, we do not discourage the defensive end from doing just that. To the backside, we attack the B gap with our running game. We do it three different ways. We offset the I-formation and run a cutback isolation play into the B gap. From the split-back's set, the base play is a lead draw play into the B gap. The third play is the counter play.

We must make the defense play their B gap defensive tackle into the wideside. The way you do that is to attack the wideside of the field and have success doing it. If you can do that, the defense gives you a wideside 3 technique and a backside 1 technique at the tackles. If you cannot get the backside tackle to move into the A gap, simply run or attack into that gap. We want to run the ball to the bubble in the defense. The bubble is the gap that is the responsibility of the linebacker.

Our ability to run into those gaps and control the backside defensive end was critical to our success in our conference championship and national championship games. Hash marks used for high school football gives you a true wideside. If you have a fast running back, you can develop a play to get outside. We want the running back to turn the corner and meet the first tackler on the boundary with his inside shoulder.

To the weakside, you have to attack the bubble because there is not enough room into the boundary. The running plays I will talk about are the cutback isolation, lead draw, and the counter. All three of these plays are not quick-hitting plays. In the cutback isolation, the running back starts one direction and cuts back to the hole. The lead draw has the element of a five-step passing scheme. The counter play is just what it says; it is a counter play. It is a misdirection play starting to the wideside and coming back to the weakside.

We have three solid plays that we can teach. These plays fit in with the basic pass we use to the weakside. The first play is the cutback isolation (Diagram #1). We run this play from an I-formation or an offset I-formation to the weakside. The angles for the guard and tackle are excellent. The guard blocks down on the 1-technique tackle. The tackle turns out on the defensive end. The center attacks toward the weakside and gets up on the Mike linebacker.

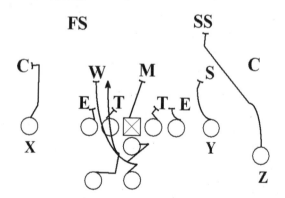

Diagram #1. Cutback isolation

The strongside offensive guard and tackle use cutoff blocks on the 3-technique tackle and 5-technique defensive end. The tight end gets upfield on the Sam linebacker and blocks him. The fullback or the offset-back leads up on the Will linebacker. The running back starts strong and cuts back to the backside B gap. The quarterback steps out strong and hands the ball back to the tailback going weak.

We can change up the blocking scheme on this play (Diagram #2). We can trap the defensive end or tackle with the lead back and bring the tackle inside on the Will linebacker.

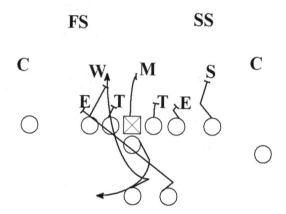

Diagram #2. Cutback isolation/back

The lead draw (Diagram #3) looks like the five-step passing game. The offensive tackle pass sets on the defensive end and invites him upfield. If the defensive end charges upfield, he keeps him going deep and pushes him out of the play. The guard executes a pass set and takes the 1-technique tackle inside. On this play, we allow upfield penetration by the defensive linemen. We want them to charge upfield after the quarterback. We also want the linebacker and defensive backs to retreat into coverage. The linebackers may not retreat until the quarterback passes the backs, but they will not attack the line of scrimmage unless they are on a blitz. We want to create separation between the defensive linemen and the linebackers.

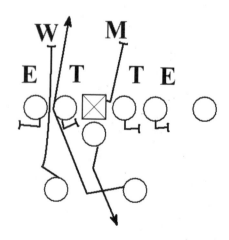

Diagram #3. Lead draw

The center executes a pass set for a count of two and releases up on the Mike linebacker. The strongside guard and tackle pass-set and block their assignments. The receivers release on their patterns and stalk block the defensive backs.

The quarterback takes a five-step drop and hands the ball to the running back on his third step. We like to run this play from a split-back look. The split back to the backside sets in his pass set for a count of two and leads up on the Will linebacker.

If you have success with these plays, the defense starts to drop the free safety into the box. When they drop the safety into the box, we must get another blocker into the play. We can do that by running the counter play (Diagram #4).

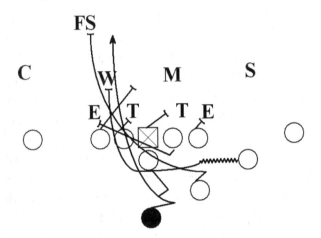

Diagram #4. Counter play

On this play, the strongside guard pulls to the backside and kicks out the defensive end. The extra blocker comes from the second back and the tight end. We put the tight end into a slot position and put him in one-step motion. He him follows the pulling guard. The blocking back sets in a strong halfback set and follows the tight end. That lets the tight end pull through the hole to block the Will linebacker. The fullback follows the tight end and takes the free safety. We cannot use the tackle to pull because he is too slow.

The defensive end may close because the offensive tackle goes inside for the Mike linebacker. If that happens, the guard logs the defensive end and everyone goes around the corner. The center and backside tackle are blocking back in this scheme.

All three of these running plays are delayed action plays designed to attack the bubble area on the backside of the defense. These are three solid plays you can teach and which fit into the basic passes we use to that side.

If you asked the players at Mount Union what Coach Kehres does at practice, they will tell you I teach the out route to the quarterbacks. Coach Montgomery mentioned that the design of the trips formation was to single up the X-receiver to the backside. The passes he showed for the X-receiver were the quick post and the X-choice. Over the years, we learned that you must have a pass you can utilize when you have to get a first down.

At the split-end position, I want an athlete that plays football and basketball. I want the type of athlete who can get his hands on the ball and handle it well. He does not have to have great speed. I do not believe that is critical. However, he must have a desire to go get to the ball and catch it. In basketball, they call him a rebounder. At the X-receiver position, that is the type of young man we want. If he has great speed, that would be an additional asset.

In high school, you have to look for these types of kids and go recruit them to play for you. If you cannot find one at your school, start looking for one in the junior high schools. Recruit him and get him ready for the future. The same thing holds true with quarterbacks. Do not allow a player to play quarterback just because he comes out for that position. The quarterback is too important to an offense. If you do not have a quarterback, go find one or make one.

A quarterback must have certain skills to play the position. A habit of mine is to go to summer baseball games. I go to the little league and Babe Ruth league games. The best throwers on those teams will be the pitcher, the catcher, and the shortstop. If you watch those young men, one of them is a potential quarterback. Locate the candidates and make yourself a quarterback.

The quarterback at Mount Union has to complete the out route. We want to isolate the X-receiver with the corner and throw the football to him. At my level of football, I expect a quarterback to be able to throw the ball from hash mark to hash mark on the out pattern. I do not expect him to complete an out route when he has to throw the ball beyond the hash marks from the middle of the field. The quarterback should be able to throw an accurate pass on the out route from the middle of the field to the hash marks. He can do that a high percentage of the time.

To teach this pattern, I need two or three receivers and a quarterback. In teaching the pattern, I always have someone snap the ball to the quarterback. The play is a timing play that starts with the center snap. The most important thing the center does on the team is snap the ball. You can never work too much on the center-quarterback exchange. The most important thing the quarterback does is receive the snap.

When we work the quarterback in the shotgun snap, we do not use the second quarterback to toss the perfect balls to the first quarterback. We do not want a perfect snap in the shotgun set. If you have the second quarterback deliver the snap most of the time, the ball comes from a standing position with a short spiral and right into the hands of the quarterback. That is a perfect snap in the shotgun. We want to practice something else. We want the imperfect snap to practice for that situation when it occurs in a game.

The ball comes from the ground on the center snap. When the center snaps the ball for the shotgun set, it is a blind snap. As the quarterback watches the shotgun snap, the ball comes from the ground. Bringing the ball from the ground is the starting point for the quick-out drill. The snap in practice has to be similar to the game situations.

Coaches who coach the quarterback in the shotgun snap talk about the quarterback feeling the snap. If the quarterback is under center, he can feel the ball and look at the defense at the same time. In the shotgun the quarterback has to look at the ball for some portion of the time, it takes to start a play. If you are going to be in the shotgun, make the

quarterback look at the ball coming from all angles. There are no perfect shotgun snaps. In practice, have your second quarterback or manager deliver the ball from the ground and not always in a perfect place.

I belabored that point, but I think it is significant if you want to go through a season and not screw up any snaps. We just got beat in the national semi-finals. Our lead started to designate when the center's shotgun snap hit a man coming in motion. You cannot blame the loss on that snap, but the momentum began to shift at that point. That was the first time something like that ever happened to us. We work tremendously hard to keep that from happening again. Work on the snap whether it is from under the center or shotgun. Make the snap part of the drill.

In this drill (Diagram #5), you need two receivers, two running backs, and a quarterback. You do not need any defensive personnel except for a Will linebacker. I play that position. I stand in the position of the Will linebacker, where I can see the quarterback. As the quarterback takes the snap, the Will linebacker is his main concern. The safety can tell the quarterback the defensive coverage, but the Will linebacker's drop is critical to the play.

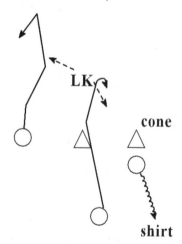

Diagram #5. Passing drill

The quarterback takes his drop and the receivers run their patterns. I play my role as the Will linebacker. If I drop under the out pattern, the quarterback dumps the ball to the back that checks the Will linebacker. He releases into the area the linebacker vacates and hooks. I do not take a complete drop and sprint back under the receiver. I give the quarterback the picture of what the Will linebacker will do. If I move toward the line of scrimmage, I expect the running back to get into position to block a blitzing Will linebacker.

I tell the quarterback to throw the ball in the "box." You can check your quarterback completion rate in practice, but I want to check his accuracy. Have the receiver hold up his arms as if he were receiving the ball. If you draw a straight line from elbow to elbow and fingertip to fingertip, that is the "box." I want to know the number of times the quarterback throws the ball in the "box." If he throws ten passes with nine in the box, that is a good day for him. If the receiver catches eight of the balls, the quarterback still threw nine accurate balls. That statistic is the one that interests me. If the receiver has to jump or go down to catch the ball and still makes the reception, the receiver did a good job. However, if the ball is in the box, the percentage of balls caught will be higher. The off-target ball is a hard catch and causes a low percentage of receptions.

You need to give your quarterback some specific information responses about the throw. I have a shirt at the correct depth to mark the quarterback's drop. He drops and throws the ball according to the movement of the Will linebacker. To make sure the quarterback is watching me, I flash a number using a hand signal. After he delivers the ball, he flashes the number he saw back to me. We check the quarterback's position straight back from the center, proper depth, right read, and if the ball is in the box.

We teach those basics in this one pass. It is a simple out route. However, if it is a third down and seven, you must go to the first down maker. When you complete this pass for 11 yards, you keep the chains moving.

We know if we go to a trips set to the wideside of the field, the coverage on the X-receiver is one or two coverages. The corner and Will linebacker are

the only defenders to deal with on the weakside. The corner plays either man-to-man coverage or cover 3. The Will linebacker plays man-to-man coverage or reads and drops into zone coverage.

The responsibility of the success of this play lies with the head coach. As a head coach, you have to be responsible for the most difficult thing you have to do. I do not want to tell myself that the first team quarterback does not know what to do on third and seven. Teach the quarterback what he needs to know to be successful.

With every pattern the receiver runs, a box exists. The quarterback always has a definition of what is an accurate throw. If the receiver runs an out-and-up, the box is in front of the receiver. Throwing to the correct receiver is of tremendous importance for the quarterback. He has to make the right decision. In the film I will show you, there are some out-and-up routes. The receiver breaks wide open. The balls on some of these plays appear underthrown. However, the underthrown ball is better than the overthrown ball.

The first pattern we throw to the backside involves an out cut to the weakside (Diagram #6). The X-receiver runs a 15-yard break back to 12-yard out cut. The running back has a check-down route based on his blitz pick up block. As an adjustment to this pattern, we may run a hitch with the X-receiver. That type of pass improves the percentage of the throw. The hitch pattern is a first-and-ten type of throw. It is not a third-and-ten throw.

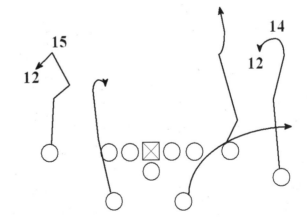

Diagram #6. Basic backside pass

The X-receiver adjusts his split to run the out pattern. He needs room to get back to the sideline. He uses a near split instead of a maximum split. The receiver drives at the outside number of the corner back. Our receiver is not a speed receiver; therefore, he cannot get the maximum depth on his pattern. The essential point is planting the foot and coming back into the sideline. He uses his head and shoulder to turn back to the football and get separation from the defensive back. The companion of the out pattern is the out-and-up route. If the out pattern is successful, the out-and-up is a distinct possibility.

When we run the out-and-up pattern, it is important for the receiver not to loose his speed. We do not run the pattern with the feet; we run the pattern with the head and shoulders. If the receiver beats the defender on the break, he looks for the underthrown ball.

The corner in most cases has to stop the out and out-and-up. That is too much for him to play by himself. If the running attack is successful, you put the corner on an island because the Will linebacker creeps toward the line of scrimmage in run support. The same thing happens to the free safety. The defense brings him into the box to help with run support.

To the frontside of the pattern, the primary combination is the curl-flat pattern. The Z-receiver runs the curl pattern and the back from the backfield runs the flat pattern. We run the Y-receiver up the seam to keep the strong safety from robbing the curl pattern.

If the defense rolls the coverage to the weakside in a third-and-ten-yard situation, our automatic is the curl-flat to the frontside. When the backside is the designated side, we run the curl pattern two yards deeper. If the Z-receiver runs his pattern at 14 yards and brings it back to 12 yards in normal situations, he goes two yards deeper. If the throw is supposed to go to the backside, the Z-receiver goes to 16 yards and comes back to 12 yards. That gives the quarterback time to come off the backside and go to the strongside without losing the timing of the play.

I also feel the X and Z-receivers can beat man-to-man coverage. Man coverage is not hard to beat if the quarterback throws the ball on time. If the timing is off, the defender reacts and covers the receiver.

I teach the curl-flat combination the same way I teach the out pattern to the backside. I put a manager in the flat area to teach the quarterback the proper reads. We spend time working on these patterns. That is how we train the quarterback.

I want to be responsible for these two ideas in our offense. That is my job. If I count on using these ideas the entire season, and we lose a game, it is my fault. It is the head coaches' fault when your team makes a big mistake. In the playoff game, we lost because of the muffed snap when we used a silent count. At the start of the year, we did not use that count.

When we snapped the ball and hit the man in motion in the knee, I knew I violated one of my golden rules in coaching. If you add something during the course of a season, you take a chance. When it does not work at some point in the season, it is your fault. It may not be your suggestion, but you allowed it to go into your offense.

I picture football as a great big circle. If you put head coach by your name, you are responsible for the entire circle. The head coach can slice the circle into a pie with as many pieces as he wants. You cannot use all of the pie. If the quarterback cannot run the option, that is a piece of the pie you cannot use. When you plan your offense, you may have to throw something out. Whatever you plan, do it early and do not add anything during the season. If you add something, it is your fault.

If your team is good, the all-star committee selects you to coach in one of their games. They selected me to coach in one of these all-star games. Since I was a Division II coach, I kept my mouth shut when all the coaches got together. That is the only time I have coached the offensive line because none of the other head coaches wants to coach it. In the coaches meetings, I listened to the other coaches talking about the offense. As I listened to the conversation, the curl-flat route kept coming up as the primary route. These conversations took place among great coaches from conferences that have powerful teams. The curl-flat is a basic pattern in everyone's offense.

If you want the 4-3 defense to become predictable, you have to attack it to the wideside of the field. Run the toss or option play into the wideside to keep the defense from rolling into the boundary. The 4-3 defense is the most common defense we play against. An odd-front defense is generally a 4-3 defense that overshifts onto the nose of the center.

In the 4-3 defense, we know the backside defensive end is coming hard up the field. We have to block him on the pass play and run the ball inside of him. The cut-back isolation is a good play to run against that defensive end.

If the defensive tackle plays a 2 technique on the guard, the guard is unsure which gap the tackle has. The lead draw is a great play to run. That allows the guard to pass set and let the tackle take the gap he wants. The lead blocker and running back reads the block of the guard. If the tackle goes into the A gap, the lead back can assume the Will linebacker is in the B gap. The lead blocker has to read the defensive tackles move.

The offensive tackle pass blocking on an athletic defensive end presents a problem. We help him by running the ball inside of him. If we are effective enough inside of him, it slows his pass rush. The blocking on the lead draw has to look like the blocking on the five-step passing game.

We play our home games in Northeastern Ohio. Late in the season and playoff time, it is hard to complete 60 percent of your passes because of the weather. So many times, we must battle the snow and cold conditions. We would like to pass more, but the weather gets in the way of high percentage passes.

Get a couple of very specific ideas and work on them with great repetition. Use them enough so over time you become confident in them. I am confident you will not stop our out pattern. I portray to the players that I will teach them these ideas. I will participate in the teaching of the idea and it will work. If you become the first-team quarterback at Mount Union, you can throw the out pattern.

On third down and ten, what are you going to run? You must have an answer for that question. The players on the field probably know the call if you have taught them well. The players are confident, too.

When we start planning. We consider players, formations, and plays in that order. The first category is players, because players make the different. Analyze your players. Since we have spring practice this year, our entire staff spent a couple of weeks talking about the players. We ranked all of our players. We wanted to come up with the top eleven defensive football players. What are you going to do if, of the best eleven players, only three of them are defensive backs? Can we get our best eleven defensive players on the field? You, as the head coach, may not be seeing what there is there to see. Make sure your assistant coaches have every opportunity to tell you what they think about the players.

After you decide something about the players, pick the formations that fit what your players can do. The young coach we hired wants to run the empty set as part of our offense. When we ranked our players, the number-three ranked player was a running back. It is not in our best interest to run a formation that keeps one of our best players off the field. We do not have a tight end in our program right now. If we cannot find one, we must adjust our formations. The quarterback this year was too short, so we used more of the shotgun set in our passing game.

The last thing you want to consider is plays. There are too many plays in football to run all of them. What you need to do is pick a few that match your player's abilities. The same plays that worked this year may not work next year. The players change and your plays have to adjust with the players. We have to be flexible in our ideas and thinking. That is it. Thank you very much.

POWER RUN AND POWER PASSING GAME

Arizona State University

From a philosophical standpoint, we are a big play-action team at Arizona State. We believe in running the football. We count on runs to match our play-action. We match as best we can the same action on the pass as we do on the run. We especially match up our personnel groups with our formations and our motions. When we make up our game plan for the week, whatever we are doing out of our 22 personnel with flanker movement we want to be able to run and pass out of the 22 flanker movement. We do the same thing out of our "bunch" personnel and it does not matter if we are running from our 11 or our 12 personnel. We are going to be able to make it look the same to the defense.

Over the last ten years, we found that 51 percent of our offense came from these plays. When we are run-downs, we were in these situations. It was first and ten yards to go for the first down, or second and one to six yards to go for the first down. You should study what the situation is for your offense. You can waste a lot of time if you are not practicing on the plays and situations you face in the games. We want to be 50-50 on run-downs. We do not want the defense to know if we are going to run or pass on each play. We give teams a "run look" and try to run the ball. If we cannot run the ball on them, we go to play-action passes and try to throw the ball over their heads. If we make them defend our run, and they stop us, we are going to try to throw the ball over their head. That is our whole deal.

The power play is not the main play in our offense. It is about our fourth or fifth play. We are a zone-threat counter team. With the zone- and counter-type plays, it makes the power our fourth or fifth play. The beauty of the system is this. When we are blocking power, it is the same blocking as counter for us. Because we are a multiple offense,

everything we do in our system—run and pass—we are trying to make it user-friendly for the quarterback. The second consideration for us is user-friendly for the offensive line. I do not can if it is ever user friendly for the receivers, tight ends, and running backs. Those people must learn the offense. They must be the adjusters. In our offense, the quarterback and offensive line have a lot to retain in our offense so we want to make it as easy as we can for those players.

We run the power play several different ways. I was with Boston College in the mid-1990s with Coach Dan Henning. We are a multiple tight end offense. Right now, we do not have any fullbacks in our program. We are playing with two tight ends. We are primarily a one-back team but we want to get into a two-back look. What Dan Henning taught me about the power play was this: pretend you are always running the power to the split-end or open side of the formation. At times we do run to the tight-end side but our base scheme, when we put the play into our offense on day one, we are always running the power to the open-end side of the formation. The tackle on that side never has an option block with the tight end on the open side.

This scheme will always work for you as long as you are running against a six-man box. It will always work against a six-man front or an eight-man front. This scheme is not sound against a true even defense with seven men in the box. You are short one blocker. As I have the play set up, we do not have a man to block the Will linebacker (Diagram #1). If we face a team that plays an even front, we are always going to use formations to try to get them to switch the defensive front to a six-man or eight-man front. How do we get them to switch the front? We do that by formations.

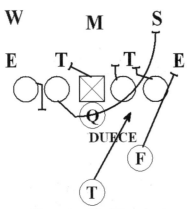

Diagram #1. 24 power

If we play a team like Washington State that is a great 4-3 defense, and they refuse to get out of their 4-3 defense, we must figure out something else if we want to run the power plays. For us, power plays may not be in our game plan every week.

We want to run the power plays toward the 3 technique if we can. We want to get a "deuce block" on the linebacker. We get a double-team in the B gap and get the deuce block on the backside linebacker. We are always going to have someone on the move to kick out the onside defensive end. I said someone on the move. I said that because defenses are so good that they can read the down block by the tackle, they are going to try to "wrong arm" him. Defenses have improved so much in the last ten years on the power and counter plays it is ridiculous. We are going to move a tight end or a fullback across the formation or fake motion and get them inside and outside and get a man on the end before he can use the "wrong arm" on the tackle. I will show you 30 film clips today, good and bad clips.

We always block back to the weakside with the center. We prefer our center blocking on a shade nose or against a 1 technique, as opposed to blocking on a 3 technique on the power play. We wrap the guard on the first linebacker inside the box. The backside guard hinge blocks on his side.

We do have different combinations we use with our tight end. If we had a tight end, his rule is to arc block number four. He has the first man outside the box. That is our power play. It is plain and simple.

If we face a seven-man front, we are going to lose the backside linebacker. We tell our tailbacks to run the ball in the A gap on power. We want to run at the double-team block. We have our tailback drop set and then we want him to go straight downhill. On the tapes, you will see how we want the tailback to get his shoulders square to the line of scrimmage in the A gap. We do get some bounces on the play. What happens is a team will fast flow over the top and we get the backside A gap.

I want to go over the next plays very quickly so we can get to the film so you can see the plays in action. I want to show you how we block power against different defensive schemes. I just covered this for the most part.

One defense I am sure you see is the Bear defense or the six-man defense (Diagram #2). For most of us, the power play is a decent play for us. It is good news/bad news. The way we scheme the play we are always going to get the play started. We are going to down block because we have great angles. That is the good news. The bad news is the fact that you are going to be short on a man to block the backside linebacker. We cannot get him blocked on the Bear look.

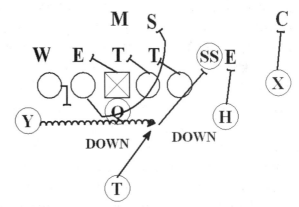

Diagram #2. 24 power versus Bear

Why do teams use the Bear defense? They are going to overload against the offense. They like to play man coverage behind the bear front. It is not a bad answer but we can still get the ball moving.

A defense we are facing more and more is the 30 stack look (Diagram #3). We are still in good shape against that look because we can start the play downhill. I am going to leave it here and get to the film.

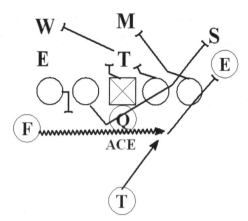

Diagram #3. 24 power versus 30 stack

The next aspect of the offense is our power pass. Earlier I said everything is easy for our quarterback and offensive line. Our power pass protection is the same for our offensive line as it is on our quick protection. It is the three-step drop protection. It is gap protection. It is the same as everyone in the PAC 10 runs the protection. The back goes to the hip of the offensive tackle. Everyone is blocking back one gap. We are secure from C gap to C gap (Diagram #4). If anything comes off the edge, you must react because the ball comes out quick on the play.

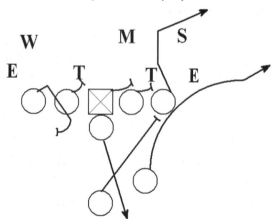

Diagram #4. Power pass protection six

When we put several pass routes in the offensive line coach cannot complain because we are using the quick pass protection. We must decide on how many pass patterns our offense needs.

One point different on power passes and most play-action passes is this. On the play-action passes, our quarterback is in a high-low progression. He is looking for the big gain first and then he checks down to the shortest gain. Power passes are just the opposite of this. Because it is a

six-man protection, we are reading the pass low to high. The old power passing game consisted of a man in the flat and someone running a flag route behind the flat man. We tell the quarterback not to pass up the man in the flat if he is open. We are not running this play on third and ten for the first down. Go back to the start of the lecture. I said before, 51 percent of our plays are on first down and ten, or third down and less than five yards to go. If we call it on third down and five yards to go and we only get three yards on the play, that is my fault. We will take the low to high play and be happy with it. If you want to go high to low, you can call another type of play.

A second point if we are running the play to the tight-end side. Sometimes the tight end is not good enough to beat the strong safety on the flag route.

In our power-pass plays, we can have many different combinations. If we call power pass right, we can "tag" it whatever we want. All of our backside routes are by rule. What we call it in our package as power pass, zone pass, or whatever, our backside receivers know what they are going to do based on the formations. For example, we love to run the post-curl route on the backside. We very seldom get to it in power pass because the ball comes out fast in power pass. We throw it high. However, I would much better not get to the post-curl route and have the quarterback know what he is doing, for the one or two times a year we are going to have an opportunity to come to the post-curl route. The other factor is the fact that the post-curl route carries over into the rest of our offense.

One point we consider in building a play-action play. Try to make the play so the backside rules are consistent. It makes the teaching a lot easier.

The reason we like the post-curl route to the backside is this. It gives the quarterback an outlet pass if the play-action pass is not open on the frontside. He will always have the low throw staring him in the face when he has to come back to the backside.

Another rule we have built into our power-pass offense is for the inside-slot receiver on the backside away from the power pass. The slot man runs a drag route. (Diagram #5). That is our backside route. The inside receiver runs the drag and the outside receiver runs the post-curl route.

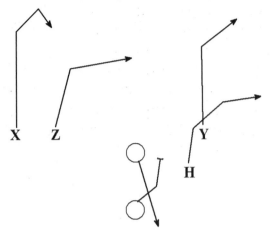

Diagram #5. Power pass rules

If you are a backside tight end, your rule is to check number four and then run a flag route. You may ask why we have our backside tight end check number four. We are in six-man protection. We have five men on the line plus the tailback to pass protect. Defensive teams like to blitz on the backside and I do not want to get the quarterback hit in the back of the head. We are not going to throw the ball to the tight end in the progression of the route. His rule is always the same: check number four and then run a flag route.

If you want to use a multiple offense set up the rules to fit more than one offensive concept. It makes it simple for the players.

As we got into the power offense, we started liking it a lot. We decided we needed more plays in this offense. You can always have more offense, right? When we faced teams that did not blitz on the backside and played the flat against our pass, we needed a third option for the quarterback as the play unfolds. We wanted to build a triangle. That is how you attack zone defenses.

We added one tag to our power pass and it gave us a third option on the play. We ran the power pass on one side and then ran an "under" route behind it. Now we have built a triangle. If you are a basketball coach, you already know this. Some teams call the route "shallow crosses" (Diagram #6). The receiver

runs underneath the coverage. If no one is underneath the receiver, he keeps on running. If there is someone waiting on the receiver when he gets to the backside tackle, he wants to hook up and show the numbers to the quarterback.

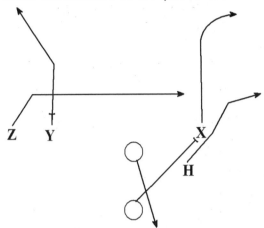

Diagram #6. Power pass — under route

We only have to spend 15 minutes on this at the start of the season. We do not have to spend any more time on it the rest of the year. We started "tagging" some power passes with some backside under pass patterns. We liked this particular passing game package.

The next thing we did was to throw curl routes off power passes against zone defenses. We built our curl package against the zone defense. We see two main types of defensive coverage in the PAC 10. We see everything but we see two main types. We see "quarter" teams and we see "man" teams. Everyone has a wrinkle to throw at you but, for the most part, we see those two defenses.

When we run the curl package against a "quarters" defense, we use "quarter busters." We run the number-two receiver on a vertical route. We take the number-one receiver and run him on a curl route instead of the flag route. We still run the man to the flat. We still have the man coming across on the under route (Diagram #7).

We still have the same triangle that attacks quarter coverage. We are clearing the area so the quarterback can read the receivers. When we started running these routes several years ago, no one used quarter coverage. Everything on defense was a two-deep, three-deep, and man coverage.

The coach that started using quarter coverage was a smart coach. He has been a pain in the rear for all offensive coaches.

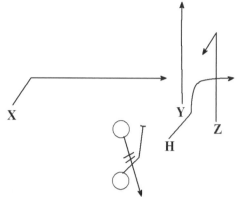

Diagram #7. Power pass — quarters buster

Because we are in a six-man protection, when we are in power pass we cut down our curl route from ten yards to eight yards. That is because the ball comes out of the hands of the quarterback faster. We like to run the curl route out of reduced formations. That means we are going to motion the man across the formation and send him to the flat (Diagram #8). The under route is the same. We want to make it look exactly like our running play.

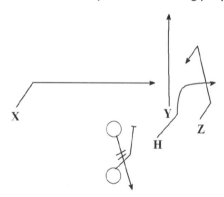

Diagram #8. Motion power pass/curl — flat

The other way we run the same play is from the "bunch" formation. In the bunch formation, we take a reverse seam for two to three steps and then push the route up to eight steps and then we break it off at a 45-degree angle. If you run the pass this way, the timing will be exactly the same as if your quarterback was taking a five-step drop and throwing a drop back curl route. We do not want the route too deep because we do not want the quarterback to be waiting.

When we play against "man" teams, we do not run the number-two receiver running the vertical route. We want the number-two receiver running a flag route (Diagram #9). This play is good against zone coverage but it is great against man coverage. Sometimes we will get the man to the flag route and sometimes we will not get there. Again, we are not going to pass up the flag route.

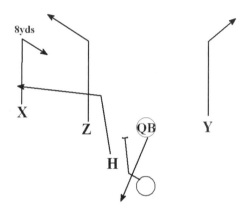

Diagram #9. Flag route

By adding one "tag" to our power route package, we have a different pattern: power-pass left - curl. In addition, we have power-pass left - tag. In our offense, anything that is a curl read for our quarterback has a "horse" name on it. We have several horse names on the patterns. Our quarterback has to be veterinarian to play for us.

In the film, I want you to notice the relationship of the curl and the flat receivers. When the ball is ready to come out of the quarterback's hand, we want the flat receiver to always have out-leveraged the curl runner. Why is that? It is because we do not want one defender to cover both receivers. If the flat receiver is under the curl receiver, one defender can cover them. We are in six-man protection. Because of the protection, the quarterback does not stand in the pocket and hold the ball. The ball has to come out of his hands quickly.

We have several combinations of the curl-flat routes with a vertical pattern bringing someone under the receivers to create a triangle. We have our combinations with the curl-flat with an under receiver. We run these patterns from the open side, bunch side, and to the tight-end side.

BALANCE IN THE PASSING GAME

Texas Tech

Thank you very much. It is nice to be here. When I speak at clinics, most of the time I have a crummy joke to get started. However, I have not heard any good stories recently so I will get going and talk about football.

You can imagine the beating we take from our critics about the balance of our offense. I think we have a very balanced offense. I do not think balance refers to running or throwing the ball a certain number of times. Many of our thoughts on offense come from the wishbone offense. That surprises many people because they think about the Oklahoma teams of the past and the Air Force Academy today.

Wishbone teams run the ball a lot and we throw it a lot. I identify with the wishbone offense because it is a distribution offense. One of the objectives of the wishbone is to make sure all the backs in the backfield touches the ball. They want to make sure the defense is accountable for every offensive skilled player.

I believe you have to utilize all your skilled players. My thoughts would be the same if we ran the ball all the time. We throw the ball to many different receivers. We use all our skilled players in our offense.

We chart the results throughout the season to see if we use all our players in our offense. There are good and bad reasons not to utilize a player. If the problem occurs, it could be with the coaching staff or the player. If it is problem with the coaching staff, we want to correct that immediately. If the problem is with the player, generally it has to do with talent. If the player is short on talent, we can improve that situation through hard work or find a specific role for him to play in our offense.

We have standards, goals, and expectations for each of our skilled players. We play most of our snaps with a four-wide receiver package. We have an X-receiver, who is the split end. We have an H-back, who is a slotback. We have a Y-receiver, who is also a slotback and a Z-receiver, who is the flanker. In the backfield, we have a quarterback and an F-back.

We want our four receivers to contribute 1000 yards each to our offense. That total is not just receiving yardage. We expect him to rush or throw for some yardage during the course of a twelve-game schedule. We exceeded the goals at the X-, H-, and Y-receivers and were under expectations at the Z-receiver.

We played a freshman at the H-receiver position for most of the season. His numbers are slightly better than 1000 yards, but will get better with experience. It took him some time to work into the offense. The Z-receiver contributed 768 yards. We are in the process of going through the cut-ups of last year's game films, to see how we can get the ball to the Z-receiver more.

From the F-back's position, we wanted 1400 yards and hoped he could exceed that. The quarterback was a non-factor because of the sacks he took during the season. Last season he had minus 136 yards. Balance in our offense is how we are distributing the football.

Most of our tricks come with our sets. Our offensive plays are basic in the passing game. From the defensive standpoint, we want our offensive plays hard to sort out. However, we never want to outsmart ourselves. Plays are only as good as the stupidest player executing it at the point of attack. As a coach, you may be a genius and you may have several players who are extremely smart, but the success of a play depends on the dumbest guy at the point of attack. Everyone has to execute for a play to have success.

If you are running right and the backside receiver does not understand the concept of the play, that does not hurt the play. He will not hurt the play because he is not at the point of attack. Everyone at the point of attack had better understand exactly what you are trying to do on that particular play.

It is not enough to have great ideas on paper unless you have the ability to teach them to your players. Your players should have the ability to absorb your offense in the time available to present it. We have a limited amount of time to spend with our players. If we cannot get the players to execute the plays, we have not accomplished much.

In our offense we take a basic play and run it from as many formations as is possible. The variations of the formations lead to the diversity of the play.

I think it is important to use your skilled people. All our formations are generally four-wide receiver sets. However, we do run conventional formations with tight ends involved in the offense. In our offense, we have packaged all types of formations. In our package, we run one-back sets as well as two-back sets. We have packages that involve one and two tight ends. We try to match the formations to the types of defenses we play against.

The H-Back and Y-Receiver may not be good tight ends when we play them tight with their hands on the ground, but they have the ability to move into those positions. A two tight end set presents some problems to a defense that may not be present in a double slot formation. All the formations we present are hard to prepare for in the limited amount of time the defense has available.

We do things on offense to create space. We do it with our offensive linemen as well as our receivers. Many coaches have said you need to throw short to people who can score. I think that is a bit overstated. One of the most effective things

we did last season was to throw the vertical passing game.

The one thing we think about is putting the ball into all our skilled players' hands. That means the defense has to cover five potential threats. They cannot double on two receivers and keep us from throwing the ball down field. It forces them to play us honestly, just like the wishbone attack.

The easiest player to get the ball to is the F-back or fullback. He is the closest player to the quarterback. We can hand the ball to him, throw it to him, and throw the screen to him. He is the best player on our offense. He is the best player because we ask him to do everything. He has to run the ball, catch the ball, and block. We hoped it would be easy for the F-back to get 1400 yards because he touches the ball so much. The receivers do not touch the ball as much as he F-back, but their plays should go further in yardage.

The slot receivers get more catches than the wide receiver, but their yards per catch are not as great as the wide receivers. They make possession types of catches that keep the chains moving. The wide receivers make touchdown catches and big plays. The catches will differ a bit, but we want everyone to have many catches.

Our line splits for our linemen start out at three feet. If the offensive linemen start to lose the battle with the defense, we tighten the line splits. If we are handling the defensive front, we widen the splits. That helps our running game by creating gaps for the backs to run into. It helps our passing game by creating throwing lanes. If you have one lineman who has to cut his splits drastically, we help him with a back or another uncovered lineman.

The offense has to force the defense to defend the field both vertically and horizontally. We want to spread the defense from sideline to sideline and make them defend the deep pass at the same time. We do not want to become simply a short passing team. If all you can do is throw short, the defense will crowd the receivers and choke off the short passing area. We want the defensive backs to know we will go deep from all our positions and do it often.

I see offensive plays all the time that look impressive. We could add them to our scheme very easily. If we start to add new plays to our scheme, we have to subtract some of the plays we already run. The worst thing you can do to an offense is to overburden them with new plays. We are already good at running the plays we have in our offense.

I think it is important to control the ball on offense. It does not matter whether you run the ball or throw it, the worst thing you can do offensively is go "three and out." We are a passing team but we take pride in controlling the ball. We set the record in college football this year for most first downs in a season. We had 418 first downs this year.

The offense has to focus on converting third downs. I do not spend a lot of time thinking about time of possession. I can go "three and out" and burn a tremendous amount of time off the clock. What I focus on is the number of plays we are running per game. If our team had 85 plays and the opponent had 60 plays, regardless of the time of possession, the opponent's defense played 85 plays. The time of possession may have been in their favor, but we had 25 more chances to score than they did. Their defense spent 25 more snaps on the field than ours.

There is a tremendous debate about how to install your offense. We install our offense in three days and repeat it over the entire spring practice. In spring football, we have three different scripts, which we repeat four times within the course of spring practice. We put one third of our offense in the first day of spring practice. On the second day, we put in one third of the offense. At the end of third day, we have installed the entire offense. On the fourth day, we start back at day one and begin to repeat the first day's script of plays. We keep working on the scripts and timing them until we can execute them very well.

We install one third of the seven and five-step passes, the quick game, the screen game and the running game schemes each day. The first day we did this, our practice was not bad. The second day the practice was so-so. However, the third day, they were having trouble keeping things straight. By the time we completed the second cycle through the offense, they were secure in what they were doing. The third time through the scripts, they could practically do it in their sleep.

We want to attack the field in a variety of ways. There are three plays in our offense that I want to show you. After I talk about them, I will show a little film on them. These plays come at the defense at different angles form different places on the field with good distribution.

The first pass is the four-vertical scheme. There is a variety of reasons to run the vertical game. This past football season was the best year I have ever had in throwing vertical passes. We spend a lot of time working on the vertical passing game. This year we were 51 out of 95 passes thrown in the vertical game. That is 53.6 percent completion rate. We had 927 yards of offense in those passes. We averaged 18.1 yards per completion. In those passes we threw 13 touchdowns and had three interceptions. Going back and looking at these statistics, I feel like an idiot for not calling it every time.

I have some definite thoughts on vertical routes. They are worthwhile if you can complete 33 percent of the passes. It is a low percentage pass. Usually we are in the low- to mid-40 percents on vertical passes thrown.

One of our favorite ways to throw the vertical game is from the trips formation. There is a variety of ways to throw the vertical game (Diagram #1). From the trips set, the wide receiver on the three-receiver side aligns at the top of the numbers. As he does battle with the corner heading upfield, we do not want him to get below the numbers. The quarterback looks for pressed coverage by the defender or an inside leverage position. That makes it easier for the receiver to get deep.

The landmark for the outside slot receiver is the hash mark. On his release, he has to go either inside or outside the defender, depending on what kind of games they are playing in the coverage. Regardless, the receiver has to declare his route quickly so the quarterback can identify what he is doing.

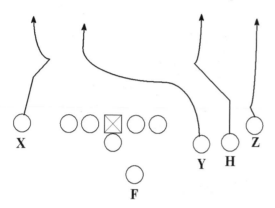

Diagram #1. Four verticals

The inside slot goes across the middle to get to the opposite hash mark. He looks early for a hot throw coming off a blitz. Usually if the ball is throw to the inside slot, it occurs early on the hot read, between the linebackers, or over the ball. Seldom does he get a throw down the hash mark.

The back can run a variety of patterns from this set. We can work him on an option route. On that pattern, he works downfield on a linebacker. He finds the coverage and works away from the defender. The four vertical routes have a tendency to clear out the defense. When that happens, we run a swing or flat pass into the area cleared by the three receivers. Against some teams you may want to run the back on a swing away from the trips set.

The backside wide receiver is generally single covered. We can tag the play with a special pattern for the single receiver side. If the defender aligns to the outside, the slant pattern is open. If the defender gives a large cushion, we can run the curl or stop pattern. We can get some mismatches and gain an advantage based on the leverage of the defense.

If you go by the book, the receivers go vertical against press coverage. They run fade routes and try to get behind the defenders. The defense has gone to four defenders across against the four vertical routes (Diagram #2). That is supposed to stop that pattern. When you try to attack

defenses, you take some licks trying to improve your game. There are some days your quarterback looks bad as we try to improve on our scheme. When teams play us with a four across scheme, we have a great deal of success in the seams of the four defenders.

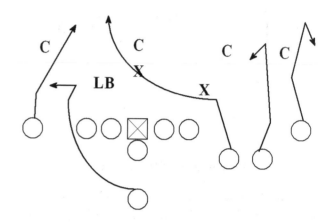

Diagram #2. Four vertical versus four across

The slot receivers find open areas in the seams by selling the deep verticals, breaking the patterns off, and setting down in the underneath holes. The second option against four across is the single receiver. We call three verticals and tag his pattern as a curl. We like to see the four across alignments in the secondary. We feel the quarterback and receivers are on the same page and know how to attack that look.

We also like to run a slant-corner combination from the two-by-two set. We can run it to either side (Diagram #3). If you hit some fades on the defense, they will over play you for the fade. Against University of California, they showed us an alignment that gave us the fade route. They aligned head up the receiver, but at the snap of the ball, they jumped outside in their alignment. We ran the fade into the coverage.

It took me much too long to make the adjustment. I felt like a moron for a quarter and a half. I forced the fade instead of running the slant. Most defenses drop the corner to a depth of six to seven yards and shade the receiver outside. The other adjustment the defense makes to prevent four verticals is to align inside the slot. They want to force the slot off the hash mark and carry him deep. We accommodate them and run the corner.

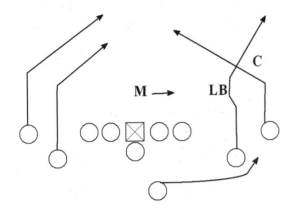

Diagram #3. Slant-Corner

The linebacker walls the slot off the hash mark and carries him to the safety. We run the corner route behind the corner defender, who is playing the slant, and flare the F-back into the flat underneath the patterns by the twin set.

On the backside, we run a double slant by the wide receiver and slot. Sometimes the quarterback prefers to check to the double slant. It is an easy pass to complete and hard to cover. If the quarterback cannot read the strongside coverage, the double slant is a safe and high percentage throw for us.

I like to run the mesh play (Diagram #4). People have gotten away from running a lot of crossing routes. I do not know why, because they are effective passes to throw. The crossing patterns give defenses problems. Defensive coach can show you how they cover them on the chalkboard, but it is difficult to do on the field. The play in the diagram comes from a two back set.

The wide receiver to the two-receiver side runs a corner route. If the corner plays inside leverage, the wide receiver is the number one choice of the quarterback. We take that pattern right now.

The split end and flexed tight end run the mesh pattern six yards deep in front of the linebackers. The mesh pattern is a double cross by the receivers. If the coverage is zone, the receivers want to find a hole and sit down after making the cross. If the coverage is

man-to-man, they continue to run after the cross. Once the receivers reach the hash marks, they turn their patterns upfield. They want to start getting depth to make the throw easier for the quarterback.

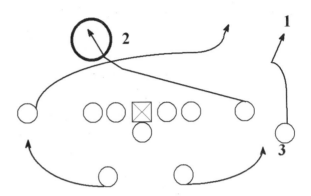

Diagram #4. Mesh play

If they continued to run their patterns across the field, the throw became a long throw to the outside, which is dangerous. If they gain depth, the quarterback can put air under the ball and throw into the seams. The mesh pattern is the second choice.

The back to the two-receiver side runs a flare or flat pattern behind the corner route. The running back to the backside runs into the flat. The third choice for the quarterback is the F-back running the flare.

The thought on these plays is to stretch the defense. The central play is the four-vertical route. That takes advantage of the popular way corners like to play wide receivers. They like to play them with a press or inside shade technique. To stop the fade route the defense over plays to the outside. They back off the receivers and play with outside leverage. That brings the other concept of the quick slant inside and quick throw as the option for the quarterback.

As you can see, we try to attack the entire field. We try to get the ball in the hands of all our receivers. The plays we run are designed to cause the defense as many problems as we can. When the defense tries to defend the entire field, it becomes a match-up game. The defense has a defender for all the receivers, but they cannot double cover everyone. The quarterback goes through his reads and throws to the receiver that is not double covered.

I will show you the film and you can see the schemes. The first point I want to make is about the receiver's break. If the receiver wants to create space to run his pattern, he leans into the defender on the break and accelerates out of the break.

If you throw the ball, the receivers must work on their releases. People talk about releases more than they work on them. I think releases are important because more defenses are into man-to-man coverages. If the receiver can prefect his releases, he can do damage to a defender who is a relatively slow player.

In the vertical game, you give the defense the option of covering your deep routes or the horizontal flares. They will cover the deep routes first and try to break back to the shallow routes. Our backs do a good job of running the option routes off linebackers. We had a back lead the nation in receptions one year and most of his receptions were option routes.

In the vertical game, if all the receivers hit their landmarks correctly, someone has to be open. The quarterback can release the ball relatively early even when the defense runs a blitz at him.

On the goal line, we like to go under the center with our quarterback. By doing that, the quarterback is able to secure the ball better, there by reducing the chance of a fumble, and he throws the ball quicker. When we run our patterns, we do not know exactly where the receivers will come open. As the players get used to the scheme, they will get a feel as to when they come open. Our receivers do not run their patterns and only look when they come out of the break. The receivers look the entire way after the break. It may cost us a step, but I believe we have more opportunities to complete the ball.

If the outside receiver gets a good release and the quarterback throws the ball on time, the receiver should not be any deeper than 28-33 yards from the line of scrimmage. I have charted our games and other people's films, and the distances came out the same. The deeper throws occur when the quarterback does not throw on time and holds the ball.

Defenses try to confuse the receivers by playing press on one down and bailing out on the next down. It is easy to check to the vertical game. If the wide receiver gets a bail out by the defensive back, he can break off his route and run the curl. That is also an easy read for the quarterback.

If you look at the vertical route, you can see the back in the flat. Even though the ball was thrown deep and the receiver made a great catch, had the quarterback taken the short, easy throw to the flat, the back could run as far as the completion. I am not second-guessing the quarterback, but the throw to the flat is a pattern he overlooked.

The more you run the vertical game, the quarterback and receivers start to read each other's mind. That is why the quarterback throws the ball so quickly on certain fade routes. In the vertical game, the receivers can see the blitz when it comes. They know the ball is coming out quickly and to prepare for it.

I am not trying to convince anyone to run a bunch of vertical patterns. You have to figure out what you want to be good at and invest the time. If you invest the time, you will get good at what you do. We do not run the no-back set. I did not want to commit the time it takes to get good at running that set.

The quarterback has confidence in his receivers. He can throw the ball up and know the receivers will go get the ball. The receiver knows if they do not go after the ball, they look bad.

In the corner-slant scheme, the corner route run by the inside receiver is hard to cover. The safety is in a bad position to cover the corner route and it forces the corner defender to take the slant or the corner pattern. He cannot cover them both. The same thing is true of the linebacker. He has to cover the slant or the flat. Either way he gives up good yardage.

If you can attack the defense from a variety of angles, they have trouble taking patterns away from you. The receivers must counter punch the defenders. If the defenders take something away, they open something else. We must be versatile enough to take advantage of what the defense gives. You must give the defense reasons to move around.

In the vertical game, we do not want to become one-dimensional. We want to throw over the top of the coverage, into the holes of the zones, and use short, quick throws underneath the coverage.

When we run the mesh play, we run a number of receivers on the mesh route. Depending on the formation, we can involve any receiver we want on the crossing routes. Do not allow your receivers to stay covered. If someone covers them, they have to move.

In football, we teach some techniques and players pick the techniques up quickly. To me, the shotgun snap is an easy delivery of the ball. I feel a lot of coaches over-coach some techniques. The mesh patterns cross at six yards in front of the linebacker. If the coverage is zone, the receivers sit down in the seam of the defense, and continue the run if it is man coverage. The mesh route is one pattern that sounds easy to teach, but it is extremely difficult and takes many reps to perfect.

When a receiver runs a horizontal route, after he catches the ball he needs to go straight upfield. The quick move upfield catches the defender off guard. He makes the catch, turns upfield, and makes whatever yardage he can make. If the receiver splits the defenders, they get a surprising amount of yards after the catch.

The uniqueness of this type of passing game is the number of different receivers that are open on the same play. The first time we run a particular play, the wide receiver may be open. The next time we run the same play, the slot is open. We may run the same play a third time and the back out of the backfield may be open. The changes in coverage the defense plays, is not the only reason for different receivers being open. The executions of those coverages become a problem for the defense. The offense presents enough problems to the coverage, to cause mistakes in the execution. If the defense executes the defense perfectly, we are out of business. However, that normally does not happen that often.

Defensive players have to make quick decisions and react to patterns in a split second. We practice our patterns day after day and can execute and change quicker than the defensive player. We move the receivers around in different sets, but they have the same routes.

We like to run wheel routes as part of our pattern adjustments. We do not run these patterns to try and get completions. The wheel route is a good pattern because it stretches the coverage and opens the post and mesh routes to the inside. The wheel route is as hard to complete as it is to defend.

I have a word of caution to coaches about adding wheel patterns into your offense. The quarter-back throws the wheel as his first choice for about three days. He becomes infatuated with the pattern.

I tried to cover things that may help everyone's offense. I know not everyone runs our offense, but these things can be useful. The main idea from this lecture is to get the ball into all your skilled players' hands. Make sure you use all of your receivers.

The way you practice is the most important aspect of all the things you do. You have to guard against doing too much in practice. You must do the same drills daily to build confidence in your players.

There are some important things to consider in the philosophy of teaching. The teaching from your assistant coaches must have consistency in the way they instruct players. If the quarterback coach tells the quarterback the receiver is running a certain route a particular way, the receiver coach must be teaching it that way. Everyone on your staff must be on the same page.

To have a successful program, you need chemistry within your team. That refers to the coaching staff as well as the players. I relate chemistry to loyalty. Included within the loyalty is the fact that your team likes being around each other.

Everyone needs to respect everyone's job and believe in what he does. Football is redundant. We run the same plays repeatedly. In the course of doing that, you have to find ways to make it fun. The only way to build consistence is to do it repeatedly.

In practice, we do not stress making big plays. We want our players to make all the routine plays. The most valuable player you have on your team is the guy that can make the routine play. Big plays happen in a game and should if you have an extremely talented player. However, the player who makes the routine play every time is the most valuable. Those guys are the players that keep the chains moving.

Make sure what you do in practice is consist with what you want to get accomplished on the game field. We have the same practice schedule every week. Every Tuesday practice is identical to every other Tuesday practice. When we go to a bowl game, it may fall on different days of the week. The fact that the bowl game falls on a Monday night does not matter to me. What matters is our practices preceding the bowl game are like every Friday, Thursday, and Wednesday during the season.

The most important thing you can do in practice is get in the reps you need to be successful. You must specifically identify what you want to do and feature that in your practices.

In your system, be simple and have a philosophy that reflects what you want to accomplish. Coming into a game, you must have a plan on what risks you are willing to take. What are you willing to do to secure an edge for your team? Generally, that refers to fourth-down plays and special teams.

During the course of a season, you must find ways to keep players fresh both mentally and physically. To keep them fresh physically, you have to cut down the number of reps in practice. The more focused the players are, the less amount of time you must devote to repetitions. The harder a player focuses, the more stress he puts on himself mentally. That is the sixty-four dollar question. How do you keep the players fresh both mentally and physically? If anyone knows the answer, call me immediately. Find and devise ways to loosen up your players and gauge when to relax them. Keeping your players physically fit and healthy is critical in your program.

If there is anything we can do for you at Texas Tech, please call on us. It has been my pleasure to be here. I hope to see you. Good luck to all of you next season.

Jay Locey

DEVELOPING TEAM CHEMISTRY

Linfield College

It is a lot of fun for me to be here. I want to talk about developing team chemistry. I have a highlight tape that will set the stage for the lecture. The tape is on our last three playoff games as we won the national championship. We had a great year and felt that we had great team chemistry that went a long want in helping us win that national championship. [Tape]

We were fortunate to have a great staff last year. We started turning the program around in 2000. It was a big year for us. Prior to that, we were just pretending to be a good football team. We ended up going 9-0 in 2000. At that time, we were contending for the league championship in 2000. In 2001, we tied for the league championship but we did not get to go to the playoffs. However, I did get to the NCAA clinic and I went to see the National championship game that year. I did not really know much about Division III. I had a chance to see what it was like. I watched Mount Union College of Ohio beat Bridgewater College. Mount Union has won several championships and has a very successful program.

When I came back from Virginia and the National Championship, I set our goals for the next year. Our goal was to win a national championship at Linfield College. On the way back on the airplane, I wrote down some things that I though would be keys to our program. I listed the things I believed it would take to have a team that could play for a national championship.

First, I believed we needed to have a "great scheme." The schools in our conference all have great scheme teams. Our conference is a good testing ground. In 2002 and 2003, we were in the playoffs and played St. John's. They had a great team and made very good adjustments at halftime. I felt it was very important for us to have a great scheme. We knew we had to be good on offense, defense, and in special teams.

Second, we had to develop the players in our program. We needed to take what we had and develop the talent in our program. We do not always get great athletes. However, we did have some good athletes in our program. We wanted to develop our players physically. We knew we had to work on speed, agility, and quickness. We want to increase our size and strength. We needed to improve our position skills.

We wanted to improve the players' knowledge of the game. We want them to be football smart about the game.

The other thing we wanted to accomplish was to help the players grow as people. We wanted them to improve in character. We wanted them to develop a positive attitude. We felt that was important for our program.

The fourth point we wanted to develop was team unity. We needed to be a team and we needed to play as a team. We wanted to be great in team unity. It was the same spirit as the New England Patriots developed. In the Super Bowl, the TV officials wanted to introduce the Patriots offensive team. The Patriots said, "No, introduce all of us. We do not want to be introduced as individuals. We got here as a team and that is how we want to be introduced." They broke the barrier on teamwork and they have been doing it ever since. That was the attitude we wanted to develop.

Another important factor was to recruit good players. In addition, we needed to retain the players we did have. Those were our thoughts on what we needed to do to win a national championship.

We were aware that schemes had nothing to do with people and nothing to do with chemistry of the team. All of the other points had everything to do with chemistry. It was about changing human skills and the chemistry of the team.

I have a quote by Tom Osborne from his book written in 1999. The name of the book is *Faith in the Game*. It is a tremendous book in my opinion. In the first chapter, he talked about team chemistry. This is what he said:

> "In the beginning of the season there are 15 teams that have the ability to go on to be national champs. They have the coach and they have the talent. They are capable of winning the national championship. What factors are going to separate the winners? The fact that determines which team finishes first, tenth, or fifteenth, is largely a matter of character. Those teams that develop a unique chemistry based on factors such as honesty, hard work, self-sacrifice, faith, and loyalty out-perform teams of comparability that lack those traits."

I think Tom Osborne is a coach that would know about winning championships. He won three national championships.

We listed some guiding principles that we could hang our hat on. I call them guiding principles. These priorities were the things we felt we could use to develop team chemistry. We establish priorities with the following areas:

- Faith
- Family
- School
- Football
- Social

In the 2003 season, we tested one these principles. We had a starting player that had a brother that was getting married on the East Coast during the season. We tried to work it out where he could attend the wedding and still make the football game. It did not work out for us. The player went to the wedding and missed the football game. We listed the things we believed in and he chose family. What could we say? That issue was an example of how we came together as a team.

Here is another guiding principle that we used in developing team chemistry. In the spring of 2002, I went to a spring clinic at Oregon State. Coach Jerry Pettibone welcomed all of the coaches. He opened up with a story about a high school coach from Brownsville, Texas, named Gordon Wood. Gordon Wood was a very successful championship coach. He won the state at the 2A level, at the 3A level, at the 4A level, and at the 5A Division. They kept bumping his teams up in class and he still won the state. He was an amazing coach. Pettibone recruited that area and he asked Coach Wood how he won all of those championships.

Coach Wood answered very slowly. "CWLP: Coaches Will Love Players!" He asked Coach Wood, "Is there anything else that helped your teams win?" He replied, "Yes! CWLC: Coaches Will Love Coaches." Is there anything else Coach Wood? "PWLP: Players Will Love Players." Pettibone asked one more time, anything else. Coach Wood said, "PWLC: Players Will Love Coaches."

What is love? It is treating the people as you would like to be treated. I think that is the strongest motivator there is. We tell our players there are going to be problems in our lives. We want to work on a relationship that will make us a better team.

I want to continue with the guiding principles. If I am a new head coach, I want to determine the pillars on which I will base the program. These factors are not new and most of you have seen them. Four words make up the acronym TEAM.

- T-eam
- E-xcellence
- A-ttitude
- M-ark of Class

We leave our "mark" wherever our team goes. A pillar of our program is T-E-A-M. For us to be successful, we must play as a team. We build on the team aspects of the game. We want to do the mundane things to the best of our ability in all phases of our live.

Attitude is important. We hear a lot about mental attitude. Attitude is a big factor in everything we do. Something I want our team to do is to take charge of their attitude. It is a pillar of our program. We made a big change in attitude in 2001. We were 1-2 early in the season.

In the fourth game, we were on the road. We got behind 27 to 9 to start the fourth quarter. Our first quarterback got hurt and we put in the second quarterback. The big question now was the attitude of the team. Our offense was on the field and our defense was on the sideline. The defense started chanting, "Believe! Believe! Believe!" We were down 27-9. The new quarterback went into the game and threw a touchdown. That made the score 27-16. Now our offense came off the field and that started chanting on the sideline. "Believe! Believe! Believe!" The defense stopped them and we got the ball back. We started driving the ball down the field. The defense was on the sideline chanting, "Believe! Believe! Believe!" We scored again and that made the score 27-23.

The defense was on the field and the offense was on the sideline chanting. They drove the ball down to our one-yard line and fumbled the ball and we got it back. Our offense came on the field and now the defense was on the sideline chanting. We went on to drive 99 yards for a score and won the game 30-27.

The poise we showed to win that game was because of our attitude. The chanting on the sideline made a difference to our team. That won the game for us.

Other things we do to improve our attitude is this. If we turn the ball over, we do not want our defense complaining about the offense not holding on to the ball. We tell the defense to go out and make it a "three plays and out" to help the team.

That is the attitude we want them to have when they go on the field after a turnover.

If the opponents make a quick score on our defense, we want the offense to develop the attitude that they will "get it back" for the defense. We want them to have the attitude that they want to get the score to take the pressure off the defense. It is the job of the offense to get the score back for the team.

We talk about the three phases of the game. Which phase will win the game? We want the offense to step up and say, "The offense will win the game." We want them to take it on themselves that they will win the game. The defense does the same thing. They take it on themselves that they are going to win the game. Any of the three phases of our team can win the game. They must feel that they will win the game for the team.

We are going to leave a mark in whatever we do. We may not always leave a good mark. We want to leave a mark of class in everything we do at Linfield. We want to steer kids in the right directions and reinforce things they get at home. Usually, we get kids with good backgrounds. It may not be as challenging for us because most of our kids do have a good attitude when they come to us.

In the championship game, the people that run the game make it a bowl game atmosphere. They had several activities going on. We arrived in Virginia for the game at 2:00 AM. Our players had a chance to go to a Children's Hospital on Friday morning. I told the team to go to visit the kids at the hospital while I stayed and worked on our game plan. Later after we returned home, I got an email from one of the nurses from the hospital.

"I want to start off by saying congratulations for winning the Amos Alonzo Stagg Bowl and for winning the Division III National Championship and finishing the year with a perfect season." She gave her name and said she was working at the hospital in Richmond, Virginia the day the team visited the hospital:

"I was impressed by the number of players and coaches that participated in the visit with our patents. Being a former college athlete, I know there were times when we were told we were to participate in community activities. I saw your players come to our floor to visit our patients. I was truly touched to see your young men when they came to our floor. I saw compassion and concern with the way your players interacted with our kids. One small boy that had cancer was scared to go to see them first as he had just undergone some treatments. He was uptight about the visit. The players came to him first and gave him a hat and then read him some stories and showed him that someone cared about him. His mother chose not to stay with him during the time he was undergoing chemotherapy treatments.

"Some of the players went to our intensive care unit. The players game one of our patients an autographed hat that all the team has signed. The patient gave them his autograph in return. The players were willing to go to the rooms of the patients that were not able to come out of their rooms. The fact that your players got down on the floor, played with the kids, and took their time to show the kids they cared for them, to me, that was a victory in itself. I hope you are truly proud of them because they made a lasting impression on me and on our patients. Not only are they national champions on the football field, but they are national champs in life. Never let that spirit die. I would appreciate it if you could forward this on to your players. I wish you and the players a Merry Christmas. You made us all proud."

That was a "mark of class." What I am saying is this: we have a chance to make a mark of class many times, in what we do on and off the field. For some reason with football players, many people assume the worst. We got a chance to show a mark of class and that is what we want to do both on the field and off the field.

The next point I want to cover is staff expectations. I do not have to post them because our staff has been involved with our programs for a number of years, either as a player or as a coach. Most of the staff have figured all of these points out but I do post them on our staff board:

- We want our staff honest with our players in everything we do.

- We want to have a strong work ethic in everything we do.

- We want to have established priorities.

- We do not want to leave out our personal health.

- We want to show poise under pressure.

- We must avoid swearing. Both the coaches and players do a good job in this area.

- We want our coaches to encourage and build up our players. We want them to be positive. We do not want to tear the players down.

- We want our coaches to be problem solvers and not whiners.

- We must acknowledge our mistakes. I make mistakes. We all make mistakes. Let us solve the problem and move forward. We want our kids to be able to admit they make mistakes as well.

- We want to strive to improve.

- We want to demonstrate compassion for each other. We want our staff to develop a feeling for the players. We want them to develop an attitude the staff loves them and cares about them.

- We are role models for our players. Players will learn more from our actions than they will from our words.

I will go over the next part fast, so bear with me. I am going to cover some of the aspects of the coaches' relationships with the players.

- Learn names of the players as soon as possible.

- Have compassion for the players. Be consistent, be truthful, and be honest.

- Build trust in the players.

- Develop great feedback with the players. We want our coaches working on every play. We want a positive ratio of 9 to 1 in feedback. It is like working with your wife; it should be 9 to 1 positive. If you can do that, you have a better chance of things working out for the best.

- We want coaching to be relevant, and not just "Hey, good job." We want to tell the players *why* it was a good job. We want to give relevant information.

- We want to sandwich a correction in between a positive.

- We hold kids accountable to doing things right. If we have to correct a person, it is better to do it privately rather than in front of the group. We are trying to build team chemistry and we do not want tear the player down in front of his peers.

- We do not coach by using "put downs" and by being sarcastic. If we make a mistake with a player, we need to be man enough to apologize.

I want to cover some "team building" things that we do. I will go over the different things we do and then I will show you a video of what we do.

We have a "hot dog and chili night." This is in the first week of pre-season practice. We are not like high schools where everyone knows each other. We have several new players each year. We used this as an ice breaker where everyone could get to know his teammates. We are trying to be more relationship oriented. We do not have scholarships so we needed to retain our players. We had seniors organize the big night and ran everything. It worked out very well for us. We invited some parents and we had a silent auction.

Here are some of the things we have fun with during the pre-season and we use a few of these fun games during the season.

We have a game we call "blob tag" which I will show you in the film. We have "hand fighting" where the players stand nose to nose to see who can knock the other man off balance. We do "finger dagger" which you will see in the film. We have "sumo wrestling" which has nothing to do with football but is a lot of fun and the players get a kick out of doing it.

We have a "swimming olympics." We have a "big splash contest." We have a "feet-first relay." We have a "medley relay" and no one on the team can do the butterfly stroke. In addition, we have a "synchronized swimming group." They come up with their own rendition of the act they are to perform for the night. It is a fun night.

We have a team council where we give the players an opportunity to provide us with input on the team. The earlier we can get the seniors involved in providing leadership, the better we are going to be as a team. The seniors can provide team leadership in conditioning drills before the season starts.

In the off-season, we have a senior—coaches—summit. We have the players select goals, come up with slogans, and list ideas of how we can build the team, and what we can do to improve the team.

We do some silly things to work on team chemistry. It has been fun for us. At times when we get to the middle of the season, we have to come up with some new games and new ideas to keep the players interested. We want kids to care and relate with each other. We think this is how we build team chemistry.

Thanks again to the high school coaches of the state of Oregon. Thank all of you for helping us.

Mark Mangino

PLAYS TO SLOW DOWN THE PASS RUSH

University of Kansas

Thank you very much, I am happy to be here today. In our first two years at Kansas, we broke almost every offensive record at the university. However, our defense has made the most strides since we took over. This year we did not do as well offensively. The fact that we used four quarterbacks because of injury was part of the reason. I think we set a NCAA record this year. We had a quarterback hurt in the first half in three consecutive games.

At Kansas, we do not get the best offensive linemen. We have to do things to counter fast and physical defensive fronts. We slowed the defensive line and cut down on their aggressiveness by using screen passes. After looking at our offense, we decided we had too many screens and draws. We condensed them and coordinated them with our trap game.

We do not have big, offensive linemen—and they are not very athletic—but we are successful on offense. We move the football because of our mentality of keeping the defensive fronts off balance.

On offense, we force the defense to defend the entire field. We try to get the number advantage in the box so we can run the football. We want to run the ball and run it well. When the defense fills the box with defenders, we go to our screens, three-step, and five-step passing game. We use the five-step concept to keep the safeties deep and make the linebacker drop. In our offense, we operate about 75 percent of the time from the shotgun formation. We want to attack the entire field and make sure the defense has to defend that area.

To pass the ball effectively, you have to protect the quarterback. Part of the protection theory is to use traps and screens to slow the defensive front down.

The first things I want to talk about are three keys to protection proficiency. We use "multiple launch points" for our quarterback. We use roll-out passes, bootlegs, three-step passes, and five-step passes to change the point from which the quarterback throws the ball. We never call three straight five-step passes because that gives the defensive front a consistent rush lane.

We have a base protection concept that allows for a "flexible number of protections." We have a system that allows us to protect with five-, six-, seven-, and eight-man protections. We take the aggressiveness out of the defense by "making the defense play assignment football." We are an option team and love to run it.

The first way to slow the defensive rush is with the trap play. We want to run the trap play into the reduced side of the defense at the 3-technique player. The trap controls the interior penetration of the defensive linemen.

There are definite advantages to running the trap game. The trap game gives the offensive linemen good blocking angles on the defense. The trap play has flexibility with multiple personnel groups and formations. It hits the line of scrimmage quick and tempers the penetration of the defensive line.

There are some problems to running the trap game. If the front is a double-eagle front or bear look on defense, we automatic out of the play. It is not a good play against those defenses. The offensive line has to recognize the front, know the numbers in the box, and be able to communicate.

We first installed this play with our four wide receivers set. However, we run it from any formation. On this play, the offense has to control the backside end. We have that capability in a number of ways. The tight end can take him in a blocking scheme. We have three options we can run at him. We have the ability to read the backside end and pull the ball if he closes.

The next part of the scheme is the actual mechanics of the trap. In the diagram, we are in the shotgun set. We can run the play from one or two backs in the backfield. I feel the best way to run the play is from the I-back set. In the diagram, we do not have a tight end in the box area.

We want to run the trap to the reduced side of the defense at the 3-technique player (Diagram #1). The onside tackle is responsible for the onside linebacker. He steps with his inside foot and takes an inside angle as close to the 3 technique as possible without running into him. The linebacker steps up when he reads the blocking scheme. The tackle comes flat and puts his nose on the inside number of the linebacker. All we want him to do is get a stalemate on the linebacker.

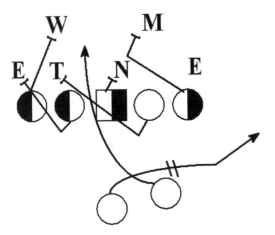

Diagram #1. Trap

The onside guard influences the 3-technique player by taking a quick set as if he were blocking for the three-step pass. We want to influence the 3 technique to start to lift his head on a rush pattern. The onside offensive guard traps the 5-technique defensive end. That is a hard block because the tackle does not set to influence the defender. The

tackle took a tight angle to the linebacker, which makes the defensive end squeeze the play. The worst thing that can happen to the guard is for the defensive end to get inside his block.

The toughest block in the trap game is the center's block. I coached the offensive line for a long time and every line coach in America has a different way to block the cut-off block. Our center was 6-0 and weighted 285 pounds. We'd tell him to step with his right foot and get his head into the far armpit of the shade nose guard. That gives him a chance to get his head in front. He must snap his hands up as quickly as he can, get them on the near rib cage of the nose guard, and run his feet. The center has to get his eyes up. If the defense has some kind of game on, he has to wall off the nose guard.

The backside guard is the trapping guard. I have changed my thinking about the steps of the pulling guard. It is not natural for players to open with the near foot in the direction they want to go. The guards with good feet take a jab step with their far foot, turn, and run. I tell the guards to run through the rib cage of the center, trap with his nose on the far numbers of the defender, and keep the feet moving.

If the trap defender runs upfield, the offensive guard does not worry about his head position because the defender has run outside of the play. However, if the influence by the onside guard does not fool the defender, the trapping guard has his work cut out for him. He has to be ready for a collision. The pulling guard does not know when the contact is coming when he pulls. We tell the guard as he pulls, he must be ready for a collision the moment he leaves his stance.

The backside tackle has a tough block. He has the backside linebacker, who aligns inside of him. He has to get to him quickly because the linebacker heads downhill as soon as he sees the pull of the offensive guard.

The quarterback is in the shotgun set. He makes the play look like the weakside zone play. The quarterback puts the ball into the running back's pocket and reads the backside defensive end. He runs the play like a veer read. The running back is two feet away from the quarterback on alignment. He steps in front the quarterback's feet and makes a pocket to receive the ball. His aiming point is the onside leg of the center. He looks for movement and hits the A gap.

That is the way we run the trap from the double slot formation. If the defense plays a double-eagle front, we check out of the play and go to the three-step pass (Diagram #2). We run all hitches for the receivers.

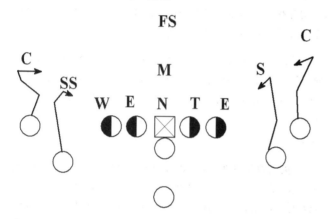

Diagram #2. Double-Eagle check to three-step

If the defense goes to a 55/33 front, we check to the inside zone play. A 55 front puts the defensive ends in 5 techniques with a 0-technique nose guard. The 33 front has 3 techniques to both sides. There is too much confusion on the outside to run the trap play.

The wide receivers on the trap play have to block for the play to be successful. From the double slot formation, the receivers run the defenders off using vertical routes. As they run off, they adjust to an outside shoulder alignment of the defenders. If the strong safety sits down in his cover, the backside slot player blocks him at that spot. If he retreats, the slot bypasses him and runs what we call a "backside stovepipe" to the free safety.

If you become successful at running the trap, the weakside linebacker will start cheating back into the box. When we see that, we run a "switch pattern" for the receivers on that side and throw the ball (Diagram #3). The wide receiver comes

down tracking the outside linebacker. The corner reads that move as a crack back block and follows the wide receiver. The wide receiver continues on to the post route to keep the free safety out of the play. The slotback runs up the field and wheels to the outside deep. We can automatic to this play and catch the defense flatfooted.

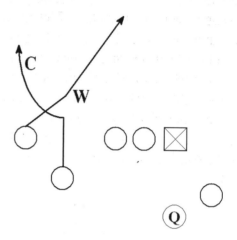

Diagram #3. Switch pattern

On occasion, we use the switch route rather than the four verticals to keep the secondary out of run support. The teams in our conference do not hesitate to put seven defenders into the box against four wide receivers. They play a man-free coverage and dare you to throw the ball.

Another play we use from this scheme is the "dart play." This play is similar to the trap except the backside tackle pulls instead of the guard. The dart brings the backside tackle up on the frontside linebacker. We run the dart play for two reasons. It gives us counter action and controls the pass rush of the defensive end. This is important to us because we play against the type of defensive ends that get to play on Sundays. Our tackles are tough kids, but not good athletes.

We want to screw around with the defensive ends and run some games on them. In a pass formation, the defensive ends have their ears pinned back coming off the edge. We trap the defensive end. When the end starts looking for the trap, the offensive tackle can run him up the field. It helps our offensive tackle by slowing the attack of the defensive end. This is the only way we can be successful on offense at this time. We have some good linemen that are developing and we signed some good junior college linemen. By using these types of techniques, we get a chance to throw the football and be effective.

We run this play from one or two backs in the backfield (Diagram #4). The "Queen set" from the shotgun has a split two-back look. The onside back goes first and sprints to block the defensive end to the backside. His aiming point is the inside leg of the backside offensive tackle. If the defensive end follows the tackle's pull, the back has to get inside leverage and block him. If the linebacker blitzes, the tackle traps him. The back reads the block of the tackle and takes his cut to the inside of the block of the tackle.

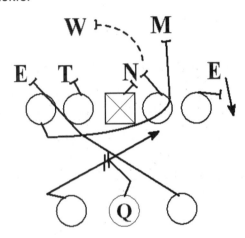

Diagram #4. Dart from Queen set

The tailback to the backside keeps his shoulders square, shuffle steps away from the hole, and starts downhill. He meshes with the quarterback and takes the ball. His aiming point is the outside leg of the onside guard at the snap of the ball. He follows the pulling tackle. The coaching point is to keep the back off the tackle by at least a good yard so he can read the back of the tackle on the linebacker. He gets on his outside hip as he turns into the hole.

We run the dart play at the shade nose tackle. We get a double-team between the center and onside guard. The onside guard looks for the first thing inside of him. When our offensive line becomes more accomplished, we will knock the

nose tackle off the ball. However, right now we use an upright combo block on the nose tackle. The center and guard step like a three-step pass protection. They get hip-to-hip and combo block the nose tackle. If the backside linebacker tries to run inside to the A gap, the center comes off and blocks him. If the linebacker tries to come over the top to the B gap, the guard comes off and blocks him.

The onside tackle turns out on the defensive end. He turns out and kick-steps outside and uses a five-step pass drop technique. We hope the defensive end runs upfield in a pass rush. If the defensive end starts upfield, the tackle uses his momentum and runs him upfield.

The backside guard drive blocks the 3-technique tackle. He cannot pass set because the backside tackle is pulling. He steps with his inside foot to prevent from getting cross-faced by the tackle. He cannot give up the inside leverage on this play.

The backside tackle steps with his right foot, aiming for the heels of his offensive guard. I do not care if he takes a little shuffle step to get his hips turned. The backside tackle pulls with enough depth to read the onside linebacker and get his hips turned. That depth is about a yard behind the double-team block. If the linebacker attacks downhill and the tackle gets too flat, the only thing he can do is trap the linebacker. He wants to turn into the onside B gap, and attack the outside two thirds of the linebacker. We want outside leverage on the linebacker.

If we call the play, the handoff is predetermined. If we tag the term "read" onto the play, the quarterback reads the defensive end. If there is no safety rolled up and the defensive end chases down the line of scrimmage, the quarterback pulls the ball and runs to the backside. He slides both hands out to let the tailback know he has the ball. If the quarterback slides one hand out, the tailback knows he runs the ball.

We can run the play the play two different ways from the one-back set (Diagram #5). If the defensive end is closing down the line, we send the one back to block him. That part of the play is like the two-back scheme. However, in this phase the quarterback fakes the tailback, pulls the ball, and runs into the B gap following the tackle pull. If the defensive end plays backside for the bootleg or quarterback run, we can run the play another way. If the end is not chasing down the line, the tailback takes a counter step toward the quarterback, receivers the ball, and runs the dart play.

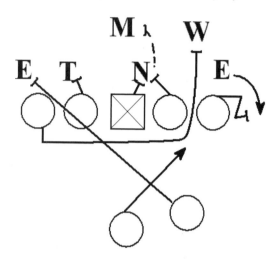

Diagram #5. Dart from one-back

The wide receivers on the dart play run the same technique they used on the trap play. They run off the defenders attacking their outside shoulders. If we read the secondary cheating into the box, we run the switch pattern.

Too many coaches come to clinics and talk about plays that work every time. They do not warn you that things can go wrong with the play. That is what we do with our players. The quarterback has to recognize the front and know what play to check. If your quarterback cannot do that, you cannot be successful with this philosophy. Line twists are a problem for this play. However, if a team is using line twists, it means they are not confident that they can handle you by playing straight.

We must control the backside end by using a tight end in the box or the quarterback reading him. The quarterback has to be smart. When teams read the backside end, the defense rolls the safety up to take the quarterback. The quarterback has to see both the end and safety. That is extremely important.

We could run this play from under the center,

but the design of the play is from the shotgun. The timing of the play is not the same from underneath the center. We do not run the play from underneath the center.

The second way to slow the rush of the defensive ends is to use the screen game against them. If your offensive line cannot match up to the defensive personnel you play, the screen game is something you should consider.

When we throw our three-step passing game we use a slide protection with it. That means we slide the offensive line to the right or left and put our back on the outside man on the line of scrimmage away from the slide. When we run our three-step game, the defensive line comes off the ball, gets their hands up, and tries to knock the ball down. Putting the running back on a defensive end is a mismatch in our protection scheme. The screen can help him block a defensive end.

We can run the screen out of any formation. We call it an investment play. Once you burn the defense with the screen, it slows their aggressiveness. We handle the squeezing of the box by using the same automatics we used in the trap and dart game. The play has three-step tempo. You must be able to account for a linebacker or safety outside the defensive end.

We throw the "rip screen" to the right side (Diagram #6). The offensive line slides to the left in their pass-blocking protection. The tailback attacks the defensive end to the right side. He stays high and blocks the defensive end near the numbers. We do not want him tangled up with the outside number. The tailback carries him upfield and slips off inside the end. He falls into an area one-and-a-half yards outside the offensive tackle and one-and-a-half yards deep. He makes the defensive end think he has beaten him. He has to set his feet and become a good target for the quarterback.

The frontside tackle in his slide protection has the B gap. He slides to the B gap and blocks the defender in that gap. If there is no defender in the B gap, he slides to the inside, counts two, and climbs for the frontside linebacker. He has to take a good angle to get to him.

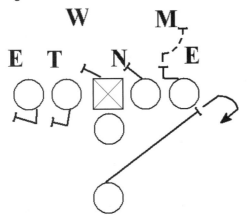

Diagram #6. Three-step rip screen

The frontside guard has the same technique. He is responsible for the A gap. He slides to the A gap and blocks the defender in that gap. If there is no defender in the A gap, he slides, counts two, and climbs to the frontside linebacker.

The center, backside guard, and tackle, block their normal slide protection away from the call. That is exactly the way we run our three-step protection when we throw the ball. The difference is that no offensive linemen leave the line of scrimmage.

If the quarterback is under the center, he takes three steps and throws the ball. If he is in the shotgun, he takes a rocker step, freezes, and throws the ball.

In the diagram, we run the "Liz Screen" against a 4-1 defense (Diagram #7). The screen blocking against this defense is easier. There are five defenders in the box as opposed to six.

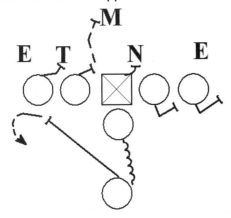

Diagram #7. Three-step Liz screen

The three-step passing game is a big part of our offense. That is why the three-step screen is also effective. The perimeter blocking on the screen is important (Diagram #8). The outside receiver to the side of the screen runs off the defender in man coverage. If the coverage is some type of zone, he has to stalk block on the defensive back. The inside receiver runs past the strong safety and stovepipes the free safety on the trap and dart. On the screen, he cannot bypass the strong safety because he is at the point of attack. He runs at him, breaks down, and stalk-blocks.

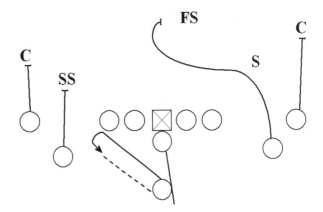

Diagram #8. Perimeter blocking versus cover 3

The backside slotback runs a stovepipe to the free safety. He gets on his outside number and blocks him. It is essential for him to stay on his block. The backside wide receiver uses a stalk block on the backside corner. Against a cover-4 defense set, the outside receivers stalk block on the corners (Diagram #9). The slot receivers make the safeties believe they want to get deep. They break off their patterns and stalk block on the safeties.

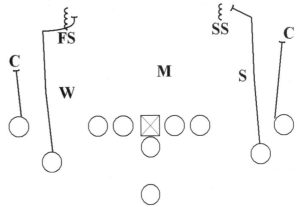

Diagram #9. Perimeter blocking versus cover 4

We also run the five-step screen play. We can run this screen from any set we have. The five-step game takes longer to get the ball thrown. To slow the rush, we use the screen (Diagram #10). The offensive line blocks their five-step protection scheme.

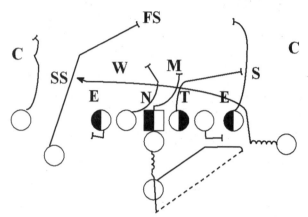

Diagram #10. Five-step right screen

The frontside tackle pass sets and invites the defensive end upfield. He tries to get him five yards deep. If the defensive end drops and no one crosses his face, he goes after the end and blocks him. If the defensive end pinches, he passes the end to the guard and goes after the flat defender.

The frontside guard pass sets and blocks the man over him for one count. After the count of one, he throws the defender upfield, releases outside, and blocks the flat defender. If he gets a pinch from the defensive end, he takes him and stays with the block.

The center blocks the A gap defender, which in most cases is the nose tackle. He stays with his block for the count of one and releases for the frontside linebacker. If there is no playside defender, he holds for a count of one and gets up on the onside linebacker. If the nose tackle uses a spy technique, he stays on him and blocks.

The backside guard is responsible for the backside linebacker. If he has an A-gap defender on his inside, it is a tough block. He has to pass block him for the count of one and release on the backside linebacker.

The backside tackle executes his pass block as usual on his assignment. He does not have an active part in the screen. He has to keep his man off the quarterback.

He is a two-by-two formation with a tight end to the screen side. The tight end's rule is to get upfield and seal the free safety. We run the Z-back on what we call a "Z Shallow." We bring him in motion and he runs a shallow crossing pattern. We throw the screen from where he came. The motion alerts the linebackers to a crossing pattern. They get involved with passing the cross to the next defender and lose the screen play.

The backside slot receiver runs a stovepipe block at the free safety. If the safety runs away from him to the screen side, the tight end blocks him.

If the quarterback is under the center, he takes five quick steps. If he is in the shotgun, he takes three steps. He looks opposite the screen and starts to drift. He locates the tailback and throws him the ball.

The tailback sets up on his pass responsibility in the protection. He pulls out into the tight end area on a count of 1001. He does not release until the frontside guard moves into his downfield blocking scheme. He catches the ball on the run and thinks boundary first.

We screen away from the trips set (Diagram #11). We crack the wide receiver on the Will linebacker. The center blocks the frontside A gap and releases for the flat defender. The frontside guard climbs up on the backside linebacker with the backside guard.

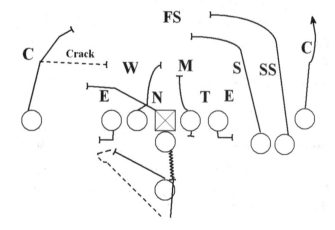

Diagram #11. Five-step left crack

I want to thank you for your attention.

THE NO-HUDDLE SPREAD OFFENSE

Bowling Green State University

Thank you for the introduction. I want to talk about our offense and some of the things we did that helped us to become a better team last year. We led the country in third-down conversions. There were many reasons for that. That is a huge deal for us. Our defense has a goal to be successful on 40 percent of the third-down plays. We averaged four yards per run on offense, which gave us a 55 percentage.

I am going to talk about our spread offense and our running game. When most people think about the spread offense, they think about throwing the ball all over the yard. The last two years we have had a runner gain over 1,000 yards each year. We were the only team in the country that had 4,000 yards passing and a 1,000-yard rusher. We are going to run the football. Two years ago, we were second in the MAC in total rushing offense. We are going to run the football and we are going to run it efficiently. It is not about how many yards we get; it is about how efficient we are.

We scored a touchdown 66 percent of the time when we reached the red zone. When you get in the red zone, you must score and we teach that to our players. On Wednesday, we work on the red-zone offense. On Thursday, we work almost exclusively on red-zone offense. We spend a lot of time on our red-zone offense.

We averaged 26 first downs per game. We had five plays of over 20 yards or more per game. We do not stress the big plays. We are not worried about the long plays. Those things will happen if we are doing the other things right. We have to find a way to make big plays.

I will give you some of the running plays we use, but I want to go in the direction of the "no-huddle offense." I want to give you an idea of where we

come from in our thinking. We like to use the no-huddle offense. That is what we do. That is who we are. It is not something that we just dabble in occasionally. Here is why we use the offense.

First, it is about controlling tempo. Being an offensive coach, I have a problem allowing the defense to dictate what plays we have to call. I do not like to call plays just to get us out of a bad play. I want to dictate to the defense what they can do to our offense and what they cannot do to us on offense. That is our mind-set. We want to control the tempo and I will cover that later.

Using the no-huddle offense gives us more time in practice. We signal the plays to the offense in practice. We can run a ton of plays. We get several reps in practice. Our practice tempo includes several reps and we get it going very fast. Practice is a lot faster than games as far as the tempo is concerned. When we get in a game, it is slow to our players because the officials have to set the ball ready for play.

We tell our offensive line and receivers to lineup and conserve energy until we signal the next play. They like it when they do not have to go back to the huddle on each play. They like setting up at the line of scrimmage and ready to go. We conserve a lot of energy doing this simple thing in a game. The defense still has to go through all of the things they usually have to do.

The two-minute offense is no big deal to us. That is what we do. The difference is that we are stopping the clock. Therefore, we are used to running the two-minute offense. That is who we are.

Running the no-huddle offense, it minimizes defensive packages. We do not want the defense to be able to call everything they have in their defensive package. If we force the tempo, it limits the defense on what they can use against us. We want to simplify what the defense can do against our offense.

We are able to look at the defense and call the play. At the start of the 25-second clock, we can look at the defense to make a decision on what play we want to run. We can call the play from the box down to the sideline or we can actually call the play from the sideline.

Our offense is different for the defense. They must hurry to line up and be ready to set their defense. They must hurry to get set against our offense. We want them to play defense for 25 seconds of the shot clock. As soon as the whistle blows for the 25-second clock, we want them to be ready to play defense. We may snap the ball in the first few seconds when we line up on the ball. We can let it run down to 15 seconds and then snap the ball. Or we may let the clock run down to the last couple of seconds and snap the ball just before we get a delay of game call. We want to force the defense to concentrate for most to those 25 seconds. We do not have that many players that can concentrate that long. Our offensive players know when we are going to snap the ball. That is how we are going to control tempo.

Our offense fosters communication skills. It does not matter what you think; the players still have to get the job done on the field. It is the ultimate team game. Coaches may actually have less to do with what happens on the field in football than they do in baseball or basketball. In football, players must communicate. We practice the same way as we play the game and the players must concentrate in practice to know what is going on with our offense. Our defense has to be on the field with their players in practice to get them lined up in the proper positions. The offensive coaches are off on the sideline signaling the plays in to them. They must communicate in practice as well as in the games.

I know kids want to spread the field and throw the football. In our offense, it is not just one man

getting the football. It is not just one receiver on the boundary sideline that is going to get the football all of the time. Our four wide receivers had 50 or more catches each this past year. I told you we had a running back that gained over 1,500 yards rushing. He also caught 40 passes. We spread the ball around and we throw the football to more that one receiver.

There are negatives to running this type of offense. You need to know these points and you have to work on them. The first negative is that we are limited in what we can run on offense. We cannot do everything running this offense. I have studied several programs and I have visited several different schools looking at the things they do on offense. It amazes me to see some big-name schools that run a play in a game and have great success the first time they run the play and they never come back to the play again in that game. I have seen teams that have run 70 different plays in a game without duplicating a single play. To me, that does not give continuity to your offense. However, you have to minimize the plays you can run from the offense we use. Players can only get so many concepts down for the games.

We know we are going to have communication breakdowns. You are going to have them. You must negate the possibilities that you are going to have those breakdowns. We still have a player that misses a signal. We may have a player miss the direction he should have gone. The quarterback can miss a call on the check off. We understand this and we must live with it and go on.

The other drawback is that we have to be secret about our method of signaling the plays to the quarterback. We may have two coaches giving signals and we can have another player giving the signals. Only one person is going to be giving the live signal. The other two people giving the signals are dummy calls. That is how we beat the secret aspects of the system.

Our system must have unifying principles that are simple and identifiable. The system must use common words and they must be easy to say. We use words such as city, state, color, numbers, or mascot.

It can be what you want them to be. It is your terminology. We want to use short, one- or two-syllable words. These words may represent blocking schemes, formations, plays, and other information.

The signals should be distinct and they should follow a pattern. They must mean something to the players. A lot of the time we have the players make up their signals. Our wide receivers get different signals than what the quarterback, running back, and tight end get. It means the same play but the signal is different

The system is the same today as it was three years ago. It is the same system. We build on it and we subtract from it. If you can keep the same system for four years, the players should be good at the system by the time they get to be seniors.

We want the signals to be simple and through so the players can play without thinking so much. We want to keep it simple, yet give them some flexibility in the system. We want them to be able to focus and play, and not think so much.

If you get anything from the lecture today, this would be the point I would consider worthwhile. If you were thinking about running the no-huddle offense, these would be the reasons why you should run it.

Our no-huddle offense consists of five phases. It is important to know why each phase of the offense is used. We can use these phases anytime during the game. First, I want to talk about our procedure on the line of scrimmage. I am not going to give you the exact detail of how we call our plays, but this is how you implement the phase.

The quarterback will be responsible for alerting everyone for the change in tempo. We are going to change the tempo as we go up and down the field. The quarterback will always give the play to the offensive line. We are not going to ask those five big bulls to look to the sideline to get the signal on the play. The quarterback will tell the line the play.

The receivers and tight ends get the information from the sideline. As soon as the previous play is over, they start looking to the sideline to get the

signal where they are to line up and what the play is. The quarterback gives the snap count to the offensive line. All of the receivers, including the tight end, must watch the football.

The first tempo is what we call our "sugar" huddle. We are three to four yards behind the ball. The line faces the football. The quarterback can line up in front of the line or he can actually line up behind the line. It is a normal "sugar huddle." We do not use this very often. We use it when we are milking the clock, or trying to slow down the game.

The second tempo is our "fastball." We line up and run a play in any formation in our offense as fast as possible. The quarterback calls out "fastball, tastball," and everyone lines up as quickly as possible. He does not have to give them the formation because they know the formation from the signal from the sideline. The quarterback only has to tell the linemen a few words. He may call out to the linemen, "read right, read right," and that is all they need to know. We can snap the ball on a regular count or we can go on a fast snap count.

We want to go as fast as we can when we call fastball. We can change the formation on fastball. We can call "right to left" and change the formation but we are going to do it as fast as we can. We want to catch the defense looking to their sideline to get their defensive signal and we run the bubble off the back door. We want to create those for the defense where can take advantage of those type of situations. We want it very simple so we can run the plays.

Our third phase is our "super fastball," or a "two-minute offense" tempo. We line up and keep the receivers on the same side of the formations. We are going faster and we are going to snap the ball as fast as we can get set. We can call "smash - smash" and the line knows what we are doing. We snap the ball and away we go. Again, the receivers stay on the same side of the formation.

The next phase of our tempo is what we call "glance." Now, I am not going to give all of our codes or signals here today. They will get back to our opponents fast enough. This is how we do this tempo. The quarterback calls any play and we line up on the ball. He continues to go through his signals for a set amount of time on the 25-second play clock. When the play clock gets down to about 18 seconds, the quarterback and the receivers all glance over to the sideline to get the signal for the play we are going to run. We snap the ball with three or four seconds left on the play clock and away we go. That is our simulated glance tempo. We want the defense to get use to the fast and then we slow it down. We call a lot of our offense from that tempo.

The next thing we do is to simulate check. It is the same thing. We go "fastball, fastball" and then the quarterback calls a color. That alerts the offense that we are not going to go on a quick count. The quarterback may call out "red - 15, red - 15." Then the quarterback looks to the sideline and if the play is what we want he will call the snap count, "Go." We are snapping the ball at 14 to 15 seconds on this tempo. We do not want to give the defense a chance to reset their defense.

In our tempo, we can snap the ball from the beginning of the play clock all the way down to the end of the 25-second clock. We want the defense to show what they are going to do and we want them to play defense all the way through the 25-second clock. Now, it is like shooting fish in a barrel.

The offensive coordinator is in the press box and he can see what the defense is doing while we are waiting for the defense to line up. As soon as he sees how the defense is going to play us, he can look at his chart and make the best call for that situation. It gives the quarterback a chance to look at the defensive rotation and figure out what is going to happen on the play. Our quarterback could make the all without looking at the sideline based on what we have worked on in practice for that week.

We have four base running plays. I may not get all the way through the four plays. We have a "read" play, which is our zone play. It is a zone read play. We have the "speed option." We have a "trap" play and we have a "rep" play. I will only have time to cover the first three plays. We run these plays in a one-

back set. We run the zone plan in our one-back and we run our zone plan from our empty set with our quarterback. We run some of the other plays out of the empty set. We can run the trap with our one-back set or we can run the trap with our quarterback running the "two-trap."

First, I want to talk about our zone plays. I am coaching with the best offensive line coach I have ever coached with in my coaching career. He is phenomenal. He does a great job with our zone plays. On our zone plays, we must be able to run the plays out of the spread look with a tight end or without him. We must have the flexibility to run the play with or without the tight end.

We can do the same thing without a tight end. We have a covered principle and an uncovered principle. It starts outside. If the guard is uncovered, he helps the tackle. The tackle is going to make the call. The guard can make a call to override the tackle.

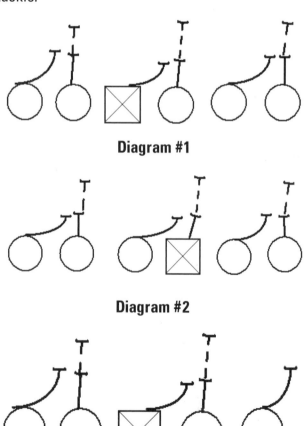

Diagram #1

Diagram #2

Diagram #3

If the guard can come outside and help the tackle, he is going to make the call. That tells the tackle he has a block with the guard. It is the same when the tight end is in the game. If the tackle cannot go help the tight end, then the tight end has the man one-on-one. The rules are very simple to follow. Our linemen can play any of those positions because they know the type of blocks to use on the line. We could play them at any of the line positions if we had to do that. We are going to play our five best players at those line positions. If a player gets hurt, the next best player is going in the game.

Our first play is "14 read." We are running this to the playside. The deep-back is set at five and one half yards deep (Diagram #4). He lines up over the offensive tackle. Last year we went to big splits in the line. If the tackle splits wide, the mesh point is a little different. We give the back the freedom to adjust on the play. He must be three steps to the mesh point. He has to have a feel for that mesh point. We work on mesh point everyday with our backs. We do ball handling everyday. We run "14 and 15 Read" everyday in our individual period.

Our quarterback lines up with his toes five yards deep. He is slightly ahead of the running back. He catches the snap, takes a rocker step, and rides the tailback as he comes through the mesh area.

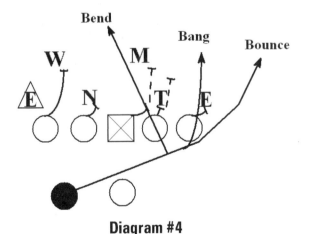

Diagram #4

Everyone up front is zone blocking. It does not matter if we have a tight end or not, we are still blocking zone. The key to the play is the tailback. He must get two steps past the mesh. He takes three steps to the mesh then he must go two steps toward the line to set the blocks up for the linemen up front on the linebackers. He must make the linebackers move.

The back has to make the play go. After he sets up the play with the two steps past the mesh, he must make a decision on where he is going to run. He can bounce it, bang it, or he will bend it back. He reads the first covered lineman past the center and then his eyes must expand after that. He gets as close to the tackle as possible before he makes the cut. We use the term "bend back," but it is more of a bend up on the cutback. That is what we do for the tailback.

The tailback must be patient on the play. The closer he can ride the tail of the tackle, the better the play will be. He must allow the play to develop and that takes time. At the very last minute, he breaks the play to the open area.

If the tailback breaks too quick, it makes it tough for the linemen to block their man. It is the responsibility of the tailback to set the blocks up for the linemen.

As long as we have five defenders in the box, we are going to block five defenders. We see six defenders in the box most of the time. We see some type of shade with six defenders in the box. There are two things we are concerned about when this happens. First, if you are in a 4-2 front we are going to block the six defenders near the line and read the outside man with the quarterback (Diagram #5). Everyone else blocks zone. The quarterback must determine if the defensive end can make the play at the point of attack just behind the tackle or on the line of scrimmage. If the end can squeeze the play down enough, the quarterback must determine if he should pull the ball or not, or if he is going to give the ball to the back on the zone play. It is the same as if you were running the triple option. It is no different.

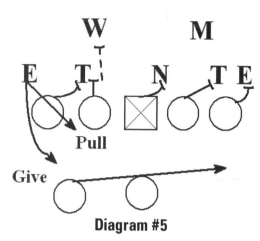

Diagram #5

This is what I tell the quarterback. One, width is more important to judge than depth or turning the shoulders. If the end can squeeze the play down and stay inside with his shoulders square to the line of scrimmage, he can stop the handoff. If the end comes up the field and does not squeeze the play down, he may not be able to get back inside to stop the play. We tell the quarterback width is more important than depth. It is more important than how much he turns his shoulders on the play.

The other thing we tell the quarterback is to read the eyes of the defender. The quarterback is not responsible for the mesh. The back is responsible for the mesh. If the quarterback can see the end's eyes looking at him, he gives the ball to the running back.

The other thing that we see is the odd alignment. As long as there are five defenders, we are going to block five defenders (Diagram #6). That is easy.

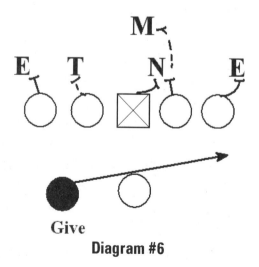

Diagram #6

Normally on the perimeter, if we are running "14 read" and we keep the ball against the six-man front, the slot man blocks the second defender off the line of scrimmage. He does not know if the quarterback is going to keep the ball or not. It is straight zone block for the H-back (Diagram #7).

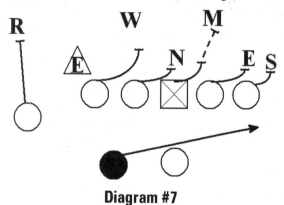

Diagram #7

The other thing we do is to run the read play and tag it with the option. Now we do not block the end. If the quarterback sees the end is outside, he is going to give the back the ball on the zone play. If the call is a read and the end stays outside, the quarterback hands the football off on the play.

If the end comes down inside now, the quarterback pulls the ball and comes outside toward the end. We said we do not block the end on this play. Now the quarterback is going to option on the end (Diagram #8). That is another way to incorporate the read or the option.

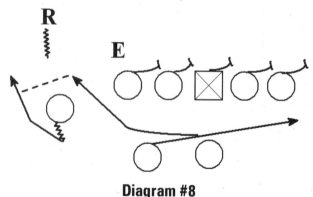

Diagram #8

I will cover a couple more things on the option play. The offensive line inside is still running our zone schemes that we talked about before. This is our equalizer. We check to it when we expect the blitz, or when we are in the red zone. We can run it with or without a tight end.

The big key is this. The tackle and the end receiver must both be on the same page. The first thing we want to do is to option the end man on the line of scrimmage (Diagram #9). If the defensive end is not coming, the tackle drives to the Will. The outside receiver is going to cruise upfield and check to make sure the tackle has taken care of the Will linebacker. If the Will is blocked, the receiver takes the next man that shows.

If the linebacker is wide, and there is someone else backing the blitz such as the strong safety, then the tackle is not going to drive for the Will linebacker. He can see the strong safety has a chance to blitz. The defensive end lines up tight. He is coming inside. We still want to option the end man on the line of scrimmage. Now we option the Sam linebacker. Now we are going to "gang" it.

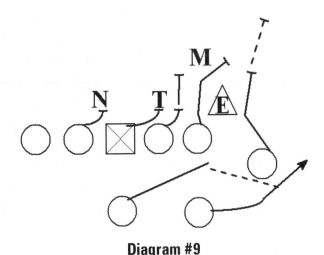

Diagram #9

The receiver sees the same thing. Now, we "gang" the play down the line. We pitch off the end man and away we go on the speed option. If the tackle is in doubt about what to do, we tell him to gang the play.

We can run the play with a tight end in the game. He has the same rules as the linemen. We still want to pitch off the end man on the line of scrimmage. Now it is just one hole removed for the play.

The end works upfield to the linebacker. He may not get the linebacker. He may end up blocking on the safety. We want to get a hat on a hat.

This is how we approach the pass protection. We have principles to cover the blocking. We work

on this from day one in the spring and fall. We have a period where we are going to work on the quarterback checking to as many bubbles as we can. That is the first thing we are looking for.

We go through the following things in checking to the play we want to run. Our thought process at the line of scrimmage is this. First is the bubble route. If our inside receiver out-leverages the defender over him enough to catch the bubble pass and run away from him, we are going to check to the pass and run it.

The second principle we apply is to check the second level defender (Diagram #10). If the defender is 10 yards deep, we will audible to a buddle call. We can check off to the play from the shotgun or from under the center.

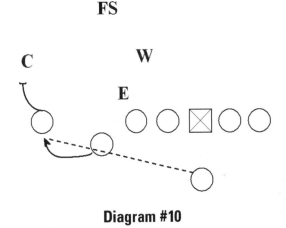

Diagram #10

We would like to run everything from the shotgun, but that does not always happen. The bubble is a lot quicker if we run it with the quarterback under the center.

If the quarterback is under the center of the bubble, he is going to crow hop back and throws the ball. He gets rid of the ball very quick.

The receiver has a normal alignment with the inside foot up. He opens and crosses over, and then starts downhill. He must know he is going to get the ball a lot quicker if the quarterback is under the center than he would if the quarterback is in the shotgun. The quarterback wants to throw the ball to the front shoulder of the receiver.

If the quarterback is in the shotgun, the pass is going to be slower now. That means the receiver is going to change his route on the play. Again, the quarterback takes the long snap and crow hops. He wants to get his momentum going toward the receiver. He wants to get the ball out to the receiver as quick as he can.

The receiver knows the quarterback is in the shotgun so he knows the pass is not going to come as fast. The receiver must adjustment his alignment. It is not a big adjustment, but he does back off and gets a little deeper. His first step is an open step. The second step is a crossover step. On the third step, he continues laterally on the route. He wants to stay on the same path as before. We do not want every receiver running the route differently.

If the receiver is "uncovered," it is different for the receiver. At the snap of the ball, if there is no first level defender on the receiver, we run the play the same as we do on the bubble. If the second defender is over 10 yards deep, we run the bubble. The quarterback and receive must be on the same page. The receiver opens up his shoulders and turns his head toward the quarterback as he comes off the line. The quarterback must deliver the ball immediately on the snap. We call this awareness. If the quarterback does not throw the ball to the receiver, he must continue on his step on the route called.

We go over the different defenses we see and give the quarterback the responsibility of making the decisions on throwing the bubble or not. He has a couple of things to consider in making his decision to throw the bubble or not. He must consider down and distance. On first and second downs, we will show the "awareness" no matter what the defense does. On third down, he must decide if the receiver will be able to get the first down or not. We do not give the receiver the choice to run the route or not. We let the quarterback determine if he is going to throw the bubble pass or not.

The third consideration is the "hitch" route. It is the easiest throw in football. We will throw the hitch route to any receiver as many times as we can all the way down the field. We are going to throw the hitch route as many times as we can. It does not matter if we throw it to the field, to the boundary,

or in the middle of the field. If it is an inside hitch we want the receiver to run five steps, turn around, and catch the football. We will continue to throw the hitch until the defense comes up and takes it away from us. When they do that, we go to some of our other plays in our package.

Our players know we are going to have a period each day where we work on the three principles. We work on the bubble, the uncovered, and the hitch routes.

I touched on running certain concepts a bunch of times. We want to run a few things and run them well as opposed to running a large number of different plays all over the place. We ran some form of four verticals over 100 times. Our players got good at running four vertical routes. They knew the adjustments on the routes. We are going to run four verticals as many times as we can.

The basic premise of the four verticals is to stretch the field. The two outside receivers are going to be at the bottom of the numbers. For the two inside men their alignment is two yards outside the hash marks. That would be on the high school hash marks. The back runs a "dump" route over the middle of the football (Diagram #11). We are going to have someone in the middle so the quarterback can dump the ball off if he is in trouble.

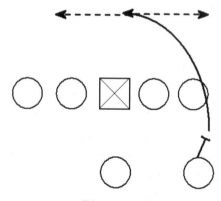

Diagram #11

We do a couple of things a little differently. The outside receivers are going to run a vertical route. If the outside receivers cannot beat the defender by 12 yards, they are going to run a drop out at 15 yards. This keeps the defender from turning and running up the field as hard as he can go.

The two inside receivers are going to get on their seams and run the route deep. That is an easy throw if there is only one safety playing deep. If there are two high safeties playing, we want to have one of the receivers run a "bender post route." It is a post route back into the middle of the field. Normally that bend receiver is our straight side receiver. He is going to run the post back inside.

If we are running 60 protection, which is six-man protection, the back can stay in and block on the play. If we have 50 protection, it is a little different. The read for the quarterback is important. He knows how far his drop is going to be. He knows his movement key and what he is looking at, and he knows he has a progression on the read. For all of our routes the quarterback has those three points to consider.

We work against the safeties. We go one high safety, or two high safeties. The quarterback looks at the two inside seams if we get only one safetyman. He looks the safety one way or the other. He is going to throw the ball to the open seam receiver. If the seam is not open, he reads the outside receivers. If they are not open, he looks for the back on the route. Those are the reads for the quarterback.

If he reads a "two high safeties", he looks for the "bender" receiver. He looks for the inside post and then to the outside fade route, and then to the back. Those are his reads with two deep defenders. He is going to read the safety to the boundary side. It could be "bender," "drop out," and then the back. Those are his progressions.

The last look is our three-by-one deep look in the secondary. We have our "all go" routes called across the formation. This tells certain receivers they are on certain landmarks. You will have to determine that with your terminology. Normally we are working shortside to the wideside of the field. Against the three-by-one, if it is a one high look, the read is the same. We read the free safety one way or the other and read the inside seams, to the drop out on the side the quarterback looks toward, and then to the back on the "dump."

Let me go to our empty set. It really gets interesting in this look. Between these two concepts, we threw the four vertical routes over 100 times. We are still going to set the receivers on their landmarks. We call a receiver's identity tag and throw him a special route. We still have the two deep routes on the outside, and we have the two inside receivers on the seams. The called receiver runs a simple "jig" route (Diagram #12). The receiver running the jig route comes across inside. He slams on his brakes, comes back outside as if he is going to run a pivot route, and then he works across the field. He has some parameters in this area. If no one comes outside with him, he can settle and look for the pass. If the defender goes with him on the pivot, he comes back underneath to the inside and look for the football. That is the jig route.

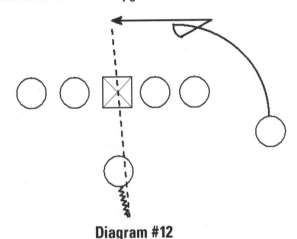

Diagram #12

The quarterback is still reading four verticals. Now his reads are a little different because he has to read the jig route. If it is a one high look, he is still reading the seam or the free safety. He looks one way and throws the ball back to the other side. If he does not throw the ball to the inside, he still has the man on the outside on the drop out route, and we have the man on the inside on the jig route. If we face two high safeties, we still have the bender route deep. He is reading bender to jig and then to the drop out route.

The movement keys are the same for the quarterback. It is no different for the quarterback. He has thrown the pass over 100 times, so it is no different for him.

Let me show the tape on our passing game. If you have questions, I will be out in the exhibit hall. My time is up. Thank you.

READ, READ OPTION, AND SHOVEL PASS

University of Florida

When I was recruiting in Florida (as an assistant coach at Notre Dame), I had to drive to Lake City, Florida, to see a recruit. As I was driving up the interstate, I kept seeing exit signs to Gainesville. One after another, the Gainesville exit signs came up. I had a couple of hours to kill before I got to Lake City so I decided to go see the stadium and the campus at the University of Florida.

I pulled off the interstate to go to the stadium. I parked my car and walked on the University of Florida campus on the way to the stadium. I waked on the campus in the middle of January and I saw all kinds of students engaged in different activities. If you have been to South Bend, Indiana, you know you would not see that in January at Notre Dame. The students at most campuses I visited at that time of the year were not very happy. At the University of Florida, everyone was walking around in golf shirts and was having fun.

I walked into the stadium. At other college stadiums, you find a padlock on the stadium gates because they are closed when not being used. I went into the stadium and there were people in the stadium running around in the middle of the "swamp." It was in the middle of January and they were having a great time. I walked down the stadium steps, and walked out on the field. I walked to the 50-yard line. My heart rate increased and the hair stood up on my arms. I called my wife and told her, "This is the place." This is the best place to be in college football. The reason I say that is simple. I am so happy now because I can recruit the kids in Florida and tell them to come to Gainesville.

I am excited about being the coach at Florida. I know you are supposed to stay calm, cool, and collected when you talk about the school where you coach. Nevertheless, I am excited about the coaching staff we have and I am thankful for the opportunity that I have to coach at Florida. This is the job; this is it. Some of my friends asked me if I was interested in coaching in the pros. I think the Miami Dolphins have the best offensive coordinator in the game today in Scott Linehan. I have visited with him over the years and I have a great deal of respect for him and many other professional coaches. I do not want to coach professional football.

The head coach is the person everyone looks to in all phases of the football program. I want to say a few things about the academic situation. That is the job of the head coach. Everyone is counting on us as a head coach to see that the athletes get an education. That is part of the hard job as a head coach. The little things are the hard things to accomplish. You have to make sure everyone on the staff does their job. The head football coach should have control over everything. I am in my third job as head coach. If our assistant coaches "suck," we will not be here very long. If our academic support system is not good, we will lose our players. They have been terrific after two-and-a-half months. We have a new weight staff. We have a good training staff and we are re-doing our entire training room.

My advice to you is this. Get your hands on everything that involves your program. If they touch the players in any way, you need to get control of them. If they are exposed to the players, you need to know what they stand for and how they work with the players.

One thing I have learned from some fantastic coaches that I have worked under is the fact that everything is systematic. The way we do things and how we operate is very systematic. This is the way we plan things. The perception versus reality is something else. Some people think we run the "Star Wars offense." They think we do not pay attention to special teams and that we do not pay a lot of attention to defense. This is our plan to win football games. For the last four years, we have used this plan and it is a plan to help you win. It is not something we just scribbled down on a chalkboard. We do not list 18 different things that we have to accomplish. When you are dealing with kids, you cannot keep their attention after you get going.

We have four keys to winning. Every day in our program we are involved in these four keys. Everything associated with our program revolves around our fundamental plan to win. We expect our players to know this plan. Every pre-game talk we relate to the keys to winning. Everything we do we base it around these keys. It may get boring but that is tough. This is how you win with time. It is time tested; it is has been proven. When I talk about the spread offense, it fits into these keys.

Four Keys to Winning

- Play great defense
- Teach to force turnovers
- Score in the red zone
- Win the kicking game

The first key is to play great defense. Many teams say this but never do it. This is how we play great defense. We never put our defense in bad position. I say never, but that is our goal.

When we talk about our players, I like people to break down what they are saying about them. If it is broken down, I will know exactly what they mean. Here is an illustration of this point. This is a statistical analysis of what happens in the course of a game or in a season.

A team will only score three times in 100 tries when it starts behind it own 10-yard line. If you drive a ball for a score and you start inside your own 10-yard line, you are only going to score three percent

of the time. You are only going to score three out of 100 tries. What does this tell us?

If we receive the ball back behind our 10-yard line, we need to be aware of the statistics that I just talked about. We want to make sure we do not turn the ball over. We are not going to be afraid to punt the ball when we are inside our 10-yard line. We can play great defense and that should lead to a better field position on the next series.

A team will only score 10 times out of 100 tries when they start from the 20-yard line. That means nine out of ten times teams do not score points from this field position. That is a big advantage.

You can see what happens when we cross the 50-yard line. We have a much better chance in scoring.

If we have the best defense in the world and we start turning over the ball deep in our end of the field, we have problems. I know this may sound like Football 101, but your players must really understand this point.

We do not want to put the ball on the ground and give the opponents a short field. When we get out to the 50-yard line, we can open up the offense and run some great plays. We have a "hook and ladder" play in our offense. In one of our staff meetings one of the bright assistants asked, "Why don't we run the hook and ladder coming out from the 20-yard line?" I told him we do not run that play when we are behind our 20-yard line on our end of the field. We run it from the 16 going in for a score. Even if we turnover the ball, it is worth the risk to run that play when you are going for a score.

The second key to winning for us is to teach the defense to force turnovers. This is how we teach this technique. We teach the players the proper techniques in holding a football. We teach them to cover the point of the ball and to squeeze against the rib cage. We have added one thing that some teams do not teach. We teach them to lock the elbow down to their body. When we get into traffic, we want them to take the meat hand and secure the ball.

All of our coaches teach this the same way. We do not have one coach teaching it one way and another coach teaching it another way. If a player puts the ball on the ground in practice, we get personal. In a game, if we see the ball is starting to come away from the ballcarrier's body, we take him out of the game before he fumbles. We do not want them to develop bad habits. If we see a loose ball, you are out of the game. If we see a loose ball from the quarterback, he is out of the game.

The next point is to score in the red zone. In our practice sessions, we spend as much time on the red zone as we do anything else. I think that is one reason we are good on offense. We work on our red zone package in spring practice. Then we finalize it in the summer. In the training camp, we go over the different areas of the field. We review plays from the 10- to 15-yard line, and the 20- to the 25-yard line, By the time we get down to the red zone we take over from there. By the time we get into the season the quarterback knows what we are going to do because we practice it so much.

I have been on teams where we did not practice much on the red-zone offense. They would tell me we run our base offense in the red zone. That is not what we want to do in the red zone. We want to be able to run the ball because we have four downs to get the first down. In the red zone, there is no vertical stretch because the defense is up tight on the receivers.

We have been very good in our kicking game. We have been sound in everything we do in the kicking game. The kicking game is an important phase of our keys to winning.

I do not want to bore you but, once again, those are the fundamentals of our program. Those are the four keys to winning for us.

I want to get to our top three plays. I want to cover our read play, our read option, and our shovel play. On perception versus reality issue, there is controversy as to who we are. Some teams refer to our offense as being wild. The shovel pass is not a wild offensive play. Everyone may think it is a wild

play but the room for error is very small on the play. If the back does not catch the shovel pass, it is simply an incomplete pass. It is not hard to explain. We are not a "Star Wars," wide open, gimmicks offense. We are similar to a single-wing offense. We work very hard in getting the football snapped to our quarterback on the off-tackle power play. We do not think that is a wild offense. We run the shovel pass with power blocking. We run the play from the spread formation because we can run the play with only five or six defenders in the box instead of nine or ten in the box. We take great pride in the fact that we are a ball control team. This is something I evaluate. Earle Bruce said it best. He said, "Offensive football is a ten-yard game. You need to win each game." That is the mentality of the game.

We are a "run first" team. We averaged close to 250 yards running per game last year, and we averaged close to 250 yards passing. We are a balanced offense particularly for our red-zone offense.

Why did we put this type of offense in our system? I think this is interesting. If I had my choice, we would have been a wishbone team. We understand some of the fans do not like this type of football. As the head coach, I know we must put fans in the stands. Still, I love the type of offense the Air Force runs. When I was at Bowling Green, the teams we played had better players than we did. The offense we ran gave us our best chance to win that first year. We did not run the wishbone but we did use several of the concepts of the wishbone offense with our quarterback in the shotgun set.

Our offense is very difficult for the defense to prepare for in two days. Greg Mattison, our defensive coordinator, is working on our defense and he will only have two days to get ready for our offense. Each year we set up our offense in a way that will give defensive staffs headaches when they start preparing for us on Sundays. Here are the things we do to make it hard to prepare for us.

The first thing that comes up in those discussions is the option. Option football is a pain in the butt for the defense. Next, we run from an empty set four or five times a game. If you do not know what you are doing against our empty set, you will have a hard time defending us. We may run the empty set four or five straight plays in a row. The defense better be ready for this when they play us.

The third thing we do is to run from a three-by-one formation. What do the defensive coordinators do in those Sunday meetings? They get up and draw an I-formation set and line up the defense against that look. Then they draw a two-by-two one-back formation and make their adjustments. They go over how they are going to disguise the defense. They do not go over the true spread formation or the three-by-one formation. This is when we apply pressure.

We recruit the type of players that like our style of offense. Our style of offense motivates our players. It can be tough to go into the meeting room everyday to get your players motivated for practice.

It is hard to motivate players when they give a great effort and the play is not successful. The end makes a great block, the tackle seals inside against the linebacker and the running back makes a great cut, but the play only goes for two yards. By design, the play did not have a man to block the tackle sitting in the gap and he made the stop for a short gain. We tell our players, "If you do you job, we will score." That is motivation. We want the players thinking, "If I do my job, we can score." We want to create interest with our offense where the players want to share the ball. We want to spread the field to equate the numbers.

This is who we are. First, we want to be physical. Our offensive line must play physical. Why did we win 12 games last year? Our offensive line beat people up. Our offensive linemen go after you. We are aggressive and we are physical. If the ball is on the ground, the play is out, and if the ball is on the ground, the player is out. I do not want to hear them tell me that it will not happen again. If the ball is on the ground, they are out and they go to the end of the line.

When we get the ball in the red zone, we apply the pressure. We are not going to be satisfied to kick a field goal. That is not what coaches get paid to do. We want to apply the pressure to score a touchdown. That is who we are.

I am going to show you our playbook scheme. I am going to talk about the mechanics of the play. People do not know this but the first coach to use the read concept was Bill Snyder of Kansas State. This started back around 1993 when I was an assistant at Colorado State. They had an athletic quarterback and they would pull the guard and tackle, and run the counter. They would read the defensive end. If the defensive end chased the counter, the quarterback pulled the ball, kept the ball, and went down the field.

At the time, we had about 27 different running plays. We started playing around with the read concept. The plays we used on the read looked like crap because we did not work enough on the play. The play did not work for us and as a result, we dropped it from our offense and moved on.

A few years later, Northwestern and Clemson jumped all over the spread offense. The whole intent was to "read" one defender, and to equate numbers, and block the rest of the defense. As long as there is a safetyman in the hole and you equate the numbers, there is a chance you will run into the cover man. That is the reason we have to include screen passes and bubble plays in our offense to keep them honest. We want to force them to cover our outside receivers. We have several ways to force the defense to cover us on the outside.

This is the 14 read, which is the zone-right play, and 15 read zone left is the base play we start with (Diagram #1). In concept, this is a zone play. We run the play the same as most other teams run it. The exception is that we do not block the backside end. We read the backside end. We read the backside C-gap defender. It could be the end, or it could be a linebacker if they are blitzing. We are reading the backside C-gap defender.

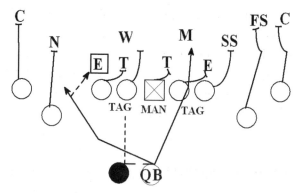

Diagram #1. 14 read

You can see several different defenses against most offenses. Against the spread offense, we only see the three following types of defenses (Diagram #2). We see the one high safety. It could be cover 1 or cover 3.

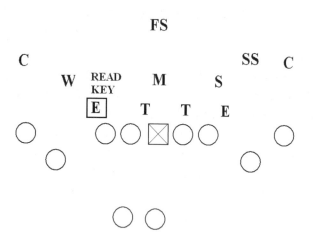

Diagram #2. One high safety

The other type of defense we see is one with two high safeties (Diagram #3). It could be cover 2. It could be quarter coverage with five underneath players.

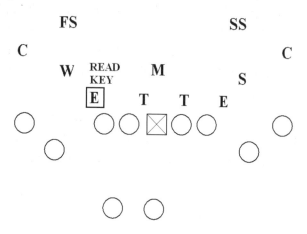

Diagram #3. Two high safeties

The third type of defense we see is with no high safety (Diagram #4). This is where defenses try to sneak someone back into the hole.

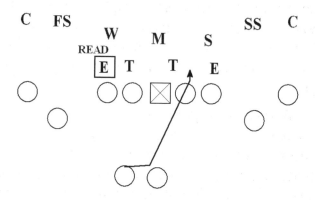

Diagram #4. No high safety

In 1997, I went to visit the University of Louisville. Scott Linehan was the offensive coordinator. We went down to Louisville to spend about four hours with them. We spent almost three days with them. We wore the same damn clothes for the entire time we were there. The Louisville theory was this: "We are going to run the ball at you. If you keep a safetyman in the hole, we are going to run the ball at you." If a team decides to stop the run, they must bring that safetyman up in the box. In theory, you are opening up the defense to a risk. If you do not have the deep safety, you have a problem.

We have a one high safety look. The defense is going to match up. They have six men in the box. We have five blockers in the box. In our style of offense, we are always going to read one defender. If we have five blockers and the defense has six in the box, we read one defender and run the ball. If we do a good job of scheming and we do a good job working and equate the numbers, we can run the play.

Let me go to the two high safeties. Teams are dreaming if they think they can line up and play cover 3 all day. They think they can rush four defenders and set back and defend with seven men. That is not going to happen. If a team plays two high, we may not throw a pass the entire day.

When it is third down and 12 to go, many teams believe you must throw the ball down the field 12 yards. We have to give the defense some credit.

How deep are the linebackers on third down and 12? They are playing 12 yards deep. They are playing two-deep coverage with five defenders underneath. Where are you going to throw the ball? We are going to run the ball and do the best we can. If we do not make the first down, we are going to kick the ball and play defense. That is our style of play.

Against two high, we are going to run the ball at the defense as often as we can. If you do not have success on third and 12 to go you should stay out of those situations. Get the first down on the second down and you will not have those third and 12 situations.

I was the "third down and 12 yards to go" coach at Notre Dame. When it came up third and 12 the offensive coaches would yell at me, "Coach Meyer, what do you want to call?" On the next day, or Sunday in the staff meetings, I would get my butt chewed out because we were not successful on third down and 12 to go. My reply was always this: "If the first down coach had done a better job, it would not have been an issue I would have had to deal with."

What does everyone on defense try to do today? They try to get an extra man in the box to stop the run. They want to be sound so they play cover down. The do not have a man in the hole. They have seven men in the box, we only have five blockers, and we read one man. They have one more man than we can handle. Now we must do something different. We call "no defender" to indicate the defense does not have a man in the deep hole. In our system, either we run option football at them or we find a mismatch for that equalizer. You can throw the ball if you find that match-up you want.

I want to go over the base-run play. I will give you the rules, but not so much for the line because I do not have time to go over everything with you on the line blocks. You can come see us if you want to know more on the line blocking rules.

Our quarterback toes are at five-and-one-half feet from the ball. The toes of the tailback are at six-and-one-half feet deep. The tailback is on the inside leg of the offensive tackle. He has his hands on his knees in a two-point stance. He is in a good football position. Our footwork on the play is this. We are going to run at the rear end of the right guard on 14 read. The back must set up the blocking for the line. The only way to do that is to get a slow read by the back. We want to get as many double-team blocks as possible upfront. That is a four-hour discussion and we do not have time to get into that today.

What we have come up with for the tailback is this. We open step, shuffle, shuffle, and then go. We want to go over the butt of the right guard.

The quarterback is extending his arms. If the tailback gets in a hurry, it forces turnovers. We want the quarterback to be able to get full extension on the play. We want him to get more width on the play. We want him to open up and read the defender. He must extend the ball and let the ball come through. We tell our quarterback if the end can tackle the play for two yards or less to pull the ball. When in doubt, the quarterback gives the back the ball.

The rule for the onside receivers is simple. We want their nose up inside the numbers. On the backside, we do a different type of block. Their only responsibility is if our quarterback pulls the ball and keeps it to their side. If the two defenders on that side pursue the ball on the "give", we are not going to chase them. We bide our time and stay outside. Many times the quarterback ends up with the ball, the defenders try to get back outside, we have the angles, and now we can block them. If the quarterback pulls the ball, he attacks the next defender outside.

On the trips set, we run the 14 and 15 read option. We start the slot man in motion and we pitch the ball to the motion man on the read. We want to keep a good pitch relationship with the quarterback and back in motion (Diagram #5). Again, we are reading the end.

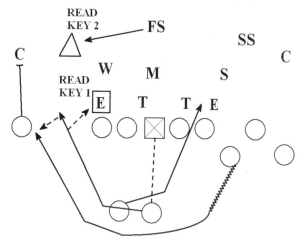

Diagram #5. Read option

On the 6 and 7 shovel play we have a read key and a pitch key. The quarterback must read the end and the second defender to show on the play. He can pitch the ball to the tailback, keep the ball on the run, or he can make the shovel pass to the back coming in motion.

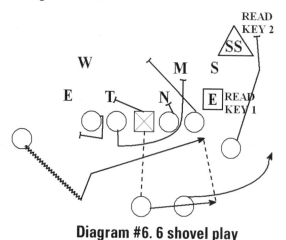

Diagram #6. 6 shovel play

You will see many different defenses and as a result, we have to be able to read that second defender. In our offense, we have built in misdirection plays. We felt as if we needed a counter play. However, we only have four run plays in our offense. We run them repeatedly so we can run them against most defenses.

If we want to run the play to the tailback, we make it look the same as we ran it before. We start

the slot man in motion until he gets to the position where the tailback would line up if he were the tailback on that side of the formation. After he gets to the area where the tailback would be lined up the ball is snapped. He reverses his position and looks for the pitch on the option play. Now the tailback is going to run the shovel route underneath (Diagram #7). The defensive end is the read key and the linebacker is the shovel key. We read the C gap and shovel off the D gap.

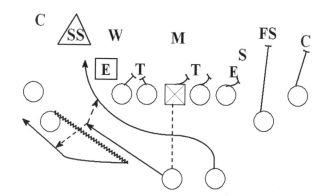

Diagram #7. 7 shovel play

In conclusion, let me say this. If you do not have a quarterback that can run this offense, you should not use it. Run what your quarterback does best.

Another point I want to make relates to the snap by the center in the shotgun. You have to work on the snap every day. When our snappers get through lifting weights, they still must go out and snap the ball 75 to 100 times. After two years, the snappers at Bowling Green State and Utah could snap the ball between the quarterback's numbers. At Utah, the center could put the ball between the two 1's of our quarterback, Alex Smith. His number at Utah was 11. After one year, they became better snapping the ball. They could lead our quarterback on the snap on certain plays that allowed the quarterback to get a jump step on the defense. The key is the snappers must work on the snap until it becomes automatic.

SUCCESS IN THE PASSING GAME

Miami University (Ohio)

It is good to be here. I have been traveling a lot this past week. Early in the week, I was in Japan for six days. I was there to speak at a clinic for John Pont. He is a former coach at Miami of Ohio and has coached in Japan for the last twelve years. I was in Atlanta yesterday and it is good to be back close to home.

Today, I will talk about the passing game. At Miami, we have been successful at throwing the ball. It helps to have a good quarterback. But it goes beyond that, because of the way we threw the ball this year with a new quarterback. I will talk about protections, routes, and a little philosophy.

We do many things in the passing game. I put a tremendous amount of responsibility on the quarterback. We try to take some of the responsibility off him in the running game. We run the inside zone play, the power, counter, the draw, and a little bit of speed option.

We do not try to do too much in the running game. We run four or five different plays and run them from each formation. We ask the quarterback to get us in the right play. We do not use too many "check-with-me" calls at the line of scrimmage. We give the quarterback a few audibles, but we try to get in the right call by formation. We ask him to do so much in the passing game; we do not want to bog him down with automatics in the running game. He has to know protections and conversion routes in the passing game. He has to check the protections and make good decisions when throwing a conversion route.

In the running game, we do not run things just to be running a play. We want to be successful in the running game; however, most of our adjustments come from personnel and game planning. There are a few times we let the quarterback check us from one running play to another. That is why we run the inside zone and power play. You can run those plays against almost any defense.

There are some factors to being successful in the passing game. The first one is to throw high percentage passes. We throw the ball a good deal of the time. It is important for us to throw the high percentage passes. I will show you about four or five different routes. We consider those patterns high percentage passes. We are fortunate to have good quarterbacks, receivers, and protection schemes. The scheme we use fits what we try to do. We played 27 games in the last two years. We played 14 games the year before last and 13 games last year. In 24 of those games, we completed over 60 percent of our passes.

When you throw the ball 30 to 40 times per game, 60 percent is a high percentage of completions. You have to find out what your high percent passes are. Not every quarterback throws the same ball or has the same strengths. Two years ago I had Ben Roethlisberger, who was extremely accurate. I was not limited with him. I could throw anything we had in our offense. The quarterback we have now, Josh Betts, is a good quarterback. He had a great year and threw for 3600 yards. However, I had to limit our offense and take some of the passes that Ben could throw out of the game plan. He probably has a stronger arm than Roethlisberger, but is not as accurate.

The second point is to throw on first down. The last two years we have been successful on offense. We broke down our offense and found we ran the ball 53 percent of the time on first down and threw it 47 percent. People see us as a passing football team, so we need to throw the ball on first down. Our goal is to get four yards on first down regardless of the play we run.

We like to throw the ball downfield to set up a second down and medium or short yardage situation. If we do not complete the pass, we have second and ten and that is still a running down for us.

If you throw the ball as much as we do, you must have a sound protection scheme. If you cannot protect the quarterback, you do not give your offense a chance to be successful. If you run only one protection, you limit yourself to what you can do. You do not have to run six or seven protections, but you need to be sound in the way you protect.

The first thing we do each week as we start to break down the opponent is to look at their blitz package. We list the formation we like, and which ones let the quarterback see the entire picture. Your formations have to allow sound protections against the blitz package of the defense. In our game plan, we want at least two different dropback pass protections. With those protections schemes we incorporate play-action passes, three-step passes, and bootleg protection schemes.

We want to be sound in protection so our quarterback does not throw hot all the time. If he does, you are asking for trouble. We are predominately a one-back team. One-back teams have to throw hot unless they keep the tight end at home in pass protection. We do not want a defender coming free every time, to force the quarterback to throw hot.

The fourth point in our success is to have an answer for the pressure scheme. I give the quarterback some audibles for each game. However, I will not have five or six. Having that many audibles requires too much practice time to perfect their use. The quarterback has one or two audibles for each game. In the passing game, the audible may be a check to a sprint-out pass. That gets the quarterback away from a blitz coming up the middle of the field.

The fifth point is to give your quarterbacks some outlets to throw the ball on each pass.

Situations occur in football that drives me crazy. One of those situations is the team who comes to the end of a game and has to throw the ball. They throw a two-man pattern with maximum protection. That does not make sense to me. In our drop-back passing game, we want to send out five receivers. The back or tight end may be checking a defender before they release, but we want them to release whenever possible. That gives the quarterback some outlets and somewhere to throw the ball. The quarterback has to know where his check-down routes are on every play.

In a perfect world, the quarterback has three seconds to go through his reads and pick out the open man. Realistically, the quarterback gets pressure early about one-third of the time. He has to dump the ball before he is ready. When the quarterback gets pressure, he has to know where the outlets are. The outlet patterns are the throwaway patterns. The quarterback does not want to throw the ball away downfield. If the outlet pattern is covered, at least the quarterback can throw the ball out of bounds.

The sixth point in the successful passing game is to be able to convert routes. We are not going to run a hitch or a quick-out into cover 2. If the receiver reads cover 2, he stems his release inside for about four steps. He pushes vertical to a depth of 12 yards. If the coverage is a soft corner, he runs the curl. If the coverage is cover 2, he runs a corner route. The best throw against cover 2 is the high throw into the corner, not the curl-flat combination. That is an example of a converted route. We do not want the quarterback throwing a hitch route into a hard corner.

If we have a deep post route called, we can turn that pattern into a streak. There is no sense in running a deep post into a cover 2 defense. When the receiver reads cover 2, he turns his post into a streak to widen the corner and get the safety off the hash mark. By doing that he can create and opening for someone else in the pattern.

The last point is to emphasize red-zone and third-down plays. We work on this situation constantly. In the red zone and on third down, the defense gives the offense some different looks. In a third-and-long situation, you get an all-out blitz or a maximum coverage with eight men. We do not practice on Mondays. On Tuesday, we work on base offense. On Wednesday and Thursday, we work extremely hard on third-down and red-zone situations with our quarterbacks and offense. That way the quarterback knows what defense he will see in each of the third down situations.

The red zone is probably the hardest place to throw the ball on the field. It is so constricted and the defense does not back up in their coverage. You have to hit them underneath and break a tackle or get behind them. You must practice these situations and practice them hard. When you get in game situations, the team will know what to expect. The absolute cardinal sin in the red zone is to turn the ball over on an interception. If you cannot get the touchdown, you want the chance to kick a field goal.

Four years ago when we installed this offense, we were primarily a spread offense. We had three- and four-wide receivers on almost every snap. That was particularly true during Roethlisberger's first two years. We have progress to the point where we are 60 percent shotgun and 40 percent under the center. When we go three- and four-wide receivers, we are in the shotgun. When we play with two tight ends and two backs, we are under the center. That simplifies our teaching. I do not have to signal shotgun if the personnel grouping in the game are three- or four-wide receivers.

For every rule, there is an exception. There are certain plays where we want the quarterback under center with three- and four-wide receivers. There are particular times we want the quarterback in the shotgun when we have two tight ends in the game. When we go to our spread formation, we see an abnormal amount of zone blitzes. Because of that, we favor the three-by-one or trips formation. Aligning in a trips formation keeps the defense from disguising the coverage. It makes them declare sooner and gives the quarterback more time to read. The defenders have to move earlier to get into position to play. Most of the routes I will show you are from a three-by-one formation.

Our best receiver will be the single receiver to the backside of the formation. If the defense tries to double the backside receiver, we will attack to the field or run the ball. In this formation the defense will show a cover-2 look, but normally go to cover 4. The free safety in cover 4 has to take the number-three receiver to the trips formation side.

Our favorite play is "Utah" (Diagram #1). The X-receiver on the backside runs a five-step man post. It is really a five-step slant pattern. He runs the pattern based on the leverage of the defensive back. If the corner is soft and head up, he runs the pattern skinner up the field. If the corner plays cover 4 and aligns inside, the receiver stems inside and flattens the pattern.

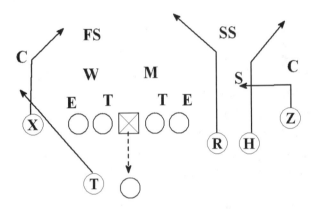

Diagram #1. Utah

The tailback aligned to the split end side runs a check-flat pattern. He checks the Will linebacker. If the Will linebacker does not blitz, he runs to the flat. In the protection scheme, the five offensive linemen are responsible for the four down defenders plus the Mike linebacker. The Sam linebacker is the defender we cannot block and becomes the hot read if he blitzes.

Defenses look for tendencies. A lot of the times we set our tailback to the wideside of the field. We run many zone plays into the boundary. Our number-one protection is the tailback double reading the Mike and Sam linebackers. When we put the tailback into the boundary, we need to make sure we are not throwing the football all the time. To break these tendencies, we call "Flash" (Diagram #2). The tailback sets to the field and on the snap of the ball he flashes to the weakside. His blitz check is the Will linebacker. It actually gives the tailback a better angle to block a blitzing Will linebacker. He does not take him straight up, but from an inside angle.

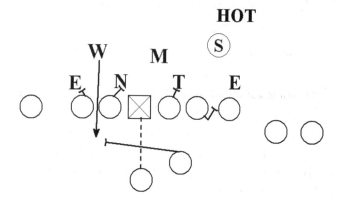

Diagram #2. Flash

We can tag the route of the tailback in the Utah pass. We call this "Utah T-wheel" (Diagram #3). By doing this, we can get the tailback matched on a linebacker going deep. If the corner pays too much attention to the split end, the tailback can get up the sideline.

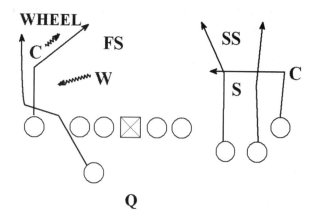

Diagram #3. Utah T-wheel

On the three-receiver side, the inside slot could be a wide receiver or tight end. His route is a vertical route splitting the hash marks. The outside slot or number-two receiver runs a six-step corner route. He breaks his pattern at about 10 yards and runs to a depth of 20 yards.

The Z-receiver runs an under route. He pushes to a depth of six yards, hesitates, and comes underneath. We tell him if the defender sits inside, he stops his pattern and stays outside on the

pattern. If the defender runs at him, he gets underneath the defender and continues to the inside on his pattern.

We do different things on the hot side, which varies, from game to game. We run all three receivers on hitch patterns. We run double and triple slants. We run the inside slot on his normal pattern and run the H- and Z-receivers on a flat-curl combination. The H-receiver runs the flat and becomes the build in hot pattern for the quarterback.

The quarterback reads the free safety. On this combination route, the ball could go to either side. There are certain routes in our passing game where the quarterback is strictly working one side. If the quarterback works one side, he reads the safety at the snap of the ball. It is too hard to read a safety, corner, and a linebacker.

We build combination route that can handle all types of coverages. The combination is a cover-3 or cover-4 route beater on one side and a cover-2 beater on the other side. The first thing the quarterback has to do is check for a hot read. If there is no hot read, he needs to find the weak safety. That is generally the safety aligned over the quarterback. That safety will tell the quarterback what type of coverage he is facing.

If the safety drops straight off the hash mark, the coverage is cover 2. If the safety sits or comes across the field at a flat angle, the coverage is cover 4. If the safety takes off to the middle of the field, the coverage is cover 3. We base our reads on the free safety.

On this pattern, the quarterback reads the hot first than looks to the free safety. If the free safety moves flat toward the X-receiver, the quarterback goes to the post by the inside slot receiver, or R-receiver.

If the safety runs to the middle of the field in a cover-3 move, we go to the X-receiver. He is one-on-one with the corner and the safety is gone.

If the safety stays and appears to double the X-receiver, the quarterback goes to the field side. His first look is to the post down the middle of the field.

We rarely throw the corner route into the wide field. The only time I tell the quarterback to look for the corner is in the red zone. The reason we send the two and three receivers on vertical routes is to hold the safety. Without the threat of the corner, the safety could jump the post route.

The quarterback takes five steps if he is under the center. If he is in the shotgun set, he takes three steps. From this pattern we adjusted and ran a choice route on the backside. We call "Utah X-choice" (Diagram #4). We run the same patterns on the frontside and tag the X-choice to the backside. The X-receiver cuts his split on this route. He runs an inside stem, pushes vertical, and wraps around the Will linebacker. The tailback checks the Will linebacker for blitz and runs a flare.

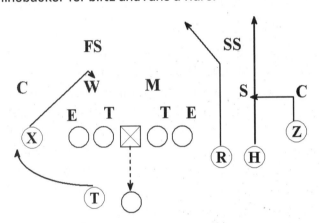

Diagram #4. Utah X-choice

When the Will linebacker drops into his zone, he keys the tailback. When he sees the tailback flare, he has a tendency to lose the X-receiver. The X-receiver takes advantage and wraps around the Will linebacker before he can find him. This is a great first-down route if you know the blitz is not coming. It is a short easy throw of 10 yards. The depth of the choice route is six to eight yards. The X-receiver replaces the Will linebacker in his alignment. We do not want the receiver to snap his pattern to the outside. Actually, the ball on the post and the X-choice arrive about the same place when the X-receiver catches them. The only difference is one pattern moves and the other is stationery.

We like this pattern against a 4-3 defense because the number-three receiver going vertical

holds the Mike linebacker. The pattern is not good against a 4-4 defense because there are two underneath players to the weakside. To the frontside, nothing has changed. We can run all the same combinations.

If we want to eliminate the hot read for the quarterback, you can run a two back protection. The R-receiver aligns in the area of the tight end and checks the Sam linebacker. If the Sam linebacker blitzes, the R-receiver blocks him and the quarterback does not have to read hot. You can align the R-receiver in the backfield or bring him in motion to his blocking position.

We played Toledo twice this year and they were a 4-4 defense (Diagram #5). If we play a team that plays cover 3 in the secondary, we run four verticals all day long. We could not do that against Toledo. They have very athletic outside linebackers. They were more like safeties than linebackers. They ran and chased our receivers' almost like man-free coverage. We wanted to run the X-choice, but Toledo presented a problem for us. To solve the problem, we went to a double formation.

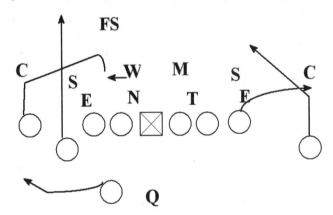

Diagram #5. X-choice versus 4-4

We brought the second receiver to the X-receiver side. If we ran the slot receiver deep, the linebacker ran with him and got depth off the ball. That put the X-receiver into the situation of working on one linebacker underneath.

If we want to run the same play to the other side, we call "Z-choice" (Diagram #6). To the backside, we can run a double slant, which takes care of the hot routes. To the frontside, we run the tight end vertical to take the linebacker deep and run the Z-receiver on the remaining linebacker. If the linebacker blitzes, he pushes upfield and looks for the ball. He does not wrap around to the inside because there is no one inside.

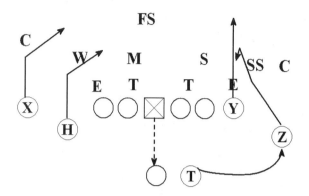

Diagram #6. Z-choice

When you are a one-back team playing against an eight-man front, there is a possibility of having both sides with a hot read. In our entire protection scheme, we protect the inside of the formation. We never hot read on a linebacker blitzing up the middle. In the game plan, we build in hot routes for each game. Against the Toledo's 4-4 defense, we ran double hitches and slants as our hot routes to the backside.

The tailback runs a flare route to the outside of the set. He open steps and loses ground to get some depth. He tries to get his shoulders square so the pass is easier to complete. He wants to catch the ball two yards behind the line of scrimmage running downhill.

The quarterback has to be on the same page with the receivers and the offensive line. When he comes to the line of scrimmage, he calls out the linebackers. He identifies the middle linebacker by his number and gives a direction call for the Sam linebacker. We run the no-huddle offense and communication becomes tremendously important. If the quarterback comes to the line of scrimmage and calls "44-Left," the offensive line knows the middle linebacker is number 44 and the Sam linebacker is on his left side.

That helps the offensive linemen identify their blocking assignments. In certain pass protections,

the linemen's assignment is to block the Sam or Will linebackers. They know the Sam linebacker is to the call and the Will linebacker is away from the call. They do not need to know the formation or the strength of it. The quarterback can declare a defensive back as a linebacker by his call. The quarterback points hot every play even if the play is a running play. If there are two hot reads, the quarterback calls the number and direction and points to both the hot reads. That lets the receivers know who the hot read is on every play. We do the same thing every play so we do not tip the defense to a pass play.

The next route is a conversion route. It is an elementary curl-flat route. We call this route the "fish" route (Diagram #7). We usually run this from a two-by-two formation. The outside receivers run a curl and the inside receivers run a flat. The tailback checks his blocking assignment and leaks through the line of scrimmage and curls over the ball. He stays inside and away from the outside patterns. The patterns to both sides are the same.

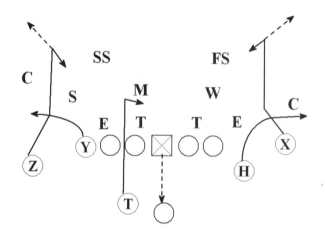

Diagram #7. Fish route

The receivers running the curl routes release to the inside and proceed up the field for four steps. The receivers do not want to get too flat. They must gain depth as they go up the field. After the fourth step, they go vertical to 12 to 14 yards. As the receiver releases inside the corner, he keys his movement. If the corner bails out of the flat coverage, the receiver continues his pattern and runs a curl route. However, if the corner stays outside in the flat, as he gets to 12 to 14 yards, he runs a corner route. That gives us a high-low pattern on the cornerback.

The quarterback reads the cornerback's adjustment. He reads the cornerback and knows the receiver will run a curl if the cornerback bails out and a corner route if the corner plays hard. If the quarterback gets cover 2, he throws the ball into the boundary. To throw a high ball into the wide side of the field gives the defense a chance to react to the throw and is hard to complete. The ball is in the air for a long time.

We tell our receivers, if the ball is on the hash marks, run the curl route into the wideside of the field. They do not convert the route to a corner route and run their curl routes regardless of coverage. If the ball is in the middle of the field, both sides are converting their curls to corners depending on the defensive reaction.

This pattern has built in hot routes to both sides. The flat patterns convert to hot patterns depending on the slide of the offensive front. If we ran this play against a heavy blitz team, we put the back on the wideside and hot the flat pattern into the boundary (Diagram #8). That is a shorter throw and easier to complete. Generally if a team blitzes, they do not play cover 2 behind the blitz. We do not have to worry too much about the corner rolling into the hot route.

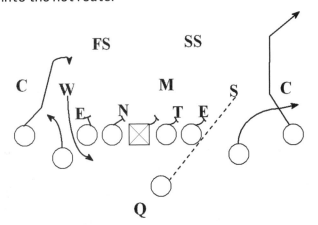

Diagram #8. Protection and hot route

If the defense is a cover-3 scheme, we look to the wide field for the curl-flat scheme (Diagram #9). There is more room to the wideside and the read on the strong safety is easy.

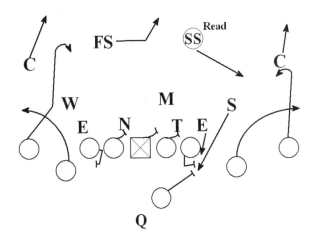

Diagram #9. Fish versus cover 3

Against a 4-4 defensive scheme, we want to throw the curl-flat to the wideside because it is a form of cover 3. The outside linebacker has flat to curl coverage into the wideside of the field. The read for the quarterback is the outside linebacker. If he runs to the flat, he throws the curl route to the outside receiver. If he retreats into the curl area, the quarterback throws the flat route. If he blitzes, the quarterback throws the hot route in the flat.

Teams do not play us in a cover-3 scheme when we are in a four-wide receiver set. If they play cover-3, we go to four vertical routes. The curl-flat and four verticals pattern are the best throws against cover 3. The high-low corner pattern or someone down the middle of the field are the best throws against cover 2.

We do not want to run the curl-flat pattern against cover 2. If we have that pattern called, we convert it to a high-low corner route, which fits that coverage. When the wide receiver stems his pattern inside, the cornerback squeezes, releases the outside receiver, and jumps the flat pattern. The outside receiver reads the cornerback and converts his curl route into a corner route.

Those are four drop-back passes we use every day. They are very simple and we run them out of different formations. We usually run the Utah and X-choice from the three-by-one set. We installed the Z-choice late in the year to combat teams who run the 4-4 defense. Toledo and Western Michigan both ran the 4-4 defense and we needed another adjustment to be effective against that scheme. We ran the Z-choice from the double wide-out set. The curl-flat is very elementary, but I wanted to show you how we converted the pass to fit the coverage.

We have a double screen, which is our main screen pass (Diagram #10). We only run the play one way because of our right-handed quarterback. It is a flare screen right to the tailback and a receiver screen left to the wide receiver. We can run the play from any formation, but we usually run it from the two-by-two set.

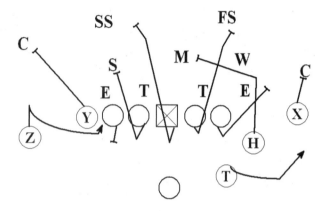

Diagram #10. Double screen right

The wide receiver to the right has the cornerback. If the cornerback is soft, the receiver runs him off. After the defender recognizes the play, the receiver cuts his pattern and uses a stalk-blocking scheme. If the cornerback is a hard cover-2 corner, the receiver comes off and blocks him. If the cornerback is a press corner, the receiver runs him off with a deep vertical pattern.

If the defense is zone coverage, the number-two receiver blocks the first linebacker inside the tackle box. He pushes upfield two steps and tries to pin the upfield shoulder of the Mike linebacker.

The rightside offensive tackle quick sets and opens the gate for the defensive end to rush the passer. After the defensive end passes, he comes flat down the line of scrimmage. He looks for the alley player. In the diagram, the Will linebacker is the alley player aligned on the inside receiver. The tackle wants to kick him out at the point of attack. The coaching point for the tackle is his angle to the flat. If he goes upfield too much, the alley player can beat him to the flat. If the tackle stays flat to the

line, he can kick the linebacker out or be in position to turn up and block.

The right guard quick sets on the man aligned on him. He holds for two counts and releases up to the next level. He blocks the inside linebacker first. If the slot receiver has the inside linebacker, he proceeds up to the free safety.

In a 4-3 defense, the center needs to check the Mike linebacker first and but has strong safety. He quick sets, goes through his two counts, and blocks the safety. If the Mike linebacker blitzes, he blocks him for two counts.

The left guard quick sets on the man covering him. He goes through his count and releases on the left alley player. That is generally a linebacker. In the diagram, it is the Sam linebacker.

The backside tackle sets and stays on his block throughout the play. He takes the backside defensive end. The tight end to the left side is the number-two receiver. He is responsible for the cornerback.

The wide receiver to the left takes two steps up toward the line of scrimmage. He works from there back behind the line of scrimmage to an area inside the tight end's alignment. He makes sure he is behind the line of scrimmage. If he drifts over the line, we have all kinds of linemen downfield. His path has to be two-three yards behind the line of scrimmage so the quarterback does not throw the ball over the line of scrimmage. The quarterback has to deal with the rush of the released linemen and cannot determine the line of scrimmage.

The quarterback takes his quick three steps and reads the widest rusher on the right side. If there is no blitz, it is the defensive end. If the linebacker blitzes, he is the quarterback's read. If the widest rusher attacks the quarterback, he dumps the ball to the tailback. We throw the ball from the shotgun so the quarterback can get depth and does not have to throw over anyone.

If the widest rusher takes the tailback, the quarterback drifts and hits the wide receiver screen to the backside. The good thing about this screen is the quarterback has a choice and not forced to throw the ball to one receiver. In a predetermined screen, the quarterback has no place to throw the ball away.

We have a jet screen to the wide receiver. It is a predetermined screen. We adjusted the play to give the quarterback something to do with the ball in case the defense reads the screen. We flare the tailback to give the quarterback somewhere to outlet the ball.

In some passing games, the quarterback has to have a strong arm to work the scheme. If you notice, these passes are not long passes and do not require the ball to be zipped to the receiver. These passes are timing patterns and conversion patterns, which come from recognizing the defense. I think quarterback play is 70 percent mental. If you take a quarterback such as Tom Brady, and put them in a quarterback completion, they would finish in the middle of the pack. However, their understanding of the offense makes up for their deficiency in their physical skills. A quarterback such as Tom Brady, can perform more effectively than the physically gifted quarterback, who has no understanding the scheme.

The fact we had Ben Roethlisberger for three years was a big factor in our success his last year. In his first two years, he struggled trying to pick up what we wanted. By the third year, he understood the system and everything ran smoothly. You have to build your system around what your quarterback can do. Ten or fifteen years ago in high school, coaches put their best athlete at tailback. In today's football, coaches are putting their best athlete at quarterback because they want the ball in his hands.

You need to build your offense around what your quarterback can do. If he is a passer and can make all the throws, you can do most anything offensively. At Miami, the last couple of years we had quarterbacks, who could make all the throws. If you do not have one of those guys, you must find the best five or six routes the quarterback can throw and work the game around them.

You must have a base set of passes. You cannot go game to game and keep changing things. We run the same passes game to game. We find different ways to run the same passes. The Z-choice pattern we ran against Toledo was that type of pattern. We had to find a way to run the same pass against a special defense. You want to put yourself in the best situation for the quarterback. The quarterback must be comfortable in the pocket.

If there is anything we can do for you, we are right up the road. Thanks for having me here and if we can help you, please let us know.

SPECIAL EMPHASIS ON SPECIAL TEAMS

University of Kentucky

Thank you very much. It is a pleasure to be here representing the University of Kentucky. My topic tonight is a very specific one. I think it will be interesting to special teams coaches, head coaches, and those who aspire to be head coaches.

Talking about the special teams is a boring topic. I coached special teams in the NFL for 18 years. The beginning of special teams coordinators in the NFL was in 1976, when George Allen was the head coach of the Washington Redskins. I will relay some things to you that reflect what I believe about football in the NFL. That will not be entirely *apropos* to you. However, if you translate what I say, it will be.

I am now coaching special teams in the SEC, which is different from coaching in the NFL to an extent. Coaching the kicking game in high school is different from the college level. Some of the things I consider important, I will relay to you. I think you can get some basic principles from my lecture.

In the game of football, one of every five plays is a kicking game play. I consider the kicking game to have seven levels of special team play. On each play in the kicking game, one or more of these three events take place:

- A direct attempt to put points on the board
- A change of ball possession
- A sizable amount of yardage is involved (40 yards of more)

If you are a good team, the ratio is about one in every six plays is a kicking game play. If you are not a good team, it is one in every four plays. The kicking game plays have the potential for big momentum swings both positively and negatively. Kicking game plays weight heavy as they affect the tide and the outcome of the game.

Many of the big "breaks" in a game occur on a kicking play. Breaks usually happen when a team or a player is unprepared for a situation. When a team is prepared, the chance to capitalize upon a break presents itself at the most opportune time. The kicking game breaks mark the difference in winning and losing.

In my opinion, the kicking game is relative to about 35 percent of the game. If we talk about the kicking game being one in five plays, that relates to 20 percent of the game. The momentum plays and the weight of the momentum in the kicking game is probably as important as the 1/3 offensive and 1/3 defensive plays in a game.

ELEMENTS OF A SUCCESSFUL KICKING GAME

Elimination of Mistakes

Most mistakes made in the kicking game are caused by a lack of belief in its importance. Lack of belief leads to a lack of concentration and from that follows poor protection, poor coverage, and slipshod application of the complex kicking game rules. *Belief in the importance of the kicking game is the key to elimination of mistakes.*

Intensity

Although intensity is essential in all areas of the kicking game, it is best observed in how you cover kicks. Covering kicks is one of football's great tests of courage. Intensity shows up in the return game in a team's commitment to physical play, yet never at the expense of the yellow flag.

Fundamentals

Kicking involves many precise skills. Time and distance requirements require *precise* skills and constant attention. Precision is attained only through practicing with concentration. Each special team skill can only be acquired through practicing with the speed and intensity of game conditions. There is *never* enough time to acquire all the simulation needed, so focus and intensity must prevail each time a skill is practiced.

It is difficult to practice the kicking at any level of football. It is difficult to do in the NFL because of the intensity with which the players play. It is difficult to do in college football because of NCAA restrictions on time. In high school, in my opinion, the quality of your kicker to an extent will not allow you to practice kicking effectively.

We have a kicking game philosophy that we use at the University of Kentucky. The philosophy of the Kentucky Wildcats special teams is to produce the greatest amount of field position possible on each kicking exchange. We want to use special teams as a weapon for producing this yardage as opposed to merely a unit for smoothly affecting the exchange of the ball in the kicking situation. Because the offense and defense will affect (and be affected by) the kicking teams, offensive and defensive philosophies should determine the specific philosophy of the kicking game.

The offensive kicking game philosophy is to gain the greatest field position and/or to produce the most points possible. *Elimination of penalties is vital to our success.* The defensive kicking game philosophy is to gain field position by limiting our opponent's returns. There must never be a protection breakdown. The punting team must think, "Get the ball out." They must think, "Turnover." The keys are second effort and reckless pursuit.

We consider the punt return and kickoff return to be the first play of an offensive drive. The field goal is the final play of an offensive drive. Defensively, the punt coverage team and kickoff coverage is big parts of the defensive philosophy.

The field-goal block team is the third phase of the defensive kicking game.

Each of the teams represented in this room tonight has the right and an opportunity to be good in the kicking game. There is no excuse for us to walk away from each season and not have a good kicking game. The move from good to exceptional requires some things to happen. To be exceptional rather than good, you must have a punter. You need a great snapper. You need to have a good kicker. The fourth element is a classy return man. To be exceptional in the kicking game, you need those four elements in that order.

In my opinion, special teams are a way for lesser or younger players to find a role in your football team. You have to do that in the NFL, but you can do it in college and high school and be comfortable. The one element you cannot sacrifice in the kicking game is speed. You cannot play with players in the kicking game that cannot run. If they can run, they need not be the best or toughest players on your team.

You can get a player to buy into a role in the kicking game and it becomes his special area. Players who are not ready to play on offense or defense will buy into a role in the kicking game.

I want to tell you a story. Probably one of the best players I ever coached in the kicking game played for me in the pros. We do not have this kind of player east of the Mississippi River. The player was a PAC 10 player from the University of California. His name was Jeff Barnes. He was a defensive player in college but could not play defense in the NFL because he never understood what was going on. He was a great special teams player and Jim Plunkett's best friend.

I coached 14 seasons with the Oakland Raiders. In 1982, the franchise moved to Los Angeles. We still practiced in Oakland but played our games in Los Angeles. We had not moved the team at that time and flew to Los Angeles each week for our games. One night we flew back to Oakland. Upon landing in Oakland while we taxied to the terminal, one of the wings of the airplane ran into a food truck on the runway. It jolted everyone on the plane and knocked some players out of their seats. The plane got quiet and from the back of the airplane I heard Barnes say, "Man, I'm glad that didn't happen while we were in the air."

One night we were at the training facility in Oakland and had a horrible electrical storm. It hit the power lines and everything went black in the facility. All the projector and lights went out throughout the building. From the corner of the room, I heard Barnes say, "Ah man, now I am in trouble. I've got a speaking engagement at 6:00 PM and my car won't start."

Those kinds of people can play in the kicking game if they can do two things. If they can run and understand how to get their fits into the particular scheme, they can play on special teams. I am not a big statistic person, but I think we lead the nation last year in blocking kicks. We had a player that blocked seven field goals this season. His name is Lonnell Dewalt and he is a freshman. ESPN ran a poll and they selected him as special teams player of the year.

He is a good player, but is not ready to play on offense. He is a wide receiver and is truly a phenomenal athlete. If you ask him what position he plays, he will tell you he is a kick blocker. Our offensive coordinator will have trouble getting him back as a wide receiver because he thinks he is a kick blocker. That was his role and he became a phenomenal player last year. I believe things like that can happen at any level of football. It is a place for people to find a niche and improve your football team.

There are seven areas of special teams. I will try to talk about six of them if I have the time. The onside kickoff return, or better known as the "hands" team, is the seventh area. I will start with the other six teams and talk about how we put them together.

I believe you coach against what you fear. In other words, you put in offensively what you most fear defensively.

FIELD-GOAL TEAM

The first area is the field-goal team. Our goal for this team is to make every kick we take. We install the field-goal team on the first day of practice and do not change another thing in that part of the game throughout the season. We have only one meeting with the field-goal teams a year. We meet the first day and that is all for the season. From the field-goal formation, nothing ever changes.

We spot the placement of the ball at eight yards from the line of scrimmage. I think it is a mistake to spot the ball at seven yards, even in high school. Kicks are blocked inside by a ratio of ten-to-one over kick blocks from the outside. Unless a team has an exceptional sprinter coming off the outside, you will never get a kick blocked from there. That is of course, if the snap, hold, and kick takes place in 1.35 seconds. In practice, we accept 1.4 seconds. The adrenaline will bring the time down to 1.35 seconds in a game.

We tell our kicker if they are faster than 1.35 seconds, they need to slow down and not rush the kick. If the kicker kicks the ball in 1.35 seconds, the ball will cross the line of scrimmage in 2.0 seconds.

In the offensive linemen's alignment, we ask them to squeeze upon the ball as much as they can. We do not want the defenders to get a big run to the ball. We want the linemen to see the ball. That is not hard for the guards and tackles, but the ends may have a slight problem. The holder calls "set." After that command, no one can move and the center snaps the ball when he is ready.

When the center snaps the ball, the line takes a short set step and gets their cleats on the ground as quick as possible. The next thing in field-goal protection is the target. We are not a man protection team. On field goal, we are a zone protection team. The linemen never move the outside foot. Make sure the linemen *never move forward*. The defender can jerk the offensive lineman forward using his momentum and create holes inside. The eyes tell the offensive linemen to get his pad level under the defense's pad level. That is the entire game in field-goal protection. The offensive linemen get their pad level under the pad level of the defense and deflect the momentum of the defensive linemen upward.

The only way the field-goal protect team can lose is for them to try to block someone aggressively. They have to take their set step and absorb the blow coming from the defense. They can never attack or hunt a defender. They have to hang on for 2.0 seconds. If they hunt a defender, we get beat. You have to convince your offensive linemen to get their pads under the defender and stun him. However, other teams do the same thing we do and it becomes a headache for your offensive line. They will get their bells rung.

In their alignment, we want them with their hand on the ground. The center gets down first and everyone takes his alignment off his stance. We align foot-to-foot with a wider stance than on an offensive play. The guards and tackles never move their outside foot.

The offensive ends on the field-goal team never move their inside foot. He has to stay square to the line of scrimmage because the C gap is the toughest gap to secure. The wingbacks on the field-goal team align at a 45-degree angle with one foot inside the outside foot of the tight end. The tight end drop sets a half yard with the outside foot and does what we call a pivot. When he drops his outside foot, he interlocks with the inside foot of the wingback. He punches the rusher in the C gap and catches the second rusher on his hip. The wingback does a ricochet block. He hits the second rusher coming off the tight end's hip with a punch to the chest and bounces out to get a hand on the outside rusher. In both cases, the block is a disruption-type of block.

This team never changes. From August 8 to January 1, these rules never change. We have a meeting on the first day of practice and do not meet again.

In the NFL, the goal post uprights are as wide as the hash marks on the field. College goalposts are wider than pro posts. Since I came back to college

football, I have learned one or two things. We play Georgia, Tennessee, and Florida every year. They have some major athletes that scare head coaches by the way they come off the corner. If you are worried about the wide field rusher on the field-goal attempt, bring the backside tackle over and go unbalanced to the wideside. Teams do not work on the short rush from the outside enough to hurt from that side.

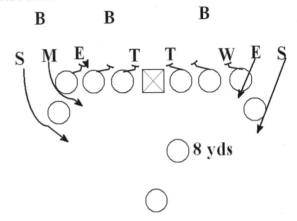

Diagram #1. Field-goal protection

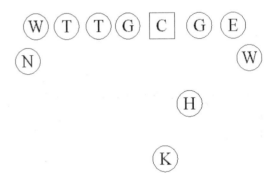

Diagram #2. Unbalanced to wideside

All they have to do is hold for 2.0 seconds. If they do, the game is over. All we ever talk about on field goal protection is "see the ball, quick set, and pads under." These things have to happen in front of the football. In my experience, in front of the ball is where the kick block occurs. There is a very narrow space where the defense can block a kick.

If the ball is on the right hash mark, the kick comes straight over the left offensive guard's butt. The left guard and tackle must be strong in their set and not get pushed backward. To protect the outside into the wide field, we ask our players to "cheat for inches." If the guard, tackle, and end get four inches wider in their stance, we can put the outside rusher one-foot further outside in his alignment. That means he cannot block the ball unless something goes wrong. Elements for blocking the ball from the outside are time and distance. Unless the defense has a stud speedster outside, they cannot get to the ball.

FIELD-GOAL BLOCK TEAM

Our goals for the field-goal block team are to block one kick or have the kickers not make 50 percent of their kicks. To block the kick, you have to apply the same rules to protect the kick. If we try to block a kick, we want to get ou.r blocker hands in the lane where the kick travels. For the kick to be good, it has to travel in a very small lane. Every kick block is designed for a point on the field where the ball has to travel to score.

Ninety percent of teams spot their placement of the ball seven yards off the line of scrimmage. The NFL kicks from eight yards deep. They know seven yards is too close to the line of scrimmage. We do not rush gaps. Rushing gaps is too hit-and-miss. We rush over a man on the offensive line. We align four defenders in the middle of the kick formation and sprint them as hard and as fast as they can go into the offensive linemen. We want the four players who have the ability to get off on the snap and sprint through someone for two seconds. They want to block the kick with the body of the offensive linemen. In this position, you could use offensive players. They will not block any kick, but they can cause huge headaches for the offensive linemen.

We look to knock the offensive lineman one yard back from his alignment. In 2.0 seconds, the ball crosses the line of scrimmage at a height of 11 feet. If we can knock the offensive lineman one yard off the line of scrimmage, our jumpers can try to block a ball at the height of 10 feet. If we can knock the offensive lineman one-and-a-half yards off the line of scrimmage, they cannot get the kick off.

We tell our jumper to get behind the four sprinters. When the kicking team snaps the ball, the sprinters take off and get as much depth as they can over the offensive linemen. We tell Dewalt that

he has two seconds to get as close to the four sprinters as he can and jump. He blocks kicks with his hands and can see the ball come off the ground. He steps into the vacuum created by the sprinters. If they get one-and-a-half yards, he can block any kick. If they get one yard, he has to get into the proper lane where the kick travels.

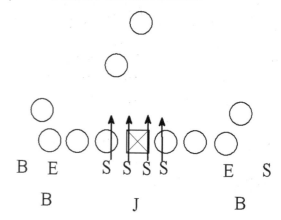

Diagram #3. Field-goal block

We align two of the sprinters on the inside shoulders of the center and roll him out of line. You cannot hit the center in the head, but we have never been called for this type of charge on the center. The other two sprinters align over the guards and blast them. Our best sprinter is a freshman by the name of Jason Leger. He is a 6' 1" and 283-pound player. He is built low to the ground and has a dynamite take off. He is super quick and tough as a pine knot. His chief goal is to stun the 350-pound guard and drive him back two yards.

That lane changes as the position of the ball changes. The jumper has to move to get his hand position in the proper lane. That is up to the coach to get his player aligned properly on the field. There is nothing more fun than the sprinter's position. The offense line cannot strike back. They absorb the blow, while the sprinters blast them.

Teams got to the point where they did not want to kick the ball against us. Twice last year, we had teams driving deep in our territory inside the last 30 seconds needing a field goal to win the game. It happened against Tennessee and South Carolina. South Carolina was down by one point and Tennessee was down by two points. Neither team wanted to try a field against us. Most teams milk the clock down to nothing and kick the ball as time runs out. They took the chances on scoring touchdowns instead of going for the field goal. Against Tennessee we blocked two field goals and against South Carolina we blocked one.

If we cannot get penetration from the guards and tackles, the jumper cannot get the ball. Eleven feet is too high for the jumper. If we can knock the lineman off the ball, we can get them all. If we do not block the ball, it is because the ball goes through the hands or under them. That is our field-goal block.

You coach against what you fear. What I fear on a field-goal block is a field-goal team that runs a fake. We have six defenders dedicated to defending the fake. We have five players to block the kick. The remaining six players are playing containment and coverage. The only middle of the field kicks are extra points. Everything else usually comes from the hash marks or slightly out of the middle of the field.

Anyone can run a fake field goal if they know where the defense will align. Each week we change the alignment of our six remaining defenders. The only reason I bring anyone from the outside is for the opponent's scouting report. We are window dressing with our six defenders.

The field-goal block team meets every week to talk about the game plan. One reason we block so many kicks is that we identify a weak link on the opponent's team. When we get the opportunity to rush that player, we want to make good. We may only get one opportunity a game to take advantage of that player.

You have to sell your players on your scheme. The secret for the four rushing linemen is to get under the offense's pads. We teach pad under on the block team and pads under on the field goal protect team. Special teams in the NFL are 100 percent match-ups. It is a little less in college because you do not know as much about the special team players. If you can get people matched up on the individual, kicking teams you will hurt them.

Our objective for our kicker is to make every single kick he attempts on the field. We tell our kicker if he misses a kick, to miss short. At least by being short he had a chance. If he is wide, he never had a chance to make the field goal. If the kicker misses a kick, he should miss it short and blame the miss on the coaches.

We have our kickers kick to a point behind the goalpost. We never kick at the uprights. If he is more than three feet right or left of that point, we jump all over him. The kick was good, but it was not good enough. If a kicker makes it in the NFL, he has to be consistent. He has to kick from the 30-yard line, which is a 40-yard field goal, and make 17 out of 20 kicks in the middle six feet of the uprights.

In 1975, when I started coaching in the NFL, there were 26 teams in the league. There were probably 35 kickers in the world that could kick in that league. There are now 32 teams, but the number of kickers has jumped to over 100 kickers. Including this year, there have never been enough punters to outfit every team. Punters are very hard to find.

While we are on the subject, if I were in high school I would never punt the ball. I would placekick the ball. Every school in America can find a soccer player to kick the football. However, you cannot find a punter to serve that purpose. They can place the ball all over the field. I would never punt it again.

Our goal for the punt team is to net 40 yards on the punt. Our goal for our punt-return team is to net 30 yards per punt. Our kickoff coverage goals are to hold the opponent at the 20-yard line or less. Our kickoffs return goals are to return the ball to the 35-yard line.

Assuming you punt six times a game and receive six punts a game, the yardage gained is 60 yards. If you kickoff six times and return six kickoffs, the real estate gained is 90 yards. That amounts to 150 yards in the kicking game or 15 first downs. If you reach your objective in a football game, you can gain between 100 and 150 yards.

PUNT AND COVER TEAM

When the punt-coverage team comes off the field, they know that if the punt nets 40 yards or the ball ends up inside the 15-yard line, they have met their goals. There are time elements involved in the punting game.

The center strives to get the ball back in 0.7 to 0.8 seconds. The risk of getting a punt blocked goes up with each tenth of a second beyond 0.8 seconds. However, a snap that comes back in 0.9 and is accurate is better than one that comes back in 0.8 and is wide, high, or low. The punter must be able to get the ball off within 1.1 to 1.3 seconds. Any time taken beyond this margin is not sound. With the coverage personnel waiting to release with the punt, time is extremely important. They have a clock in their head that says "2.0 equals go!"

Good snappers are like money in the bank. The defense cannot block the punt if you have a good snapper. I would rather have a snapper than a kicker. It is critical.

The "elapsed time" is the combined snap and punting time. With the center getting the ball back in 0.8 and the punter getting it off in 1.2 seconds, the elapsed time will be 2.0 seconds. With our protection and our release, a 2.0 get off time is critical. The "hang time" is the time the ball is in the air. We must keep the ball in the air 4.75 seconds. A punt hanging for 4.65 can be covered and the return held to a minimum with a punt of 45 yards.

Coverage time for a punt can be calculated. Since the punt takes approximately 2.0 seconds to get off, you have approximately 7.0 seconds to cover the ball from the time of the snap. If the punter is facing a 10-man rush, he must get the ball off in 1.2 or less. He may have to use a two-step approach.

To keep the punt cover at net 40 yards, the wide cover men have to get in front of the return man immediately (Diagram #4). That keeps the return man from catching the ball and getting the first ten yards up the field quickly. They have to make the return man run right, left, or fair catch the ball.

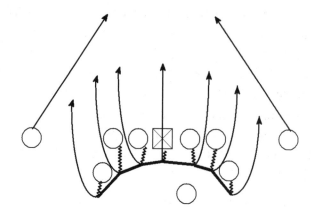

P

Diagram #4. Punt formation

If you punt the ball 40 yards and the return man fair catchers the ball, that is net of 40 yards. If you punt 50 yards with not as much hang time and the punt return man brings it back 10 yards that is a net of 40 yards. However, they are not the same situations. The fair catch cannot be returned for a touchdown. The other punt can. Any time the coach gets nervous about the coverage team, kick the ball on the ground. The football is not round and has odd bounces. Make the return man make a play on the ball before he can return it. He will not make all the plays. Do not gamble with a great turn man. Kick it away from him or out of bounds.

College football has a new invention in the punting game. Some teams are using the rugby type punt. To return that ball, you have to get lucky. You could not do this in the NFL because only two players can release in coverage until the ball is kicked. I hate this kind of punt because I am not in control as a punt-return team.

PUNT-RETURN GAME

In the punt-return game, the wide coverage men have to be blocked. We have to do whatever we can to keep them from getting in front of our return man. By blocking the wide coverage men, we are buying grass in front of the return man. If you can buy 15 yards of grass in front of your return man, he will hurt people. If we have to double both the outside men, we will. That means we have five players involved with two defenders.

I will use two blockers on one man, if we run directionally. When we run a directional return, we start everything at a 45-degree angle. We must get the first 10 yards immediately. We never run laterally or backward. I also will double-team the containment man to the side of the return. Every punt coverage team has a player responsible for containment. If they lose their containment man, they are in trouble.

In the punt return game, there are six "don'ts." Don't:

- Be offsides
- Rough the punter
- Clip
- Let the ball bounce
- Let the kicker run the ball
- Field the ball inside the 10-yard line

I think the worst thing you can do in the kicking game is to put your defense back on the field. That is a psychological killer. I do not like to rush a punt on fourth and less than five yards for a first down. If you have a guy who is keyed up to block the punt and jumps offside, that gives the offense a first down.

The same rules hold for roughing the punter. Do not rush the punter in fourth and less than five yards for a first down. If two or three rushers run into one another and one bounces off and hits the punter, you put the defense back on the field.

Do not block anyone when you cannot see the numbers on the front of their jersey. That is a disciplinary thing for the return team. We do not block very much downfield. We tell our return team to find the return man so they know where the return is. They run to a point on the field where the return is coming. We hold up defenders and run to that point, trying to put our bodies between the defender and the return man. All of our returns are man-to-man blocking schemes. We do not run any wall returns.

The return man will beat the coverage coming late. What he cannot beat is the quick speed in front of him. If you let good return men start running upfield at coverage players, they will beat most of them on their own. Teach your return men to run at coverage personnel and make a move. When the return man runs away from the coverage, he puts all of them in the pursuit game. Everyone who can run will run down the return man. However, if he runs at them and freezes the defender, he can get by him.

In my opinion, this is how you should teach punt return. The punt-return team is a brutal special team. If you have a star and want to help him out with special team play, do not put him on the punt-return team. It is sheer hard work. The most important single factor in a punt return is your honest conviction that the play will succeed. Most punt returns teams play as follows.

The first time the opponent kicks, they make a reasonably good effort to return the punt. However, the kick is short or high and no return opportunity develops. This is discouraging. On succeeding punts, their effort dwindles, and they never get in position to execute a successful return. Finally, they do not even try to make a coordinated team play.

If our opponent punts the ball to us five times, we can return one for a touchdown. However, we are never sure which of the five punts it will be. If our head is in the game and our effort is there on each punt, we will make the big play on a punt return. A big punt return can turn the momentum in a game. Your players have to try as hard on the fifth punt as they do on the first one.

The punt return team knows when they come off the field that if the ball is 29 yards from where the ball was punted, they did their job. We want a net 30 yards on every opponent's punt.

KICKOFF COVERAGE

I am going to kickoff coverage. I think I can help you on your kickoff coverage. What we look to do on kickoff coverage is cut the size of the field. Your players can buy into your program and be major contributors in the kicking game if they can run. The kickoff coverage team is the team where that fact is especially true. The kickoff is 75 percent covered before we kick the ball.

We number our personnel from the inside out. Our R5 player is the last man to the right and the L5 player is the last man to the left. Teaching kickoff coverage is almost like the field-goal team. Theoretically, you do not have to practice kickoff coverage after the initial practices at the beginning of the season.

The kicker's steps into the ball will be the same on August 8 as they are on January 1. We kick the ball angled into the sidelines. We hope the ball goes to the numbers on the right or left. We go through entire season kicking the ball to one direction or the other. All we coach to the players on kickoff coverage is to time up their run to the ball.

We do not care where the players line up as they run to the ball. We want them to pick out a spot on the grass. When the kicker passes that spot, they can begin to run a hundred miles an hour and never look at the kicker again. When the kicker's foot hits the ball, the coverage man is within a half yard of the ball. The key to timing up the run is going 100 percent full sprint. If you do not do it that way, the time element changes. If they go 100 percent, they can start the same place for every kickoff and never be offsides.

That is important to the kickoff coverage because the game only amounts to the five blockers on the front line of the kickoff return team. We sell our coverage men on the idea that if they run past the front five blockers, the game is over. No rule in football is as skewed as the kickoff — kickoff return differential. The rules are written so heavily in favor of the coverage team that no kickoff should ever be returned for a touchdown.

As soon as the kicker's foot hits the ball, the coverage team finds the flight of the ball. As their eyes come back to the field, they take lanes on the football. As they cover, a blocker will come into his vision. They should know quickly how to avoid the block, while remaining in the lane. The coverage team should always keep their feet moving to the football.

When the kicker hits the ball, the coverage team is at full speed. The front five blockers stand dead still thirteen yards from the kickers with their

backs to where they want to go. By the time the ball crosses the 30-yard line, the coverage team has run 35 yards and the return front has run 22 yards. The coverage team should be running past the front five blockers on the 30-yard line. At that point, the game is over because there is nowhere to run.

The depth of the ball does not matter as long as the kicker can hang the ball in the air for 4.1 seconds. You do not need a stopwatch to check the hang of a kick. If the ball is still in the air as your players cross the 30-yard line, the kick is at least 4.1 seconds. It is that simple.

As the coverage team runs down the field to cover the ball, they must think, "fits." We kick the football to the right numbers (Diagram #5). We cover with nine men. We cover with five men on the right side and four men on the left side. The L5 is the safety and the kicker comes down on the ball. The R5 coverage man is the outside containment to the right side, but he is almost against the sideline. The R4 comes down the field and is under the first blocker to his side. It does not matter who it is because the R5 is over the top of him.

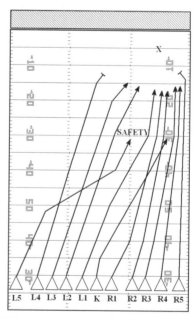

Diagram #5. Kickoff coverage

To the backside, it becomes more critical with the relationship to fits. The L4 is the backside containment. However, he is a hard, go-after-their-butt containment man. His job is to find the last opposite-colored jersey outside his way. He does not cover grass; he squeezes the widest blocker, keeping his outside arm free. Never cover the field; run to blocker in the return game.

If we kick the ball to the five-yard line, the return team will never have more than 17 yards to space to their players. With the coverage team coming down into that area, there are nine coverage players in that area. The return team will have 10 players in the return. That means there are 19 players in that 17-yard area. There is no place to run the ball.

The opponent cannot run a kickoff return if the kicker can hang the ball 4.1 seconds and cut the size of the field. The coverage team has to get their fits, and there is nowhere to run the ball. The backside L4 man squeezes the last man to the widest side. The backside L3 man is under one blocker. The backside L2 man is under two blockers. It does not matter who the blockers are. The frontside R5 man squeezes the last blocker to his side. The R4 man covers under one blocker. The R3 man fits under two blockers.

We meet two or three teams a year where discretion is the better part of valor. In those games, there is no reason to kick to certain people. We held teams to an average of the 17-yard line, but we do not play with fire. In our league, there are some super return men. If we can kick the ball deep into or out of the end zone, that stops the return. If your players understand that fit and are timed up, there is nowhere to run the ball.

We do not practice kickoff coverage very much. As a player runs downfield looking for his fits, he has limited options. As he gets to the 35-yard line, it becomes apparent someone is trying to block him. He has only two options. If he feels he will not outrun the blocker, he goes to the blocker. He plays "hands-under-pads" and keeps running. He never uses a forearm. If the blocker is set up, he runs at him to freeze the blocker and avoids the block to the side of the kick.

The thing that kills kickoff coverage is one player avoiding the block to the wrong side. That wipes out every coverage man outside of him. He has to avoid the block to the side of the kick. The coverage team penetrates until they are within five yards of the ballcarrier. When that occurs, they break down and get ready to tackle. Until the ball is at the coverage team, they run their butts off, penetrate, and chase the ball.

We are at the end and I did not get to kickoff return. However, I want to take five minutes and review our kickoff return. When we talk about kickoff return, we think about the other side of the coverage team. The thing the return team has to do is buy grass in front of the return man. The hardest position in football besides the quarterback is the interior blockers on the kickoff return team. They must be good open-field players.

We drop our front line to the 33-yard line in front of the wedge. We ask our open-field players to do one thing. We want him to force his blocking assignment to run over him. We promised them that no matter what happens, there is no laughter when we review the tapes on Sundays. If they force their blocking assignment to run over them, they buy grass for the return man.

I think the middle wedge is a great return scheme. Vanderbilt led the league last year in the kickoff return and never ran anything but the middle wedge. The middle wedge is a great return for high school.

I am completely out of time, but if you want to stay around, I will talk to you about the middle return. I appreciate the opportunity to talk to you. I hope you were able to get something out of this lecture. The best thing I talked about is the kickoff coverage. You have to believe that is the real deal, because it is. If you go to the converse on the kickoff return, it is all about buying grass for the return man. Thank you for your time.

SECONDARY TECHNIQUES AND DRILLS

Indiana University

Thanks for that introduction. I just returned from a clinic in Japan. Terry Hoeppner, Shane Montgomery and Brian George put on the clinic for former Miami and Indiana Coach John Pont.

I am going to talk about three things. First, I will talk about our base defensive coverage, which is corner coverage. Out of that coverage, we do something different in that we press with the corners. I will get into "press cover techniques" and how we teach the coverage. We use some unusual techniques in our coverage. At the end, I want to talk about defending the spread offense. The trend in offense is to spread things out. It has filtered down from the pros to the youth leagues. We saw some of it in Japan. I had many questions in Japan about the spread offense. "How to you stop the shotgun offense?" That was the big question.

I want to start with a little of our philosophy. We do not have cut-ups from Indiana at this point so you will see the Miami cut-ups. I believe this is what makes us good on defense. We play a lot of base defense. We play more base than usual. We get a lot of reps on the base defense in practice. I think it is important for the players to understand what they are doing so they do not have to do a lot of thinking on the field. We played our base defense 70 percent of the time at Miami. That included everything against our opponents. We offset that by using about 30 percent of zone blitzing. We will get into our 3-4 scheme and do some zone blitzes in nickel-and-dime situations.

We want to make the offense earn everything they get. We want to eliminate the one-play drive. In our corner package, we may give up some soft plays underneath but we want to make the offense drive the ball the length of the field to earn their points.

The thing that really makes us good is the way we practice. We get a ton of reps during practice. We have our players running all of the time. We use the two-whistle drill. The first whistle blows the play dead. The second whistle lets the players know when they can stop running. They are all running to the ball until that second whistle blows in practice. It is good not only for physical conditioning but also good for mental conditioning. Our pursuit is excellent.

Our base defense is an attacking front-seven defense. The cover 4 that we play allows us to use the front seven to attack the offense. The linebackers are coming downhill. People think we blitz a lot in the games. That is not true. It looks like we are blitzing but that is our linebackers coming downhill fast. The safety coverage in cover 4 allows those linebackers to play that way.

The other point that helps us is the way we disrupt routes. Cover 4 is not a new concept of what we are doing. We want to make the reads more difficult for the quarterback.

This is our tight alignment. We play the end to the boundary in a 9 technique. The tackle is in a 5 technique, the nose is in a shade, and the backside end is in a 5 technique. The linebackers are line up five yards deep. The Sam and Will linebackers lined up in a 50 look and the Mike is in a 10 technique.

To the boundary side we have our halfback on the wide receiver. The corner is on the opposite side on the wideout. The safeties line up on the outside of the linebackers.

The front rules: Roger or Larry call to the tight end.

- Two tight ends with two backs — check to hawk, check to curl, check to bulldog

- Two tight ends with one back — Check hawk (Call to field — Game plan)

- No tight end — 1) Hash call to field; 2) Middle of field call to strength of formation

- Balanced formation — 1) Hash call to field; 2) Middle of field call to strength of quarterback.

Position	Alignment and Techniques
Ends	Call side • Tight end, 9 technique • No Tight end — Loose 5 technique • Flex tight end, three-yard rule
Tackle	Call side • 3 technique
Nose	Away side • 1 technique • 2i with check hawk call
Sam	50 technique to call side or strength. Bump all trips and two wide receivers based on converge called. No tight ends — align to field.
Mike	10 technique to call side. Bump to a 30 technique versus all trips based on coverage called.
Will	50 technique away from call or strength. Bump all trips and two wide receiver formations based on coverage called. No tight ends — align to boundary.

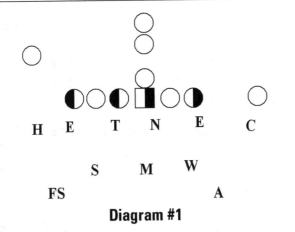

Diagram #1

This is our cover 4. Our front four linemen set up the same way (Diagram #2). Let me cover the alignments, keys and techniques, and coaching points and adjustments.

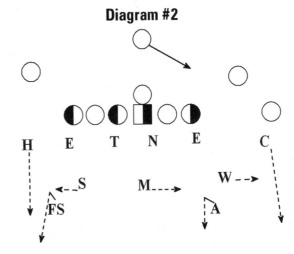

Diagram #2

Position: Sam
Alignment: Play front
Keys and Techniques: 2 Match
Coaching Points and Adjustments: Bump trips, check curl, yo-yo-yo

Position: Mike
Alignment: Play front
Keys and Techniques: 3 Match
Coaching Points and Adjustments: Bump trips

Position: Will
Alignment: Play front
Keys and Techniques: 2 Match
Coaching Points and Adjustments: Bump trips, check curl, yo-yo-yo

Position: Free
Alignment: 10 X 2 Inside Edge of #2 Skill
Keys and Techniques: Stick Q 2-1
Coaching Points and Adjustments: "I've got trips," yo-yo-yo, trips, cross key #22 and #3

Position: Apache
Alignment: 10 X 2 Inside Edge of #2 Skill
Keys and Techniques: Stick Q 2-1
Coaching Points and Adjustments: "I've got trips," yo-yo-yo, trips, cross key #22 and #3

Position: Halfback
Alignment: Press-Inside Eye, Off, 7 x 2 Inside
Keys and Techniques: Press-shadow technique, off, drop Q 1-2

Coaching Points and Adjustments: Possible check curl, yo-yo-yo

Position: Corner
Alignment: Press-Inside Eye, Off, 7 x 2 Inside
Keys and Techniques: Press-shadow technique, off, drop Q 1-2
Coaching Points and Adjustments: Possible check curl, yo-yo-yo

I want to cover our techniques and drills that we use with our secondary. I will cover the techniques and then talk about the drills we use to teach the techniques.

STANCE — PEDAL — WEAVE

Off Stance

Keeping the feet within the framework of your body, take a heel-to-toe relationship stance slightly tilted toward the quarterback. Balance your weight evenly with mental weight favoring your upfield or outside foot. Safeties will set slightly higher enabling them to see the "big picture."

Backpedal

Great defensive backs stay in their backpedal as long as possible. By staying in a good backpedal, keeping good cushion, and not biting on the wide receiver's first move, you will put yourself in position to play the thrown football. The backpedal is the starting point for becoming a fundamentally sound defensive back. The following checklist points out the area of emphasis:

- Shuffle (slow backpedal) out of your stance clearing three-step pass.

- Keep numbers down with our chest slightly over your knees, weight on the toes, not the heels.

- Maintain good knee bend, hips behind you, elbows tight to the body.

- Control, control, control. Keep the wide receiver where you want him. Stay quick and crisp with every step.

- Break on the football keeping your feet under your body.

- Keep your cushion as long as possible with proper leverage. Anticipate the wide receiver breaking your cushion. You must swivel in one movement running with his upfield shoulder and working to get your hands on him at the cutoff point.

Read Pedal

From a good soft stance, the corner will shuffle out reading the quarterback for the three-step-throw. If the quarterback stops to throw the three-step-route, the corner will snap his eyes from the quarterback to the wide receivers outside shoulder driving through the outside and upfield shoulder to play the ball. On a hitch-and-go or out-and-up route we should collision and run with the wide receiver.

Speed Pedal

Once the quarterback has dropped more than three steps, the corner will go from a read pedal to a speed pedal. The corner will snap his eyes off he quarterback and onto the wide receivers inside hip. He will simultaneously square up into a speed pedal. Keys to good speed pedal are:

- Keep the chest slightly forward over the toes. Do not lean backwards.

- Use the arms to balance the backpedal, but do not over exaggerate the arm action.

- Control your speed! Be quick and fast, but not hurried.

- Keep the feet close to one another.

Weave

Weave technique allows the defender to not only keep proper vertical cushion, but also horizontal leverage. The three main components of the weave are:

- Step behind

- Stay square

- Maintain good pedal technique

Drills

- Stance and Start
- Slow Pedal - Fast Pedal
- Pedal and Weave
- X-Drill

CHANGE OF DIRECTIONS (FOOTWORK)

Break and Drive

Once the defensive back reads the break of the wide receiver he must establish a break foot and drive foot almost simultaneously. Keeping the feet within the framework of the body the deepest foot should break the speed pedal with a little help from the front foot. Momentum must be transferred from the break foot to the drive foot in one quick moment. The defensive back will keep his feet under his body and dip his shoulder out over his upfield foot thus beginning the drive. The defensive back should drive to the wide receiver as if he is coming out of a 40-yard dash. Once again, do not hurry or rush the technique, be efficient in transition. Do not round off the breaks! All breaks should be sharp angles.

Key Coaching Points: Plant, point, accelerate

Drills:

- Pedal turn and run
- Pedal and break
- W-drill
- 2-line (slow turn/speed turn)
- Pedal open 45 degrees
- Pattern dances

BODY POSITION (IN PHASE)

When covering a receiver down field it is important to be in proper body position. We call this proper body position "in phase." To be in phase means that the defender is in a hip-over position and should be able to look in the ear-hole of the receiver.

Drills:

- Out of Phase
- In Phase Squeeze Drill

Cover 4 started out as a red-zone coverage, but now it has become our base coverage. We run it a lot. We may run it a little too much. We like it versus the run because it allows the linebackers to come down hill on the run. We do not teach gap concepts to our linebacker in cover 4. We tell them to "go get the ball." It allows our linebackers to play fast.

We also like cover 4 against the pass. It is a relatively safe pass defense. We put our best pass defender at the free safety position because he must cover more slot receivers. If the offense does run vertical routes, it ends up being a man situation with the vertical receivers. Therefore, you must have someone that can run in that free safety position.

Let me talk about route tendencies by releases. When you are up in the receiver's face, he has no choice but to go inside or outside of you. He is not going down the middle to try to knock you down to get open. If he executes a release inside, there is a tendency he will run certain routes. You cannot say it is going to happen one hundred percent of the time, but there is a heavy tendency they are going to run a particular release. It could be a quick slant. They could be going inside to crack block on the safety. With our safeties coming down to make tackles, that is what offenses like to do against us. However, most of the time the inside release is going to equal a curl, dig, or post route. It could be a post corner. On the inside release, the receiver releases early enough that we can coach or defenders to play against that release.

When we get an outside release the play is usually going to be one of the following routes. It is going to be a fade or a go route. It is going to be an out route or a comeback route. It could be a run-off.

Let me talk about the crack block just for a second. Teams try to use this against us. They know our safeties are coming down fast. I tell the safety to come down fast, defeat the crack back block, and make the tackle. The corner must read if it is a crack back block or not. A good coaching point is this. When that receiver is going to crack block, he turns his shoulders perpendicular to the line of scrimmage. The corner can tell when he turns his shoulders and he knows it is going to be a crack block. He is not going to run the crack and go route.

We drill our corners to come off the receivers butt when he turns his shoulders and starts inside. We do a crack replace and fill the seam. We bring the safety and the corner into fill the hole. We get eleven players in a bunch where they are trying to run. The corners can read the shoulders to determine if the receiver is running the crack block when he turns his shoulders inside or if he is coming straight down the field.

Let me talk about the corners. Let me get to the press coverage. This is the teaching progression for the "bump and run" press techniques.

- Philosophy: We feel the "bump and run" or "press" technique that we employ forces the offense to adapt to a few factors that are not normally presented with versus traditional soft coverage techniques. The offense must adapt to the following:

- The press technique forces the wide out to show us this release immediately, thus revealing route tendency.

- The press technique forces individual pass routes into taking more time, thus buying time for our pass rushers to get to the quarterback.

- The press technique forces routes to be inconsistent in where they finish.

- The press technique forces the timing and spacing of routes to be inconsistent.

- The press technique lets our players play within our attacking philosophy.

- The press technique gives the quarterback a "murky" look at the wide-out forcing throws to his secondary reads.

BUMP AND RUN TEACHING PROGRESSION

Alignment. Inside eye on wide out with your eyes focused on his numbers.

Stance. Take an inside foot staggered stance with feet within the framework of the shoulders. The defensive back should be able to rock back and forth comfortably. Hands should be in front, over the knees, with the arms bent at a 90-degree angle, and he fingers alive. Weight should slightly favor the "up" foot for shadow.

Shadow Technique. On wide receiver movement, the defensive back will slightly "shadow" his release, staying within arm's length distance keeping your shoulders square with his shoulders. The "shadow" begins with a push-off with the up foot. The defender waits until the receiver makes his move inside or outside before he goes on to phases two.

The defensive back should never initiate the first move; he should always be the "reactor" to the release of the wideout, unless using a *quick-jam* or *fake two-hand* change-up.

If the wideout "dances" from his stance, hold your water. Do not let him invite you to attack him. When he is dancing, he wants you to be impatient and attack him. Do not buy it. We must learn to be aggressive moving backward.

Once the wideout has declared the direction in which he will try to clear you, we will become aggressive. If he takes a release to your right, you must flip your hips leading with your right foot at an angle to meet him on his stem. Almost simultaneously, you must punch the arm opposite to force his release wider than he wants it to be. As you punch him, grab his near number and pull yourself into and over his near shoulder and hip.

Pester the man. Once you have established "hip-over" leverage, it is now your duty to disrupt the route. If he took an outside release, hammer him out of bounds.

Finish. Once the defensive back has moved into a hip-over position and is in a hands-on relationship with the wide receiver, it is time to be a playmaker. "Finishing" is what separates the good cover players and the great cover players. Attitude must be that once the ball is in the air we become the wide receiver.

Quick jam. A quick jam is used as a "change-up" throughout the course of a game. The corner must show a normal, staggered stance and, upon the wide receiver's movement, deliver a jam to the inside chest plate while stepping between the wide receiver's two legs and splitting the crotch. It is essential that corner get his body to a full quarter turn so he can turn and run immediately following the quick jam. Again, this is used as a "change-up."

Fake two-hand jam. The fake two-hand is another "change-up" to be used throughout the course of a game. The corner should throw his hands out in front of his body at the wide receiver forcing him to swim on air. The key is to "shadow" back at the same time. Do not stop the feet when throwing the hands. Keep good shadow relationship throughout the fake two hands.

- Wedge the fade and squeeze

- Flip to the post first

- Quick turn

- Dip to pressure for the push-off

- Flatten the quick slant

We do not jump on the receiver when we press them. One out of ten times, we will make contact when we are pressing. We are playing inside leverage on the receivers. We are playing with the inside foot up. As the players get used to playing with the inside foot up, we start moving them up to play with their feet parallel. We want them to give a little ground as they move their feet up to a parallel stance. They must be patient.

Next, I want to talk about alignments. We have the corners in a press position. We are facing a true spread formation with two wideouts to each side and the offense is in a shotgun set. We tell the linebackers to split the difference between the end man on the line of scrimmage and that removed

receiver. If they are going to make a mistake, we want it made a step less than splitting the difference. I want them more toward the ball than toward the receiver. They are taking a read step toward the box on the snap of the ball. We are going to get them involved in the run from this alignment. The safeties line up slightly inside the slot receivers.

When you face a spread offense, this is the question you must ask about them: Is the quarterback a threat to run the ball? That is what you must look at.

We are going to kick the front away from the running back set opposite the quarterback. This is where we start in our alignment. If the quarterback is not a threat to run the ball, we kick the front away from the running back.

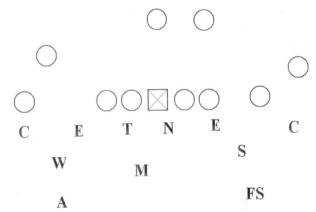

Diagram #3. Front = away from the back

That gives us a 3 technique and a 5 technique on the side opposite the running back. We want to take away the running play first and, typically, it is the zone play. When we have a B-gap and a C-gap player on the same side of the line of scrimmage, it tells the end he must become a shuffle player.

If the quarterback is a threat to run the ball, we are going to set the front toward the running back. We want a 3 technique and a 5 technique on the side of the running back. That 3 technique tells the 5 technique he is inside and the end knows he is a shuffle player (Diagram #4). The end must play square to the line. He does not want to get upfield. He plays with his heels at the line of scrimmage.

When the quarterback pulls the ball on the play toward our end, he is in position to make the play. He cannot do that if you are playing with a shade technique on the center and a 5-technique end. The 3-technique man must be the cutback player on the inside. We want the 3 technique and the 5 technique on the side where the quarterback is going to keep the ball on the option.

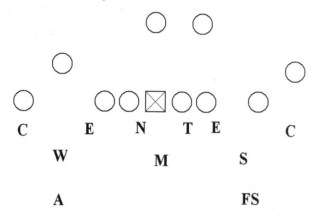

Diagram #4. Front = to the back

From a regular T-formation, we have our linebackers key the backs. Once a team starts running the shotgun formation, we have the linebackers key the linemen. Flow does not do much for you anymore. The offenses run so much mis-direction now that it confuses the linebackers to read the backs. Now when we face a spread formation team, we have our linebackers read the linemen nearest to them. We call it "linebacker gun reads" (Diagram #5). The outside linebackers key the two tackles and the Mike linebacker keys the center.

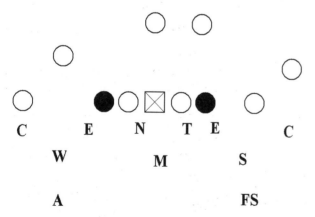

Diagram #5. Linebacker gun reads

This gives us a better read on what the offense is doing. Just by changing the reads for the

linebackers, it helps us a great deal. It gives us faster run reads.

When teams see what we are doing with our linebackers they start running the bubble play with standup blocking by those tackles. If it is an early down, we can run some stunts or run a gap call where we move the 5 technique into the B gap. It allows the linebacker to play outside on the bubble screen play (Diagram #6). The linebacker can widen out and move up toward the line of scrimmage more to stop some of those bubble passes.

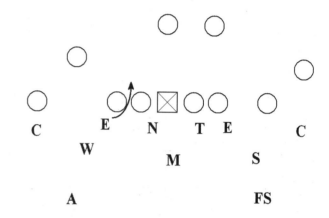

Diagram #6. 5-technique movement

Any time there is a tight end in the game we always kick the defensive front toward the tight end (Diagram #7). You must be aware because the offense can still run the counter option weak on you. If the run the cut back play the end on the splitside must be able to cover that B gap.

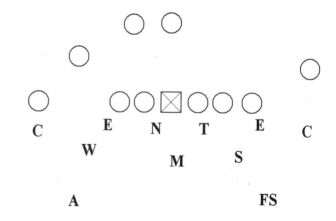

Diagram #7. Front = to the tight end

Let me give you a three-by-one formation. The key for the safety is always the number-two receiver. If you look at the trips set, you see our Apache does not have a second receiver to his side. So who does he key now? He keys number three on the opposite side of the formation. He is reading the number-three receiver. If the number-three man runs a vertical route, he must go get him.

If the number three receiver runs an out route, or does not run a vertical route, the Apache can look to the backside of the formation or he can help the cornerback. We do cheat the Apache over toward the trips side. We tell him he can never cross over the ball. If the offense has a trips set with a tight end on the trips side, he does not have to cheat over as much.

Against any type of trip formations, we are going to "bump trips" with the linebackers. We are going to bump everyone over toward the trips. We automatically call the front away from the trips (Diagram #8).

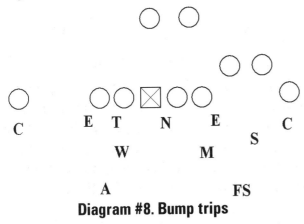

Diagram #8. Bump trips

Anytime we get three receivers to one side, we make a call in the secondary. The safety to the three receiver's side calls out: "I have trips! I have trips!" This tells the backside safety and the corner "Yo-Yo." This stands for "You're on your own!" He gives the warning to the corner to let him know he will not be getting help on his man. He may have to take more inside leverage on the receiver. If the number-three receiver does not go vertical, the safety can look to the backside and help the corner.

Our last formation is against the empty formation. We do not have a set call that we play against the empty look. If it is late in the game and the offense comes out in an empty set, we may blitz them. We play what ever we have called. If we have cover 4 called, we stay in that coverage. We just make one adjustment (Diagram #9). The offense has a split end and a back to one side and a split end and a back in the slot to the other side.

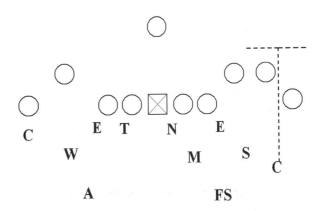

Diagram #9. Empty formation

We pretend the third man to the field on the trips side is not there. We play cover 4 and the safety reads the number-three man on that side. We did a study and found that most offense teams very seldom throw to that outside receiver in the trips set. So we take the corner and play him at a mid point between the outside two receivers. He lines up, splitting the difference between the number-one and number-two receivers. If they all three of those receivers go vertical he is going to lean on the inside man. If the ball is thrown to the outside man on a deep route, the corner will have time to get over the top on that outside receiver. Very rarely are they going to send all three receivers vertical. If one of the receivers run an out route or an in route, the linebacker covers the flat. As soon as one of the three receivers does not run a vertical route, the corner picks up the deep receiver to the outside. The safety takes the second man inside and we have them all covered.

Let me get to the tape to show you what we are doing with our secondary. I will cover all of the sets I talked about against the spread formation.

DEFENSIVE END PLAY

University of Pittsburgh

It is an honor to get to talk to you. As I go to more and more clinics, I realize the things I hear only reaffirm what I am coaching.

We play with a 6-technique defensive end. He is head up the tight end and is a C-gap player. The 5 technique starts to vary as we align in different calls. The 5-technique player's toe is shaded on the offensive lineman's near toe.

The 3-technique player is toe-to-toe on the offensive guard. The nose is in a toe-to-toe alignment on the opposite guard or inside shade in a 2i. I want to give names to alignments or stunts that have recall value for the players. We have a technique called a "slope 5 technique." This is a slightly tilted technique on the offensive tackle. It is an alignment to get the defender to his pressure key. He aligns his hand five inches outside the foot of the offensive tackle. We should be able to draw a straight line from the defenders tail pad straight through his spine to that outside point of the offensive tackle.

We adjust all the techniques from their straight alignments. We have a slope, closed, and a tight 5 technique. That gets us beyond the simple 5 technique in the outside shade.

In our pre-snap progression, we want the players to know down and distance. We want them to know the personnel and formation in the game. We try to read the stance of offensive linemen.

When the defense is aligning and getting ready for the play, the defenders call out colors to each other. If the defender sees two linemen aligned with their weight back in their stance, they call "blue." That alerts everyone that it could be a pass play. If the defender reads a heavy stance by the linemen,

they call "red." That is the alert call for run. The "yellow" call alerts a pull technique for the guard. That is when we read heavy alignment to one side and light to the other. The colors are based on the offensive linemen's alignment and body language.

We have a key progression. The first thing we key is the ball. Our next key depends on where we align. The defender has a primary and a secondary offensive lineman key. If he is a 6-technique player, his first key is the ball. Once the ball is snapped, he transfers his eyes from the ball to the inside plate of the tight end. The inside plate is the inside half of the player. He does that as he steps upfield. His primary key is the inside plate of the tight end and his secondary key has to be the offensive tackle. The tight end is his pressure key and he should be able to feel him. If the tight end and offensive tackle are working a combination block on the 6-technique, he feels the pressure from the end and sees the offensive tackle.

If there is no pressure from the primary key, the 6 technique's eyes should focus to the inside. The hands are another set of eyes. The third element of the key progression is the scheme used by the offensive blockers.

I need to back up a bit and talk about stance. The stance of the defensive linemen affects the get-off and his steps as he comes off the ball. A lineman with a narrow stance steps out on the first step instead of up the field. If his stance is too narrow, widen him so he can get off the ball and get up the field. We want them in a shoulder-width stance with a toe to mid-foot stagger. We want them in a shoulder-width stance so they do not take big steps coming out of the stance.

The down hand in the stance is in front of the back foot. If he puts his hand down in the center of his body, the stance is twisted. Putting the down hand in front of the back foot squares the stance. Do not create a tripod with the down hand. Reach out with the hand so that 75-percent of the weight is on the hand. That helps the defenders get off the ball.

The defensive linemen want to take two short steps coming off the ball. The first step is a direction step and the second step is a set step. We want to get both steps back on the ground as quickly as possible. They do not react to the scheme until the third step. If a defensive lineman takes long steps, he gets reached. The third step is the reaction step and is based on blocking scheme.

Instead of talking gap responsibility, we talk lines and plates. I teach the 6-technique end he has the inside plate of the tight end. That is how I begin to teach responsibility. The end is not worried about a gap; he is thinking inside plate of the tight end.

The 5-technique end on the open side of the set spills any blocker that comes at him. The problem is when the defender gets too far upfield and has to turn to get under blocks coming at him. The way we avoid getting upfield is by "chasing plates." His pressure key is the outside plate of the offensive tackle. If the offensive tackle blocks to the inside, the defensive end chases the plate to the inside. That puts him under all blocks coming at him. He has to work on the bootleg coming his way but we teach running straight lines and chasing plates as his get-off technique.

When we talk to our defensive end about pass rush, we talk about straight lines to the quarterback. We do not want them to arc and get off the straight-line attack. I know when they use pass rushing techniques such as spins, they get off the straight-line concept, but they must try to rush in lines.

The next fundamental we work on is the hands. The punch with the hands has to be an eye level punch. When players first start to punch, their mistake is punching too low. The elbows are in and the thumbs are up in the punch. When you punch, do not expose the chest. The weight room is a great aid for the hand punches. We have a great strength coach. Everything he does in the weight room is truly football-oriented.

Instead of bench press, he does dumbbell presses. He does one arm at a time and turns the weight at the end to simulate the punch. He uses a medicine ball punch drill to work on the linemen's punch. Two players partner-up and use the medicine ball drill. They sit on benches opposite each other and throw the medicine ball at one another. One player chest passes the ball to the other player. As the ball comes to him, he uses his punch on the ball. The strength coach does all kinds of drills that carry over to the football field. They are simple drills but make sense. He also does some position pattern running designed for particular groups. Everything he does in the weight room tries to build good habits and ingrain skills.

I have some drills that you can do in the off-season. This first one looks like a linebackers drill, but it works on the hand punch (Diagram #1). We set up four tube dummies and put a defensive end on one side and a simulator with a hand dummy on the other side.

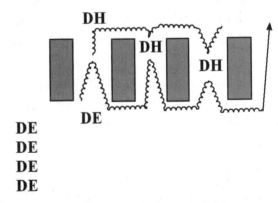

Diagram #1. Punch drill

The dummy holder and end start in a two-point stance. They enter the first chute and approach one another. The end delivers a punch with both hands locks out and drives the dummy holder out of the chute. They retreat into a backpedal and enter the second chute and do the same thing. He slides to the third chute and repeats the drill. The emphasis in the drill is hand explosion and knee bend. We want the elbows in and the thumbs up in the hand explosion. The defensive end bends at the knees and not the waist.

We do board drills to help the defender focus on keeping his base. We do the drill like a board drill with a dummy holder on one end of the board and a defender on the other end. They move onto the board and the defensive end punches the dummy, locks out, and drives the dummy off the board. The punch is the same as the in the punch drill. The emphasis in this drill is to keep the base wide so you maintain stability. This helps us in playing blocks. When blocks start to move, this helps keep our base and not cross over in our footwork.

We do the same drill in a partner drill. We fit the defender on the offensive player. He places his hands on the chest of the offensive blocker. On a command, the defensive player snaps his hips and locks out on the offensive lineman. He moves him back five yards in the locked out position. They switch roles and go the other way. We do the drill twice looking for the full body snap.

To teach punch, we use a punch progression drill to emphasize what we expect. We can start players on their own by aligning them around the wall in a weight room or workout room. The players get down on their knees and punch out into the wall. This is nothing but an upper body shoulder punch. That gets them ready for the explosion drill by working the punch part from their knees. The next part of the progression is to get the defender into a six-point stance against a dummy.

To start the drill, we lift the toes off the ground and snap just the hips exploding into the dummy. From there we ground out the toes and do the six-point explosion drill. When they explode, they do not rock back on their heels and come forward. They sink their hips and explode with the hips behind the shoulders. From that position, we get into a three-point stance and explode with one step.

After the player goes through the progression with the repetitions he needs at each position, he begins to see where his power comes from. From

the one-step explosion, we get them into a two-step punch on a wall.

Another drill we use is a ball drill. When a defensive player plays in a game, he is not punching a wall; he is punching a moving target (Diagram #2). This drill works on that concept. The players get into a three-point stance aligned on a ball on a stick. The ball on the stick is for the get-off. The medicine ball is for the punch. This helps the players train their eyes to hit a moving target. The eyes take his hands to the target. As soon as the ball on the stick moves, the medicine ball is rolled at the defender. The defender gets out of his stance and punches the ball. If the ball is rolled inside that is where he attacks the ball.

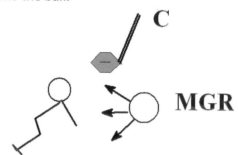

Diagram #2. Medicine ball punch

The next drill is the "sumo drill." This is a drill that emphasizes hand battles. This is a partner drill. We have two defensive linemen facing one another. They get in a good bent-kneed position with their heads back. One player gets his hand inside on the other player's chest. The opponent has his hands outside the other player's hands. On the command "go," the players try to get the inside hand position and push the other player backward. We do not want the drill to turn. We want it to go straight back as the players work for inside hand position while moving their feet.

This is a competitive drill and best done with the headgear off. If you take the helmet off, the players are less likely to use their heads to butt the other player.

The next drill is a "get-off bag carry drill." In this drill, we have someone hold an agility bag opposite the defensive player. As the defensive player gets off, he punches and makes contact with the agility bag. He grabs the bag and carries it five yards up the field. The focus is getting off the ball and shooting his hands. If the bag were not in the drill, it becomes a five-yard get-off drill. We want concentration on hand placement. We make sure when we work get-off that we get something in front of them to work their hands and feet.

You can do the next drill any number of ways. You can use an old mattress, a high-jump pad, or a stack of tumbling mats. Have the defender take one or two steps and lunge forward on the landing pad. That gives the player a complete extension of his legs, through his hips, and behind his shoulders.

We have a simple "get-off and react drill." The defender aligns on the line of scrimmage with the get-off ball. I stand five yards away from the defender. As the ball moves, the defender charges off the ball and attacks toward the coach. I give him a right, left, screen, or draw call and he reacts accordingly to the command.

Make sure you show your players how the skills they work on in drills apply to game situations. Use game films to illustrate the skills they work on in drills. If you do not, they will not work hard in drill work. They have to know what they are doing can be used in a game.

We do all kinds of drill in the chutes. You can invent anything that has an application to game situations. We work our line stunt games through the chute. We do straight get-off drills. We line a defensive lineman on the pole of the chute and let him cross face an offensive blocker. That keeps him low and attacking with his shoulders forward. In all the drills you do in the chute, the theme is the same. You want them to work with their pad level down low.

Another drill we do is "closed-eye pressure drill." We do the drill as a one-on-one or two-on-one drill. We tell the players they have two sets of eyes. They have a set of eyes in their head and a set of eyes in their hands. In the 6 technique on the snap of the ball, the defender steps with his inside foot. He gets his hands on the inside plate of the tight end and feel the pressure coming from the tight end. The hands on the tight end are his first set of eyes.

He feels the pressure from the pressure key and turns his eyes inside to see if the tackle is coming out to try to overtake the end's block. He feels the pressure and sees the blocker. If the tight end releases, the defender focuses inside on the tackle. He reads the tackle in the pass-blocking mode and gets into his pass rush.

In the "closed-eye drill," the defender gets into a fit position with the blocker. On a "go" command, the offensive blocker simulates a block, release, or some kind of line maneuver. The defender has his eyes closed, plays the pressure key, and fights the resistance. When he feels the pressure of the block, the defender pushes and pulls to escape the block. We do this every day.

We work the "hoops" with a wrinkle in the drill. We put a simulator in the middle of the hoops with a hand dummy. The hoops are five to six yards in diameter (Diagram #3). We want the defender to try to cut the circle off, but the simulator will not let them. He is banging the hoops runner as he goes around the hoop. The simulator has to work hard in the drill to make the defender work hard. The defender gets in his stance and gets-off. He gets his hands into the simulators dummy and works his charge. If the defender can turn early, he will. The hoop is there to give him a mental concept of what we are doing. If he can turn the simulator and run right through the middle of the hoop, we consider that a great job by the defender.

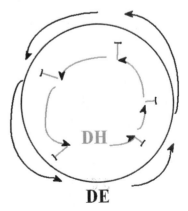

Diagram #3. Hoops drill

This drill is the "catch drill." It teaches the defender to get off on the movement of the offensive lineman and catch him as quickly as possible. The offensive lineman has a defender about one-yard-and-half in front of him. We have a shirt five yards behind the offensive lineman. The offensive lineman retreats in his pass set. The defender gets off the ball and has to catch the offensive lineman before he gets to the five-yard cutoff point.

We tell the defender where his shade is on the offensive lineman so he can make contact with the proper plate on the lineman's body. When the defender gets to the plate, he has to execute some kind of escape move on the offensive lineman. He can use a push, pull, rip, or whatever you have taught him to escape the pass block.

I want to get into some pass-rush drills. We start with a "one hand mover." The defender puts one hand behind his back. As he gets into the offensive blocker, the blocker starts to fire random hand shots with one hand at a time to the body of the defender. The defender uses his one hand to knock off as many of the offensive blocker punches as he can while working around the corner of the blocker.

We continue the drill except the defender uses both hands to ward off the punches of the blocker as he works around to the outside. The next part of the drill is similar, except the offensive block shoots both hands at the defender. The defender tries to grab the wrist of the offensive block and gain control of the blocker's wrist.

From the wrist control, we teach them a move called "airplane." These are individual moves. The players can work on them all the time. In the airplane move, the defender grabs the wrists of the offensive blocker. He splits the hands by pushing his outside hand high and his inside hand low. He forms the wings of the airplane. He gets his body on the offensive lineman's body and releases the inside hand as he steps with his outside foot. When he releases the inside wrist he gets back on the line to the quarterback.

Another move is the "heart pick." The defender attacks the blocker and attempts to grab the

wrists. He gets the outside wrist but misses the inside wrist. With the inside hand, he punches the offensive blocker in the chest and pulls with the outside hand so he can step through to the outside. When the offensive lineman pulls his hand back, he opens his hips and gives the defender a great line to the quarterback. Even if you cannot gain control of both wrists, as the offensive lineman start to panic, he opens the gate for the defender.

Once you teach the players a few moves, put them in a "gauntlet drill" (Diagram #4). You do not need to teach ten moves to every player. They cannot use them all and will not be able to do some of them effectively. They pick two to three moves and prefect them. Once your players learn and become good at a couple of moves, it is all they need. I like to use people holding dummies instead of just dummies. Have the defenders work through three dummies using a different pass-rush move on each dummy. At the end of the gauntlet drill, we make them perform a form tackle on a simulator as the quarterback.

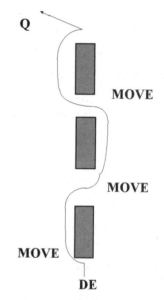

Diagram #4. Gauntlet drill

When I first learned these moves, I thought there would be no way our players would pick them up. I did not think they would be able to execute these moves, but I was wrong. When we taught these moves to our players, they started to understand a concept of how they could control the body of an offensive lineman. The first move is the "samurai rip." As the offensive lineman starts to punch the defender, the defender grabs the blocker's outside elbow two feet in front of his torso with his outside hand.

The offensive blocker will try to pull the arm back. The defender wants to hold on to the elbow and rip with his inside arm. The blocker's body will start to turn and open the defender to the quarterback. When the defender gets his inside triceps on the blocker's outside triceps, the deal is over.

The "samurai swim" is the same concept. The defender grabs the blocker's elbow two feet in front of his torso. The blocker's upper body goes down as the defender gains control of the elbow. The defender takes the inside arm and swims over the blocker's outside shoulder and gets on the line to the quarterback.

On the "samurai bull," the defender tries to grab both elbows. When he gets control of the elbows, he tries to drive them back into the shoulder blades. The same thing can happen with a combination punch. If he only gets one elbow, he uses a heart pick, and tries to throw the elbow over the blocker's helmet. If you get body position and control of the blocker's upper body, you can do anything you want to him. It is not a matter of strength.

In our pass rush, we take what the offensive linemen give us. If they let us get into their upper plate, we bull rush through the blocker. If they try to punch, we use whatever works for us. Some players work on the wrists and others work on elbows.

If the blocker gives the defender his head by leaning forward to butt the defender, he uses that momentum to pull him forward. He grabs his jersey or wrists and reaches for his back plates. He opens his hips, pulls the blocker forward, and goes around him.

The defensive linemen read all different types of pass sets. If the blocker sets in a short pass set, it is one of two things. It is either a hot or quick pass, or a draw play. We want to squeeze the blocker into our gap and get our hands up if the play is a pass. If the play is a draw play, we do not want to run up the field on a short set. That is what the offense wants

us to do. If we get the short set, we squeeze then respond to the play.

If the blocker short sets and releases, we play the wide receiver screen or a short screen to the back. If the blocker deep sets and tries to cut the defender late, bend the knees and play off the block. Retrace your steps back to the line of scrimmage because the play is some type of slip screen or wide receiver screen.

We practice under moves all the time. We want to use the under move at the same depth of the quarterback. If you are not at the depth of the quarterback, do not take the under move. When the offensive lineman turns his shoulder parallel to the sideline, he is in trouble. As long as the lineman has his butt to the quarterback, it is hard to get under because he is in control. When he turns his butt to the sideline, the defender takes one more step upfield and works under the blocker. We use the "hump move." Reggie White made that move famous. It does not require tremendous strength. You use the momentum of the offensive lineman to keep him moving the way he is going. Use the inside hand, throw the blocker upfield, and rip underneath. You can use the heart pick and rip underneath. They both are the same concept.

Another move your player can use is an outside spin. The rusher plants on his outside foot, sinks the hips, throws the outside arm, and gets himself to the quarterback. However, do not use this move until the rusher is at the depth of the quarterback.

When we get into pass-rush scheme, we have to decide what types of protections the offense is using. Most teams slide the center one way and use man protection the other way with the back reading the linebackers for blitzes. We focus on which way the center turns before we decide which games we want to run. We chart the center's movement. We chart him to or away from the running back. He could go toward or away from a tight end set. The other two checks we make are to the field or to the passing strengths.

In our pass-rush games, if we read run the game is off. If we run the "me" game (Diagram #5), the defensive end takes two steps up the field, plants on the outside foot, and drives underneath the offensive tackle. When you run stunts, you cannot have a selfish attitude. On this stunt, the end is trying to free up the tackle. As the defensive end comes underneath the offensive tackle, there could be separation between the guard and tackle, which means man-to-man blocking. If the guard and tackle come toward, they are blocking zone and will pass the stunt off from one to the other. If they come toward, the end grabs the tackle/guard, and holds on. We hope the defensive tackle gets around to the outside and gets the sack. If there is a hole and the tackle is chasing him inside, the end takes the gap and goes to the quarterback. The defensive tackle is in a heavy technique on the guard and releases outside.

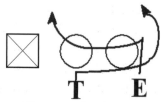

Diagram #5. Me game

The "you" game (Diagram #6), is the opposite stunt. On this stunt, the defensive tackle has a technique we call CTB. That means he charges through the B gap and works for containment to the outside. The end is the second defender coming inside over the offensive guard. We tell the end to expect one of two things as he comes inside. He could see the guard trying to pan back into position to pick him up. The end can use that momentum against the guard to try to get to the quarterback. He could see the center sitting and waiting for him. If that is the case, the defensive end has two to three yards of momentum built up and blasts the center.

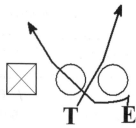

Diagram #6. You game

We have a "coast" call (Diagram #7), which is a "me" game on one side and a "you" game on the other. We base the stunt on which way the running back sets or what the game plan shows. If the center turns away from the running back, we know the "coast" is available in our stunt package. With the center sliding right, we run the "me" game to the right and the "you" game to the left. The defensive tackle to the "you" side does everything he possibly can to draw the guard out so the defensive end hit frees up the middle. We want to run the "you" call to the side of the running back.

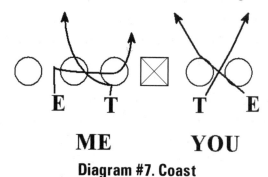

Diagram #7. Coast

Another stunt we use is "Falcon" (Diagram #8). This is a four-man game based on our scouting report and film study. We rushed the defensive end to the side of the slide into the man-to-man side of the protection. The defensive tackle to his side has a CTB technique and rushes hard to the outside for contain.

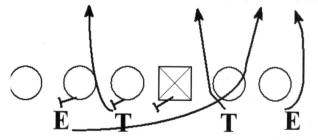

Diagram #8. Falcon

The defensive end to the man-blocking side is a true containment man. He has to stay on the outside and cannot go underneath the blocker. Even if the under move is there, he cannot take that move. This stunt was good for us a couple of times this year. In all these games, if the read is a running play, the stunts are off.

I want to go to the film and show some of the things I talked about in the lecture. I hope you got something out of this. If there is anything I can help you with, please let me know and I will be happy to visit with you.

EIGHT-MAN FRONT MULTIPLE DEFENSE

Texas Christian University

Thank you it is good to be back in this area. Some coaches come to these clinics and do not tell you anything because they think they have something unique. Men, there are very few original thoughts in college football. Everyone steals from everyone else. Coaches that take the old ideas and innovate them have the popular schemes. A few years ago, the hot defense was the 46-defense used by Buddy Ryan in Chicago during their Super Bowl years. There was a book written in 1954 on the 46-defense. The brochure for this clinic lists me as an innovator of the 4-2-5 defense. The eight-man front has been around forever. What we do with the eight-man front is get as much speed on the field as we can and be physical.

At TCU, we have almost an 80 percent graduation rate. Every six weeks we have our players fill out an evaluation form. We have everything on the form that reflects every aspect of their athletic ability, intelligence, personality, and behavioral traits. There are a number of choices available. We list a variety of ideas. We have quotes from "refusing to lose" all the way to "it does not matter." The players fill out the form and rate themselves. The coaches also fill out a form on each player. They rate them according to what they see. This form lets the player relate his self-image as to the kind of player and competitor he thinks he is. When freshmen come into our program, they usually rate themselves at the top with nines or tens. Usually the coaches rate them at five or six on the scale.

Other categories on the form are talent level, speed, toughness, awareness, intelligence, commitment, work habits, durability, coach-ability, strength, character, trust level, academics, leadership, and MTXE (Mental Toughness, Extra Effort). We give them a grade on what they do. If they get over 60 on the test, they generally are good players and accountable within the system. That means they will go to class and be in the program for four or five years.

When you talk to incoming freshmen and give them the test, about 50 percent of them walk out of your office and believe what you tell them. The other 50 percent do not think you know what you are talking about. We keep the results and review them each year. The results are funny because, at the beginning of the players' freshmen year, the players and coaches are on opposite ends of the spectrum. It is remarkable how each year the players and coaches get closer on the scale. By their senior year, the players and coaching staff are thinking the same way.

That gives you a good feeling because you know they have matured and are accountable. They get their degrees and are closer to knowing what they want to do with their lives. This form serves a great purpose for us. If you want a copy, drop me a note and I will send it to you.

Each year during the off-season, we get a feel for what type of football team we are going to have for the next year. We give each year's team a motto to guide them throughout the season. Two seasons back, we almost broke into the Bowl Championship Series because we were undefeated for most of the season. Last year I got tired of our players talking about playing in the BCS. I told the players, no more talk. If they thought they belonged in the Bowl Championship Series, "Show me."

After the first four games, we were 2-2 and there was no more talk. We did not get accomplished on defense what we needed to do. We lost eight players from the defensive team to NFL camps. We had to play with younger talent and did not work as hard in the spring and summer as we needed to maintain our level of play. Then to compound matters, we lost a starting corner to grades.

Regardless of what happens each year we start our season the same way. A program is build upon tradition. The tradition at Texas Christian is the base of our pyramid. We start at the bottom with the players' commitment to attitude, chemistry, family, and accountability. This preparation starts in January. We work by position groups. We bring the skilled athletes in together to lift and run. We group the big men in one group, and the standup players in the other group.

I keep my offensive and defensive coordinators off the road and they work with these groups. The reason I do that is to ensure there will be improvement within the course of the off-season program. If I have to go to war with a redshirt freshman, I want to know he has worked in the off-season. The way to do that is to put the coach in charge of playing time during the season, in charge of the workouts. If they want to play, they will improve. Within the off-season program, we want them to start to mature.

We move up the levels of the pyramid to get to the top. Within those levels, the goal is not just winning. We want to teach the value of being honest, not cheating, and not stealing. Sometimes young coaches do things that are not good for the program. They do not tell the exact truth. They do not do it on purpose. They do it because they want people to be happy with the way things are going. The bottom line is trying to get our players where they are accountable and understand what we want to accomplish.

Mental toughness is part of the tradition and essential in the offense, defense, and the kicking games. That, in addition to being prepared, goes a long way to the success in a program. The players have to play one game at a time. They cannot beat themselves and must find a way to win. The biggest and hardest thing to get over to your team is to believe.

Each year the road to success changes for each team. We feel we must win the games played in Texas. The fact that we recruit in the state of Texas almost exclusively is the reason we feel we must be successful in Texas. To be a championship team you need a home-field advantage and you must win at home. If you cannot win at home, you will not win anywhere. We have a 16-game winning streak at home. If you want to be a special team, you have to win on the road.

Our motto from two years ago was: "Count me in." In 2001, my first year as head coach, I made a mistake. I talked too much about the 2000 team. The 2000 team was a great team. We had three-year starter on defense and led the nation in defense. We had players on that team that started 40 games for us. My first year as head coach we went 6-5 and I resolved not to make that mistake again. The motto of the 2002 team was: "Count me in." We had young players that had to step up their level of play. They wanted to be "counted in" on the road to success. In 2002, we went 10-2. That is the way we must do things in our program to be successful.

If you want a good program, you have to think on the positive side. Being a defensive coach, sometimes I think we are second-class citizens. If the offense is moving the ball all over the place, they get the recognition. The defensive coaches do not get any recognition. I joke about that.

The top of the pyramid is a national championship in the BCS. At Texas Christian, as many people call a mid-major team, that may be out of reach. However, they probably thought the same thing in Miami at one time. There are two things you need to win a national championship. You must have the resources and a recruiting base. Just like in Pennsylvania, we feel we have those two things in Texas.

We call our defense multiplicity with simplicity. I still believe in the KISS method, but I have found out there are a bunch of coaches that are paid to do a good job. If you do not have a way to get an edge or a different way to teach your players when they do not understand, you could be in trouble. We want to make sure our players can finish the drill and play. I am going to talk about how to get into a seven-, eight-, and nine-man front when you have five in the secondary and six in the box.

The second thing I will talk about is blitzing from man coverage or a zone void scheme. It is easier to do both when your defense starts as the nickel package. The third thing is the double rotation zone and how we play both man and zone in the same coverage concept.

We consider four things in recruiting. The number one asset we look for is speed. We recruit speed over size. If we can get speed and size in the same player, that is great. We do recruit for size, but with certain restrictions. You have to find ways to be successful. We coach our defense like offense. The free safety and the weak safety are the quarterbacks of our defense. Our fronts and coverages have nothing to do with each other unless I want that to be the case. If you run your scheme that way, you must be able to communicate. The last thing we look for is strength and work ethics.

I came from a town of about 175 people in western Kansas. The reason we played sports was to keep from throwing bales of hay or riding the tractor. You had a choice, but the biggest thing was the girls were at the track meets.

I want to talk about our fronts. The first front is the eagle front. We align the eagle front four different ways. We line up to the tight end, to the split end, toward the field, or into the boundary. In the eagle front, someone on the line of scrimmage is in a 3 technique. We use the terms "rip" or "Liz" to designate the side for the 3-technique tackle. If the tight end breaks the huddle and aligns on the defense's left, the eagle linebacker calls "Liz." The 3-technique tackle aligns on the left outside shoulder of the guard and the nose tackle goes to the right. Our defensive ends do not flip-flop from one side to the other. The reason we flip the tackles is our inability to find two tackles with the ability to run. In our 3-technique tackle, we want a 300-pound tackle that can run 4.6 in the forty and take on a double-team.

The defensive end to the tight end side plays a 6-technique head up the tight end unless he gets over a three-foot split (Diagram #1). If he gets over a three-foot split, he moves to a 7 technique on the tight end, which is the inside shoulder. If there is no tight end, the defensive end plays a 5 technique or outside shoulder of the offensive tackle.

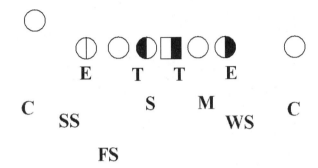

Diagram #1. Basic eagle alignment

If the defensive call is "field" or "boundary," the linebackers align before the offense breaks the huddle. If the call is tight or split, we have to let the offense align before we declare. The rip or Liz calls are for the 3-technique tackle alignment only. If you want to stop teams on offense, you have to take away what they do well. You have to put more defenders in the area where they run the ball, then they can block.

The second thing you must do is pre-play plays. In a two-back system when we call an eagle defense, a linebacker alignment is at four-and-a-half yards. We do that to give our linebackers a chance to fast-flow and get downhill in a hurry. We can fast-flow both linebackers because we overlap with our safeties in the running game. That lets us get the extra linebacker across the stacks on the isolation and power plays from the two-back set.

If we play the up defense, it is the same adjustments and calls of the eagle defense. We run tight, split, field, and boundary as we declare the defense. We run the Liz and rip calls for the 3-technique tackle. The difference is the depth of the linebackers. If the set is a one-back formation, the zone play is the popular play from that set. If the linebackers play eagle against the one-back set, they are at the depth of four-and-a-half yards. That puts the 320-pound guard base blocking on a 230-pound linebacker at a depth of four-and-a-half yards. That is a mis-match. We move the linebackers up to the depth of two-and-a-half yards and play gap control instead of fast-flow. We play the play in this situation.

In the last eight years, we have never been out of the top 25 in run defense and have finished first twice. One of the keys is to pre-play plays and take them away from the offense. We can play with 220-pound linebackers because they can make plays and run. From the one-back set the offense runs the inside and outside zone play and the counter. The play that can hurt us in this alignment is the counter because the linebackers may end up getting pinned inside. I will tell you how we play the counter later.

I have faced the problems of playing with smaller players my entire college career. I have been at the Naval Academy, Utah State, and New Mexico. Those are not the top spots of major college football. At each place, we had to find ways to make our players successful. We slant, stunt, and gamble at Texas Christian. If we had better players on a daily basis, we could play a straight up game. The key is to establish the defense, run to the football, and give your kids a chance to be successful.

In our pass coverages, cover 2 is our robber coverage. That means the free safety to the strong side has the number-two receiver. If the number-two receiver does not run a vertical route, the safety robs the curl and post patterns of the number-one receiver.

Our quarter coverage is "blue." We changed it to cover 4 and played it like crap, so we changed it back to blue coverage. Our cover 5 is squats and half coverage.

There are only three kinds of looks in football except a quad set. The offense can have a pro set, twins set, or trips set. That gives the offense one, two, or three receivers to the passing strength side. For this example the formation is a pro-twins set with one-back set in the backfield. That gives the offense a twins set to one side of the defense and a tight end and flanker back to the other. The passing strength of

that formation is the "twins" side. The running strength is toward the tight end. If we have called a tight eagle defense, the eagle linebacker calls rip. That means the tight end is right and the 3-technique tackle is set to the right side of the defense.

The free safety calls left and plays "25" (Diagram #2). He aligns into the twins side of the formation. If the formation had been a tight end and flanker back, his alignment is over the strongside guard. In the twins look, he splits the difference between the offensive tackle and the slotback in the twins set. If run shows the free safety is an alley runner and quarterback player. The strong safety aligns on the number-two receiver and is the force player on the run and the pitch player on the option. The free safety is the communicator to the strongside and communicates the coverage to the corner, strong safety, and linebacker to his side.

If a pass shows, the secondary plays cover 2 to the strength. The free safety keys the number-two receiver. If he goes vertical, he takes him. If he does not come vertical, the free safety robs the number-one receiver on the curl or post pattern. If the number-two receiver does anything fewer than eight yards, the strong safety sets on him. If the number-two receiver goes vertical, the strong safety turns his attention to the number-one receiver.

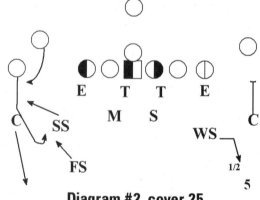

Diagram #2. cover 25

The backside is the weakness of the coverage. We play cover 5 to this side. The weak safety is the communicator and talks to the corner and the linebacker to his side. The corner and weak safety play cover 5, which is squat and halves coverage. The corner plays the backside flat patterns with the weak safety playing over the top in half coverage. The linebacker to that side is involved in their coverage.

In the first day of two-a-day practice, we teach cover 2. That afternoon we teach blue coverage and the next morning we teach cover 5. When we teach these coverages in practice, we teach them across the board to both sides. From that point forward, we never call them by themselves again. There are two sides in the defensive secondary divided by the football. If we call "25," we are playing cover 2 to the passing strength of the formation and cover 5 to the backside.

In the 4-3 defense, the toughest thing to play when you mix coverages is change of strength motion because linebackers have to bounce in and out of coverage. To solve that problem, we try to recruit a player at the strong safety position that can play some man-to-man coverage, blitz, and play like a Will linebacker. We want him in the 6'1", 215-pound range and he does all the adjusting in the coverage.

In our fronts, I drew up a tight eagle look for the alignment. We have a Liz call to the tight end and the nose tackle is on the backside. The tightside defensive end aligns in a 6-technique head up the tight end. The defensive end to the backside has no tight end and aligns in a 5 technique. All our defensive linemen use two techniques when slanting. If they want to control the gap, they use a "loop step" (Diagram #3). That is a flat step down the line of scrimmage. If the blocker tries to down block, the defender can play across his face. That keeps the defender from being cut off from his gap. If we use a loop step, the eyes of the defender go to the next blocker on the inside. If the blocker is coming at him, he gets upfield, keeps the outside shoulder free, and squeezes inside. That is the "ricochet technique."

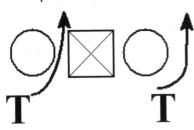

Diagram #3. Loop

If the defensive linemen cross the blocker face on the snap of the ball, we call that technique a "slant step" (Diagram #4). It is more aggressive. The defender takes a short step to the inside, a cross-over step, and rips with his outside forearm through the gap. He keys the next blocker to use the ricochet technique if the blocker comes to him.

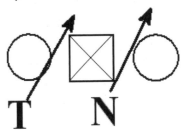

Diagram #4. Slant

We have line calls to move the defensive line on stunts. If we give a "toro" call, that moves both tackles on a stunt to the strongside (Diagram #5). The 3-technique tackle and nose tackle slant right or left depending on the line strength call. If the call is "rip toro," both tackles slant right through the next gap. A "Liz toro" is still toward the tight end but slants left.

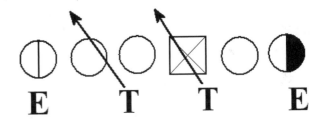

Diagram #5. Rip toro

If we want to move all four of the down linemen, we call, "rip tank" or "Liz tank" (Diagram #6). That moves all four defensive linemen toward the call made by the eagle linebacker.

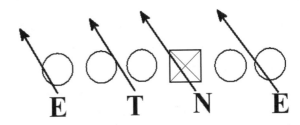

Diagram #6. Rip tank

If the words are "army" or "aim," we go away from the call made by the eagle linebacker. If we call a "rip army," all four defensive linemen go away from the call. Since the call was rip, they slant to the left. Aim is the tackle stunt away from the call. The terminology does not matter; use the terms you want, but make them simple.

If we call the eagle defense by itself, the nose tackle aligns on the backside shade of the center. If we add the letter "G" to the call, the nose tackle aligns in a 2 technique on the guard with an inside eye shade (Diagram #7). If the call is "tight-G," the 3-technique tackle aligns toward the tight end and the nose tackle aligns on the guard to the weakside.

Diagram #7. Tight-G

I want to talk about a couple of other fronts. We have what we call an "Indian front" (Diagram #8). The Indian front is a specialty front to play against inside zone teams. Both defensive tackles align in the "G" position, which is the cut-back running lane of the inside zone scheme. The linebacker still gives the rip and Liz call and the tackle flips, but the 3-technique tackle goes to the inside shade on the guard. The linebackers move wider in their alignments.

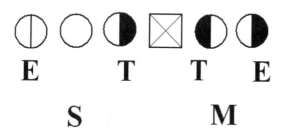

Diagram #8. Indian front

The "outlaw front" has both tackles aligned in 3 techniques (Diagram #9). Both linebackers align is the A gap. If you watched the Super Bowl, New England played the outlaw front most of the game. The reason for playing that type of front against Philadelphia was the running of McNabb. Both defensive ends came up the field and did not let him

run out of the pocket. They played a coverage man on the tight end and both linebackers played inside.

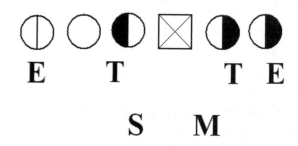

Diagram #9. Outlaw front

Playing two 3-technique tackles gave the offense no option on running the zone play. If the offense wanted to block back and pull a guard, with the linebackers that tight it gave them a run-through lane. We play the outlaw front against teams that play one-back and two tight ends

If we call an "Indian tight," we align in the Indian front and slant into the tight front. If the line call is Liz, the slant is left. If it is rip, we align in the Indian front and slant right into the tight front.

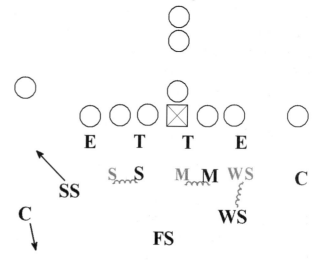

Diagram #10. Slide alignment

The next adjustment is a "slide alignment" (Diagram #10). I stole this from a defensive coach by the name of John Goodner. When I started using the eight-man front, we got 175 plays from a two-back formation all running to the tight-end side. If you align your Sam Linebacker in a 3-technique tackle stack or in the A gap, you are a half man short in the off-tackle hole. The answer to that problem is the "slide alignment." We still call the front with a "tight" call because it has nothing to do with the front. There is a slide call in the secondary. In the secondary, we call cover-2-sky-slide.

The free safety sees the tight end come to the left side of the defense. He calls left as passing strength. The linebacker calls Liz for the left alignment of the tight end. The weak safety sees a two-back set with the fullback in the I-formation, in the strong back position, or the tailback shift to the trips set. The weak safety calls slide and moves up into a position of a Will linebacker to the backside. The Sam and Mike linebacker slide to the tight-end side. They play like true 4-3 linebackers. To stop people, you have to overplay what they do well. We open with Oklahoma next year. We must already have everything in our package we need to stop them in the running and passing games. We can teach it in the spring and two-a-day practices in the fall.

The last five days of spring practice, we work on the mid-line veer and triple option. We devote the last 20 minutes of practice to that scheme. We start preparing our players in spring ball. Every third day during two-a-days we will work on the triple option. Every Sunday night we are going to work on the triple option. When we get to the Air Force game, that Sunday night we will have the game plan. Be prepared for what you have to play. You cannot get ready for a triple option team in one week.

Since we put the slide alignment into our package, we have not had over 60 plays of two-back offense run at us in 10 years. We had 55 plays in the slide package this year. Of those 55 plays, 26 of them were passes. The big thing about defense is to know what to go to when things go bad. If you cannot fix the problem, the defense is no good. People will try to exploit what you do. If you do not know the defense, you cannot fix it. If the offense started to take advantage to the weakside with the run, we have a number of things we can do. One solution would be to slide the defensive line into an "under" defense. The free safety has to be the alley runner to the weakside in this defense.

The key to the slide defense is not to line up in the defense but to move to it late. You have to

disguise so the offense does not know what you are doing. The weak safety in the one-back set plays at eight yards so he can help on three verticals run to the strongside.

To the backside in the slide alignment, you have two choices in pass coverage. You can play zone or man coverage. As a head coach I try to study the opponent's defense during the week. The opponent's offense will be the best at what they play against in their practices. When we played Colorado State, their defense zone blitzed, and played squat and halves in their secondary. They did not play a man-to-man press defense. That is what I ran against them. They did not handle the press-man coverage very well.

I want to show you some film on our defense. The brochure says we are going to talk about the blitz package. The next thing we do is to combine the calls in combinations. For instance, if we want to a run defensive call and bring the safeties off the edge, we can call "smoke." The smoke call brings one or two safeties off the edges of the defense. If we call "field-G army, field smoke" (Diagram #11), that means we are in a field eagle defense into the wideside of the field. The line is slanting into the boundary. The nose tackle is aligned over the guard in a 2 technique. In the secondary, we are playing man-to-man coverage. The corners match up on the wide receivers. The free safety slides over to take the tight end. The Mike and Sam linebackers have the remaining backs in the backfield. The strong safety blitzes off the edge.

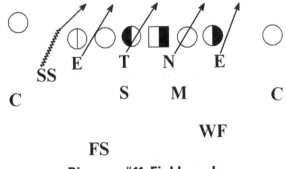

Diagram #11. Field smoke

If we want to bring the smoke from the other side, we call "short smoke." On that call, the weak safety runs the blitz off the edge from the boundary. If we want to send both safeties off the edge, we call "double smoke."

In our blitz package, you can blitz a thousand different ways. When we call "bullets", we are blitzing inside linebackers. The secondary does not know what kind of bullets the linebackers are running and do not care. All they know is the linebackers are going. The free safety wants to know with whom he is playing coverage. The corners are out of the mix because they always match up with the wide receivers to their side. The free safety plays coverage with the strong and weak safeties. If we call double smoke, the free safety is playing coverage with the two inside linebackers. The free safety knows he has to communicate with the linebackers.

Teams try to attack us to the backside when we slide our linebackers. We change the front by how we call the coverage, not by how we call the front. Our secondary wants to accomplish their goal of not talking to the front six players. In this defense, we call tight-G with the Sam and Mike linebackers playing eagle defense because there are two backs in the backfield. In the secondary, instead of playing cover-2 we go to a blue coverage (Diagram #12), which is quarter coverage. In the blue coverage, the weak safety drops down into a hip position of the 2-technique tackle. The linebackers slide to the strongside and we look like a standard 4-3 defense.

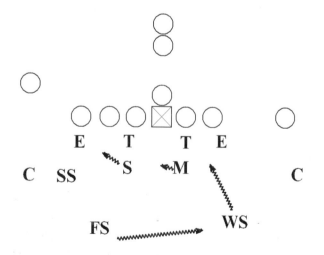

Diagram #12. Tight-G blue coverage

The next example of calling coverages and moving the front is the "power call" (Diagram #13). On this defense, we call a split-G. If the offense comes out with a pro set to the left of the defense, the eagle linebacker calls rip. That sets the 3-technique tackle to the right side of the defense. The defensive end to that side aligns in a 5 technique because he has no tight end. To the tight-end side we are aligned in a shade 2 technique by the nose tackle and a 6 technique by the defensive end.

On the tight-end side, I want to play a 59 alignment to the tight end. I signal a power-blue call as the coverage. The power call drops the strong safety down into a 9-technique on the tight end. He has to communicate with one player. He tells the defensive end to move into a 5 technique on the offensive tackle. I play with a 215-pound strong safety and he does not play like a 250-pound outside linebacker. He cannot play head up on the tight end. He gets into an outside shade and tilts to the inside. This gives us an adjustment to the stop teams from running to the split side with a two back attack

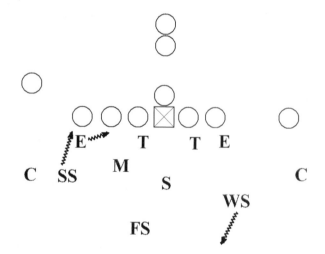

Diagram #13. Split-G power blue

We play blue coverage in the secondary. That means the weak safety drops into a quarter coverage with the corner on his side. The free safety plays a quarter coverage with the corner on his side. That gives us a chance to stop the attack to the weakside.

Those are two ways to help us on weakside. The third way is to bring a smoke stunt from that side and cause problems in the backfield. That brings a 4.5 speedster into the backfield to try and wreck things before they get started.

We coach our defense differently than most teams. We have only one defensive line coach. I put the graduate assistant with him. If he is working with the defensive tackles, the graduate assistant works with the defensive ends. When he works with the defensive ends, the GA works with the defensive tackles. That does not happen every year. In some years we do not have a graduate assistant who can help in the defensive line. We try to get the best graduate assistant that can help our program. That generally is someone who is good at computer skills. Because there is so much computer skill involved, the graduate assistant has to be competent in that area. We have to hire the GA who is best for our system.

We have a linebacker coach. We have a safety coach that works with the strong, free, and weak safeties. We have a corner coach who works with the corners. If you put your corners on islands, you must find a good cornerback coach to work with them. He has to work with the corners exclusively. We do not recruit big corners that play squat coverage. We want corners that can play in space, play one-on-one, and have ice in their veins. This year we signed two corners that are 6'2" and 190-pounds. One of them ran 20.9 for 200 meters. If you can get size and speed in the same athlete, that is a bonus.

Let me talk coverage for just a minute. If we split the sides of the defense at the center, the free safety works in coverage with the strong safety, corner, and linebacker to his side. The weak safety works with the corner and linebacker to his side. They never work together unless there is a trips set. In all of the zone coverages we have, the inside linebackers play the number-three receiver.

We even try to take coverage away from our linebackers. The away-side linebacker in our coverage either is a wall player or slash player. A wall player keeps people from getting into the middle of the field or up the seams. A slash player is a player that keeps leverage on the flat routes.

The mistake coaches make is getting bored with teaching the same coverage. They start to add coverages and before they know it, they have about 20 coverages. We do it, too. About five of those 20 coverages do the same thing. That is when you have to ask yourself why do you play the coverage? In our scheme, robber coverage is the one we want to use. It gives you great run support, angles, and the eight-man front. From the robber coverage, you can overplay offensive strategies and it has good adjustment to any scheme. Against the one-back set, it is weak because the linebacker has the number-two receiver on the verticals route.

The defense is weak against play-action. We want to keep the strong safety force and still protect against four vertical routes. We can do that with blue coverage.

Before I get into this next situation, I need to explain "wheel coverage" (Diagram #14). The free safety keys the number-two receiver. If the number-two receiver runs a route to the outside, the free safety makes a wheel call to the corner. That tells the corner he has an outside route working in his area. The corner continues to play the number-one receiver, but his eyes go to the number-two receiver. The wheel call tells the corner the free safety has the post by the number-one receiver.

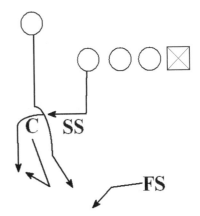

Diagram #14. Wheel coverage

The corner squeezes the number-one receiver to the free safety and comes off on the wheel pattern run by the number-two receiver. We do not want the strong safety to take the wheel route. If the offense sees the strong safety taking the wheel route, they will bring the third receiver out of the backfield into the flat.

If the offense came out with a trips set with a tight end into the trips side, we make a tight eagle call. The pattern that drove people into three deep sent the number-three receiver deep and ran the number-one and number-two receivers on an out-curl pattern. That pattern kept the corner and free safety deep. The offense ran the out-curl pattern and high-lowed the strong safety. We run an automatic call for the weak safety (Diagram #15). He runs with the number-three receiver on the deep pattern.

The backside corner is in man coverage on the number-one receiver to the backside of the three-receiver set. The backside linebacker has the short and long wall on the next receiver his way.

That frees the free safety to run cover-2 robber with the corner and strong safety. If the number-two receiver goes out, the free safety robs the curl by the number-one receiver. We turned the number-three receiver over to the weak safety and played cover-2 robber on the two outside receivers. If the number-two receiver runs an outside route, the free safety calls wheel to the corner. The number-one receiver runs deep and to the post. The free safety and corner play wheel coverage on the number-one and number-two receivers.

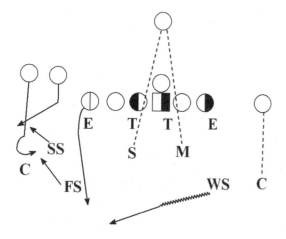

Diagram #15. Trips adjustment

A coach told me this story about Dan Fouts of the San Diego Chargers. Dan Fouts had three offensive coordinators in five years. One of the coordinators began to tell Dan what he wanted him

to read. Dan told him the only thing he had to know was who was playing one-on-one coverage. The key for us in these coverages is to disguise them so the offense cannot find the one-on-one match-up.

To the backside, we want to disguise what we are doing. We have to play squat and halves, quarters, man to the off-side trips, and man coverage. We are trying to make the perfect call to cover everything the offense can do. The way to make that call is call two coverages that do not have anything to do with one another. Another important fact is the coverage does not involve the front six defenders in our defense.

If I can give you one point that helps you, then I consider my lecture a success. I coached at a place called UC-Davis. They won 20 straight conference championships. The head coach was Jim Sochor, who was a good friend of Bill Walsh. They called everyone by their first names and did not use a whistle on the practice field. They were a non-scholarship school and had 180 players out for football every year. The key to the situation was what they taught me about personnel. They played with 230-pound defensive linemen against 290-pound offensive linemen. They taught me there was no such saying as, "I cannot do that." Their answer to "I cannot" was "I will". It may take us a little longer to accomplish the task.

I was a young coach and thought I had all the answers. I found out I did not know anything and still do not. Every day I learn something new. The key is to make sure you continue to keep learning.

One of the things that make you a good defensive team is how you start practice each day. We have two "take-away" circuits with four stations in each circuit. We do not call them turnovers because that indicates the offense gave the ball to you. We also have a tackling circuit. We put all the stations in close proximity to each other on the practice field. In the stations we want more than tackling, striping the ball, and catching the ball; we want to create enthusiasm. The stations are fifteen yards apart. We have four groups going at the same time. We spend five minutes in the circuit.

Everybody gets a rep at each station and rotates to the next station.

We have the defensive line, linebackers, safeties, and corners grouped at the four stations. On Tuesday, we have a tackling circuit and a take-away circuit on Wednesday. We do the tackling circuit in pads or no pads. They are tackling bags not people.

The first station in the tackling circuit is our "string out drill"(Diagram #16). We have a defender and a blocker. The blocker is on all fours. He launches himself at the defender's inside leg and tries to cut him. The defender punches the blocker down and tries to turn the head or pad. After the defender comes off the block, he comes forward to the cone to assimilate a tackle.

The second station is the "box tackling drill." This is a sideline tackling drill. We do not tackle people; we tackle dummies held by players. I hate the "buddy" drill because it is too inconsistent with the effort you want. Using bags keeps the players healthy and allows us to tackle longer. The bag holder runs straight to a cone on the sideline. The tackler attacks across with the head and works his feet around to get square on the bag and drive the bag back.

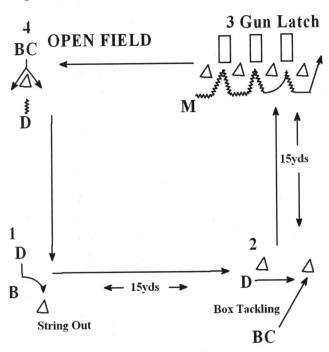

Diagram #16. Tackling circuit

The third drill is the "gun latch drill." This drill is a session of two cones with a bag in between them. The tackle comes up between the two cones, tackles the bag, wraps up, and drives his feet through the tackle. On the whistle, the defensive backs and linebackers backpedal out of the first chute, slide over, and tackle the second dummy. The defensive linemen turn and sprint back to the next chute when the whistle blows. We are teaching technique tackling in this drill. We teach hand, eyes, and run-through. A coaching point for the bag holder is to step forward on contact. If they do not the tackler steps on his feet, he falls, and ruins the drill.

The last tackling station is an "open-field tackling drill." This is the game situation drill. This is tackling in space. The tackler and ballcarrier start on opposite sides of a cone. The bag holder runs to the cone and makes a move to the right or left. The tackler approaches from the other direction and makes the tackle. The two mistakes that occur in an open-field tackle are the tackler dives or, on contact, he does not move his feet. Those are coaching points and emphasis of this drill.

We do the same thing in a take-away circuit. In take-away circuit A, the first station is "scoop and score." In this drill, we step them over a series of bags, drop a ball, and they scoop and score. If they do not get the ball on the first attempt, they fall on the ball and cradle it.

The second station is a "strip and scoop drill." We have a dummy with a Velcro-ed ball on it. We align two defensive players at the end of the line of scrimmage. The dummy is in the middle at five-step depth. The two defenders attack at the same time. One strips the ball and the other scoops and scores.

In the third drill, we use a "strip and punch drill." We have balls with handles on them. That keeps us from chasing balls all over the place. We work in a partner drill. One player carries the ball and the other strips. The defender attacks from behind. He makes the tackle and tomahawks the ball out of the ballcarrier's arm. The ball comes loose, but the handle prevents it from getting away from the ballcarrier. In the next part of the drill, the defender attacks, performs a tackle, and punches the ball from underneath to knock it out.

The fourth drill is a "break on the ball" drill. This is the game situation drill. We have backs and linebackers breaking on a thrown ball. For the secondary backs, we may have a deep ball drill. They take one or two steps, the coach calls ball and throws the ball over the opposite shoulder. The back looks up on the command ball and has to find the ball. The circuit is set up like the diagram for the tackling station.

We have a take-away circuit B. In this circuit, the first drill is a double strip. The first man makes the tackle; the second defender strips the ball. The second station teaches players how to fall on a fumble. In the third station, the defensive backs execute a backpedal, plant, and drive on an angle through a bag holder. The third station for defensive linemen is a "hands up drill." We charge two defenders at a coach who imitates the throwing motion of the quarterback. The lineman on the side the ball, as directed, gets his hands up to block the ball. The other defender runs through the quarterback.

This teaches the defensive linemen who are not in the quarterback's face not to jump or hold their hands up. If both linemen jump on the quarterback pump, the quarterback may escape. However, if the quarterback pumps toward one lineman and pulls the ball down, the other lineman runs over him. You can put the problems your players are having in a game situation into these stations and make them part of the circuit.

The last drill is a "big ball drill." The defender attacks the quarterback. We roll the big ball at him as he comes in on the quarterback. He has to punch the big ball with his hands and get a piece of the thrown ball by the quarterback. Pass rushing and knocking balls down is like tackling; if you do not use your eyes, you cannot perform the drill.

You have been a great audience. I wish we could recruit up here, but for players to come from Pittsburgh to Texas Christian he has to fly over several good schools. I know you have good football in this state. I am humbled and privileged to come and be a part of it. I hope there will be a time I get to come back for a visit. Thank you for your hospitality.

SPECIAL TEAMS AND THE PUNTING GAME

Ferris State University

Let me give you a little about my background. I have been at Ferris State University for 21 years now. I started my coaching career in the Upper Peninsula of Michigan as a football coach. I graduated from Ferris State in the 1970s and I coached high school football for five years. I understand the things you are going through. It is all about working with young people. It is satisfying for me to see the young people grow up.

I came to Ferris State 21 years ago as a graduate assistant. After that, I became the linebacker coach. Then I became the defensive coordinator. I have been the head coach for the last 10 years going on my 11th season. It is an interesting time for me. It is all about working with young people. I give the high school coaches a lot of credit for what you are doing. We are in the business that molds young lives. We can never forget that point. That is the most important thing. It is rewarding for me to be able to stay at the same school for as long as I have been at Ferris State. As I travel to high schools recruiting, I see former students all of the time. It is great to see them develop, grow, and mature. Do not overlook the impact you have in working with the young kids today.

A couple of other things and then I will get into special teams. I think one of the most important things in coaching is to get kids to play for you. If you expect kids to give you everything they have, you must do that back in return. There are no gimmicks in this business. If you can show attention to your players and if you are there when they need you, they will play for you. You should treat the players the way you would want to be treated. If you do that, you will get a kid that is going to be committed to you and your program.

The next point I want to discuss will lead into my topic today. As a coach, you must be a teacher. You must be a very good teacher to be successful in our business. There is a difference between the teacher in the classroom, as many of you are, and a football coach. Many things are similar, but if the student does not comprehend and grasp what the teacher is trying to get across to him, the teacher flunks him. If the kid does not understand what the football coach is trying to get across to him, they fire the football coach. That is the difference. You must find a way to get the kids understand what you are trying to get across to them.

It does not matter what you know as far as X's and O's. If you cannot get the kids to learn what you are teaching them and display it on the football field, it does not matter. All of the guys that learned the game of football with a Budweiser in one hand and a remote control in the other hand that are your number-one critics, that do not come to football clinics but think they know every thing about football — they will be on your butt.

I am going to talk about special teams. I am going more into how we break the game up as far as techniques are concerned. In addition, I will cover some drills that we work on. I have been involved with the special teams for several years as the head coach. I want those kids to understand how important special teams are. Some teams take special teams very lightly. Some teams put 11 men out on the field, kick the ball down the field, and tell them to go get it. You can turn a game around very quickly with the kicking game. However, you have to coach it and teach it just as you have to coach linebackers. We work technique drills during the special teams sessions. Do you put players on the field and tell them what to do and then look at the film on Sunday to see if the players performed the task correctly?

You must make a commitment time-wise to the special teams. I want to cover an example of a practice plan that we use. Our Tuesday and Wednesday practice schedules are about the same. We are going to spend ten minutes a day before the stretching period on our specialist. This includes sessions with the snappers, kickers, return men, and all phases of the kicking game. In addition, we are going to spend time with the individual drills with the players. We work on the techniques in this period.

FERRIS STATE FOOTBALL PRACTICE PLAN

Game Week Wednesday—Date:_____

Offense	Time	Defense
Warm-Up	3:15	Warm-Up
Specialist	3:20	Specialist
Team Stretch	3:25	Team Stretch
Kicking Game	3:30	Kicking Game
Teach	3:35	Teach
	3:55	
Giant	4:20	Giant
Inside	4:25	Inside
Skelly	4:35	Skelly
Team vs. Defense	4:50	Team vs. Offense
Team vs. Scouts	5:10	Team vs. Scouts
Goal Line	5:30	Pursuit

Comments: The specialist period is 10 minutes.

Special Teams

5 Minutes = X-PT/FG/Block

15 Minutes = Punt, punt return, kickoff, kickoff return.

On Tuesday, we may work with the punters on their techniques. On Wednesday, we may work with the defense blocking the punt. We dedicate 20 minutes to the team portion of special teams. In the first 10 minutes, we go about half speed. We have not stretched at this point in practice. We want to make sure they understand the proper techniques. Later when we get to our 20-minute period on special teams, we can determine what we need to work on. That covers Tuesday and Wednesday.

Thursday is our review day. This is the last day we are on the field because we meet on Friday and play on Saturday. This is what we do on game week Thursday.

Game Week Thursday—Date:_____

Offense	Time	Defense
Warm-Up	3:15	Warm-Up
Specialist	3:20	Specialist
Team Stretch	3:25	Team Stretch
Kicking Game	3:30	Kicking Game
Teach	3:35	Teach
Skelly	4:10	Skelly
Team Passe	4:25	Team Pass
Team vs. Scouts	4:40	Team vs. Scouts
2 Min. X PT/FG	5:05	2 Min. X PT/FG

Comments: Specialist period is 10 minutes.

Special Teams Script - 25 Minutes

THURSDAY KICKING SCRIPT

Extra Point/Field Goal: 6 Kicks (1's)

Spread Punt: 1's and 2's one each vs. scout (full cover, tag off)

Short Punt: 1's and 2's one each vs. air (mirror)

Tight Punt: 1's and 2's one each vs. scout (full cover, tag off)

Punt Rush: 1's and 2's one each rocket vs. scouts (full return)

1's and 2's one each Lazer vs. scouts (full return)

1's and 2's one each missile vs. scouts (full return)

Punt Safe: 1 defense vs. scouts (snoop smoke 5) full return

Kickoff Return: 1's and 2's one each red vs. scouts

1's vs. surprise onside kick

1's and 2's one each Blue vs. scouts

Kickoff return after safety: 1's one time

Substitutes one time vs. air (1's only leave when replaced)

Kickoff: 1's and 2's one each RDM vs. scouts

1's Surprise onside kick

Kickoff after safety: 1's one time vs. scouts

Special onsides kick: 1's vs. air

We are going to cover every situation that is going to happen in a football game.

I am going to spend the majority of my time left talking about our punt team. The punt team is the most critical part of our special teams. If you get a punt blocked, you have a major problem. It can turn a football game around. I am going to put my best players on this unit. I will use starters on this unit. I know you want to play as many players as possible but you must decide if you want to risk a blocked punt or if you want to have the best players on that unit. Let me go over some of our philosophy and general rules on our Punt Team.

General Philosophy

- Put our defense in the best possible field position.
- Protect our punter with a full zone protection concept.
- Fan two thirds of the field in specific lanes to cover the punt.
- Speed and Effort

General Rules

- Either team can advance a blocked punt.
- A partially-blocked punt that crosses the line of scrimmage is the same as a regular punt.
- Coverage men cannot interfere with the free movement of a receiver in his effort to catch any punt.
- The return man gets a two-yard buffer zone in which to catch the ball.
- Neither team can advance a fair catch, and the fair-catch man cannot be bumped or tackled.
- A muffed fair catch is a free ball and belongs to the team that recovers it.
- The punt team cannot advance a muffed punt.
- To down a punt, the covering team man must stay with the ball until the whistle declares the play dead. (If the official does not rule the ball dead, the receiving team can try to advance it at no risk to themselves)
- To down the ball around the goal line, coverage men must not let any part of their body get into the end zone. (This means carrying the ball in or sliding into the end zone with it.)
- When we punt, we go from offense to defense at the line of scrimmage.
- Past the line of scrimmage, the opposing team cannot block below the waist.
- The kicking team is the only team that can be penalized for not having enough people in the game. (We must make sure we have 11 men on the field and at least seven on the line of scrimmage.)

Stance

- Lineman (guards, tackles, and wingmen):
  - Feet under the armpits
  - Inside foot up, heel-to-toe relationship
  - Knees over your toes

- ° Chest out, head and eyes up
- ° Hands resting on thighs
- Fullback:
  - ° Feet shoulder-width apart and parallel
  - ° Knees over your toes
  - ° Chest out, head and eyes up
  - ° Hands resting on your thighs
- Shooters:
  - ° Feet under your armpits
  - ° Inside foot up in take-off position (like a wide receiver)
  - ° Hands up in front and open ready take on defender

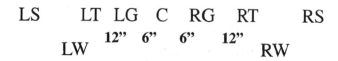

Diagram #1. Punt team alignment

Alignments

- Center: on the ball
- Guards: six inches split off of C, head on his belt line
- Tackles: twelve inches split off G and at the same depth
- Wings: inside foot behind the outside off foot of the tackle, close enough to his hip
- Fullback: directly behind the right guard, 5 yards deep
- Punter: directly behind the Center, with his toes at 14 yards
- Shooters: on the line of scrimmage, inside the numbers (distance from ball varies by position on field)

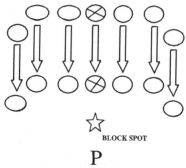

Diagram #2. Punt-team block spot

Zone Protection Scheme

- Each zone blocker has a specific area of responsibility
  - ° Your nose to the nose of the next man to your outside
  - ° Block the man or men in your zone
  - ° Use inside-out leverage
    - √ Increases his distance to the block point
    - √ Maintains kicking pocket integrity
  - ° Meet rushers forcefully so that they cannot drive you backward into the block point.
- Maintain constant split relationships to one another
  - ° Drop vertically off the line of scrimmage (straight back).
  - ° Give ground as fast as the fastest rusher outside of you.
  - ° Continue moving backward until the man outside of you stops.

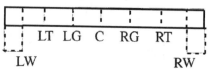

Diagram #3. Zones of responsibility

The zones of responsibility go from your nose to the nose of the man to your outside.

- Footwork: Kick slide technique
  - Keep shoulders square
  - Push off with your inside foot (front foot)
  - Place outside foot (back foot) firmly in the ground for stability
  - Slide front foot back to original stance
  - Repeat until depth is reached
  - Keep shoulders square

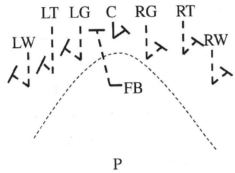

Diagram #4. Vertical set lanes: "White" call white = fullback right

- Handwork
  - Hands should raise and be ready to strike
  - Use outside hand in an extended but strong position to protect your gap (outside zone): big outside
  - Use inside hand with elbow tighter to body to assist your inside gap only when necessary: little inside
  - Meet rusher with hands and eyes under his near shoulder pad

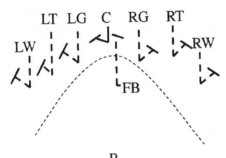

Diagram #5. Vertical set lanes. "Black" call black = fullback left

- Awareness
  - Know how many rushers can challenge your zone and the zone to your inside.
  - Never block inside even if a man crosses your face to the inside.
- Common Rush Schemes
  - One man in your zone
    - √ Drop straight back to get between him and the block point.
    - √ Maintain inside-out leverage.
  - Two men in your zone
    - √ Drop straight back to get between both of the rushers and the block point.
    - √ Keep dropping as fast as the outside rusher to use up both men.
    - √ Use your body to inside hand to take the inside rusher.
    - √ Play the outside rusher as you would a single rusher.
  - Stacked rush
    - √ Pick up the rusher that comes to your zone.
    - √ Pass the inside rusher off to the zone protector to your inside.
- Center zone technique
  - The number one objective is a great snap.
  - Get your head up to avoid being caught of balance and pulled out of the center box.
  - Give ground to fill the area between you and the left guard or right guard.
  - Release through the gap and any man challenging that gap.
- Coaching points
  - Expect a block attempt each time we punt.
  - Survey your zone and then watch the ball as it is snapped.

- ° Move when the ball moves and execute your technique.

- ° React quicker than the man or men rushing your zone.

- ° Block the rusher with proper technique.
  - √ Drive through him
  - √ Force him to restart or redirect

- ° Help your inside gap by maintaining constant split relationships and punching with your inside arm.

- ° Do not allow yourself to be pulled or grabbed by a rusher

- ° Form a solid wall. Work together!

- ° Protect first. Cover second.

COVERAGE

Phase One

- Linemen and wings fan to specific landmarks 15 yards down the field

- Keep the ball on your inside shoulder

- Shooters and fullback go directly to the ball

Phase Two

- Converge on the ball

- Keep the ball on your inside shoulder

- Never, follow another player

- Shooters attack the outside shoulder

- Full Backs play head up

- Wings have ultimate contain

Coaching Points

- Keep the ball on your inside shoulder (do not let the ball cross your face)

- Start to gather 10 yards away from the ball and breakdown at five yards, continue to find the football

- Continue to close on the ball at all times, keeping it inside and in front

- You must be ready to make the tackle

- If the ball carrier breaks up field away from you, cut toward him and get into a good pursuit angle

- Gang tackle the ballcarrier; first man secure the tackle, second and third men try to strip the ball out.

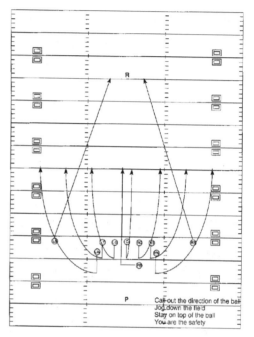

Diagram #6. Coverage phase one

The punter calls out the direction of the ball. He jogs down the field but he wants to stay on top of the ball. He is the safety man.

We tell the coverage men to fan to their landmark at 15 yards from the line of scrimmage. We set up cones on the field to indicate the lanes the cover team must fill. Here are the landmarks we want the cover team to shoot for.

Center: Go to goal post.

Guards: Go one yard inside the hash mark.

Tackles: Go five yards outside the hash.

Wings: Go to the numbers.

Fullback: Go directly to the ball through his gap.

Shooters: Go directly to the ball.

Next, we kick the ball from the hash mark (Diagram #7). This is how we cover the kick from the right hash mark. We are kicking the ball down the right hash mark unless we designate otherwise.

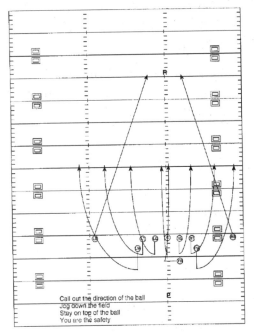

Diagram #7. Coverage: Ball on the hash mark

Again, we want the cover to fan to their landmarks at 15 yards from the line of scrimmage.

Punter: Call out the direction of the ball.

Center: Go one yard inside the hash.

Boundary Guard: Go five yards outside the hash.

Boundary Tackle: Go to the numbers.

Boundary Wing: Go three yards inside the sideline.

Field Guard: Go to the goalpost.

Field Tackle: Go to upright away from the ball.

Field Wing: Go to outside the hash.

Fullback: Go directly to the ball through your gap.

Shooters: Go directly to the ball.

We want the cover team to go into phase two of the coverage once they have reached their landmark.

We have a plan to cover the kick once the punt is away. If you have a plan, you had better work the plan. If you do not teach the plan and rep the play, it will not happen on Saturday.

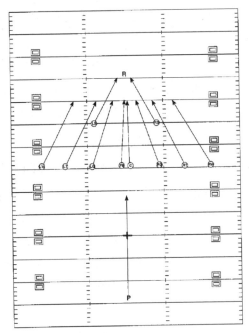

Diagram #8. Coverage: Phase two

We tell the cover men to get to their landmark first. They must adjust their lanes to close on the return man keeping the ball on the inside shoulder. They must start to gather at 10 yards way from the ball and breakdown at five yards from the ball. They must be ready to make the tackle.

We set up cones to make sure we come down in the cover lanes. We put a coach back to simulate the punt. We do not want a punter back there kicking the ball all over the field. We want to control the punt so we can check the coverage. The coach gets the ball to the return man and we work on the coverage. It is a controlled environment and we get a lot accomplished on the drill.

Let me cover the timetables on the coverage. We cover the timetable from both sides of the football.

On the kickoff, set the standard at a minimum and want to exceed it each week. Colleges and high schools kickoff are at different distance so you have to adjust to those distances.

Hang Time
Minimum 3.5 seconds / Preferred 5.0 seconds
Distance
Minimum 55 yards / We prefer 65 yards
Minimum goal is inside 30-yard line

Punt	Punt Block
Total Execution	Block Time
2.1 Seconds	2.4 Seconds or More
Snap Time	**Snap Time**
0.7 - 0.8 Seconds	0.9 Seconds or More
Release Time	**Get-Off Time**
1.1 - 1.3 Seconds	1.6 Seconds or More
Hang Time	
4.5 - 5.0 Seconds	
Distance	
40 - 45 yards from LOS	
PAT Block	**PAT**
Total Execution	**Total Execution**
1.1 - 1.2 seconds	1.3 seconds or more
Snap Time	**Snap Time**
3.4 seconds	0.5 seconds or more
Hold Time	**Hold Time**
0.1 seconds	0.2 seconds or more
Release Time	**Release Time**
0.7 - 0.8 seconds	0.9 – 1.0 seconds
Field Goal	**Field-Goal Block**
Total Execution	**Total Execution**
1.2 - 1.3 seconds	1.4 seconds or more
Snap Time	**Snap Time**
0.3 - 0.4 seconds	0.4 - 0.5 seconds
Hold Time	**Hold Time**
0.1 seconds	0.2 seconds of more
Release Time	**Release Time**
0.8 - 0.9 seconds	1.0 seconds or more

We feel a good snapper is worth his weight in gold. If you can get a good snapper to get the ball to the punter, it is a big factor in the punting game. If the punter can catch the football and get rid of it in the period we allot, you can have a good punt team.

The important of this presentation is this. You want to make sure you have worked on the kicking game so they act as if they know what they are doing in the game.

Our punt drills include the following:

Protection Personnel Drills

- Kick slide: Down the line
- Kick slide: half line
- Individual fit drill vs. Rush
- Kick slide vs. Rush (board)
- Half line vs. Rush
- Coverage lane drills

Shooter Drills

- Fit: Step and swat
- Fit drill: Swat technique
- Foot fire: Swat technique
- Release

Snapper, Protector, Punter
Team

- Team vs. Air coverage (cones)
- Team vs. Air (phase two)
- Team vs. Rush

Let me see if this tape will fit the VCR. I am technically handicapped. Here we go. (Film)

DEVELOPING SECONDARY FUNDAMENTALS

University of Pittsburgh

I want to thank Nike for giving us the opportunity to speak at this clinic. I would like to thank Coach Wannstedt and Pittsburgh for the opportunity to coach football for this great university.

Coach Wannstedt addressed a group last night. One of his themes or philosophy was to take the emotion out of what you do in decision-making. You have to take the emotion out of the decision.

That situation reminded me of a similar lesson I had learned growing up on a farm in Iowa. I came down one morning and breakfast was not on the table. I asked my mother where was breakfast. She told me I had to do my chores before I got breakfast. I was mad because I was hungry. I had to feed the chickens, slop the hogs, and milk the cow. When I went into the chicken coop, I kicked the first chicken I saw. When I went to slop the pigs, I kicked the first pig that came up to me. When I got to the cow, I did the same thing.

When I came back into the house, my mother had a bowl of dry cereal on the table for me. My mother told me she saw what I did to the animals. Because I kicked the chicken, she said I would not get any eggs for a week. Because I kicked the pig, I could not have any bacon for a week. In addition, because I kicked the cow, I did not get any milk for a week.

About that time, my father came down the stairs. The cat was walking across the floor and he kicked it. I looked at mother and asked her this question: "Are you going to tell dad or do you want me to tell him?"

It is a privilege to be here. I want to thank many of you in this room for the support you gave me during the whole process. I was very humbled and honored, and I mean it sincerely. I am very proud to be at the University of Pittsburgh working for our head football coach Dave Wannstedt.

What I want to talk about is some of the fundamentals in defensive back play. I hope I can give you some ideas that will help you improve what you are doing.

Listening to Coach Stoops last night, I came up with some things I believe I can use to tweak some of thing we do in our program. I want to talk about defensive back drill work and finishing up with some tackling that can be useful to all position groups.

In secondary play, we have a list we call the big four. If you can accomplish these four things, you will enjoy success in the secondary.

The first thing is to be a sure tackling secondary. You have to get the ball on the ground and not let it continue to run. Do not allow any deep balls to be thrown. You have to establish criteria for what constitutes a deep ball. I realize offenses had expanded and become more potent but we consider any ball over 20 yards to be a deep ball. An example would be a screen pass that goes for 20 yards. Another example would be a 10-yard catch that turns into a 25-yard gain. We consider those situations as deep balls.

The secondary cannot have a busted coverage. We cannot be playing halves on one side and thirds on the other. We cannot have people running loose in the secondary because someone is playing the wrong coverage. A big part of not busting coverages is communication.

The last thing is to cup the football. That means to contain the football. Keep the ball inside and in front of you at all times. Keeping the ball in front of you lets everyone on the field have a chance at the ball.

If you are doing these things in the secondary, you are playing good defensive football regardless of what is happening up front.

We have some secondary axiom we try to get over to our players.

- Never take an inside fake as a deep defender in the passing game.

- Play the ball not the man. Cover the receiver, but play the ball.

- The deep defender must never break on the short-arm action of the quarterback.

Being a great defensive back starts with the stance. If you get into a good stance, there is no wasted movement to get started. The stance starts from the ankles. A good defensive back has to have great flexion in his ankles. Everyone has stiff hips. You can help a defensive back who is stiff by starting at his ankles. Have them wrap a towel around the instep of his foot. Flex the ankle out and pull it back with the towel. Give resistance with the towel. If they do not have good flexion in the ankles, they cannot have a good stance.

He has to be able to bend his knees and sink the hip in that order. We talk about numbers over knees and knees over feet. To get into a good stance you have to go in order. If you flex the ankle, bend the knees, sink the hips—number over knees and knees over feet—you will find yourself in a good stance.

To be a great defensive back you must have good eyes. The defensive backs have to look where you want them to look. Some coaches tell the defensive back to read his keys. If you want him to key a tackle, make sure he is looking at the tackle. Whatever you want him keying, make sure he is looking at it. You can coach the defensive back from both sides of the line of scrimmage. I would prefer to coach from behind them, so I can see what they see and try to digest that. If I have players that are making mistakes in keying, I get on the offensive side of the ball so I can see their eyes. They all think

they can play faster and quicker by looking at the quarterback. They think that because he has the ball. If we cannot get the defensive back to look where he is supposed to look or coach him to do that, he will not be a great defensive back.

You cannot be a great defensive back without a good backpedal. We will talk about the mechanics of it later when we get to the drill work. It does not matter if you are a rolled up corner or a safety that plays with a shuffle technique; if you cannot backpedal, you will never be a great defensive back.

When we set up our spring practice, we schedule about 20 minutes for individual practice. In those 20 minutes, I want them moving. I want them moving like they are going to play the game. I want them to backpedaling and changing direction. I want them to shuffle and change direction out of that. I want them moving like they are going to play.

We want to tackle using all variations of tackling drills. We form tackle, angle tackle, sideline tackle, open-field tackle, and any other situation they may face in a game. We do tackling in a circuit as a defensive team.

The last thing during our individual period is ball drill. I want them to catch the ball using their eyes and fingers. That is my point of emphasis during this part of the period. The eyes are the first thing the defensive back uses to catch the ball. We want to look the ball into our hands without letting the ball get into the palms of the hand.

All phases of the individual period are important. However, if we have to cheat one of the three areas of the individual period to gain time in another part of the period, it is the ball drills. They will play catch by themselves. Do not cheat the movement phase or the tackling phase of the individual period.

The most important skill for playing defensive back is backpedaling. If a player has trouble with his backpedal, he will have trouble in coverage. I believe there are four phases in the backpedal progression. In the initial backpedal; it all starts with the butt. The defensive back must lead with his butt as he gets into his backpedal. If the defensive back leads with his shoulder blades, he cannot change directions.

If they are too far forward in their bend from the waist, they cannot get to the deep ball. The defensive back wants to change direction any way the receiver is going. To do that you must lead with the butt in a backpedal. That way the numbers will stay over the knees and the knees will stay over the feet. That way the defender can drive on the curl, dig, and the out and open to the post, go, and the deep corner.

When coaching the backpedal, coach it from the side because that is the best view. The backpedal is from the knees down. You do not want a player backpedaling with his whole leg. He snaps from the knees down in the backpedal. In the backpedal, the back has to drive with his elbows as he moves back. Pumping the elbow is not as much for the speed of the backpedal, as it is for the control in change of direction.

When the back backpedals, he does not lift his feet off the ground. He takes the top off the grass and he moves backward. He glides in the backpedal instead of running.

Another thing you will have to determine is the ground covered in the backpedal. If the back is not gaining enough ground, he has to reach back further with his feet. That lets them gain enough ground to keep his cushion.

After we cover the four basic phases of the backpedal, we have to drill the techniques. There are four techniques to practice in this drill. We want to work on control, speed, zone turn, and turn and run. I can set a cone ten yards down the line or we can go to the hash marks (Diagram #1). We line the defensive backs on the sidelines to start the backpedal drill. We line two defensive backs on either side of the yard line facing the coach.

The two defensive backs come out on either side of the yard line. The coach calls "Ready, ready," and the defensive backs get into a good stance. Everything we do in the drill has to be the way they play the game. I start the drill with a hand signal. The defense does not react to the game of football by sound. They react on the movement of the ball or movement of a player. The less you get them to move by sound the better you are going to train them.

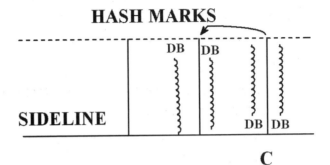

Diagram #1. Backpedal drill

The "control" part of the drill is an easy controlled pedal, where they are deciding what type of play they are seeing. In the controlled pedal, they want to know if it is a run, hot pass, three step pass, or down-the-field pass. We go nice and easy for ten yards in the controlled backpedal.

The second phase of the backpedal is the "speed" phase. The defenders start in a controlled pedal and read down-the-field pass. The defensive backs key to this phase is the quarterback's reaction. The quarterback is dropping trying to figure out what the coverage is going to be. He is looking down the field trying to pick up safety movement. The defensive back is being threatened by a deep vertical coming up the field. He has to get out of his control pedal and into to a speed pedal. In the drill, the first hand movement sends them into a control pedal; the second hand movement put them in a speed pedal.

Making sure the pad level does not change is the coaching point in this phase of the drill. When the back goes from controlled to speed backpedal, he increases the frequency of the reps in his steps. He does not raise his shoulders. The coaching point to emphasize is to lead with the butt. If the defensive back goes from a controlled to speed backpedal and leads with his shoulder blades, he cannot change direction to come forward. If he leads with his shoulder blades, he has raised his pad level and leaned back in his run.

The next phase of the drill is the "zone turn." The zone turn occurs when the receiver threatens to break the cushion of defensive back. The defensive back gets the momentum out of his backpedal and into his downfield run. If the back does not get his hips open for the turn, the receiver is going to run by him for a touchdown. There is no set distance for the defensive backs cushion.

We had one freshman defensive back that can hold his backpedal up to a distance of two yards before he makes his zone turn. He can zone turn in two yards and keep control of the receiver's upfield shoulder. We have another freshman defensive back that has to zone turn at four to five yards to keep from being run by. Know your players in relationship to the distance in their cushion. The general rule for the cushion is three yards. However, some players can stay in the backpedal longer and some shorter periods. Know your players and coach them as to what their cushion is going to be.

The technique for opening the hips is to use the elbow to the side of the turn. The defensive back throws the elbow to open the hips. That puts him in a perpendicular position to the line of scrimmage. His eyes are still on the receiver as he takes the cross-over step. In the next step, the hips are still perpendicular to the line of scrimmage. We stay in that run for three or four steps. We want to get out of that run because it is not normal or comfortable.

Receivers are coached to make the defensive backs open their hips before they make their breaks. When the defensive back open his hips, the receiver makes his break or continues to run deep. With the hips perpendicular to the line of scrimmage, the drive on a receiver's break is quicker.

The last phase of the drill is "turn and run." The receiver tries to run by the defender. The defensive back rolls his hips and gets into a full-speed run downfield, playing on the upfield shoulder of the receiver. The defensive back has to cover the route before he can play the ball. To cover the route, he has to look at the receiver. After he covers the route, he can look for the ball.

This type of drill is great work for the indoor program and spring practice. We do not have s lot of time to spend on it during the season. We do not do this drill on Tuesday. In the winter and spring, they drill until they understand the phases of their backpedal, their cushion, and their body mechanics.

In season, we wake the body up and work them on breaks and their relationships to receivers. We start every practice with what we call "line pedal" (Diagram #2). We get all the defensive backs in a line on the sideline. I start the first man in the line and the rest of the line starts each other. They backpedal in a steady stream of backs to the hash mark in a nice comfortable pedal. When they get to the hash mark, they jog over five yards to the next line and repeat the drill coming back toward the sideline.

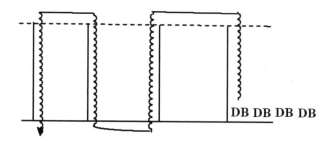

Diagram #2. Line pedal

The defensive back gets in a good stance, leads with his butt, and is in a nice, controlled backpedal. This is the wake-up call to the muscles. They are conditioning their muscle that this is the position they are going to be in for the next two hours.

The next drill is designed to stretch and strength the hip flexor. When a defensive back plants and drives on breaks, he has a tendency to stretch the hip flexor and groin muscle. This drill tries to prevent injuries to that area. If you do this drill on a daily basis, you should avoid the problems of muscle pulls in the groin and hip area.

We start in a control backpedal. It does not matter which on side you begin. The key is to exaggerate the movements in the drill. The defender opens his hips and exaggerates the rolling of the hips. The secret is to lift the leg as high as you can and get it and over to the other side. We go down the line, right leg over, left leg over, and come back on the other line, left leg over and right leg over.

We do this drill every day we are on the practice field. This is not a technique drill. Make sure they understand they are not zone turning for technique. They are doing the drill to strengthen and stretch the hip flexor muscles.

The next drill is the "weave drill" (Diagram #3). This is a partner drill. We have one back be the receiver and the other is the defender. The defender gets in his stance with his proper leverage either inside or outside. The defender looks in at me for direction. I snap the ball and look downfield. Once the defensive back finds out where the ball is going, he gets his eyes back on the receiver. The receiver runs deep, stretching the defender both vertically and horizontally. The receiver runs inside the defender and crosses his face to the outside getting width and depth as they go downfield.

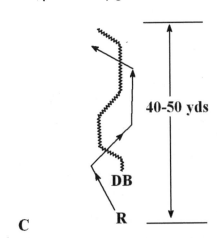

Diagram #3. Weave drill

The defender must maintain his proper cushion and leverage on the receiver. This makes the defender weave in his backpedal. He has to weave in the backpedal and not sidestep. If he sidesteps, the receiver eats up the defender's cushion. The defender has to maintain his cushion and not get beat deep. It takes a 40 to 50 yard area to run this drill.

I do not think you can truly weave with speed when the receiver is running forward full speed. I do not think the defensive back can weave and keep his

shoulders square to the line of scrimmage. The defensive back has to turn his butt in the direction he is pedaling and keep his shoulders square to the receiver who is pushing in that direction. If the defensive back has to weave right, he has to push off his left foot. To weave left he has to push off his right foot. When the defensive back plants his foot to weave, there should be a distinct and sudden change of direction.

The depth of the defenders depends on the position and technique they are playing. A safety in quarter coverage is at a depth of nine yards. If he is a safety playing loose man coverage, put him at 10 yards. If it is a corner playing man-to-man stem, he is at seven yards.

The defensive backs have a run key, a hot pass key, a downfield pass key, and a movement or play-action pass key. The three-step pass game is what we call "hot key"(Diagram #4).

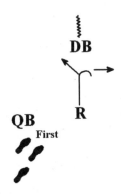

Diagram #4. Hot read drill

We play an eleven-game schedule. In nine of the eleven games, the quarterback will tell us when he is throwing the hot or three-step pass on the first step. On the first step, the quarterback looks at the flat immediately. On Sunday in our team meeting, that is the first thing my defensive backs want to know. When we play off-man coverage, we get a tremendous amount of three-step passes.

In our coverage, the defensive back looks in at the quarterback. He starts on a control backpedal. When he reads the three-step pass, he puts his cleats in the ground and settles. His eyes snap back to the receiver to ID the route run. It would do no good to break up when the receiver is slanting inside. Once he identifies the route, he drives on it. We work the hot read on a daily basis. If we are playing a shotgun quarterback that is the pass route we work against.

Tuesday and Wednesday are our heavy practice days. On Tuesday, we run a "W" drill (Diagram #5). Any type of break the offense is going to make you can do in the W drill. You do not need to take an offense and run curl, dig, out, post, or any kind of break they make at the defensive backs. You can do this drill in a fifteen-by-five-yard confined area. Defensive backs react off receivers.

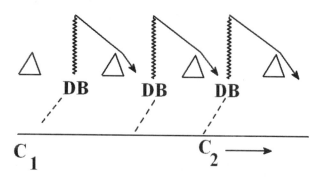

Diagram #5. W drill

The drill has four cones five yards apart, 10 yards off the sideline. I use three defensive backs at a time with two coaches. I am the quarterback and other coach is the receiver. This is a speed pedal-drive drill.

The defensive backs retreat in their speed pedal; their eyes refocus from me back to the receiver. The coach, who represents the receiver, is running in place as they backpedal. When the coach stutter-steps, the defenders plant his feet to stop his backpedal.

It does not matter which foot the defensive back plants. He plants by bringing his foot down under his body with the foot pointing open. I want the foot in the ground and a change of direction immediately. I want all the cleats in the ground. You cannot stop with your weight on the balls of your feet because there is too much force built up. If the playing surface is wet, having all the cleats in the ground aids the plant.

The coach gives the direction of the pattern with a hand signal. The defensive back drives to the cone in direction of the signal. His eyes leave the coach and focus on the cone because that is the receiver. I do not want to see them sprint for three yards and coast into the cone. I want to win the game of inches. I want to see urgency as they drive to the cone. I want them all the way to the cone as hard as they can go. The break to the receiver is to be a straight break and not rounded off.

We win games because the defender finishes all the way to the cone and does not pull up when the ball is in the air. It is not because one back runs a 4.7 and the other back runs a 4.5. They knock the pass down or intercept it. You can win the game of inches with fundamentals and techniques. If you have good fundaments and techniques, you can compensate for speed. This should be a nicely timed drill. You have three players starting at the same time, breaking at the same time, and running straight lines.

To add multiple skills to the drill, do something basic past the last cone. Have a manager drop a ball and have them scoop and score. Throw a ball to them and have them intercept it. Always have your players finish every drill full speed. This drill works on conditioning and mental toughness. If they do not go hard, they do the drill again. We usually go back and forth across the drill a couple of time. If they do not want to work hard, we do it six or seven times. Any kind of route you get in a game you can work out of the W drill.

On Wednesday, we run the "box drill." The box is a ten-by-ten-yard box marked with cones at the corners of the box (Diagram #6). I stand on one side of the box. I put two defensive backs in the box. The defensive backs are four yards into the box facing me. I give them the "Ready, ready" call, which puts them in a good stance. The next command is "feet." On that command, they start to pound their feet. I give them a quick pedal and they start back. I point in the direction of one of the four cones.

That indicates where the receiver is going. As soon as I point, I want them to plant and drive in that direction. I want them to drive in the direction with their eyes on me. I point to the second cone, which indicates the receiver has changed direction. They have to stop and drive on the second cone. When they change direction, I want them to open their chest toward me. Do not let the players get control of the drill. Do not let them chop the feet and slide instead of running. Make them run and change direction.

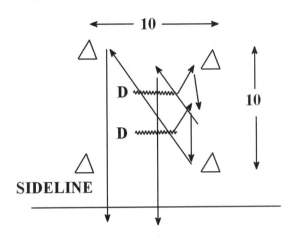

Diagram #6. Box drill

That gives you a series of breaks to the cones. The eyes are always on the coach, which represents the receiver. Each time they redirect, they open with their chest to the coach. When the coach calls them out, they finish across the sideline. When they finish across the sideline, we may have an additional drill such as a fumble drill.

We want to finish drills as we finish plays in a game. It may end with a cadence, a rhyme, a tone, with a movement, but we have an end to our drills.

I am going to shift gears and get into some tackling. When I do a clinic, I feel I can help you more with drill work than schemes.

When you game-plan and work on it all week, you expect to play well. The players believe in the game-plan and believe you know what to do. On the second play of the game, the opponent goes for 15 yards on a running play. Nine players on that team do not know that two players on the defense missed a tackle. Nine defensive players doubt the creditability of the game plan. That doubt comes because of missed tackles.

Here are some characteristics you need to be a great tackler. To be a great tackler, you must have great vision. The tackler has to see what he is going to tackle. When you tackle, you want to sky the eyes. We do not drop the head. The first thing that happens when the tackler drops his head is he is injured. I do not want to call some mother and tell her that her son is in the hospital because he dropped his head in a tackle. If you sky the eyes, you will be safe and see what you are tackling.

The tackler must see the target. The target is the hip of the ballcarrier. Make sure they are not flinching as they get to the tackle. They must keep the eyes open during a tackle.

The second characteristic of a great tackler is his *feet*. When tackling, get as close as you can then take the extra step. We want to step on the toes of the ballcarrier. Once you make contact, run the hips through the tackle. We want to tackle with the front of our chests. The first contact comes with the chest. The feet run throughout the entire tackle. The feet have to run until the ballcarrier is on the ground.

If you want to be a good tackler, you must have the *desire* to tackle. Whatever it takes to get the ballcarriers on the ground, do it. It does not matter whether it is a perfect form tackle or a shoestring type tackle, get him on the ground. Whatever it takes to get the person on the ground, I am willing to do it for the team.

The last trait of being a good tackler is toughness, or courage. All your players have it or they would not put on the helmet and pads and walk out on the field. If your kids have courage, you can develop the toughness. I believe in taking the headgear off in some tackling drills. That way you keep the head out of the tackle and tackle with the chest. It also develops toughness.

We chart our tackles. We make a board from the chart and put it up in our locker room. On top of the board, we have the four characteristics of tackling (vision, feet, desire, and toughness) and a definition of each one of them. We have everyone's name on the chart and total the number of tackles, assists, tackles for loss, and missed tackles. In the missed tackle column, we also list the reason for the missed tackle. In the reason for missed tackled column, we never want to put desire or toughness. But if we do, it is up there for everyone to see.

When we practice form tackling, we want the players two yards apart. At our practice field, we have numbers on the field. The numbers are two yards in height. That is where we do our form tackling. We put one player at the top of the numbers and one player at the bottom of the numbers. We do this drill on sound. On "go," the ballcarrier and tackler go full speed at one another. I do not want the ballcarrier to drop his shoulder or make any move. I do not want him to jump into the contact.

I want to see the defensive backs sky the eyes, hit chest first, and step on the toes. The tackler shoots the hands and brings his hip. I want to see the hands shoot and reach for cloth. I want him to wrap up and run his feet though the tackle until I stop him.

We do the same thing with our angle tackling. I put a towel down and the ballcarrier runs to the towel. The tackler comes on an angle and tries to get his face across to the opposite armpit. I do not emphasize getting the face across to the opposite arm because the player will start leaning to get his face across. When he does that, he loses all the power in his legs. I coach taking the extra step. I coach stepping on his toes, and running through the tackle. If I emphasize those things, the head will get across to the opposite armpit.

Original thoughts in football are almost nonexistent anymore. We steal from everybody. I got this from someone out west. The three phases of open-field tackling are important. Open-field tackling is the hardest part of the tackling game. That is what everyone is trying to do in the spread game. They are trying to get players in space and make people tackle them.

When making an open-field tackle, the tackler has to close the distance between the tackler and ballcarrier as quickly as possible. By closing the distance, we can minimize the gain. The next thing is balance. This is almost as if the cushion is pass defense. If the tackler does not sink his hips, get his numbers over his knees and his knees over his feet, he will miss the tackle. Coming to balance occurs at the same distance as the cushion in pass defense. The missed tackle occurs when you come to balance too late. When the tackler comes to balance, he wants to keep advancing toward the ballcarrier. He does not come to balance and sit there.

The last phase is the hit or finish part of the tackle. When the tackler comes to balance, his base widens somewhat. He keeps his feet moving but progressing toward the ballcarrier. He wants his hands in the holsters. If he gets his hands wide, he gets his base too wide. When the ballcarrier changes direction, he has to go right or left. As the ballcarrier moves, the tackler wants to step laterally. The tackler is not sure where the ballcarrier is going and, by stepping laterally, he keeps his feet under him. If the ballcarrier stays in the same direction, the tackler makes contact, tries to step on his toes, and runs through the tackle.

We drill open-field tackling in an open-field tackling drill (Diagram #7). The defensive back aligns in his defensive position. On the first "go," the back goes into a controlled backpedal. On the second "go," the ballcarrier starts and the defensive back plants and comes up to make the open field tackle. The ballcarrier gets one cut.

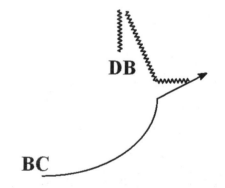

Diagram #7. Open-field tackling drill

The second drill we do in the open-field drill is an angle tackle (Diagram #8). This is like the box drill. We have a defensive back and a ballcarrier. I got this drill from the Denver Broncos. The drill is set up in the ten-by-ten-yard box. The ballcarrier works straight down the cones. The cones do not represent the sideline. The defensive back goes into his pedal, plants, and approaches for the tackle. Any time the tackler comes into balance, it is because the ballcarrier has the tackler ID. That means he sees the tackler coming. If the ballcarrier has the tackler ID, he will make a move.

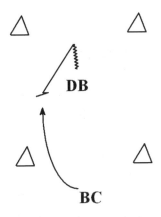

Diagram #8. Angle tackle in the box

The tackler cannot go full speed if the ballcarrier sees him. If a receiver catches a hitch route and does not see the tackler, he could continue full speed. Otherwise, the tackler has to come to balance and get ready for a move by the ballcarrier. The tackler aims for the back hip of the ballcarrier. That is his line, path, angle, and vision to the runner. He is not coming one or two yards in front of the ballcarrier. He makes a beeline right for the hip of the ballcarrier.

When you play baseball, your eyes and brain will adjust your swing for a high or low ball. In basketball, if the player shoots eight-footers or 16-footers, he concentrates on the rim. The eye will tell the brain how hard to shoot the ball. The same thing is true in tackling. If the tackler is coming at an angle and the ballcarrier moves upfield or goes to a different plane, the brain adjusts the angle accordingly. If the tackler runs up the field two yards in front of the ballcarrier and he cuts back, the tackler will miss every time.

I coach this drill from behind the tackler because I want to see the angle he is using. If the ballcarrier stays straight ahead, the tackler ends up in a good across the bow tackle. If the ballcarrier cuts back, the defensive back hits him with a solid butt tackle. The angle of the tackler is such that if the ballcarrier cuts back he run into the tackler. This is the box drill with the tackler working straight on the ballcarrier.

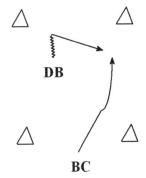

Diagram #9. Box tackling inside-out

In the second type of box tackling, we change the angle for the tackler to the inside-out angle (Diagram #9). The mechanics of the tackle is primarily the same, but the angle the tackle takes changes.

The last tackling drill we use in the box is the outside in tackling angle (Diagram #10). Again, the mechanics of the tackle are the same but the angle from which the tackler attacks changes.

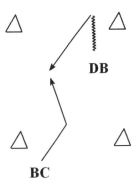

Diagram #10. Box tackling outside-in

I want to draw all these things together with a drill tape. I appreciate your attention. This is one hell of a clinic.

EFFECTIVE SCREENS AND DRAWS

Western Michigan University

Before I start drawing the X's and O's, I think I need to talk for a minute about our philosophy on offense. Where screens and draws fit into your offense depends a great deal on your philosophy. It has a lot to do with the success you have with them and how much you want to run those plays.

We are a multiple formation football team. We use multiple personnel groupings in our offense. We want to spread the field as much as possible. We are not a team that tries to complete all of our passes within five yards of the line of scrimmage. We want to throw the ball downfield. We want to attack all areas of the field. We want to be a 50-50 team in the balance between run and pass as much as possible. We do not want to become predictable. We want to mix up the runs and passes on different downs. We like to run the isolation plays and other running plays. We want the ability to be a physical football team from time to time. We want to be able to run our screens and draws on any down. We do not want to be predictable when we throw the screens and draws. We feel the screens and draws plays are more effective on the first down.

Our offense is a quarterback friendly attack. We want to make it as easy as possible physically on the quarterback. We are going to put a lot of pressure on him mentally to put us into the right play. Very rarely do we go up to the line of scrimmage and run the play called in the huddle. We are a big "check-with-me" team. We give the play to the quarterback that we would like to run, but he does not have to run that play. We give him an alternate play to run if the original play called does not look good when we line up on the ball.

The reason we do this is that we have a very limited amount of time with the players. Today's athletes have a lot on their plate. They have academics, weight lifting, and this and that and many other things to do. As a result, you do not have a lot of time to practice football. You do not have a lot of meeting time to cover all of those things. We try to give the a few things they can get good at instead of giving them many things to work on.

We are not going to run all of our plays out of all of our different looks. We use a multitude of formations but there are certain plays that we are only going to run from particular formations. I have always been in favor of telling the quarterback the plays he can check to instead of letting him pick any play he thinks will be effective. We teach the quarterback the looks and then give him the outs from those plays. It may be a run/run check off. It may be a run/pass check. It can be a pass/pass check. The big thing is not to give the quarterback the same out on each call.

As far as game planning goes, we are going to run our screens and draw plays. We have a menu that we start the season with. We will only have a total of five or six screens and draws over the course of the season. We do not go into every game with all of the screens and draws that we have in our offense. I have always been a firm believer that you can go into a game with two or three screens and two draw plays in each game.

What are we trying to get out of the screens and draws? Let me give you several points we feel the benefits of the screens and draws give us.

Benefits of Screens and Draws

- Shows the rush of penetrating and attacking defenses.

- Allows you to get the ball into the hands of specific playmakers. You can set that up in several ways.

- We have a high percentage of positive yards.

- It allows you to attack different areas of the field. We can attack various areas of the field (outside, inside, curl area). If we can find a weak defender in one of those areas, we can take advantage of the screens and draws.

- Outside Screens can serve the purpose of a toss sweep in a one-back offense. We are in this set about 75 percent of the time.

- It is an easy tie-in with check off plays (run-run, run-pass, pass-pass). Give the quarterback two looks. If the first play is not there, he can check to the other play.

- Takes hit off the quarterback. In the passing game, you do not want to get your quarterback hit on every play. The screens and draws keep the defense off balance.

- Effective versus man or zone coverage, and man blitz or zone blitz.

- The screens and draws are great confidence builders:
  - ○ Easy throw
  - ○ Calm a rattled quarterback

- Good in all running and passing situations as well as in the scoring zone, creating carry-over in your game plan.

Keys to Success

- Front and coverage recognition. Know who to block and how to block them. We are going to teach the quarterback how to read the fronts and how to read the pass coverage. The front blockers need to know who to block.

- Understand the philosophy of the play and where it is designed to go.

- Understanding of when and why the play is being run. They are to take advantage of the defense. We run the plays to:

  - ○ Attack the defense
  - ○ Soften the defense

- Patience. Play must be allowed time to develop. The mistakes I see with teams that run the screen and the draw is because the quarterback is in too big of a hurry or the man getting the ball is rushing the play. Timing is important. Let the play develop.

- Efficiency of the quarterback and timing of the receivers and ballcarriers is important. I think it is important to spend a lot of time against "air" and get the timing down. There must be good timing between the quarterback and receivers. This is especially true early in the season.

- Effective practice time and tempo can be utilized. The first thing we do in each practice is to run a drill we call "take off." We used to line the offense up at the ten-yard line and run the play into the end zone. We used it to stretch and warm up. Now we have turned that drill into our screen and draw session. Now the drill is doing two things for us. We get our warm-ups and we can practice the screens and draws.

We run the inside screen off our slide protection with 80 and 90 protection. We call the plays 41 and 42. We want to make sure we develop the screen plays off plays we run in our offense. We run the plays off the same drop-back protection we are using in the game. That is something very important. Develop the screens off plays that you run in the game.

The 42 and 43 Screens are C-gap screens. It is off our three-step protection package. We want to use that same protection and give that same look to the defense and throw the screen play off the action.

The first play is our 42/43 screen. It is a tailback screen run from our 80 or 90 protection (Diagram #1). This is a three-step screen play. Let me give you the coaching points on the play.

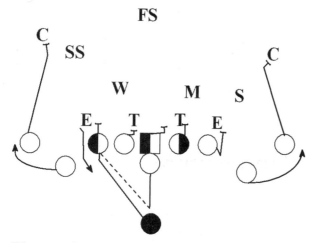

Diagram #1. 42 Bengal right / 43 Bengal left

We want a 1.5 second count release for the offensive linemen. Our frontside tackle blocks the near linebacker. If he shifts out of the box, he must be alert and block him after blocking protection. We use names and we use numbers to call our screens. We use all kind of combinations to call the screens. If we call 42, it is Bengal right with 80 protection. If we call 43, it is Bengal left and we use 90 protection.

FST: 80/90 protection for 1.5 seconds; Release to near linebacker.

FSG: 80/90 protection for 1.5; Release and block linebacker inside of offensive tackle.

C: 80/90 protection.

BSG: 80/90 protection.

BST: 80/90 protection.

R: Run ring/lock.

B: Attack inside shoulder of defensive end, bang and pivot inside for the ball.

QB: Five-step and drift. If invert to Bengal side, throw ring. No invert, pump bubble on drop, drift and throw to B.

X: Push crack

Z: Push crack

T: Run ring/lock

We want the line to slide away from the area where we are trying to create the screen pass. We must be aware of the fact the defense may have extra players in the "box."

We want to create a running lane between the B and C gaps. The onside tackle must make contact with the end man or outside man on the line. After he has cleared, he wants to move up to the Will linebacker. We slide the protection on the rest of the line. We want to force the end outside and throw the screen in the area underneath the defensive end.

The key coaching point is this. That deep back must make the play look like a three-step drop play. The quarterback must drop the three steps and then drift on his fourth and fifth step. The timing must be good on this play. We want the defense to think it is a three-step play.

On the 48/49 screens, we want to throw to the wide receivers using quick Ray or Leo protection (Diagram #2). The coaching points on the play are simple. We call quick Ray pro for tiger left. We call quick Leo for tiger right. There is no "man" call used with quick Ray or Leo protection on tiger screen.

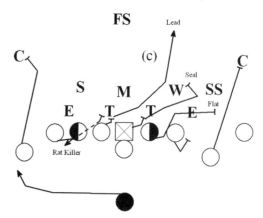

Diagram #2. 48/49 Quick Ray/Leo

48/49 QUICK RAY/LEO

FST: Block C gap, cut run defensive end. If defensive end fills inside, release and block flat.

FSG: Quick set B gap, club and sprint to block flat defender. Block defensive end filling inside.

C: Quick set A gap, club and sprint to block hook defender.

BSG: On, inside, club and sprint to block next defender inside hook.

BST: On, inside, force defensive end wide and become "Rat Killer."

Y: Inside release to safety.

RB: Automation flare away from throw.

QB: Five-step and drift, timing, make throw firm and put on receivers sternum.

X: To: Three-step stutter, attack heels of end man on line of scrimmage in controlled sprint, catch the ball five yards outside tackle. Away: Fake X tiger.

Z: To: Three-step stutter, attack heels of end man on line of scrimmage in controlled sprint, catch the ball five yards outside tackle. Away: Fake Z tiger.

T: Block first outside defender.

We run our 44/45 quick wide screen using 80 or 90 protection (Diagram #3). The coaching points include the following points. We are going to block the gap to the called side. If we call ring, it is gap to the right with 90 protection. If we call lock, it is gap to the left with 80 protection.

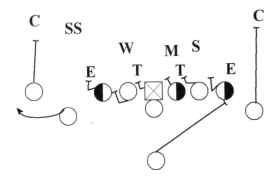

Diagram #3. 44/45 Quick – wide screen

FST: Gap to call side, cut defensive end, C-gap player.

FSG: Gap to call side, block B gap.

C: Gap to call side, block A gap.

BSG: Gap to call side, stay square.

BST: Gap to call side, stay square.

TE: Inside release to safety.

RB: Block 80/90 protection.

QB: Under center - One-step and throw. In shotgun - Catch the ball and throw.

X: Fake tiger screen.

Z: Block first defender outside.

T: Open parallel to line of scrimmage; catch the ball, work upfield on fifth step.

My favorite screen play is one I took from a friend of mine. The outside screens are great to get the ball to the outside receivers. The bubble screen is a great way to get the ball to the inside receivers. The three-step screens are great ways to get the ball to the running backs. The poor tight ends are feeling left out. In many protection schemes, the tight end is involved in the protection. We run the tight end middle screen that we can run from an empty look, or off motion to an empty look. You can send the tailback the opposite to make it look like it is hot protection. It is amazing at the running lanes that open up inside when you empty the set.

This play has the same effect that a draw play has. It is a two-count middle screen. We call it "Hot 72/73 Y slip" (Diagram #4). We are running our five man-to-man protection. You can use slide protection and gap protection and the play will still work.

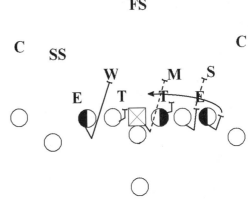

Diagram #4. Hot 72/73 Y slip

The coaching point is for the frontside guard. Against the 3 technique, he must allow compression to clear the route for the tight end.

FST: Set two counts, double duty to Sam to support man.

FSG: Soft set onside, inside.

C: Soft rock/load.

BSG: Soft rock/load.

BST: Set defensive end, double duty to backside linebacker.

TE: Two kick steps for width. Look for the ball at the B gap.

RB: Flare away from tight end.

QB: Five-step drop. Hit and throw to Y in the frontside B or A gap.

X: Clear

Z: Clear

T: Block the defensive man over, against man coverage clear the area.

On the snap of the ball, we want the tight end to take two shuffle steps for width. We stress the fact we want him to get wide. We want the end to get side so the man over the tackle has time to clear the area. We want the end to catch the ball in that B to C gap. They have a tendency to want to cross the football. If they take the route vertical, we have a chance to make a big play. The minute they catch the ball, we want them to take it north and south. This is true on any screen we run. We want the ballcarrier to get vertical.

We never tell our quarterback to set his feet to throw the screen pass. It takes the hit off the quarterback. There will always be a defender that comes clean on the play. We do not want that quarterback to set his front foot and have a defender hit him in that position. We want him to throw the ball as he gives ground.

In the next ten minutes, I want to talk about two draw plays. We can run the play to the open end or we can run the tight end draw. We tell the tight end to take the frontside linebacker. This is a play where the quarterback must understand the defensive set. We do not want to run this play into a pressure defense. We want to run this play against the soft zone defense. We want to run this play when we see those linebackers dropping back as

soon as they see our quarterback drop on his pass steps.

This play is off our man protection. We package the play with plays we like to run against pressure defense. If we call the draw and the defense is in a pressure set we check out of the draw play.

The play is a one-back draw to the tight end side (Diagram #5). The tight end blocks the frontside linebacker unless we give a tag call by the frontside tackle or frontside guard.

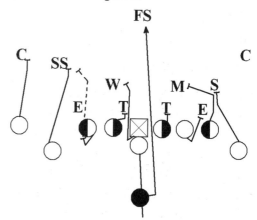

Diagram #5. 52/53 Draw

Here are the coaching points on the play. We must be alert to the frontside linebacker in threatening position. If the linebacker is on, use the tag block depending on our game plan. We show the pass on the draw play. The center and guard use a rock/load for the closest defensive tackle and the backside linebacker. The quarterback must eye the frontside linebacker. If Y cannot block him on a blitz, throw the hot route to our Y end. The backside tackle has double duty on the outside linebacker and safety.

FST: On, outside.

FSG: On, outside.

C: On, rock/load riggin/liggin vs. odd.

BSG: On, Rock/Load, C block.

BST: Double duty.

TE: Best release, block playside inside linebacker. If the linebacker is void, look for hot ball. Use "inside" call to alert C/G that you will block middle/Mike with no Sam in the box.

RB: Openside to playside, take handoff from the quarterback between his third and fourth step. Read the first down lineman to the playside, and then look for the tight ends block on the linebacker.

QB: Open to your throwing arm and show dropback pass. Keep head downfield two steps. On third step, overtop exchange with the running back. On 53 draw, keep the head downfield for one step, reverse beyond six o'clock on second step, overtop exchange, set to pass.

X: Push crack.

Z: Push crack.

T: Block inverted defender.

It is a patient play for the running back. You see some running backs that get over-anxious and want to attack the line of scrimmage. We teach them to take an open step, square to the line of scrimmage, and wait for the ball. We want the back to simulate some type of pass protection look as much as possible. The deeper we can get the ball to the running back, the more vertical separation we can have against the defense. Now we have some creases and we have a chance to hit some of the holes in the defense.

On the next play, we run off the draw action, or the counter look. You can run the play out of the spread formation or with the quarterback under the center. You can run the play form the spread with the running back lined up on either side of the quarterback in the gun. It is the same draw blocking as 52 draw.

FS

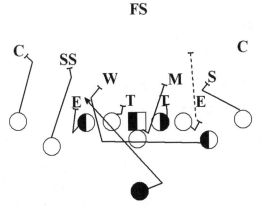

Diagram #6. 56/57 Texas draw

This play is virtually a lead draw. It is our 56/57 Texas draw (Diagram #6). We have the tight end lined up off the line of scrimmage off the tail of the tackle. We bring him across the ball to block the frontside linebacker.

Coaching points include the following techniques. A deuce call by the frontside tackle indicates seven defenders: a) box, b) C/G's work to middle linebacker, c) backside tackle pulls for the frontside linebacker. We want to use short set draw technique.

FST: Draw/Short set on, torque outside, hammer call against the linebacker on line of scrimmage, outside, Jump/Drive.

FSG: White Castle on, nudge inside. Use hard post.

C: Nudge free safety, Hale backside, slow slip versus Mike stack, be alert for deuce call.

BSG: White Castle on, Hale inside, MOCK, Ron to near linebacker versus guard bubble.

BST: Double Duty.

TE: Fold for the first linebacker in box, be alert for hammer/linebacker on line of scrimmage, deuce if seven in box.

RB: Open step, slide to opposite hole. Run to bubble B gap to C gap read. Spread offensive set, open step, shuffle, and square to quarterback.

QB: Open to your throwing arm. Show dropback pass. Keep head downfield two steps. On third step, overtop exchange with the running back. On 56 draw keep the head downfield one-step, reverse beyond six o'clock on second step, overtop exchange, set to pass.

X: Stalk block and seal, against man coverage run your man off.

Z: Play away, cut off the safety, push crack.

T: Block inverted defender. If he disappears, go to the safety.

It is difficult to create deception in the one-back set. You can run counters, but you have to spend time working on it. The draw is a play you do not have to spend a lot of time on it.

SHOTGUN WIDE OPEN SPREAD OFFENSE

West Virginia University

My topic tonight is "Running Out of the Spread Offense" which I have been doing for 15 years. I heard Urban Meyer talk about the things he has done at Utah. Everyone has some version of the spread offense running game in his package.

I started running this offense when I was the head coach at Glenville State College, a Division II school in West Virginia. I want to give you some of the background as to why I went to this type of offense. The offense is a shotgun wide-open spread offense and a zone-read scheme.

I stayed there seven years and then went to Tulane University to have some fun down there. When I started running this offense, I had a six-foot quarterback. We started running the zone play out of the shotgun. I was not smart enough to think about the read option from the play. My quarterback was smarter than I was. This kid scored about 1600 on his SAT test.

We practiced the zone play all practice and the defensive end kept making the play on the ballcarrier. After practice, my quarterback told me he would take care of the defensive end tomorrow. I asked him what he planned on doing. He told me he would "read" him and pull the ball if he came down the line after the ballcarrier. That was in 1990, and we stumble onto the read on the zone play by accident.

We had some good years at Tulane when Sean King was the quarterback there. When we went to Clemson, we developed another diminution. We had a quarterback in our offense that ran the ball like a tailback. That added a diminution because of the faking and the ability to run a quarterback trap and other companion plays.

The biggest coaching point I can give you about offensive football is to find something you can hang your hat on. You have to be flexible but simple and fit your offensive schemes to the personnel. I know you cannot recruit in high school, but if you have a big, strong athlete, build the offense around him.

If we can recruit a great athlete that can run and throw, we emphasize those parts of our offense. Our offense is flexible enough to take the things he does well and build the offense around those skills. Your offense has to be simple enough for everyone to understand.

If you have eleven dumb players and can only run one formation, make sure you can execute that formation. It is not what the players know; it is what they can execute. If you cannot execute the zone-read plays, do not run them.

The more people run a particular scheme the faster the defense catches up with what the offense does. Defenses are finding ways to get more defenders into the box. We still run the ball, but we found it goes much better if you can be versatile with your formations.

We hang our hat on the zone scheme. Rick Trickett tells his offensive line we will run the zone play each game as a major part of our offense regardless of what the defense does. If the defense gives us what we want, the play gains 10 or 15 yards. If the defense does a good job, we still gain something positive. Our players believe in the zone play. If the numbers are in your favor, the four- or five-yard runs become 10- or 15-yard runs.

I am going to get into my clinic talk and I go fast. If you have a cell phone, turn it off or put it in your pocket. I do not like the phone ringing because it interrupts me. Besides, having the cell phone in your pocket on vibrate is fun sometimes.

The offense has certain advantages. They know where they are going and when they are going. That means they know the play and the snap count. The offense can establish the tempo of a football game. In our no-huddle offense, we have three tempos that we use. Our regular tempo is a quick tempo as compared to other teams. We have a tempo called indy. The indy tempo is fast but we sometimes change the play we have called. The last tempo is get tempo. The get tempo is a tempo that says, "As soon as the umpire spots the ball, get the hell out of the way. We are running the ball." We practice all three tempos and they are part of the game plan. If the offense knew the defensive alignments before the snap, they could call a play that would go 100 percent of the time. When you control the tempo of the game, that is the situation you get into. We snap the ball so fast that the defense we saw on the last down is the one we see on the upcoming down. If we do not huddle, the defense cannot huddle. I can call the right play for the defense, but we may not execute it or we might be whipped.

Another reason we change tempos is to prevent the defense from stemming from on defense to another. When they align, it is hard from them to communicate a change before we snap the ball. What you see is what you get. On occasion, we have to wait for the defense to align because we are ready to go before they line up. In that case, the quarterback is not sure what the defense is.

Even if I were a huddle team, I would still use tempo to make it hard on the defense. On one down, I would sprint to the line out of the huddle and snap it quickly. On the next down, I would use the regular tempo and try to draw the defense off sides. I would keep them off balance and make them stem early or not at all. When I talk to our defensive staff, they tell me the change in tempo screws them up as much as anything.

I prefer to have fewer schemes and more formations. It is easy to teach formations. I would rather take one run and run it from a multitude of formations than add another run. The first thing the defensive coordinator does on Sunday night as he puts the game plan together is list the formations the opponent runs. He lists all the formations, all plays run from each formation, and how he will line up against them.

We use the no huddle because we can control the tempo. The no huddle eliminates disguises and stem by the defensive line. If you ever watch the classic games of the past on ESPN, the teams that played in those games ran one front, one formation, and only one pass coverage the entire game. They ran power and isolation and had one play-action pass. In present times, nobody does anything like that. Every one is in multiple fronts and formations. They run all kinds of coverages and blitzes. By going to a no-huddle scheme, we eliminate many those types of things.

Running the no-huddle scheme gives the coaches time to change a play. The quarterback does not make an audible and change a play. Although a quarterback is a junior or senior in our program, he uses the checks we call. He knows what are good plays and bad plays, but the coaches make the audible. I trust our coaches more than I trust the quarterback. Some quarterbacks can handle the audible, but most of the quarterbacks I coach watch cartoons on Saturday mornings. They are not watching film of the opponent. Therefore, I trust my judgement and the decisions of my coaches in the press box before those of the quarterbacks.

If you are a no-huddle team, you have more practice repetitions. In a five-minute period, most teams run seven or eight plays. We run 13 plays in a five-minute period. We go fast and get more repetitions for our time on the practice field.

The last reason is important in running the no-huddle offense. It makes conditioning a factor earlier in the game. The most compelling factor in determining the outcome of a game is conditioning. That holds true for professional, college, or high school football. You run your team during pre-season and two-a-days, but after the games start there is that doubt of running them too much. Coaches talk all the time about making conditioning a factor in the fourth quarter. It may be too late by the time we get to the fourth quarter. We have to make conditioning a factor in the first quarter. Our team prides themselves on running the no-huddle offense.

In West Virginia, we have about 50 signs with our slogan posted all over the complex. It is a simple message: spot the ball. That is not just an offensive slogan; it applies to defense and special teams. When the referee spots the ball and gets out of the way, we are ready to play. We take a lot of pride in it and conditioning is a big part of it.

We are a shotgun team and there are advantages of being in the gun. Being in the shotgun gives the quarterback time when a defender comes free on a missed block. It gives the quarterback vision. If you have a short quarterback and put him under the center, he cannot see peripherally the way he can in the shotgun. If we back him away from the center five yards, he sees the outside so much better.

When a quarterback throws an interception, the reason is because he did not see the defender. That is his excuse when he comes back to the sideline after the pick. More times than not, the quarterback is right about the play. I do not expect him to say I saw the defender and threw the ball to him.

I had a 6'5", 245-pound quarterback that could throw the ball a mile. The first game he played, he threw three interceptions. I noticed when he looked to the sideline for the signal he squinted all the time. I sent him to the eye doctor after the game for an examination. The eye doctor called me after the examination and told me he should not be driving a car. The doctor fitted him with contacts and the next game he was 35 out of 45 in the passing game. Vision is important in the mechanics of the quarterback.

What I want to talk about before I get into the zone play is the game plan. When you decide what you are going to emphasize in your offensive scheme, you must have the answers to all the defensive adjustment the opponents will throw at you. We put together what we refer to as an answer sheet. The thing we look at between series, halftime, and during TV time-outs is the answer sheet. It has the adjustments we go to if the defense plays a certain defense. If a team is playing a Bear defense, the answer sheet tells us the adjustments we need to make. We have a series of plays that provide the answers to the questions.

We establish the answer sheet at the end of spring practice or at the end of two-a-day practice. We sit down as a coaching staff and decide what we should do against different defensive looks. The answer sheet does not change during the season. You must have more than one answer for each situation. The answer sheet helps our coach in the press box when thing go fast and we need answers.

An example from the sheet is a change in cadence. We are in the shotgun and the center has control of the snap. The defense watches film of the center snap. If they find the center is in rhythm from the time he looks to the time he snaps, we must have an answer for that problem. To keep the defense from timing up the shotgun snap, the center has to change up his rhythm to keep the defense onsides.

We have to do the same thing with the quarterback. He signals the center when he is ready and the center snaps the ball when he is ready. If you have 15,000 fans in the stands, you can say, "Go." If you have 60,000, it makes a difference with communication. The quarterback has an indicator to let the center know he is ready. At times, the quarterback uses a leg lift, a clap, or a finger signal as the indicator. We give false signals to keep the defense confused.

On the answer sheet, there are solutions for coverages, fronts, and stunts. All our coaches understand what how to use the sheet and what to look for. On the main page of the answer sheet is the down and distance situations. It lists calls for third and long yardage, third and short yardage, third and medium yardage, and every different situation you could possibly have.

There is a special section for a great player. If you have a great athlete, you want the ball in his hands. We list ways to get the ball to the star and beat special defenses designed for him.

One of the biggest advantages of going to a no-huddle offense is the NCAA rules that govern it. There are no NCAA rules that govern the number of players you can have on the field. If you huddle, you can only have eleven players in that huddle. If you break the huddle with 12 players, that is a five-yard penalty. If you are a no-huddle scheme, you can have the whole team on the field before the snap of the ball.

That reminds me of a story. In my early years of coaching, we were struggling with finances. I had a big booster that wanted to donate $10,000 to the football program. He had a nephew playing in our program. This boy was the worst football player I had ever seen. The booster wanted to know if he could see his nephew on the field. I told him he would be on the field for about half the snaps in our game. I told the player I wanted him to check the numbers on the field. I told him to go out on the field, run to the number, stand for three or four seconds and run right back off the field. He was on the field for 35 plays and did not interrupt anything.

I want to get into the zone play. A rip formation for us is a four-wide receiver formation. There are three principles for running the football. The principles are numbers, angles, and grass. That sound simple and it is. When we run to the numbers, it means the number of defenders to each side of the center. If there are four defenders to the right of the center and three to the left, I want to run to the left.

The grass principle relates to the wideside of the field. We want to run the play to the area that has the most room or most grass. The hash marks in the college game are 20 yards off the sideline.

The angles refer to the blocking angle we get with our offensive line. I would rather run at a 1 technique than a 3 technique. It is easier for a guard to block down on a 1 technique than it is to reach block the 3 technique. If the numbers are the same,

we run at the 1 technique.

The reason we like the zone play is the fact that the 1 technique does not stay a 1 technique after the snap of the ball. Generally, the 1 technique is slanting somewhere else. The zone play allows us to zone block on moving linemen.

We run the ball to the grass. That means if your numbers and angles are the same, we run to the wideside of the field. If the defense is head up on their techniques and evenly defended on both sides of the ball, we run to the wideside of the field. That gives us more room to run the ball.

The most important thing is the numbers. We want to run and throw to the numbers of the defense. If the defense is in a cover zero, you should be throwing the football one hundred percent of the time. If there is one safety deep, you have numbers to run the ball.

It is still a numbers game because if we run the football, we have four defenders coming to the weakside. The defense shows you three defenders weak and brings the four players from outside the box to balance their scheme. Even with the safety aligned on the hash mark, we expect to get a safety rolled into the box from somewhere. When we design the offense, we must be able to block four defenders to the weakside.

The split between the guard and center depends on the alignment of the defense. If the center has a shade technique on him, the guard is almost toe-to-toe with the center. He has to be in a position to cut off the shade in the zone play.

In our formation scheme, we play with three wide receivers on the field most of the time, and sometimes with four. We name our receivers with letters. We have an X-, Y-, Z-, and H-receiver in our offense. The quarterback is in the shotgun set with the tailback to his right or left depending on the play or blocking scheme. The zone play in the first diagram comes from a "rip Max" formation with the outside zone play going to the left. In the formation, rip means right and Max gives a two backs in a split set in the backfield. We have Y- and Z-receivers in a wide slot right, and the X-receiver in a split position left (Diagram #1). We tell our wide receivers to stalk the defensive backs unless they can run them off. It is easier to run off defensive backs than to stalk them. We tell our receivers to get in front of the defensive back and allow him to run over him slowly.

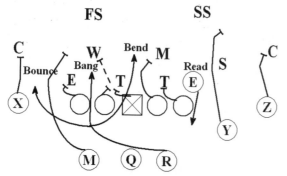

Diagram #1. Outside zone

We pick up the extra blocking on this play because the quarterback is reading the backside defensive end. If he chases the ball down the line of scrimmage, the quarterback keeps the ball and runs out the backside. That is one reason we run the shotgun.

To run the zone play, the offensive line needs to give a little ground to gain a little ground. We do not give as much ground as traditional zone teams because penetration kills you. We take a quick-set step, turn, and put the hat on the outside of the breastplate of the defender. We would like to knock the defender down the field, but many times it is not going to happen. If the offensive lineman is good enough to get in front of the defender and get run over slowly, that is good enough for us.

That theory is the same with pass blocking. In the pros, you might see an offensive lineman lock up a defensive man, but at the college level that does not happen often. We coach our players to get in front of the defensive lineman, get a good hold on him, and allow him to run over the blockers slowly. The coaching point is to make sure he comes over the top so the lineman can pull him down as he falls backward.

If the nose guard stays in a 1 technique, the offensive center gets help from the guard. The guard stays on the nose tackle until the center can come to take him over. When the center takes the

nose tackle over, the guard climbs up for the Will linebacker. The coaching point for the guard is not getting in a hurry to get to the linebacker. He stays on the 1 technique as long as he can. The faster the guard gets to the linebacker, the faster the linebacker steps up.

As long as the linebacker stays deep, the guard can stay on the 1 technique. The backside guard zone steps to the inside and climbs to the next level to cut off the Mike linebacker. The backside tackle zones steps and tries to reach the 3 technique. If there is movement in the 3 technique, the tackle cannot reach him. In that case, he pushes him down past the hole and the back runs on the backside cut back lane. That is a hard thing for a back to do initially.

The way the back runs this play is the whole key to the play. He is toe-to-toe with the tackle in his width. He opens, cross steps, and on the third step he is parallel with the quarterback. The biggest mistake a tailback can make in the zone play from the shotgun is to start immediately downhill after he receives the ball. When the back starts downhill, the Will linebacker starts downhill. When the linebacker starts downhill the guard cannot block him.

The aiming point for the back is the outside hip of the offensive tackle. After he receives the ball, he goes two more steps parallel before he starts to press his aiming point. I do not care how wide open the play looks; he must take those two additional steps. He reads both down defensive linemen to playside. He reads the end first and the tackle second. If we reach the defensive end, he bounces the ball outside.

If the defensive end beats the reach block, the running back's cut depends on where the defensive tackle is. If the center has taken over the shade tackle, he cuts the ball into the hole. If a shade tackle slides down the line of scrimmage, the tailback bends the play behind him. The tailback has three paths to run the ball. He bounces it outside, bangs it into the crease, or bends it back. If the defensive front is an even front, we generally get a bounce or bang path for the tailback. If the front is an odd front, the play is usually a bang or bend path.

It has been our experience, that we will not get a bounce on an odd-front defense. The odd front has a nose tackle, a 5 technique, and a linebacker outside of him. You cannot get outside on that type of alignment.

If we have a split backfield where we have a second back in backfield, it is a Max set. He aligns toe-to-toe behind the offensive tackle. He reads the defensive end for his blocking key. If we reach the defensive end, he goes outside and blocks on the run force player.

The left tackle splits about two feet. The split of the right tackle may be tighter because he has to cut off the 3 technique to his side. If we get the backside tackle cut off, we have a play.

The companion play to the outside zone play is the naked bootleg by the quarterback (Diagram #2). The offensive line blocks the outside zone play and stay on the line of scrimmage. They cannot get downfield. The outside receiver runs a hitch at five yards. The inside receiver runs the smash route. The smash route is a short corner route. This is a good play because both plays look alike.

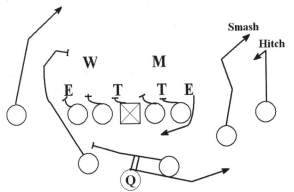

Diagram #2. Naked bootleg

The difference between the naked bootleg and the outside zone for the quarterback is the mesh. On the zone play, the quarterback does not put the ball into the pocket of the tailback and ride him. In the zone play, the quarterback does not ride the tailback and decide to pull the ball. By the time the tailback gets to the mesh area, the quarterback has decided what to do with the ball. It is not like a veer play. He gives the ball to the tailback or he keeps it around the end.

On the naked bootleg, the quarterback puts the ball into the pocket of the back and rides him. He pulls the ball after the ride and runs the pattern.

Once the backside defensive end begins to play the naked bootleg, we run the quarterback trap play from the same set (Diagram #3). The Max back comes across and kicks out on the defensive end. The quarterback rides the tailback, keeps the ball, and runs inside the Max's block. That is a nice adjustment to that series of plays. That is an answer for the defensive end playing the bootleg.

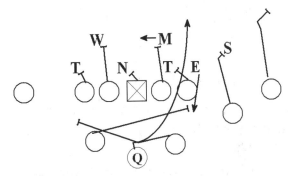

Diagram #3. Quarterback trap

When we run play-action pass, our linemen do a good job of keeping their pads down. They do not sit with a high hat to tip the defensive linemen. They go through their run blocking and assignments and try to stay down on their blocks. We tell them to go at the family jewels. We do not tell them to go at the knees. Defensive players will protect their knees, but if they are any men at all, they will protect the family jewels first and stay down.

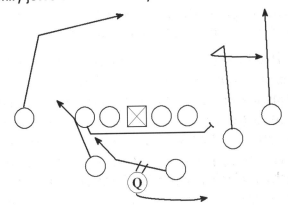

Diagram #4. Play-action pass

This is different from the naked because we pull the backside guard to protect the quarterback

(Diagram #4). To the twin receiver side, we run a take-off for the outside receiver and a snag route by the inside receiver. The X-receiver comes across the middle on a deep cross. The quarterback rides the tailback and brings the ball to the outside.

On this pattern, we go further down the field with our routes because we have some protection on this pattern. The play we like to run takes some time (Diagram #5). Against a cover-3 secondary, we want to get four verticals down the field. We use the same type of action in the backfield. To the twin side, the outside receiver runs his vertical up the numbers of the field. The inside receiver comes into the hash marks to that side. To the backside, we bring the X-receiver into the hash marks to threaten the safety right away. The Max back comes out of the backfield and runs a wheel-up route down the numbers to the backside.

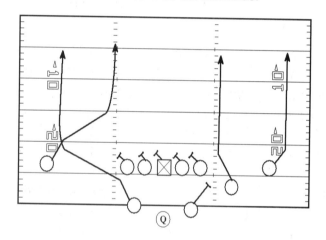

Diagram #5. Four verticals

The protection for these types of plays is gap protection. Gap protection gives you a zone type of blocking scheme for your protection. We block both backs one way and the line blocks the other. We do not have many man-blocking schemes. When you set up your blocking schemes, you have to consider your personnel.

Your blocking scheme depends on the ability of your offensive linemen. Remember you should always play to your strengths and never your weaknesses. If your linemen are athletic, you can do more man schemes. If your linemen are short, fat, dumpy players, use zone schemes.

I had one player play for me that was two inches from being a complete circle. He was 61 inches tall and 59 inches around. We tried to get him to be a complete circle. We bought him a bunch of cheeseburgers and French fries to help him make it.

I played defense at West Virginia University. When I first started coaching, I was a defensive coach. My first full-time coaching job was as a defensive coach at Salem College in West Virginia. At Salem College, if you could spell Salem they would let you enroll. If you could not spell it, they gave you the S, A, and L, and hoped you could come up with the E and M.

Corky Griffith, a coach from the state of West Virginia, was the head coach at Glenville State. I was 22 years old and this was my first full-time coaching job. I ran the defense at Glenville State. At our first coaches meeting, Coach Griffith comes in the office. He was a good ole' hillbilly and he called everyone "Jack." He told me he wanted me to run the "Cat" defense. Since he was the head coach and I was a company man, I was going to do what he wanted me to do. He told me he coached the Cat defense and one year his team got 16 sacks in one quarter using it.

I told him I had to see that defense. I asked him how to run the Cat defense. He said, "After the offensive linemen get in their stance, you flex the defensive linemen off the ball and back them up five yards." I thought he was talking about the flex defense that Dallas ran at that time. He told me, "You flex all the defensive linemen five yards off the ball. You have all the fat offensive linemen up on the line of scrimmage. We have our defensive linemen five yards off the ball.

"You get your fastest and quickest defensive back and he is the 'Cat.' You put him at the end of the line of scrimmage in front of the end man on the line. Remember, you have the defensive line backed off the ball five yards. As the quarterback starts calling out the cadence, the Cat starts walking up and down the line of scrimmage. He walks up and down the line of scrimmage mocking the quarterback. He points to one of the offensive linemen and tells him,

'I am the Cat and I am going to get you now! I am the Cat and you cannot block me.'"

Coach Griffith went on to describe the Cat defense. The idea is for the Cat to make something happen. He wants to disrupt the offense and get them to jump offsides. He goes from one gap to the next gap yelling, "Here comes the Cat! Here comes the Cat!"

Those offensive linemen start thinking, "What is he going to do next?" You know how those fat offensive linemen hate blocking those small skinny defenders. You can imagine what they are thinking. They get in their stance and then they start yelling. "Watch out, here comes that Cat. Man, I hope that Cat does not come through my gap."

The Cat is trying to get the offense to make a false start to draw a penalty. The Cat goes from one gap to the next gap screaming, "Woo-e, woo-e!" Coach Griffith is serious as a heart attack. He told me to run the Cat defense in practice. He said, "As a matter of fact, I want you to run the Double Cat too." I asked him what the Double Cat was. He said, "You get one Cat on the left side of the line and one Cat on the right side of the line. They both start yelling and screaming at the same time. When the Cat strikes, there will be a hole in the line for him to run through."

I was not going to tell Corky I was not going to use the defense so I made some notes on it. Two weeks later, we started spring practice. I got the practice schedule and saw that I had a 10-minute period to work on the Cat defense. At the end of practice, we had a scrimmage set up. I was to run the Cat defense in the scrimmage.

I had a set of twins on the defense and they were perfect Cats. They were about 5'10' and 190 pounds and they could run all day. So I worked on the Cat defense to get ready for the scrimmage. That first scrimmage we were only running the Single Cat, not the Double Cat.

At the end of practice, we came together to scrimmage. On the first play from scrimmage, the offensive right guard jumped offsides. Coach Griffith came sprinting up to me screaming, "I told you it would work, I told you it would work."

Coach Griffith told the offense to run the play again. The offense wore one of the twins out. The offensive line knocked his butt 20 yards down the field. They ran up and down the field with ease for about five plays. Coach Griffith started yelling at the defense, "You guys are doing it all wrong, damn it." I asked him what he meant by that. He said, "The Cat can't just walk up and down the line of scrimmage like that. It is all rhythmic, Jack, all rhythmic."

When I first went to West Virginia University as head coach, I was about ready to run it. I wanted to be creative, but I was not brave enough to run the Cat defense. We did have a lot of fun with the defense. If I see the Cat defense show up in Florida, I will know where it came from.

Now, most teams are going to some form of the spread offense. People think when you get in the shotgun that you lose the timing of your throws to the receivers. Our timing from the shotgun is just as efficient as it was from under the center. When we throw from the shotgun, we want the timing to be the same as it is from the three-step drop or the five-step drop. If the snap is good, we can get the ball off in the same amount of time as in the drop scheme, and sometimes we can get it off faster.

If the snap is bad, the quarterback's eyes come off the coverage to catch the ball. After he catches the ball, he has to refocus and throw the ball. If the snap is away from his face the timing is good. The timing is the same in the shotgun or under center for the five-step pass. In the shotgun on a five-step pass, we throw it with the same reaction as we do on a three-step drop. That makes the timing the same or betters from the shotgun.

If the quarterback runs a play fake from the shotgun, he has to speed up his throw to keep the timing the same. He play-fakes, sets his feet, and throws to keep the timing the same.

TACKLING AND THE 4-4 DEFENSE

Grand Rapids Community College

It is great to be here this morning. I appreciate Don Lessner giving me this opportunity to share some of my ideas on football and to represent Grand Rapids Community College.

I am going to get into the football aspect and I am going to cover a wide variety of things in this lecture. After I talk about the tackling aspects of the game, I want to cover our 4-4 defense and what we do that is a little different that may help you with what you are running on defense.

There are many innovations going on in football today from the offensive side of the ball and on the defense as well.

What is the best offense and what is the best defense? If there were a particular "best," then everyone would be running it. Everyone would be running the same damn thing. I do not care what you run on offense or defense; it still boils down to this. The best teams in junior high, high school, college, and pro football are the best football teams around are those that can block and tackle.

Here is my belief. This is the first thing we are going to cover. I do have some drill tapes on tackling and I will share those with you later. I want to tell you one important thing today. I say "to hell" with offensive or defensive schemes. Tackling is the key to defensive success. *USA Today* ran an article titled "The lost art of tackling."

Some of this will be old to some of you. I am not an innovator. I will tie in this with our 4-4 Defense. The point I want to stress is defensive quality control. It does not make any difference what you are running it comes down to defensive quality control. When we break our films down, we look at defensive quality control in four areas:

- *Scheme.* Do you have people in position? Are the players in position to make the play? Is your scheme sound?

- *Scoring Defense.* You can get all the information you need from the stats to see what has happened in the game. Every team in America has that on their scoring goals board. I am not very smart but I tell our players this all of the time: "If we do not score, we are not going to win the game." They can understand that point.

- *Yards Rushing and Yards After Catch (YAC).* Yards rushing play a big role in determining the winner of the game. That is why we play the 4-4 defense, because we want to stop the run. You do not win unless you stop the run. The other point that plays a big part in the game is yards after catch. We have all heard the acronym YAC: yards after catch.

- *Missed Tackles (MT).* How many missed tackles and who is missing them? You will be able to see the yardage for the game, you will be able to see the score, but the fourth point will not show up on the scoreboard. If you want to become involved with your defense, look at quality control and the number of missed tackles. You want to evaluate your players when you watch the film. We go through the film and we list MT for each missed tackle the players are involved in for each game. When we total up the plays at the end of the film, we list the number of missed tackles. After watching the films and counting the missed tackles, I realized if we wanted to be a better football team we had to be able to tackle.

Why do we have missed tackles? Missed tackles show up because of a lack of confidence and/or poor technique. It is very similar with the good shooter in basketball. A good shooter will keep on shooting because he knows what he is doing wrong. He is going to shoot until he gets the shots to go down. He is upset when he misses the shots because he knows what he did wrong to cause the ball to miss the basket. It is the same in tackling. You must have confidence and you must have good technique. Just as in basketball, the shooter does not say, "I hope I make it," the defensive man in football cannot say, "I hope I make the tackle." If that happens to you, you know he is not going to make the tackle.

Good practice leads to confidence. I believe this very strongly. You can put a practice schedule together that may not be very good from the standpoint of teaching the players what they need to learn about tackling. We say good practice leads to confidence.

You get what you emphasize. This is why you need a checklist to follow during the season. If you follow that checklist, you have a better chance to prevent the mistakes in the game. You may need to practice tackling every single day.

Let me talk about the perfect form tackle. It is a matter of body position. It is breaking down into a football position. The players all start clapping their hands and a coach yells, "Breakdown!" The players bend their knees and get into a hitting position. To tackle you must have good body position.

What is the football position? It is head up, neck bowed, and big eyes. Most of the players want to duck the head down. I tell them if they want me to give them a grade in the film, they must get the head up to make the tackle. I do not want to give them a MT on a play because they have their head down. In addition, I tell them if they get their neck broken by tackling with the head down, I do not have time to visit them in the hospital. I let them know nothing good is going to happen if they tackle with their heads down.

We have to be careful when we talk about protecting the head. We use a statement in tackling that we have used over the years. "Bite the ball; get the head across the bow." I am very careful not to say to put your face on the football or to put your hat on the football.

There are not running backs that are going to try to run you over unless it is down on the goal line. It is all a matter or angle tackling. If the back is running toward me and I am going to tackle him, I want to put my face on the ball. I did not say my head. I put my face on the ball so I can bite the ball. I shoot my head across the bow. We do close quarters tackling repeatedly.

We want to shoot the arms tight through the cylinder of the ballcarrier. We drop the center of gravity and shoot the arms through the cylinder of the man we are tackling. We accelerate our feet on contact. The most neglected phase of tackling is bringing the hips up under the body. We bite the ball and tackle up through the cylinder. Some teams tell the tackler to step on the toes of the ballcarrier when they are making the tackle. We want them to accelerate the feet on contact. We want a simultaneous explosion up through the ballcarrier. If the players fall down in a tackling drill, they are not doing it right. If you chop your feet, you will not fall down when you are tackling.

We are not going to talk about the "cut" or "chop" tackle. You can use a dummy to work on that tackle, but I am not going to cover it in this lecture. Instead, I am going to show you a film of our tackling drills. You can write them down and then I will show them to you on film.

First is close quarters tackling. It is very similar to the fit drill. If I line up two players 15 yards apart and tell them to come together in a form tackling drill, I am defeating my purpose. Probably nine out of the ten reps would be bad reps. Earlier I said, "Perfect practice leads to confidence." We want to line the two players up in close quarters and fit them into the perfect fit so they will know what type of tackle we want. We work together on the drill and we go from the left side and the right side. We can run this drill with pads on, or I can do it without pads. I should be able to do this drill without a helmet. I can teach this in the physical education class.

My favorite evaluation drill is what we call "off the back." I tie this in with tackling. We talked about running the feet. What do we do when we run the feet? You expose the hips or you release the hips. We have the man down on his back. He gets up and executes fifteen perfect form tackles. He must get off the ground and back into the football position. It is a great drill and it is good for evaluating players.

We emphasize the acceleration of the feet in tackling drills. We do the gauntlet drill and work on tackling. We get the cigar dummy and we have two players with shield dummies. I put the player on his back again. The two players are squeezing the cigar dummy, and the player gets off his back and executes a form tackle.

We use a blind tackling drill. It is the old "door drill." I have seen this drill where the coach actually takes a door on the practice field to execute this drill. They put a running back behind the door on one side and a tackler on the other side of the door. On a whistle, the tackler starts to run toward the tackler outside the door. The defensive man has to make that tackle on the ballcarrier. They cannot see each other behind the door.

We have worked on the perfect form tackling in several drills. We have several variations of angle tackling drills. We use them with pads and without pads.

We have one drill we like that we use on the goal line. It is a live tackling drill. Then we get specific and show a sideline tackling drill. I will cover the shed and tackle drill. At the end, I will show you my version of the skate drill. If you have seen me coach, you know we sequence out everything that I cover. We break it down and sequence it out together in smaller segments to get to the results. I want to show you these drills on the film. This is not a highlight film. It will cover the points I have covered in this lecture. (Film)

You need to practice tackling. You saw the number of reps some of our players got in that film. If you do not put tackling drills in every day, you are cheating your kids. You can tackle five minutes a day and improve a great deal. You need to emphasize what you want accomplished on that next game day.

Now that I have players that can tackle, we are going to talk some X's and O's. I want to talk about our 4-4 Scheme. On any defense you run, you need a defensive philosophy. In my defensive philosophy, the first thing is to be aggressive. "I am going to be aggressive." We put our 4-4 defense into our system in one week-and-a-half. Our players may not be able to pick up some of the classroom work very fast, but they picked up the 4-4 defense in a hurry.

The next part of the philosophy is to have a defensive package that gives you the ability to adjust the defense. You must have the flexibility in your defense that allows you to make the change up in the defense.

We want a defensive system that makes sense to the players. I want a defensive system that flows with the coaches and players. I want the defense to make sense.

With any defense, you must have a built-in disguise in the system. You do not want to manufacture a disguise; you need to have a disguise built into the defense.

We are not any different from anyone else. We play over as our base defense and we play under as our change-up defense. You can call the defense anything you want, but the key is to have flow. By flow, I am talking about alignment. It is so critical. I will show you an alignment against a pro formation. There is no such thing as stealing in football. It is borrowing ideas from other coaches and other teams. It is imperative that we have the ability to line up on defense.

This is how we line up on the 4-4 over call (Diagram #1). The end on the tight end side is always in a 9 technique. The tackle lines up in a 3 technique. The nose is in a 1 technique. The end on the split end side is in a 5 technique.

The Mike always goes with the tackle. The Will goes with the nose man. Sam is always on the tight end side. The Buck is always on the split end side.

The Will and Buck are always to the bubble side. These four down linemen and four linebackers are working together on stunts. I will show you the pressure or stunt package later.

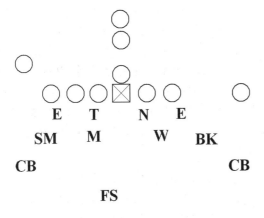

Diagram #1. Over

This is how we line up against a twin set (Diagram #2). The tight end is to the opposite side of the twins. You can see we line up the same way with the front four down men. We do adjust with our linebackers. Now Mike is in the middle of the formation over the center. Sam is still on the tight end side. Will is outside the end on the formation side. Our Buck is not in a strong safety position.

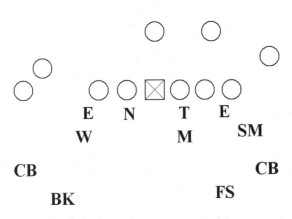

Diagram #2. Over versus twins

I am not going to get into the coverage because I have a film I will show so you can see the different coverages we play. We play different coverages including cover 3, cover 4, cover 1, and cover zero. Predominantly we played more cover 4 last year. Cover 4 is quarter, quarter, quarter, quarter across the board. We ran all of these coverages and we ran them with only a few mistakes. You must remember the disguise aspects of our defense.

On our under look, we change it up slightly (Diagram #3). Sam is still on the side of the tight end. Our Will is now stacked behind the nose man. Mike is stacked behind the tackle in the 3 technique. The Buck is on the split end side and the free safety is on the tight end side.

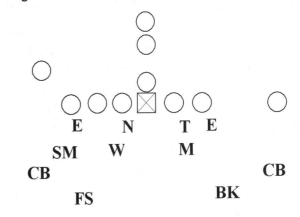

Diagram #3. Under

Against the twins set, we flip it over to the tight end side again (Diagram #4). We slide or kick down the linebackers with Sam on the side of the tight end.

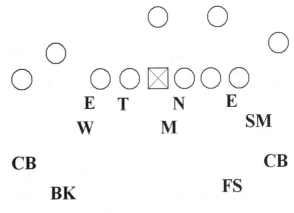

Diagram #4. Under versus twins

When we rush five players, it leaves us six defenders on the pass. When we play cover 1, we have five defenders to cover the five eligible receivers. That leaves us one man to play over the top. I am a firm believer in having a defender deep in the middle of the field. However, in cover zero, we do not have anyone in the middle of the field. However we are going to bring pressure on the quarterback and force him to throw the ball before he can find that deep receiver.

We want to use linebacker pressure. The general assumption is when we apply pressure with five men we are going to play cover 1 When we are going to bring six men in the pressure package we are going to play cover zero.

We are a zone blitz football team. We want to disguise our defense as much as possible. Here is the beauty of this defense. We can replace players in the coverage. We cannot drop a 300-pound player back into a passing zone. We could, and I am sure that would be intimidating. If we did that, the offense would run the crossing routes and pass routes where they "picked" the defense. "Go ahead and pick our 300-pound shade technique." We can go to our zone coverage and let those pencil-sized receivers come into the zones of the 300-pound shade man.

We are a gap control defense. In the over set, the Mike linebacker lines up in a 30 alignment. He is lined up behind the heels of the 3 technique. We have an A gap and a B gap. If we want to send the Mike in the A gap or the B gap, we make a simple call. If we call "Mash," the Mike blitzes the A gap. If we call "Mob," he goes through the B gap (Diagram #5). It is very simple terminology. It is Mike in the A gap or Mike in the B gap. Mike knows where he is to line up and he can read the gaps. The 3 technique knows that he is going opposite the call for the Mike. If Mike runs Mash, the tackle has the B gap. All this is to us is gap exchange. We can play cover 1, 3, or 4 with the Whip.

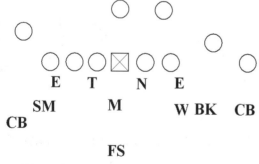

Diagram #5. Whip — cover 1, 3, 4

The other linebacker pressure package includes the Whip and Waco (Diagram #6). Whip indicates Will is going *inside*. Waco indicates Will is going *outside*. That is how we run the linebacker pressure. Again, we can play cover 1, 3, or 4 with Waco. Whip

and Waco are calls used only to the split end side of the formation.

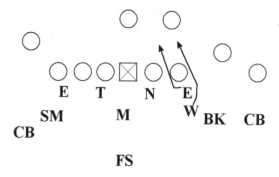

Diagram #6. Waco — cover 1, 3, 4

We do film study on the team we are going to play and decide what stunts we want to use each week. Each week you may use different stunts. We have two corners and we have two linebackers. The other deep players are safeties. It is a three-safety scheme.

We are going to show the base 4-4 look. The Will linebacker comes up on the line and now we are in a Bear alignment (Diagram #7). This is a version of Bear with cover 1. We can run the Bear cover 2 and cover 3 as well.

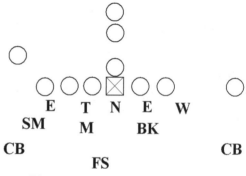

Diagram #7. Bear — cover 1

Against a trips set we can play our Bear with different coverage. We can play the same look by moving the free safety and Buck to the strength of the formation (Diagram #8). It is our Bear call with a different coverage.

Our next stunt is pop. The first thing I hear is that this call does not have anything do with a W. Pop is both linebackers pressing their assigned gaps (Diagram #9). We can play cover zero or cover 1. Here we are man-to-man.

This is a great red-zone defense. We add the word peel to the call. Peel means the end has the back if the flare shows. The end fakes the blitz and then backs out to look for the back on the flare route. If the back stays in the formation to block for the quarterback, the defensive ends retrace and step back in their original alignment.

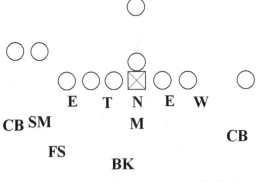

Diagram #8. Bear – cover 1, 3, 4

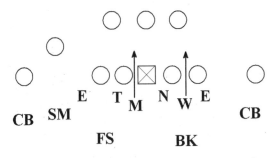

Diagram #9. Pop - cover zero, 1 - peel

We use the same concept with our cross cover zero or cover 1 peel (Diagram #10). This is a trailer blitz with the Will coming off the tail of the Mike on the crossing action. We can run cover zero or cover 1 peel.

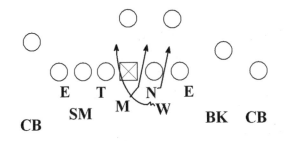

Diagram #10. Cross cover zero, 1 peel

The coverage is the same as in the cross stunt. It is a great stunt. It is a great stunt against the draw and screen Pass.

We also use the zone blitzing. This is our pop/cross/snake cover 3 or cover 4. I can run pop or cross, and run snake coverage. We can run cover 3 or cover 4, depending on the formation (Diagram #11). On the snake we are dropping the 3 technique back into the vacant middle area. How far back does he drop? I tell him to drop back and show his hands. He drops about six yards deep.

We teach the 3 technique where the hole is located. Who is the hot receiver when the tight end is in the game? The tight end is the receiver that will come into that area.

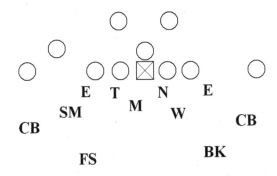

Diagram #11. Pop/cross/snake cover 3, 4

We can run pop/cross taco - cover 3 or cover 4. You ask why taco? We are dropping the tackles. We are replacing them in the zones (Diagram #12). If we call echo, we drop the ends. On taco we can play cover 3 or cover 4.

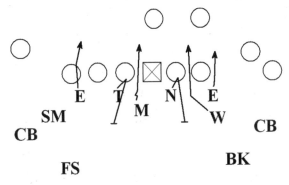

Diagram #12. Pop/cross taco – cover 3. 4

I know I talked fast but I want to show all of this on the film. (Film) This has been fun. Thank you very much.

SIX-PACK BLITZ PACKAGE

University of Oklahoma

It is great to be here with you. I say this all the time, but I do not think I can say it enough. I have a great respect for what all of you do. Coaching at any level is coaching. My father was a high school teacher and a coach for 30 years. I have an older brother who is a high school coach and teacher in Ohio. I understand the opportunities you give young people and the sacrifices you make working with them every day. I know you do not make a great deal of money. We all know you do it because you love the game. Regardless of the salary we make as college coaches, we do it for the same reason. I was talking to someone last week and I told him it did not matter what I made. This is what I am going to do. I am going to do it at some level and enjoy what I do. I firmly believe we are in a great profession.

I struggled on the way here as to what my topic should be. I just realized I had spoken here only a couple of weeks before. I spoke at the National Football Coaches Association conference two weeks ago. Today I will talk about long yardage defensive pressure from a three-man and four-man defensive front.

When we get into a long yardage situation, we use six defensive backs on the field. I will show you some film and talk about the pressure scheme we use in those situations. I want this to be informal. Anytime you have a question, stop me and ask questions. If I do not have time at the end of the lecture, write me and I will send you a copy of the lecture I used at the national convention.

The first thing I want to show you is our "dollar package" (Diagram #1). That package has six defensive backs, two linebackers, and three down linemen. We align the ends in 5 techniques on the outside shoulders of the offensive tackles. The

nose tackle aligns head up the center in a zero technique. The linebackers are over the offensive guards. We play with a dime-back and a six-pack player in the game. The dime-back goes to the strongside and the six-pack player plays to the weakside of the defense. The dollar sign in the diagrams represents the logo for the six-pack player.

From this front, we have the ability to blitz any of our linebackers or defensive backs and rotate into different coverages. The key to all the blitzes is the bluffing that takes place up and down the line of scrimmage. Any offensive line can pick up the blitzes if they know it is coming and from which side. We do our best to disguise the blitz through our fakes.

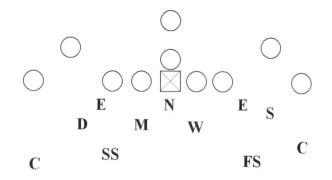

Diagram #1. Dollar package

The first blitz we run in the film is our "sugar blitz" (Diagram #2). The s in sugar tells us it is a strongside blitz. This blitz involves the strongside defensive end, the dime-back, and Mike linebacker. We bring the dime-back off the edge, blow the Mike linebacker through the B gap, and twist the end behind the Mike linebacker.

The nose tackle plays into the weakside A gap and the weakside end comes off the backside and stays outside for containment. In the secondary, we play cover 3 with the strong safety, Will linebacker, and six-pack player in underneath coverage. The corners are in the outside thirds. The free safety has the middle third. The strong safety rolls to the strong flat to curl area. The Will linebacker has to overlap the strongside and cover for the Mike linebacker. The six-pack player overplays in the Will linebacker's protection area.

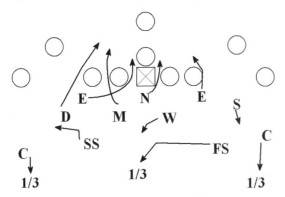

Diagram #2. Sugar blitz

The strong safety plays inside the number-two receiver at a depth of five yards. He must challenge the slant pattern if it comes inside. If the number-two receiver starts on a vertical route, he expands out and makes contact with the receiver. He jams and disrupts the number-two receiver so that he has restarted his route.

The Will linebacker slides over and becomes the short hole player in the middle of the field. If there is a trips set to the strongside, the Will linebacker has to slide out and get into a position inside the number-three receiver. If the number-three receiver comes across the field, the Will linebacker slides out and protects under number two.

We can mix in a man-free scheme in the secondary to confuse the quarterback. In our zone coverages, the corners are playing man principles in their zone coverage.

We can run a variation off the same blitz. In the sugar blitz we bring the same three players from different angles (Diagram #3). The defensive end rips inside, the dime-back comes tight off the edge, and the Mike linebacker loops around to the outside. Everything else in the defense plays the same way.

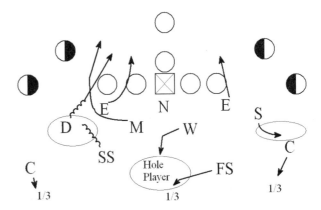

Diagram #3. Sugar blitz rip

The diagram for this blitz is a two-by-two set. The coverage is primarily the same. The strong safety and six-pack player are inside the number-two receivers to their sides. The corners are in an inside leverage position on the number-one receivers. The six-pack player and strong safety are playing under the slant by the number-two receivers and working out under the number-one receiver. The Will linebacker is the short middle-hole player.

We can run the same blitz scheme from either side. When we come from the weakside, we give our blitz a name that starts with the letter "w." The sugar blitz to the weakside is "whiskey." When an offensive team slide protects and sends a back to block the backside, we try to send two defenders at him as quickly as they can.

The "spice blitz" (Diagram #4), is another blitz involving the same three defenders. On this blitz, the dime-back comes inside and the defensive end takes a wide outside rush. The Mike linebacker comes through the A gap.

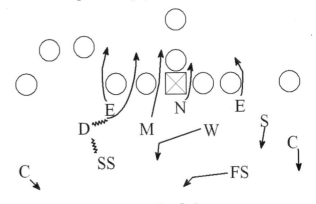

Diagram #4. Spice

The coverage principles are the same as the sugar blitz. The strong safety aligns inside the number-two receiver to the strongside and works under the number-one receiver. The Will linebacker works under the number-two receiver to the strongside. The six-pack player keys the number-two receiver weak and works out under the number-one receiver weak. In both cases, the number-two defenders align inside the receivers and pass off the underneath patterns. All of the underneath defenders stay with their primary coverage key until they are no longer a threat.

The corners align inside of the wide receivers. They challenge inside slant routes and protect against all inside routes. In their coverage, they start inside and work out on their responsibilities.

To the strongside, we run "sugar and spice." The same stunts to the weakside are "whiskey and water." The "whiskey blitz" (Diagram #5) involves the Will linebacker, six-pack player, and the defensive end. This is an effective blitz coming from the single receiver side in the three-by-one offensive set. The six-pack player is the outside rusher off the edge. The Will linebacker blows the B gap, and the defensive end loops to the A gap behind the Will linebacker.

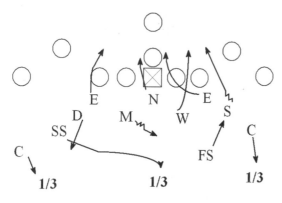

Diagram #5. Whiskey

The nose tackle must get good push on the center to keep him from coming off on one of the blitz men. If the Will linebacker can get a strong push over the guard in the B gap, he creates a pick for the defensive end looping behind him. If the offense tries to drop someone out of the line to pick up the backside edge rusher, he probably will be late. The six-pack player comes off the edge with speed.

In the secondary, the dime-back aligns inside the number-three receiver in the trips set. If the set is a double slot, he fakes the blitz and moves in and out on the number-two receiver to the strongside. On the snap of the ball, he plays the number-two receiver and works out under the number-one receiver. He stays with the number-two receiver until he ceases to be a threat. The Mike linebacker slides to the middle hole on the snap of the ball.

The free safety slides down into weakside flat area playing the number-two receiver using inside out principles. He takes the inside away from the number-two receiver on the quick slant. He takes the number-two receiver if he goes vertical. He jams the receiver, forces him off the seam, and makes him restart his pattern. He works out under the number-one receiver after he releases number-two. We hope the blitz gets to the quarterback before the receivers can execute their four vertical routes.

The strong safety aligns inside of the number-two receiver to the strongside. He fakes his alignment up and back and finally bails out into the middle third. The disguise of the defensive backs is extremely important. We cannot tip the defense until the moment the ball is about to be snapped.

With the blitzes, a fair amount of the time the offenses are unsure of their scheme. They do not know where the blitz is coming from. The blitz control protectors end up blocking or getting out late on their patterns. We render potential receivers as a non-factor because they cannot release on time. They get out so late that they are not a major threat.

Teams try to counter the blitz by inserting a tight end on the backside of a trips set and leaving him in to block. That being the case, it is easy to get over and under the number-two and number-one receivers. That leaves us in a sound secondary coverage, which can squeeze back on anything coming out late. These entire situations are third-and-long yardage plays. If the offense is dumping the ball to receivers coming out late, that is what the defense wants. If they do that, we come up, make the tackle, and get off the field.

The "water blitz" (Diagram #6) is the companion blitz to the spice blitz. On this blitz, the Will linebacker blitzes the A gap. The defensive end takes the rush off the edge. The six-pack player comes under the defensive end into the B gap.

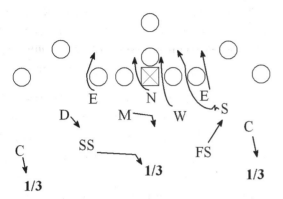

Diagram #6. Water blitz

When we blitz, we want to have the ability to come from the strongside as well as the weakside. We want to come up the middle as well as off the edge. We want to come from the wideside of the field as well as the shortside of the field. In some of our blitzes, we disregard the formation and blitz from the boundary or the wide field.

In long yardage situations, we do the best to protect deep and make the offense throw underneath routes. That way we can come up and make the tackles short of the first down markers. With long yardage, we must make the offense throw the ball quick. If they hold the ball, we should sack them.

We want the ability to bring all of our secondary personnel on a blitz. We like to bring this blitz from the boundary. The offense always looks at the Will linebacker and six-pack player as possible blitz men. What we try to do is bring the corner off the boundary along with the six-pack player (Diagram #7). The defensive end slants into the B gap and attacks upfield. The six-pack player blitzes from the outside on a tight path. We bring the corner outside of the six-pack player on a blitz. We hope the offense does not see the corner coming until it is too late.

In the secondary, we play either three or two deep. In this diagram, I will show you the three-deep

zone. Since we bring the corner and six-pack player, the Will linebacker has to get under the number-one receiver weak. The free safety rolls into the outside third behind the Will linebacker. The dime-back aligns under the number-two receiver in the trips set strong. The corner aligns inside the wide receiver. The Mike linebacker aligns in his linebacker position and slides out under the number-three receiver in the trips set.

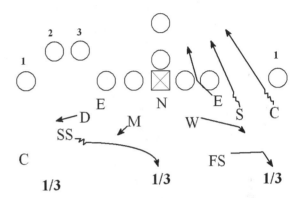

Diagram #7. Weak corner blitz

The strong safety aligns inside the number-three receiver in the trips set. He disguises and on the snap of the ball; he rolls into the middle third. He holds his position until the last second and bails deep.

The offensive blocking scheme targets the Will linebacker and six-pack player because we bring them on the whiskey and water blitzes. That is why the corner comes free on this blitz. We try to get the six-pack player and the corner on the one-back in the backfield.

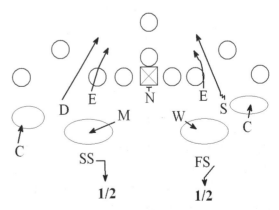

Diagram #8. Outside

The next blitz is "outside" (Diagram #8). On this blitz, we bring the dime-back and six-pack players off the edges. The secondary call is "35." That means we play either cover 3 or cover 5. If the set is a trips with a three-by-one set, we play cover 3. The bubble screen is the reason we play cover 3 against the trips formation. Any other offensive set we play cover 5, which is cover 2 to most people. The strong and free safeties drop to the hash marks and the corners roll up into hard corners.

The offense thinks they have soft corner. They think they can throw the ball quickly to the outside on hitches and outs. The Will and Mike linebackers drop into the holes on each side playing inside out on the receivers.

We can do any number of things with the nose tackle. We can drop the nose tackle into coverage over the ball. We can jam the center, play screens and draws. We can make a "Louie" or "Righty" call for the nose tackle (Diagram #9). That sends him on an outside loop with one of the defensive ends. The defensive end charges inside the offensive tackle and the nose tackle loops outside of him. We can run him either way. On this blitz, we run a "Louie with the outside blitz.

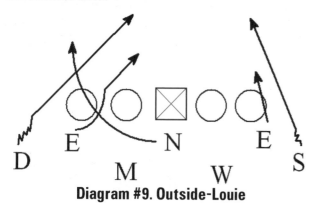

Diagram #9. Outside-Louie

The next blitz is a free safety blitz with the six-pack player (Diagram #10). In this diagram, we kick the coverage into two-deep coverage. The strong safety moves across the formation and plays the weakside half of the field. The dime-back rolls back into the strongside half. The corners roll into hard corners and the Will and Mike linebacker sit in the holes on each side. The free safety slides down and blitzes from the outside with the six-pack player.

To help us with the four-vertical route, we mix in some man-free coverage and cover 2. If the offense

knows you are in any coverage all the time, it is easy to pick apart. The quarterback gets confused because it looks like the corners are playing soft. He sees the pressure coming and throws to what he thinks is a safe pattern, when in fact he has thrown into the coverage. What we are hoping for is two defenders on one back trying to protect. When the offense sees the free safety spinning down, they think he is coming down to take the linebacker's place in the coverage. They think the linebacker is blitzing instead of covering. When the safety comes, they are surprised.

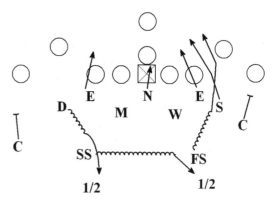

Diagram #10. Free safety blitz

The coverages compliment the blitzing game. When we put our package together for a game, we try to have man-free, cover 3, and cover 2 ready as change-up for the secondary. None of our blitzes is complicated. Any offensive line could block them if they knew they were coming.

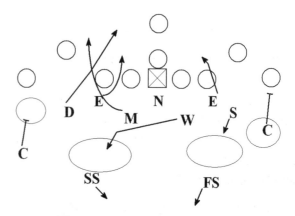

Diagram #11. Dime/Mike blitz

We can run the same basic blitz to the strongside (Diagram #11). We bring the dime-back and the Mike linebacker from the outside. The defensive end blows the B gap. The dime-back cheats and comes from the outside. The Mike linebacker slides and blitzes from the outside.

We play cover 2 in the secondary. The safeties retreat to the hash marks. The corners roll down in to the outside flats. The Will linebacker slides to the strongside window on the snap of the ball. The six-pack player has the weakside window. We try to disguise long enough to get two-on-one on the back defender. In the film, you can see the offensive linemen pointing out who is coming. We showed the blitz too early and the offense blocked it. However, we had good enough coverage in the secondary to stop the play.

Our "silver blitz" is a double linebacker blitz (Diagram #12). We have a number of ways to blitz the linebackers. The blitz I like brings both of them to the same side. We take the nose tackle to the weakside A gap. The Mike linebacker blows the strongside B gap and the Will linebacker fires the strongside A gap.

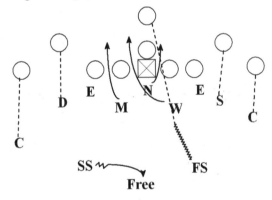

Diagram #12. Silver blitz

We play man-free coverage behind this blitz. Everyone matches up with the corners on the wide receivers and the dime-back and six-pack player on the slotbacks. We can game plan how we want to cover the back in the backfield. We can drop the free safety down into the box to cover him or spy with the defensive ends.

With this blitz, we like to bring the free safety down into the box and blitz him from the weakside (Diagram #13). When we do that, we spy with the defensive end on the back. The offense has a tremendous amount of problems blocking this blitz.

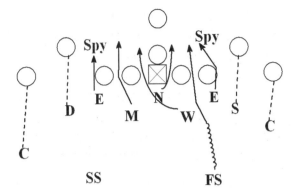

Diagram #13. Free safety silver

We worked a package this year called "spinner." We played with five defensive backs. Our best pass rusher was a 6'5", 270-pound defensive end by the name of Dan Cody. We played him in the six-pack player position. We rushed him an average of 75 percent of the time. We call him the "spinner." He walks around in our defense from the strongside to the weakside and blitzs using the fire blitz scheme. We blitzed him inside, outside, and up the middle. We dropped him in coverage about one out of every four plays.

A blitz we use with the spinner defense brings the defensive end into the B gap. (Diagram #14) The spinner came around to the outside from an inside alignment and we bring the corner off the edge. We played cover 2 behind the blitz.

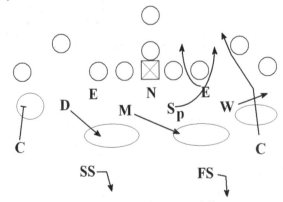

Diagram #14. Spinner blitz

The Will linebacker flies out to the corner's position. He cheats out and takes the corners rolled up position. The strong and free safeties get to the hash marks and play cover 2. The strong corner rolls up into the flat. The Mike linebacker and the dime-back play in the underneath holes to either side.

Sometimes coaches get caught up in the X's and O's of football. The situations in all of these plays are long yardage. All of the plays shown are blitzes. On this particular play, the offense ran an option play. I want to call your attention to the discipline we have on defense. We have a blitz called, but the defensive end (in the midst of a blitz) reverts to his teaching and plays the option as if he expected it. He holds the quarterback off until the linebacker can react and get into the play. Although the players are in an aggressive scheme, they do not go wild and forget their elementary football fundamentals.

All of the blitzes you see the spinner running are the same ones I showed you earlier with the six-pack player. The spinner replaces linebackers and defensive backs in the blitz scheme. When he moves from one side to the other, he assumes the alignment of outside and inside linebackers.

The defense is not magical. The offense can pick up any blitz you run as long as they know where it comes from and when it is coming. They can pick up the blitz if they are willing to commit enough men to the protection package. If we bring five rushers and they protect with seven blockers, they can block the blitz. The down side to these numbers is they have three receivers in the pattern against six defenders.

We do not come free on every blitz we run. The offense is practicing all week to prevent that from happening. That is why we must have sound coverage in the secondary. When you blitz, you want to get there the majority of the time. If you do not force the quick throw, you set your defense up for the big play. There are holes in the underneath coverage, but we try to keep the deep coverage sound. We can allow completed passes as long as we can react back to them and make the tackles.

The underneath coverage has to understand what we want to do. They cannot bite on short-pattern fakes. They must be patient in the defense and hold all catches to yardage short of the first down. We want to react, but not gamble in the secondary.

There are many things going on in front of the quarterback. When he comes to the line and looks at the defense, everyone with the exception of the three down linemen are moving. The linebackers are walking from gap to gap, moving up and back in their alignment. The outside linebackers are moving in and out from a blitz position to a coverage position. In the secondary, the corners are adjusting their position from inside leverage to outside leverage. The safeties are walking around, moving up, and back. The disguise of the defense is what the offense must sort out.

It is important to mix up your coverage so the quarterback does not see the same defense every time. Man-free coverage is a good defense, if you are satisfied with the match-up you have with your corners and their receivers. However, we do not want to use man coverage as a steady diet. In the long-yardage situation, you want to be sound and not risk taking.

We have some time left for any questions you may have on what we do. In the blitz game, you have to come from both sides and up the middle. You must change your coverage to give the quarterback a problem with his read. You must not be predictable in your blitzes or coverages. If you become predictable, the offense will pick you apart because there are many good quarterbacks in major college programs.

Once your players understand the principles of the coverage, the defense becomes easy to run. They have to learn to jam and protect seams in the coverage. They have to learn how to play in the short holes in the defense. They have to learn how to deter patterns by alignment and how to move under receivers.

The object of the blitz is to disrupt the timing of the offense. You get on the blocker quicker, make the quarterback throw before he is ready, and disrupt the paths of the receivers.

In a balanced set, we declare the strongside as the wideside of the field. If the ball is in the middle of the field, we declare to the defense's left as the strongside.

In the Southern California game, they did a good job of moving the pocket to buy time for the quarterback. They hurt us more on first and second down than the third down. They made some great catches on third-and-long and executed even when we had defenders challenging the catch. They made the plays. They did a good job on first and second downs and got some big plays. We did a poor job of playing the play-action pass and being in position. Thanks a lot for that question. You win twelve games and all they want to talk about is the one you lost. [Coach Stoops was joking with the questioner and the audience roared with laughter.]

The flat players spin down to a depth of five to seven yards. If the yardage for the first down is longer, they can be looser in their alignment. They look inside out for slant patterns. Offenses when given quick pressure try to hit the quick slant pattern to the wide receivers. They try to hit the creases of the zone and split defenders for the big play. The first thing the flat player wants to do is get in the slant window and stop the quick throw. From there, the defender tries to get even with the receiver and jam him to protect the seam. If the seam is a major threat, he protects it. As soon as the seam is no longer a threat, he works to the flat.

The hole defender's job in a two-by-one formation is to slide under the number-two receiver. If the formation is two split receivers, a tight end, and a split receiver to the boundary, he works to the major threat. That usually is the speed receiver wherever he is. Most tight ends in this formation end up blocking. If the tight end releases, the hole player goes to where the quarterback looks. If there is only one number-two receiver, he slides under him first.

If the set is a three-by-one set, the hole player slides under the number-three receiver. The safety spins down on the number-two receiver is inside out on him.

The corners start with inside alignment, unless it is a tight split. He generally looks to challenge flats and inside throws and work out from there. The middle safety is deep in the middle over the top.

We want to play the first threat. If that quarterback is looking at a particular receiver, we cover him up. If the quarterback is looking somewhere else, and the number-two receiver is not a threat, the defender drops under the wide receiver or speed receiver.

We work hard on reading the screen. The screen is a big and major offensive weapon. If you are a high-pressure team, as we are, teams try to slow you down with the screen. The more experience you have on the defense, the better you read screen. The experienced player knows when the blocker releases him and when he beats the blocker. He knows he does not come clean on the blitz all the time. They feel the screen and recognize when someone is not blocking them. Playing the screen is a feel the defense has to develop. To become good at anything, you have to practice it with repetitions.

We do not play this defensive alignment on first and second down. This is our third down and long yardage defense. Our normal front is a 4-3 alignment. We shade the center and play over and under adjustments in the base defense. We use our safeties in run support. We are not a big blitz team on first and second down. We like to be in our structured defense. We want to play blocks and technique to stop the play, as opposed to trying to trick the offense with a blitz. We do blitz on first or second down, but that is generally from game planning or tendencies.

It has been a pleasure to be here today.

LINE RUN AND PASS RUSH TECHNIQUES

Carolina Panthers

I am excited to be here. I know a lot of the coaches here today. I am going to take you through our program as if you were a rookie coming to training camp.

The first thing I teach the rookie is sound fundamental football. Everything we do in our practices we do quickly. When we move from one spot on the practice field to another, we go quickly. To have success within the defensive line, you have to be good with your hands and feet. We play hard on every snap as if it is the most important play of the game.

When we practice, we play as if we are in a game. We take what we do on the field in practice and apply it into game situations. If you think Julius Pepper is a good football player when he plays, he practices that way. The defensive line coach has to demand his players play that way.

We pursue to the ball. We do not care where the ball is on the field; we are going to run to it. The distance from the football at the end of a play measures the desire of a defensive lineman.

The defensive line sets the tempo for each game with physical play. We create contact on every single play. We tackle using good techniques. During my lecture, you will hear me talking about near foot, leg, and shoulder. To tackle an individual, you need to use the near leg and near shoulder to tackle. That gives you power to knock the ballcarrier back. If you tackle across the bow, you open up your base and have no power.

We have great team defense at the Carolina Panthers. The reason we have a great team defense is we install every thing as a team. When you install things with the team everyone is on the same page.

Players have to understand the concepts of what you are trying to do. Players will learn their assignments. The coach has to make the player understand the concept of the defense and what you want to get done. If you do not teach the concept of the defense, the player will know what he is doing but not know the weakness of the defense.

If the player understands the concept of the defense, he will not come on an inside blitz. He knows if he comes inside he loses containment and that is one of the weaknesses of the defense. We do not teach anything that is illegal, but we use our hands to get off blocks and make plays.

This next piece of information I learned from Mike Trgovac, who is our defensive coordinator. He told me the number one thing a defensive line coach had to do was perfect the art of getting off the ball. In every aspect of the game, whether it is running or passing, the defensive linemen have to get off the ball.

In every drill you do, you should have a ball in the drill because defensive linemen are coached to move on the ball. They move on movement of the ball or individual movement by some player. A defensive line coach has to have a stick-football to use as part of every drill. Every thing the defensive linemen do is predicated on the stance. The linemen have to perfect the first step they take from their stance.

The first step is a six-inch power step with the back foot. It thrushes through the upper body to get into the neutral zone. From that six-inch step, we want the player to explode. He brings his hands and hat into the explosion and keeps the feet moving. When the contact occurs, the feet have to motor so the defender can push the offensive lineman backward.

The next technique we teach is hand placement. Do not let any one kid you about hand placement. That is the most important thing you can do in playing a defensive technique. If you get your hands in the right placement and strike them properly, you can control the line of scrimmage and get off blocks. The hand placement must be on the blocker's breastplate, with the defender's hands inside the blockers. The thumbs are up in the placement with the elbows tight. The player who gets his hands inside always wins the battle.

The defensive linemen have to play with leverage. The defender's helmet must be under the blocker's helmet to win the battle of the heads. I am evaluating tape right now on our team. If you find a player playing with a flat back, you have a chance to win. If you have a player playing with his chest, you have no chance to win.

When you evaluate players, you look for flexibility in the hips, knees, and ankles. The defensive lineman playing with his chest has stiffness either in his knees or ankles. Some players are naturally loose in the ankles and knees. However, some things can be done for players with stiff joints. Every drill you do should be predicated on bending the knees and ankles and striking a blow.

The next phase for defensive linemen is the knock-back. After contact, the defensive lineman becomes the blocker and tries to squeeze the offensive lineman into the hole. We teach the defensive lineman to sink his hips and drive the blocker into his gap of responsibility. His feet must penetrate the neutral zone. He regains leverage with his head if he lost that battle on the get off, or re-establishes his knee bend if he got over extended.

To get off a block, the defensive lineman must achieve separation from the offensive blocker. When he shoots his hands, he gets into a locked position with his hands and arms. He wants to keep his hands active to prevent the blocker for holding him. You must have separation to escape.

There is a tremendous amount of power in a six-inch punch if delivered with a snap of the hips. When the defensive linemen hit the blockers with both hands and snap the hips, they can create a tremendous amount of separation between the defender and blocker. You teach this by explaining to the players that they do not want to give up what they already have gained. If they let the momentum, which they established on the initial punch, go back to their bodies, they are at a disadvantage. When they punch the blocker and lock out, they have to continue the momentum and get separation at that time. They want to identify the play and get off the block right then. They can do it by ripping or swimming. By using quickness, the defender can stun a blocker with a short open palm punch. That pushes the blocker off so the defender can use the swim or rip to disengage and get off the block.

The defender wants to escape by shedding the blocker after he recognizes the scheme. He re-establishes the lockout with his arms and uses a technique called "post and pull." Keeping his outside leverage, the defender takes his inside hand, grabs the jersey, and pulls the inside shoulder down. He uses the outside leverage hand as the post. He pulls down with the inside hand and rips or swims to escape. We want to win with speed.

We want to play fast in the defensive line. To play fast the defender needs to be in his exact alignment and assume a good stance. The defender does not need to give the offense an advantage before the ball is snapped. If the defender knows his exact alignment and knows what to do, he will play fast.

Some coaches want to move defensive linemen after they line up. Once the defensive linemen get down and are ready to play, let them play. Communication is difficult once they get ready to play. What they can see is movement on the line and in the backfield. Teach the defensive line to recognize backfield sets and motion in the backfield. Teach them when a tight end moves in motion or trades from one side to the other, blocking angles change and will effect the way he plays. He understands leverage in the defense and knows if he does not adjust his position, he has lost leverage by alignment.

In playing technique, you have to give the defender a visual key. The visual key for most defensive linemen is the V of the offensive blockers neck. Wherever that key goes, the defensive lineman keeps his leverage and alignment relative to that key.

We use the butt technique to defeat the offensive lineman with a three-point hit. The three-point hit is with the hat and the hands. He leads with his hat and hits with his hands. They want to stay low, dig in, get their cleats in the ground, and manhandle the blocker. The punch to separate from the blocker has to be violent. The defender is not coming off and running up the field. He comes off hard and reads on the run. This is what we call "in-flight adjustments."

If the offensive guard attempts to reach a 3-technique player, his six-inch step may be too long. He has to get his foot on the ground so he can get out on the attempted reach. That is an in-flight adjustment.

In this situation, the offensive guard folds around the tackle and up on a linebacker. The tackle comes down on the 3-technique player to seal him inside. If the 3 technique tries to cross-face the tackle, the offense has won because that is what they want him to do. The 3 technique has to get off and get upfield on the guard. That makes the tackle come down flatter to pick off the 3 technique. That creates a big opening in the B gap. The backside 1 technique comes behind the play and makes the play on anything coming into that gap. The guard is forced deep and the tackle has to come flat. That is because the 3 technique got off the ball and up the field.

When you play defensive line, it is not precise. They have to make in-flight adjustments, move their feet, and know what is going on. We use all kinds of calls between the defensive tackles. Those calls come from reading the offensive lineman's body language and stance adjustments. We use the terms go, Rambo, and rabbit as three of them. The go call means the offensive linemen are sitting in a pass-set stance. If the backside tackle is calling "light," that means the guard is pulling on the power. We work on them in practice because if you do not hear them in practice, you sure will not hear them in a game.

Make sure the linebackers know if it is run or pass. I learned this years ago; if you know the play, let everyone know. Offensive linemen tip plays more than anyone does. If you think you know the play, tell everyone and we will read as we go.

In the defensive line, the defender has to do his job first. He has to react and cover his responsibility. He must have confidence in his teammates because together they can stop anything.

When you play in the defensive line, go all the way to complete the job. Punish the ballcarrier when he runs the ball. Pursue the ball until the whistle blows. The defensive linemen get hot and tired, but you cannot let them be late. The defensive line coach must make the linemen pursue the ball. When we have pursuit drill, those linemen's butts are flying to the football.

When you play in the defensive line you must have concentration and intensity. You have to be assassins on the field. They must be quick and decisive in their play. My players understand and recognize a triple or double set. They recognize an unbalanced set and they know where the play is going before it is run. That is why they are able to make plays.

Diagram #1. Technique alignments

This is important to me and it is critical. Show them exactly what you mean by alignment. When we draw our defensive alignment up for our defensive team, we go in numerical order (Diagram #1). Head up the center is a zero technique and on the shoulder is a "shade." Inside shoulder of the guard is a 1 technique, head up is a 2 technique, and outside shoulder of the guard is a 3 technique. The inside shoulder of the tackle is a 4 technique, head up the tackle is a 5 technique, and outside shoulder of the tackle is a 6 technique. The inside shoulder of the tight end is a 7 technique, head up the tight end is an 8 technique, and his outside shoulder is a 9 technique.

I am sure everyone has used the numbering system for alignment for years. This is slightly different because John Fox, our head coach, said make it as easy as you can. We number in sequence from the inside to the outside on both sides.

If the defensive linemen are in a zero, 2, 5, or 8 technique, we are in a balanced stance on the nose of the center, guard, tackle, or tight end. When I say balanced stance, I mean the defensive linemen's feet align on the offensive linemen's feet. The defensive lineman's inside foot aligns on the offensive linemen's inside foot and the outside foot on the outside foot.

If the defensive lineman aligns in a 1 technique, his outside foot aligns in the middle of the offensive guard's crotch. If he goes to a 3, 6, or 9 technique, the defender takes his inside foot and splits the middle of the offensive linemen's crotch. We have a term we call "track." If we align in a "track 3 technique," the defender puts his outside foot slightly outside the outside foot of the offensive guard. The guard is not sure whether the 3 technique is on the shoulder or head up. If we play a track technique, we use the feet of the offensive linemen to align. If we play straight techniques, we use the crotch to align. If we play a "loose 3 technique," we align our inside foot six inches outside the outside foot of the linemen.

If anyone is playing any type of 46-defensive game, the key is the 3 technique. You play a zero technique on the center and two 3 techniques on the guards. Make sure the 3 techniques are in loose alignments and they can get up the field.

This is exactly how we teach alignment. All I am telling you is make it simple, make it accurate, and demand they get their alignment.

There are two main responsibilities for playing in the defensive line. They have to assist in stopping the run. That means the defensive line cannot be selfish.

There are times when they have to spill blockers and grab offensive linemen. The job of the defensive line is to cause commotion and disruption at the line of scrimmage. When they cause commotion, they knock blocker off so that linebackers can make plays. If the defensive line does things properly, they have a chance to make plays.

The second main responsibility of the defensive line is to put pressure on the quarterback. Julius Peppers has to have 13 sacks every year. This year Mike Rucker went from 13 sacks the year before to four-and-a-half this past year. Our season went that way. We do not want to hear excuses because, in a nutshell, you have to pressure the quarterback.

When we teach pass rush, we start out by stopping the run on the way to the quarterback. In the defensive line, you may get a run call and the play is a play-action pass. The defensive linemen have to convert themselves from run stoppers into pass rushers.

In their running play rules, the defensive linemen must hit their target with bent knees, fly to the ball, and swarm. In the pass rush rules, the defensive linemen must explode, play technique, close, and defend the quarterback. When we attack, we explode through the blockers, attack, and react to the offensive linemen. We play with our feet on their side of the line of scrimmage. We will hit hard and are violent on every snap. Every move that we perform on run or pass will be of a violent nature. We will never allow our opponents to get their hands on us first.

That last statement is probably the most critical thing a defensive lineman must do. The most important drill you can do at any level for the defensive football player is using the hands against an opponent. It does not matter what type of drill it is. In a pass rush drill, the defender has to get his hands on the opponent first. If a defensive back is playing press coverage or re-routing a receiver, he has to get his hands on the opponent. If the linebacker is playing a block, he has to get his hands on an opponent. It does not matter whether it is high school, college, or pro football; in defensive football, that skill is crucial. If the defensive player cannot get his hands on the offensive player, he does not have a chance in hell of winning.

If you take your players to camp, that is a time for learning as well as practice. We let our players know what to expect in a meeting. They must be on time and bring a notebook. We take notes on everything we do. If a player shows up without a notebook and nothing to write with, throw his butt out of the meeting. He is not ready to play or anything else.

In preparation for our next opponent, I draw every offensive play they run and highlight the blocking scheme from each of their runs and formations. If we are in an under front with a bubble, our players know there will be a down block, with the center blocking back, and a guard pulling through the bubble. The 3 technique knows if we get the I-formation, he gets the double-team. They know what to expect.

I want to talk a little about pass rush. When the defensive lineman goes into a pass rush, he has to change his stance. In our normal stance, most of our pressure is on our outside foot. Our feet are slightly wider than our shoulders. The stagger is a toe-to-instep relationship.

Once the lineman reads pass, he changes his stance into a sprinter stance. The most important thing is the get-off. We look in at the ball and get-off on the movement of the ball. The defensive end picks a spot three yards behind the offensive tackle's alignment. He wants to beat the offensive tackle to that spot.

Pass rushers have to get off and knock the offensive lineman backward. Sometimes the offensive tackle opens up from the get-go. If the pass rusher can get to the blockers outside wrist, he generally can beat the blocker.

Players who also wrestle know how to use leverage in the pass rush. The simplest move is the "wiper" move. Wrestlers use the move when they wrestle. If someone tries to grab them they wipe the hand off the wrist or wherever. When the offensive lineman attempts to punch the pass rusher, he grabs the elbow and pushes it inside across the chest of the blocker. After the defender pushes the elbow inside, he steps with his inside foot across to the outside. The step with the inside foot clears the hip and allows the defender to flip his hip around to the outside. Some people describe the hip flip like a reverse carioca step.

You can anticipate pass based on the game situation and formation. They have to understand what formations the pass generally comes from. The defender must respond immediately to the pass set by the offensive linemen. He wants to have no wasted movement and be quick and deceptive on the initial move. The pass rusher wants to keep his movement toward the passer. Some pass rushers in their attempt to avoid the blocker end up working away from the passer and aiding the blocker.

The quickest way to the quarterback is a straight line. I tilt the defensive end at an angle to get to the quarterback as quickly as possible. He does not know what type of set the quarterback will take. If the drop is a three-step drop, the defensive end will not get there. He has to get his hands up and try to knock the ball down. The pass rusher wants to keep his movement toward the quarterback and make him change his set.

The worst thing the pass rusher can do is being predictable. If the rusher beats the blocker with a speed rush constantly, the blocker will figure out how to block him. Change up on the blocker and keep him guessing. Every good pass rusher has one counter off his initial move. One counter move for a soft pass setter is a "single arm bar." On that move, all you do is take the inside hand and grab the outside arm of the blocker, and lower the hips.

Use the natural agility of your players. They can use head movements and fakes to make the blocker miss the rusher. Quick feet and speed are deadly in the pass rush. Quick head and shoulder movements freeze the feet of offensive linemen. If you can do that, you can use rip and flip moves on him. If he soft sets, you can thrust speed into power and push him back into the quarterback.

The pass rusher cannot give up on his initial move too quickly. He has to give it a chance to work.

The spin move is a popular move of the pass rusher, especially as a counter move. You have to get up the field before you can use the spin. If you plan on spinning to the inside, make sure you have all your weight on the inside foot. He throws his outside elbow, extends his arm, and slaps the blocker on the butt to pull himself through.

The movement games are critical for the run and the pass. We run a game called "combo" (Diagram #2). If we are in a 4-3 over defense, we put Julius Peppers in a 7 technique on the tight end. We have a 3 technique on the guard. We play a backside shade on the center with the other defensive tackle. We create a bubble to the weakside by playing the defensive end in a 6 technique.

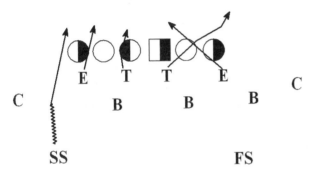

Diagram #2. Combo game

We tell the shade tackle to jam the center hard and get across the slant by the defensive end and to the outside. We have two linebackers up on the outside if anything bounces. When you are a defensive line coach, you have to know what the offense is thinking. Show them the bubble and then disrupt it.

What you do is take the same kind of running game stunt into the pass rush game. The nose tackle will probably draw a double-team from the guard and center. The defensive end makes his move upfield and comes under the offensive tackle. He is going to knock the guard off the shade tackle and let the tackle come free to the outside. They cannot be selfish. The defensive end gives him up to free the tackle for an outside rush.

You have to take advantage of weakness of

offensive blockers. If you find a slow setter, use the speed rush on him. Make him so conscious of the outside that he becomes susceptible to the under move. If the tackle false steps, we want to get to his set side arm immediately.

Speed rushers need to work on the hoops as much as they can. I put a player with a pad inside the hoop and jam the hoop runner as he goes around. That makes the hoop runner fight resistance, lean, and keep his balance as he goes around the arc. The offensive lineman can feel a rusher that is leaning too far. If they feel that, they will bury him quickly. That is why balance is important when he runs the hoops. It gives him a realistic situation.

I do not do any drills that have no carry-over value for a game situation. I try to involve some kind of contact in every drill. Very seldom does a defensive lineman get a free run at anyone.

If the linemen get into three-point stances, take advantage of that. If the defensive end is in a 7 technique on the tight end and gets a "go" call from the inside, he adjusts his alignment. The offensive linemen, once they get into the three-point stance, cannot move. The defensive end can adjust his alignment, get extremely wide, and make it doubly tough on the offensive tackle to get him.

Pass rushers make mistakes all the time. Some of them have nothing pre-planned in their mind for a pass rush and no pass rush move at all. The first move should be the speed rush. After the speed rush, we use the wiper move. If you are having success with either of those outside moves, the next move should be the inside rip. A mistake a pass rusher has is too many moves. He should find two or three at the most and make them effective.

If the defensive end gets a "go," he watches the quarterback if he is under the center. Just before the quarterback takes the snap, he steps out or sinks his tail. When the end sees the sink, he is off. You have to remind your players that during the course of a game the offense probably will adjust their cadence to draw our defense offside.

The hardest thing the defensive lineman has to do is make the transition from rushing the passer head on to some kind of play-action or sprint-out pass. I work a three on one key drill (Diagram #3) to help the defensive linemen adjust to the play-action pass. I align a 3 technique on the guard. The guard has three things he can do. He can fire out in a double-team block. He can quick set the guard or he turns out as in slide protection. The defensive linemen when double-teamed play the play like a run. If the guard quick sets, the tackle takes a step upfield and comes inside on the guard. If the guard set outside, the tackle beats the center with his speed.

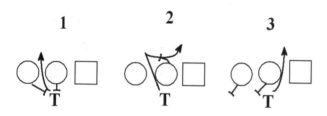

Diagram #3. Three-by-one key drill

If we read the three-step drop, the defensive lineman does not put his hands up until he sees the ball coming out. This is a simple drill to run. It is effective in making the defense read different situations.

The next thing I want to talk about is the tackle set line. That is the imaginary line drawn behind the offensive tackle to a point three to four yards behind him. This is the point at which the defensive end thinks he can beat the tackle. The point will be different from game to game depending on personnel. The defensive end has to race the tackle to the point he has chosen. At that point, the defensive end has to make a decision on which move he will use if the tackle gets to the point first.

You have to know how the tackle is going to set. If he drops straight to the point, the defensive end may have to get wider in his alignment to make his move more effective and make the tackle widen his retreat line. If the defensive end can get the offensive tackle to open up and use a cross over step, he has won the battle. When the offensive tackle does that, he loses his power in his legs. The defensive end bull rushes over the top of him.

If the tackle is retreating straight back to beat the defensive end to the spot, the defender takes

an inside move to slow his drop. If the tackle is beating the end to the spot, his weight has to be backward because of the speed he is moving. The defender uses his inside hand to push the tackle outside and uses an inside rip to get to the quarterback.

The critical thing is to put your players in a position where they are not square to the line of scrimmage. The defensive end to the open side of the set gets wider and tilts at an angle to the inside. That gives him good vision on everything inside and he can see the ball. That lets him get off the ball and do what he wants to do. We work on those little things in practice.

We have talked about the pass rush fundamentals. Now let us talk about the running game from the shade technique. You have to explain the different blocks the shade player is going to face. The first thing the shade player must understand is he will have an easier time getting his hands on the center because the center has to snap the ball before he can block. That means one of the center's hands is between his legs when the defender gets off the ball. The defender should knock the center off the line of scrimmage.

The shade player has a visual key, which is the V of the center's neck. He also has a pressure key. If his visual key tells him the center is working toward him and the pressure key tells him the guard is blocking down on him, he has to flip his hips and make himself skinny. He wants to take away a surface and make himself flat. The entry level of the pad of the defensive lineman is critical. If the defensive lineman's head is under his opponent and his hands are inside with his hips flipped to the guard, he is in good shape. He has leverage on the center and is in good shape with the guard.

If the center is trying to block back on the shade technique, the tackle wants to get off with his pad entry level lower than the center. He knocks the center back and keeps his gap side arm free. The center is the pressure key and he has vision on the guard. The running back is reading the movement of the shade tackle and running off it. If he beats the center and gets off into the backfield, he can create a lot of havoc.

If the center and guard try to combo block on the shade tackle with the guard climbing to the next level, the tackle has to beat the center. The center takes a drop step to get a better angle on the nose tackle. The tackle has to reach and grab the outside pad of the center. He will feel the guard coming down on his hip. If the shade tackle can grab the outside pad of the center and get hold of his outside triceps, the center will pull him through the block as the guard climbs for the linebacker.

If the center tries to reach, the nose tackle wants to do anything to keep his linebacker free. He grabs the center and keeps him from getting to the linebacker. If the nose tackle gets any kind of near back set, he does not step into the center. He steps into the guard. He has to anticipate reach, down block, and power. The shade tackle has to know the most popular scheme used on him is some kind of scoop or combo block. He will have two players working on him. He has to do anything he can to keep one of them from getting up to the linebacker.

The hard scoop is a popular scheme when running away from a 3 technique. The guard releases hard inside the 3 technique trying to get off on a linebacker. The offensive tackle comes down hard on the legs and ankles of the 3 technique. We drill this situation with a big ball drill. The 3 technique aligns on the guard. The guard moves hard inside. The 3 technique wants to get his hands on the guard. As the defensive lineman gets off and reaches for the guard, a manager rolls the ball at the feet of the 3 technique. The 3 technique takes his backside hand and punches the ball to get it away from his legs. That is a good drill to work on this situation.

When we teach the defensive line to get off the way we do, the defenders have to understand the angles of departure of the offensive linemen. There are two angles for the offensive linemen. There is the angle that keeps him on the line of scrimmage and the angle that lets him climb to the next level. The angle that keeps them on the line of scrimmage goes with the zone play. The offensive line tries to get the defensive line to move with the flow so they can use that momentum to wash them down the line and create a cut back lane for the running back. Because the scheme happens so fast, the defensive line is exposed. As the defensive line is working upfield, I tell them to get down and play low. Ideally, we would like to fit inside their blocks, but if we can create a pile, we have done our job. If the offensive turns someone and creates a hole, we have won the battle.

To be a good coach, you have to coach your players on recognizing the draw play. The offensive lineman takes a short drop one step off the line of scrimmage. On his next step, he screws his inside foot into the ground. The technique the offensive lineman uses is a slap technique. He invites the defender upfield and uses the momentum of the defender to push him further upfield. The offensive lineman slaps the defender on the inside pectoral muscle and pushes him upfield. As the defender feels the slap draw, he grabs the offensive lineman inside biceps. When he does that, he prevents the punch to the pecs and he can use the hold on the biceps to pull himself back to the line of scrimmage and into position. He can walk around the offensive lineman and get back inside.

Most times our defensive end plays in a track 7 technique. Playing that technique is critical for us in a running situation. I do not like to play a straight 7 technique.

If we play a straight 7 technique, we do not see the inside tackle. If he looks inside, the tight end will kick his butt every time. When we align in a 7 technique, the tight end is his basic key and we are going to beat him first.

Most tight ends concentrate on catching passes and could care less about run blocking. When the defensive end gets his hands inside, the tight end does not have a chance. He must be aware of a couple of blocking schemes. In the 7 technique the defensive end has C-gap responsibility. We can play a shade technique with the defensive end, which puts him on the outside shade of the tight end. From this position, he still has C-gap responsibility. People want to know how he can possibly be responsibility for a gap when he is one gap wider.

In this situation, two things are going to happen. He does not have to worry about the reach block. If the tight end tries to reach the defensive end, the end knocks him back off the line of scrimmage. When defender knocks the tight end back, the ball has to come inside of the tight end. If the defensive end gets a zone-blocking scheme to his inside, he takes the tight end and closes the hole with the tight ends body. If it is a pass play and the tight end releases, the defensive end has a better angle from which to attack.

If the tackle wants to combo block with the tight end, he has to bail off the line of scrimmage to get to the outside 9 technique. That lets the 3 technique get off the ball and press the hip of the offensive tackle. The 9 technique is a tight alignment on the tight end because of the run responsibility.

The reaction by the 7 technique on the drive block by the tight end is the same. His hands go inside. He steps with his inside foot to the tight end and wins the battle. On the arc block, the defensive end gets into the tight end with his hat and hands, and stays on him. Do not let the tight end get off the line. When the defensive end works on the tight end, he does not want to get flat with him. If you push the tight end back upfield, the zone play will not get off. If the defensive end lets the tight end arc to the next defender, the tackle will get his hands on him and they win the battle.

The blocking scheme that is tough on us is the scheme that New England runs. They base the defensive end with the tight end and bring the tackle on his hip trying to get his butt up inside. We tell our defensive end whoever initiates contact is the primary key. The defensive end turns on that player and kicks his butt. If the tackle gets the initial contact, the defensive end leans inside on the tackle. If the tight end initiates the contact, the defensive end destroys him.

I have to tell you a couple of theories. If we have a 9 technique end in a 4-3 defense, or if we have an outside linebacker in the 3-4 defensive set, they have to play against the counter off-tackle play. The defensive coordinator wants the end to read the backside pull of the offensive lineman. If the tight end blocks down, the defensive end squeezes down the line. He reads the pull of the backside offensive lineman. If the backside lineman is deeper than the frontside offensive lineman is, we want the end to take out both blockers. He wants the defensive end to spill the shallow pulling lineman.

The way we play our defensive end technique is to spill everything coming at us. When we see the double pull, we are not coming so flat that we hit the inside thigh pad and exchange one lineman for one defender. We use a technique called a "cheek" move. We get inside the shallow lineman. As the defensive end makes contact he strikes up into the inside breastplate of the pulling lineman. The defensive end wants to turn up on the pulling guard and try to push him up the field into the high pulling lineman.

Offenses run the bootleg or waggle pass off this action. The ends technique is a good technique to play against the play-action pass. We spill all backside-pulling linemen and cheek all tight ends, running backs, and frontside offensive linemen. In the cheek technique, the defensive end is not giving himself up to the pulling lineman. He is staying on his feet and forcing people deeper.

I hoped I helped you with some defensive-line play. Thank you very much.

QUARTERBACK DRILLS AND TECHNIQUES

University of California

It is a real pleasure to be here today. First, I want to tell you I admire what coaches do with the youth of our country. Most of you are high school coaches and I really admire what you do. I recall when I was in high school I was a young man from a single-parent home and did not have a lot of direction. I will never forget my high school coach. When I was a freshman I could walk by his office, he would invite me in, and we would talk. We talked about more than X's and O's. We talked about growing up and other important things a young person needs to hear at that age. I will never forget that happening. He did not know if I was going to be a player in the future or not. If he had not spent the time with me, who knows what would have happened to me. Coaches stand for a lot more than the X's and O's. If you see a skinny looking kid walking by your office staring at you, take a minute or two to visit with him.

I want to talk about the quarterbacks. I will start out by saying there are several ways to skin a cat. We have been very fortunate to work with some great quarterbacks over the years. We have coached seven quarterbacks that are in the NFL now. Six of the seven were first-round draft picks. Aaron Rodgers will be coming out this year and may be the first or second quarterback taken in the draft this year. He is coming out early as a junior. I have been fortunate in that I have worked with several talented young men. Each one of those seven quarterbacks had individual skills they needed to work on. Each of these players had individual problems. We worked through those problems and each became an efficient player.

I want to talk about the characteristics we are looking for in a quarterback.

- Mental and physical toughness
- Intelligence
- Competitiveness/Leadership
- Escape dimensional
- Athletic ability
- Natural throwing ability

First is mental and physical toughness. We are looking for players that win. When things get tough, he can get back in the huddle and lead the team. He has what it takes to be a winning quarterback. The physical toughness part is important. When he is hit under the chin a few times and is hit hard a few times, he has to be the type of player that will come back in the huddle and call the next play. If he can do that, his teammates will respect him.

The second characteristic is intelligence. We must have a quarterback that is going to run our offense. He has to get the play into the offense effectively and get us to the line of scrimmage. The quarterback must be a player that is smart enough to read the signals on the sideline that will enable us to do the thing we want to do in our offense.

The third characteristic we look for is competitiveness. In the fourth quarter when the game is on the line, he must be at his best. A good example of that was with Joey Harrington at Oregon. I worked with him and he led us to 10 fourth-quarter comebacks for wins. He was very, very competitive. When the game was on the line, the team had confidence in Joey because of his competitiveness.

The next point is the escape dimension. He must have some athletic ability. I can draw the plays up on the chalkboard, but in reality they do not always work that way.

The last characteristic we look for in a quarterback is some type of natural throwing ability. That is what we are going to discuss today. I want to go over the throwing motion of a quarterback. I want to talk about making a quarterback efficient in throwing the ball. I really believe this is something that can be changed. Some aspects about an individual quarterback we cannot change.

The mental and physical toughness aspects are something where some kids have it and some do not. When we talk about the throwing motion, we can work with some players and improve their throwing motion.

Our goals are to make the quarterback efficient, accurate, and consistent. Football is football, really. At all levels of competition, teams throw the flat-curl route in some shape or some form. Throughout the level of play in football is the speed of the game. That is the only difference. That makes the efficiency of the quarterback very important in getting the ball out of his hands on time. The time it takes for the quarterback to get the ball out of his hands is very critical. When I talk to the quarterbacks I have coached that are in the NFL, they talk about the speed of the game. In high school, the flat-curl route is a big play but the players do not cover much ground. As you progress to the colleges and pros, the flat-curl is much faster because the players cover more ground. It is very important for the mechanics of the quarterback be efficient.

I want to talk you through some of these mechanics and then we are going to see them on tape. I will show you some of the good and bad points of related to developing a quarterback.

The first thing we talk about is "ball placement." In ball placement, we talk about the ball on the "shelf." We imagine a shelf coming on the top of the players' numbers. We want the ball on the shelf. We do not want it down low under the belt line. We want it up on the shelf. We want the ball slightly outward. We want the ball past he midline of the body. The ball placement is something like this. It is past the midline, on the shelf, and slightly outward.

Some players carry the ball down low below the armpits. We tell them to get the ball up. The first thing they want to do is to raise the elbow. [Demonstration]

The second thing we talk about is separation. In my mind, this is the absolute key in efficiency in throwing the football. We want the ball above the shoulder. When I talk about separation, I am talking about when the quarterback releases the ball where it is at it lowest position or spot. One of the keys to this is the front arm angle.

The third point is the cocking of the football. The elbow should be at shoulders height. You will see this on the tape.

The fourth point is the release. When we release the ball, we want to make sure the elbow is at eye level. Many quarterbacks want to drop the elbow below the eye level. We tape the quarterbacks so they can see these landmarks on the release.

Next is the finishing aspect. We want to finish with the throwing hand in the opposite front pocket. We want the throwing shoulder under the chin after the ball leaves his hand. We want to exchange our shoulders. We want the quarterback to finish up with that throwing shoulder under his chin. Many quarterbacks are not consistent on their throws because their head falls off the target and the shoulder never gets under the chin. After the finish, we want to keep the head up and get the throwing shoulder under the chin.

I want to put on a tape to let you see the throwing motion of several quarterbacks. [Tape]

Once we get the throwing motion down, we must put it together with the dropback. The quarterback must be on balance and he must be under control so it all works together.

Let me give you a drill to help your quarterbacks. We do the seated drill where the quarterbacks sit on the ground and pass to a receiver in front of him. Put them about eight yards apart. It is hard to throw the ball without the legs. By taking the legs out of the drill, the quarterbacks can work on their form allowing them to get to the midline correctly. This drill forces them to get the ball back where it should be.

We sit the ball down on the ground and simulate a snap so they do not get laces every time. They must get used to finding the laces on the football. They do not get a perfect snap every time is a game so we make them find the laces and get the ball set to throw.

Next, we have the quarterbacks go to two knees and throw the ball. We want them to get the hips involved in the throw. Then we have them throw from the left knee up, and then with the right knee up. If you are a right-handed passer, you throw with the right knee on the ground and the left knee out in front of you.

I want to talk about our drop for the quarterback. First, we have to talk about our stance. We do not stagger the feet in our stance. Our feet are parallel. We can still drop back, go to the right, or go to the left without the stagger. The feet are slightly less than shoulder width. We do not want the shoulders very wide. The thing we do is to take a small "punch" step as the ball comes up on the snap. It gets the feet of the quarterback out of the hole. We do not want the quarterback stepped on as he comes out from the center. We want the quarterback to get his feet out of the hole.

Another thing the punch steps do is that it sets our feet at the angle we need to be on the play we are running. It does not matter if he is coming straight back, running the stretch play, or coming out at three or four o'clock. We want him to replace his feet, get them out of the hole, and set the feet at the angle he is going. We are not taking any false steps. We are not taking any unnecessary steps. If we are going straight back or to our right, most of the weight should be on our right foot. If we are going to the left side, it is the same thing. We want the weight on the left side. This gives us separation from the center. It set the angles where we are going.

As far as the drop is concerned, we like to have very good shoulder profile. On the dropback, we want the back shoulder slightly open. I hear coaches tell the quarterback to get the shoulder wide open so they can see the flat defender outside. How does the quarterback get his head around to see that flat defender? It starts in the feet.

We want to have our left foot slightly open. We do not get into a lot of detail on a five-step drop where you must be seven yards deep, or on the seven-step drop, you need to be ten yards deep. We do not want them concerned about gaining a certain amount of yards on the drop. Then when they get back to the drop area, they are off balance. We want them on balance when they set up.

The relationship we want will take care of this is where the weight is on the front foot heel and the ball of the back foot. We want this relationship. Anything less is stepping in the bucket. If that happens, we are sacrificing depth. We do not want to be so concerned about gaining a certain amount of yards on the drop and then be totally out of control when we get there. We want to keep the relationships with our feet and we want the front foot slightly open. If we can keep the front foot slightly open, it allows the hips to stay open. This helps you control your body. Now, this allows you to release the ball quicker, especially if you have to throw a "hot" route.

On the drop, we do not swing the ball back and forth across the chest very much. The reason we do not swing the ball back and forth across the chest is that we want the ball ready to come out as soon as possible. We have to be ready to get the ball away in a hurry on some plays.

The first drop-back drill is the line drill. We are not working on ball placement. The quarterback looks at his front foot. He wants to try to keep the front foot open. Because he does this, the front hip stays open. We do the drill on a line so we can keep the relationship with the front heel and the ball of the back foot. The purpose of the drill is to watch the front foot.

The next thing the drill does is to hold the shoulder open. We are going to exaggerate and I am going to hold his shoulder open. We are going to keep the shoulder open. We hold the shoulder open toward his back. If he has his left foot forward and you hold his shoulder forward, he is going to fall down. The only way he can drop with the shoulder like that is by opening the hips and opening that front foot. Until they learn to get the front foot open, many young quarterbacks feel as if they are going to fall to the ground. Again, this is all so we can see the field. We work on keeping the shoulder and hips open. He has no choice but to keep the front foot open.

After the quarterback gets comfortable with the technique, you run along side him and call out numbers. As the quarterback runs, he must call out the numbers you yelled out to him. This keeps the quarterback focus downfield and helps him with his awareness. The coach can be two yards ahead of the quarterback. You can get in their blind spot and work on making them see you with the proper focus.

Here is another drill we do everyday before practice. It is the board drill. If you do not have a board, the bags will work. It is use to make sure we keep our front foot angle and our shoulder the way we want it. The quarterback has the ball in his two hands and he works the pocket that way. Many times, we are able to get the pass away because we were able to slide in the pocket. We work in the pocket sliding one way and then the other way with two hands on the ball. We want to keep our hips and shoulders at a proper angle. [Film]

I want to go over our towel drill (Diagram #1). Foot angle is critical on the three-step drop pass. The second step is the stop set. The third step is the position step. You get power with the position step and you create an angle to throw the ball. We are throwing the ball to our left with a three-step drop action. The towel is just outside where he will not step on it. His first step is the punch step. He gets his feet out of the hole. The second step is the stop step and the third step is the position step.

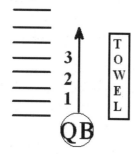

Diagram #1. Towel drill

What happens when we throw the five-step drop? We do not want to take the hitch step. Where is the break step? It is on the fourth step. Nothing changes on the mechanics. The legs are doing the work. The foot angle is critical in accuracy in throwing the ball.

Look at the shoulders. You see the legs doing the work. There is not a lot of shoulder movement. We do not change the angle of the shoulder plane and we want his hips open. He is moving but he is not stepping on the towel. Those are the steps to the left. It changes when he goes to the right side.

There is not a lot of weight on the back foot. The second step is where most of the weight is. On the throw to the right side, the key is to get his hips around or he will step on the towel.

We have the quarterback take his drop and look to the right side and then scramble to the left (Diagram #2). It is 1, 2, 3, and look to the right side. Then he goes 1, 2, 3, laterally without stepping on the towel. He turns around the towel without stepping on it. The theory for the towel drill and the straight-line steps is for the momentum of the quarterback to move in the right direction.

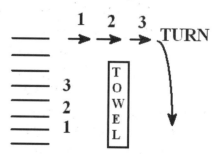

Diagram #2. Towel drill move the pocket

I want to finish with a mental drill a middle school coach gave me when I was in school. We used checkers as symbols for the players. We used one color for offense and one color for the defense. The coach calls the play for the quarterback. The quarterback has to align the offensive players in the formation the coach calls. Next, the coach aligns the defense. The quarterback moves the checkers as the play unfolds. The idea is to develop the quarterback's awareness to the overall offensive scheme as his mind works to accomplish the play.

Jon Tenuta

PRESSURE WITH THE ZONE DOG ATTACK

Georgia Tech

Thank you it is a pleasure to be here today sharing some of our defensive philosophies and schemes. The ability of your corners to play man coverage is the key to the pressure package. In the last ten to twelve years, the zone blitz, fire zone, and blitz package makes up 70 to 80 percent of our defensive package week in and week out. We believe in pressure.

We run the pressure game because it dictates to the offense what they can do. At Georgia Tech we are not as big as many people up front in our defensive line. We want to move our players around because we are a stunt 4-3 package team. First, we want to confuse the offensive line. We want to make the offensive line help and adjust every play. We want to make it tough on them with the zone scheme.

The second reason we use the pressure game is to confuse the quarterback. We want to give the quarterback a pre-snap read from one coverage and play coverage. We want to make sure the quarterback cannot read whether a second- or third-level player is coming on the blitz. We never want the quarterback to be able to set his feet. We want him to antsy in the pocket and take away his hot reads when he sees the blitz coming. When we eliminate his hot throws, the pressure can get to the quarterback.

When you break down your opponents, you want to know his blocking scheme. Everything we do in our zone-dog package is built to attack the run-blocking scheme of the offensive line. We bring our blitzes and dogs from a number of different directions. We can bring it from the tight-end side or open side. We can bring it from the boundary side or the field side. We can bring the blitz from a two-

receiver side or a one-receiver side and we have the ability to go away from the same situations as well.

The same things hold true as to the passing aspect of an offense. To pressure the passer, you have to know the protection used by the offense. Once you know how the offense is protecting the quarterback, you can attack the scheme from the areas we just mentioned in the running game.

We do not want the offense releasing five receivers on a pass play. We want to force the back to stay in to block. We know that four receivers are going to get out, but we want the fifth receiver to have to stay in and block.

We are an over and under 4-3 front. We start spring practice this week and the first zone-dog we put in comes from the field or wideside. We set our front to the boundary, which we call bench defense. The left defensive end aligns in a 5 technique on the outside shoulder of the tackle. The strongside tackle aligns in a shade technique on the outside shoulder of the center. The bench tackle is in a 3 technique on the guard and the bench end aligns in a 5 technique on the backside offensive tackle. We have a field corner that is always into the wideside of the formation and a boundary corner that aligns to the shortside of the field. Our strong safety goes to the wide field and the free safety is to the boundary side of the formation.

The call for the defense is "falcon." (Diagram #1) The F in falcon means field-side blitz. It is a zone-dog coming from the wideside of the field. This is the number one zone-dog we run. In the secondary, we play a three-under and three-deep or a four-under two-deep zone concept. The other secondary coverage is a man-free concept. The linebackers in the under defense are aligned with the Sam linebacker on the line of scrimmage in a 9 technique on the tight end. The Mike linebacker is aligned in a 30 alignment over the guard and the Will linebacker is in a 10 technique in the backside A gap. In the secondary, we show a cover-2 disguise.

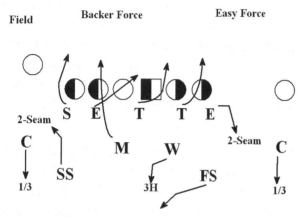

Diagram #1. Bench falcon

As I said, we run the zone-dog or some kind of blitz 70 to 80 percent of the time. We are not good enough to rush four players and get pressure on the quarterback. The falcon starts with the defensive front. I will start with the 3 technique tackles. The bench tackle's aiming point is the inside ear hole of the offensive tackle. He is a B-gap player, but if the tackle tries to collapse on him, he plays across the face of the tackle. He is the contain player on the pass play.

The shade tackle aligns in a strongside shade and cross faces the center and penetrates the bench-side A gap. The 5-technique defensive end is coming hard to the inside in what we call a "big stick technique." He has to get down the A gap. If the guard blocks down on the nose tackle, he closes the A gap and gets up the field. He is coming downhill to penetrate first. His vision point is the offensive guard. He gets to the A gap based on what the guard does in his blocking scheme.

The Sam linebacker is on the line and playing an in an outside-blitz technique. His job is to cut the field off because he is a primary contain player. He is what we describe as "backer support." Everything we do depends on departure angles. Because of our package, we spend 10 to 15 minutes a day on departure angles and aiming points. The Sam

linebackers departure angle and aiming point is a yard outside the near back or deepest back in the backfield. He has to cut the field off and has the pitch if the play is an option. He cannot go flat because he has to play run support.

The Mike linebacker aligns in a 30 technique and runs straight at the offensive tackle. He reads the tackle on the run. If he runs straight to the face of the tackle, he will know exactly what the tackle's blocking assignment is going to be. If the tackle goes outside on the Sam linebacker, the Mike linebacker goes under the tackle and becomes the B-gap player. He goes under all blocks and spills the football outside to the Sam linebacker.

The bench defensive end aligns in a loose 5 technique. He takes a flat step and has to cut the ball if it is coming to the boundary. He is what we call "easy support" or "end support" on a running play. The big thing for him comes if the ball leaves the line of scrimmage in a pass set. He becomes the two-seam defender to the boundary side.

We ask the defensive end to drop straight back and hold off the slant seam and help the corner. He jumps any pattern that crosses his face going to the flat.

The Will linebacker is the three-hook defender. Everything he does is from the flow of the number-three receiver. He tries to get to the middle of the field and play football. He moves on the flow of he number-three receiver and reads from the three-receiver to the two-receiver. He is looking to play the number-three receiver in the middle of the field or pass him off to the strong safety if he goes to the flat. In that case, the tight end is probably coming to the middle for him to pick up. When he gets to the middle of the field, he tries to help with all underneath routes. That is why he keys the number-three receiver to the number-two receiver.

In the secondary we are trying to disguise cover 2 or cover 4. The strong safety is aligned at eight to ten yards deep. When the ball is snapped he balances his feet and moves off the action of the number-two receiver. If the play is a running play, the Sam linebacker is the force player. The Mike linebacker is spilling everything to the Sam linebacker. The strong safety fills the gap between the Sam and Mike linebackers. He is filling from outside in into the C gap along with the Will linebacker.

The corners and free safety have the deep thirds if the ball comes off the line into a pass set. The corners have to be ready to jumps route as the receivers start to get ten yards deep. They cannot give up the deep third.

If the offensive set is a twin set to the field (Diagram #2) and a tight end away into the boundary, the responsibilities do not change, but the techniques are different for some people. We still have backer support toward the field and easy support into the boundary. The bench-side defensive end cannot get reached by the tight end because he is run support into the boundary.

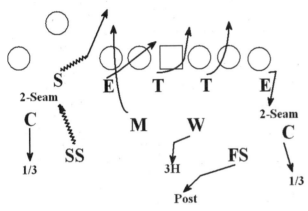

Diagram #2. Falcon against twins

The linebackers bump over to the twin set with the Sam linebacker aligning inside the number-two receiver. His departure angle is still one yard outside the near back even though he not in his normal alignment. Nothing changes from this aspect of the zone-dog.

The Will linebacker has an additional threat with the tight end aligned to his side. He is responsible for flow of number three either way, but he is responsible to the field first. He is a three-hook defender in the middle of the field. He flows to the field first and watches for the misdirection to the backside. He still plays the number-three receiver to the number-two receiver.

The strong safety is a two-seam defender keying the number-two receiver. He plays the technique from eight to ten yards in depth. He works to take the charge on the vertical route of the number-two receiver. We want the strong safety to align his body so that the number-two receiver has to adjust him pattern either inside or outside to get by the strong safety. We cannot let the number-two receiver run unrestricted down the field and get a two on one with the corner. No one is pressing the number-one receiver and we must help by rerouting the inside vertical.

The hardest pattern to cover from the four vertical schemes is the post-corner cut by number-two receiver, which we call a seven-pattern. The strong safety can run underneath that pattern and cover it. The whole object of running a zone-dog is to make sure the offense does not have time to run the entire pattern.

The adjustment we have to make to the boundary side comes from the offense breaking their set in the backfield. If they put a running back into the slot of the split end to the boundary, we must adjust. This gives the offense a pro set to the field and a twin set into the boundary (Diagram #3).

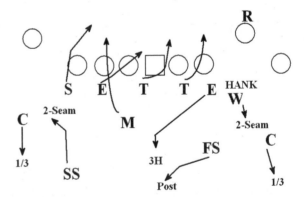

Diagram #3. 11 personnel to the boundary

Nothing changes for the Sam linebacker, 5 technique, 3 technique, or the Mike linebacker. The Will linebacker steps outside and covers the slot receiver to the boundary side. He gives the 5 technique end to his side a "Hank right" call. That tells the defensive end his is now the three-hook player. When we snap the ball, the defensive end goes to the three-hook area. He does not key anything. He opens up and runs to the middle of the field and plays like a Mike linebacker. The Will linebacker becomes the run support to the boundary side of the formation. We now have backer support to both sides of the set.

The Will linebacker plays the same technique as the strong safety on the twin set. However, he does it from a depth of five or six yards. He tries to reroute the slot back to the boundary side. If he can get his hands on the vertical route and slow him, we can stop the four verticals based on our pressure. We do not ask the Will linebacker to carry the route vertical. He wants to hold the route off as long as he can. He does not run under the short corner as the safety did in his coverage. The safety had more depth and could cover that pattern.

The next formation you deal with is some type of trips alignment (Diagram #4). In this formation, I have the tight end to the three-receiver side. That requires our front to shift toward the tight end. The 5 technique moves to a 6 technique. The shade tackle moves to a 2i technique on the offensive guard. They are still slanting back to their stunt gaps.

The boundary side end is playing easy support. In his pass coverage, he plays a two-seam coverage on the number-two receiver to his side, Or he helps the corner on the number-one receiver. The Sam linebacker walks out to an inside position on the inside receiver in the trips set. Before the snap of the ball, he stems back inside and comes off the edge. He is playing backer support as he has always done.

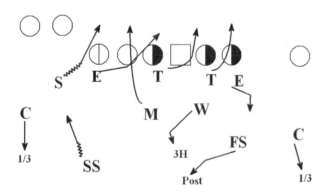

Diagram #4. Falcon trips alignment

The Will linebacker has the three-hot read from the middle of the field. That becomes the negative aspect of this coverage. If the tight end free releases, that becomes tough on the Will linebacker. He knows the tight end is hot and he has to get to him. Nothing changes for the strong safety. He plays the inside slot as he did from the twins set. He collisions on the slot receiver and helps on the short corner and flood to that side. The free safety leans to the trips side and has the tight end if he comes vertical.

The zone-dog we like coming from the bench side of the defense is the corner blitz off the edge. The blitz is "bench crow" (Diagram #5). We play cover 3 in the secondary and bring the bench-side corner and the Will linebacker. The bench tackle takes the same move he did on the falcon, except he does not have to cross-face the tackle because there is someone outside of him. He is the B-gap player and gets up the field.

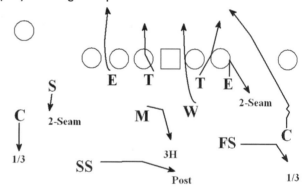

Diagram #5. Bench crow

The nose tackle gets in a heavy shade on the center and slant to the inside ear hole of the strongside offensive guard. He is the A-gap player. He wants the center to block on him and open up the backside gap for the Will linebacker. The aiming point of the Will linebacker is the backside hip of the center. He comes downhill and wants to reach the hip of the center. He goes for penetration.

The thing we have to spend a lot of time on is the 5-technique end to the field. He has a tight end outside of him. He aims toward the inside ear hole of the tight end. He cannot get pinned inside. He is a C-gap player on the running game, but is the contain player in the passing game. If the tight end comes down on him, he has to work a cross face and get up the field for containment so the ball does not get outside.

The bench corner has to steal at least two yards based on the split of the wide receiver. His aiming point is the same as the Sam linebacker on the falcon blitz. He aims one yard outside the near back or deepest back in the backfield. The worst thing that can happen is for the corner to come too flat. He has to be in a position to be in the throwing lane, if the quarterback decides to take the snap and hot throws to the outside receiver.

The defensive end is a two-seam dropper and helps the free safety who is rolling into the deep outside third. He plays the same technique he did on the falcon. He gets inside the slant move of the split end and jumps anyone who crosses his face going to the flat area. He collisions the number-two receiver if he is trying to get vertical.

The corner drops into the outside third and the strong safety rolls into the middle third. The Mike linebacker is playing three-hook. If flow comes to him he retreats to the middle of the field and plays the three-receiver to the two-receiver. The Sam linebacker is playing the same technique as the bench-side defensive end. He is a two-seam player and jumps anything going to the flat. He gets under the slant by the number-one receiver. If the tight end releases vertical, the Mike linebacker can help him because he is reading hot toward him.

The free safety takes a slide step for depth and reads what is happening to the number-one receiver to his side. If he has any doubt, he wants to get depth to protect the outside third. If they throw the hitch to the split end, the defensive end and free safety come up and make the tackle.

If there is a running play, the corner has run support to the bench side and the Sam linebacker has run support to the wide side of the field.

Obviously, we would rather have a tight end to that side. The run by the corner is shorter and there is no deep threat to the outside (Diagram #6). The tight end is the hot receiver to the bench side and the defensive end aligns over the top of him and dropping with him. On this set, we could run the Mike linebacker through the B gap and get an extra blitz player. The down side to this situation is the

pass coverage to the field. The Sam linebacker aligns on the number-two receiver. He is a second-level player rerouting the number-two receiver, playing two-seam, and has to get under the short flag to his side.

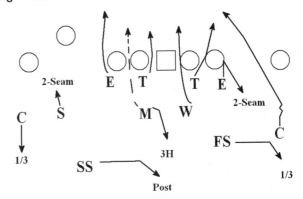

Diagram #6. Crow versus twin set

The Sam linebacker has to play like the Will linebacker in the falcon blitz. He is at a depth of five to six yards and has to get his hands on the number-two receiver as he tries to get deep. He has to disrupt the pattern and make the quarterback hold the ball. The blitzing corner will get to the quarterback fast.

The next situation is a two-by-two set with a twin set to the boundary and a tight end and flanker to the wideside. The Will linebacker moves out to play inside of the number-two receiver to the boundary. This call is "bench wren" (Diagram #7). The Will linebacker replaces the corner on the blitz and the defensive end replaces the Will linebacker on his blitz. The bench tackle slants outside through the B gap. The defensive end loops behind the defensive tackle and into the A gap. We roll the free safety down into "big sky" coverage.

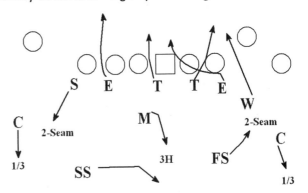

Diagram #7. Bench wren

The free safety rolls down and becomes a two-seam player on the number-two receiver to the boundary side. He reroutes the number-two receiver and can carry the pattern all the way to the short-corner route. The corner drops into the third and the strong safety drops to the middle playing the post route. The remainder of the defense is the same.

The Sam and Will linebackers are the run support personnel to each side. We call that backer support.

If the set is a trips set with a tight end to that side. we like bench crow (Diagram #8) from the backside. This is a one-back set and someone should get there quickly. Everything is the same for everyone. The danger is with the corner getting too close to the box, before he comes. To the trips side, the Sam linebacker is playing two-seam on the inside slot of the trips set. The strong safety goes to the middle third and picks up the tight end if he comes vertical. The Mike linebacker has three-hot and is on top of him. He collisions him if he goes deep. The field corner goes to the third.

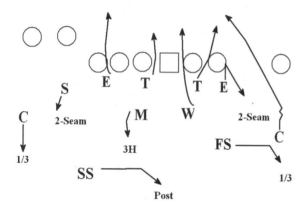

Diagram #8. Bench crow versus trips

The corner stems and blitzes off the edge and the Will linebacker shoots the A gap. The bench end comes off the line of scrimmage and plays under number-one. The free safety rolls over the top into the third.

The "spear" (Diagram #9) is a run blitz. It becomes a 4-4 type of defensive call. We get eight men in the box and come with three straight lines of pressure from the tight-end side. The quarterback in his pre-snap read sees a three-deep or man-free concept. We attack with a three-man surface to the tight-end side. This blitz comes out of an over call for the front. That aligns the defensive ends in a 6 technique over the tight end and a 5 technique to the open side. The tackles are in a 3-technique strong and a center shade to the open side.

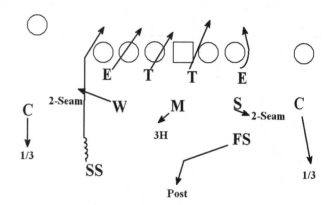

Diagram #9. Spear

The linebackers align in a normal alignment. In the over defense, the linebackers cheat away from the front. That means they are toward the open side of the formation. The strong safety walks up as if he is playing in a cover-3 zone. At the last second, we bump the linebackers to the tight end. The strong safety is coming from whatever depth he feels he can get there. He could come from four, five, or seven yards deep to blitz.

The 6-technique end is going to work like hell to ram through the B gap. If the tackle tries to block down on the 3 technique, he closes and penetrates the B gap. The 3 technique spikes or penetrates through the A gap. The key to the entire stunt is the strong safety. His aiming point is the outside hip of the tight end. He runs through the hip of the tight end and closes down. If the tight end tries to block out on the strong safety, he comes under the block into the C gap. The Will linebacker backs him up to his side that is responsibility for the support and the two-seam.

The object of the blitz is to make the ball go east and west and bounce to the outside. The Will linebacker cuts off the field and turns the ball inside. The Mike linebacker pursuit over the top and into the alley and becomes the extra player to the ball.

The Will and Sam linebackers are the two-seam defenders and the Mike linebacker is the three-hook player. The corners and free safety play three deep behind the defense. This is a big run stunt for us, but what happens if they throw the ball?

We are playing the strong safety under all blocks. He is coming off the hip of the tight end and reading the near back as he comes. As he becomes a better player, he will read the high-hat of the linemen and have a chance to ricochet up the field and contain the pass.

If the offense aligns in a twin set with the tight end to the backside, the strong safety aligns on the tight-end side (Diagram #10). We have to balance our linebacker to the slot side. The negative aspect of the defense is it is hard to disguise. The free safety moves toward the slot and the boundary corner backs up to give the appearance of a two-deep coverage. The Sam linebacker is playing the two-seam on the slot receiver.

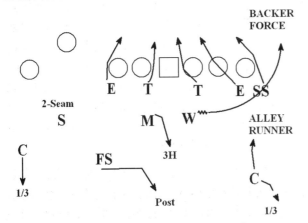

Diagram #10. Spear versus twin set

The Mike linebacker is committed to the open side on the run and cannot cheat to the tight end. The Will linebacker cheats to the tight end and is the run support to the outside. The tackle, end, and safety run their techniques and the Will linebacker cuts off the run. The extra player on the run is the corner depending on what the tight end does.

In the past, I have done the same thing running out of what I called a "load front" (Diagram #11). I did not have big strong safety or corners to run the spear stunt. Instead of using safeties and corners, I let the linebacker do the stunt. In the load front, we

played a 5 technique and 3 technique to the load side instead of a 6 technique and 3 technique. We put the Sam linebacker outside as a 9 technique on the tight end. The strong safety was the two-seam defender to the tight-end side and the Sam linebacker ran the stunt. The strong safety played run support and the Mike linebacker was the alley runner.

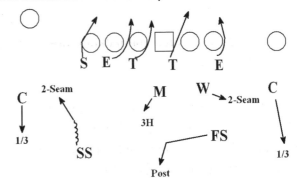

Diagram #11. Load front spear

The blitz we have the most fun with is "hawk" (Diagram #12). We have to match the secondary with this defense. From the under front we like to run the inside crossed-dog blitz. This blitz helps us in the running game because of how we are penetrating and forcing the football. We like to run this zone-dog inside because it puts a strain on the center and two guards. The key to this stunt is having a nose tackle that knows how to flash step and work himself to the B gap. If blocking scheme is a zone scheme, he has to run and shove the guard as the ball is progressing toward the tight-end side.

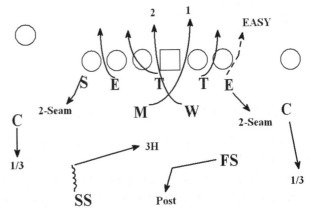

Diagram #12. Under hawk

The nose-tackle flash steps and works to his load alignment and plays the B gap. The 5-technique end works through the inside ear hole of the tight end. He is a C-gap player on the run and a containment player on the pass. He plays the same technique on the backside stunts. We teach the same thing repeated in our zone-dog package. The backside tackle plays through the inside ear hole of the tackle and is a B-gap player on the run. If the tackle blocks down, he has to cross-face and get outside to contain the pass.

The backside defensive end takes an echo step, drops, and becomes the two-seam defender. If it is a run, he is force and cuts off the ball. The Sam linebacker aligns in a 9 technique and is a two-seam defender. He has backer force depending on what the tight end does.

In this zone-dog, the Mike linebacker goes first and is the penetrator. The Will linebacker goes second and is the looper. The Mike linebacker angle of departure depends on the split between the center and backside guard. His aiming point is the hip of the guard. He is penetrating the backside A gap. The Will linebacker aiming point is the hip of the strongside guard. He comes off the hip of the Mike linebacker and penetrates the strongside A gap.

We roll one of the safeties down to become the three-hook player. He plays like the Mike linebacker. We generally roll the safety to the two-receiver side or the tight-end side into the box. In this situation, our strong safety becomes the three-hook defender. If the ball is on the hash mark, he does not have to adjust his alignment. The only thing we tell him is to be inside the tight end on alignment.

If the ball goes to the backside, he becomes a C-gap scrapper. He plays exactly like the Mike linebacker. He is at a depth of six to seven yards reading the number-three receiver moving to number-two. He gets inside the tight end and is the extra defender on the run and the three-hook player on the pass.

We use our nickel package to run some of our zone-dog blitzes. In most cases when we bring the nickel back into the game it is generally against one-back spread teams. We bring the nickel back in for the Sam linebacker. We make a front call based on where the nickel back lines up. We run the falcon

concept against one-back personnel based on where the nickel back lines up. The front call is "vulture" (Diagram #13).

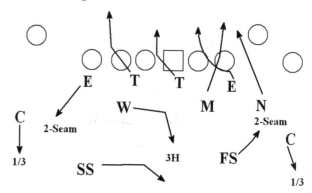

Diagram #13. Vulture versus two-by-two set

With 11 personnel in the game. we align our nickel back on the slot receiver to the twin-receiver side. The defensive end to that side aligns in a 5 technique. The tackle to the nickel side is in a shade on the center. To the tight-end side, the tackle is in a 3 technique and the end is in a 6 technique. The front slants to the tight-end side. The Mike linebacker shoots the B gap and the nickel comes off the edge.

The 5-technique tackle runs a "big stick" technique when he slants down from the outside. The 3-technique tackle has to go through the offensive tackle working for containment on the pass.

The free safety stems down to replace the nickel back and is the two-seam defender. The 6-technique end drops and becomes the two-seam player. The Will linebacker replaces the Mike linebacker in the middle as the three-hook player. The strong safety rolls to the middle third and the corners play the outside thirds.

When nickel blitzes off the edge, his aiming point is one yard outside the near back or deepest back. That includes the quarterback in the shotgun set. The vulture allows me set the front and run the falcon stunt coming from any situation I want. The falcon stunt is from the field only.

In the trips set, with the tight end to the trips side, the nickel, corner, and strong safety align to the trips side (Diagram #14). The disguise looks like we are playing a three-on-two scheme over the two wide receivers to the trips side. We slant the front away from the nickel. The Mike linebacker blitz behind the defensive end with the nickel coming off the edge.

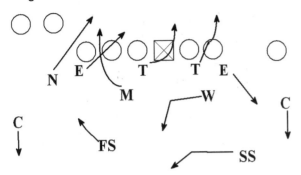

Diagram #14. Vulture versus three-by-one

The strong safety stems down to become the two-seam defender. The Will linebacker replaces the Mike linebacker as the three-hook player and the defensive end away from the nickel drops as a two-seam defender. The corners drop to their thirds and the free safety goes to the middle as the post player.

This zone-dog is "thrasher" (Diagram #15). In this formation, the nickel is set to the wide slot. The front to the nickel side aligns in a 5 technique and a shade on the center. To the tight-end side the tackle is aligned in a 3 technique and the end is in 6 technique.

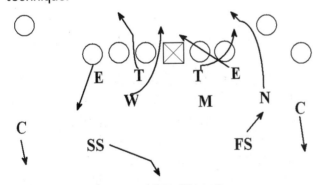

Diagram #15. Thrasher

The 6-technique end drops and becomes the two-seam defender. The 3-technique tackle drives through the inside hip of the offensive tackle. He is working outside for containment. The Will linebacker shoots the A gap with an aiming point of the hip of the center. The defensive end to the nickel side angles hard into the B gap like a big-stick technique. The tackle to that side loops outside at the hip of the offensive tackle. We call that line stunt an "ET game." The nickel blitzes off the edge and aims one yard outside the near back.

Everyone in the secondary plays cover 3 with the strong safety going to the middle and the free safety replacing the nickel as the two-seam defender.

We run a zone-dog off a hash mark call. We run this blitz off the protection scheme of certain teams. It is called "sparrow" (Diagram #16). To the tight-end side, the Will linebacker gets in a 9 technique and comes from the edge. The defensive end to that side aligns in a 7 technique and drops into as a two-seam defender. The 3-technique tackle fires into the B gap, but is a C-gap player. The tackle to the open side penetrates the A gap and tries to make the center take him. The 5-technique end contains from his position. The nickel drops and become a two-seam defender. The Mike linebacker drops to the three-hook position and the strong safety rolls to the post. The corners play the outside thirds.

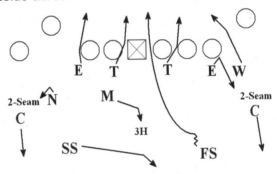

Diagram #16. Sparrow

The free safety starts high and stems down and blitzes the A gap to the tight-end side. If you wanted to flip the game over to the other side, you could bring the strong safety into the A gap to his side.

I have run out of time, I hope you enjoyed this. Thank you very much.

Mike Tressel

LINEBACKER DRILLS IN THE 4-3 DEFENSE

University of Cincinnati

I appreciate you being here today. I am going to talk about linebacker techniques.

As coaches, we need to talk with young football players about many different topics. You may think they are simple things but to the players they may not be that simple. Talking with Division I football players is a good example. We ask them to tell us what they think about on each play. We ask them what goes through their mind when they hear the played called. They respond, "the call." There is a lot more involved than just the call. We laid the thought process out for the players. Our coaches came up with five points in this thought process.

Know the situation. This point incorporates down, distance, yard line, hash mark, time in the game, and field position. The more the players know about the opponent, the more the situations will help them.

The next part of the thought process is the "base alignment." This includes calling the front for the linebackers. We set our front "right - right", or "left - left."

The third part of the thought process is "alignment, adjustments, and checks." Everyone has a few base alignment adjustments. We all have alignment adjustments but our players do not think about them. They think about lining up.

The next part of the thought process is to identify the initial key. There are keys we use to take our initial step. We have run-pass keys.

The next step is to identify the pass responsibility. We screw this up a great deal of the time. Once we read pass, we should be able to react. We need to know what the pass responsibility is on the pre-snap.

The last point is to "play fast!" When we watch film, we review these points. Take time to go over the different situations that occur in the game.

Stance is another aspect we cover in the general category. I will not spend much time on stance. We want the stance to be comfortable and we want our linebackers to be athletic. We want the feet spread narrow enough as we take the first step that we are not off balance and unable to redirect.

We all know to bend at the knees and ankles, and not at the waist. We know to keep the head up, and to keep the chest up, keep the hands off the knees. We talk about turning the toes inside a tad, but we do not want them too duck footed. The key is to be comfortable to be able to move without over-striding. We want to be in a position where we can play fast.

The next point of progression is key reads and fits. What are the initial key and the fit? The key read is to attack the line of scrimmage. This is simple but we work on this every day.

We are not foolish to think we are never going to be blocked. We know we must overcome some obstacles. Nevertheless, if we can make our players believe if they play fast, get to their gap responsibility before the offensive line gets ready to block them, they can run through and make plays (Diagram #1).

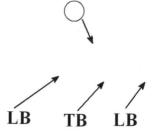

Diagram #1. Key reads/attack line of scrimmage

Drill Set-up

- Backers align at five yards depth. The tailback is seven yards from the line of scrimmage.

- The tailback uses footwork of opposing team (inside zone, stretch, power, counter).

- Linebackers key the tailback and attack the line of scrimmage. They stop at the next yard stripe, and start another rep.

- We must use the offensive line and quarterback for reads versus shotgun.

- Occasionally, we use the offensive line with the quarterback under the center to show the offensive line pulling.

Coaching Points

- Stance

- First step, no false steps

- Attack the line of scrimmage fast at the same angle as the tailback.

- Every play should be a TFL (tackle for loss of one yard).

When the quarterback is in the shotgun, we change our keys and read the offensive line. The shotgun quarterback can ride the tailback, or he can keep the ball. Our outside linebackers key the tackles and guards, or tackles and ends, but primarily they key the tackles. Our Mike linebacker keys the center and guard on his reads. When you are working on the reads against the shotgun look, you must get a scout team offensive line to work against.

We do these keys everyday for two minutes. Everyone gets five or six reps in the drill.

When we have a tight end in the game, we have to work on the keys for the Sam Linebackers. He keys the tight end for us. We line the Sam over the tight end and give him the reach block, down block, the base block, and the hinge block.

Next, we go to our next progression. It is what we call "fits versus cans." We like to use this in our pre-season camp. We line up five Trash Cans. We use coaches or scout-team players as the skilled

players. We use the quarterback, tailback, and tight end. We run the base offense and have the linebackers fit to their reads (Diagram #2).

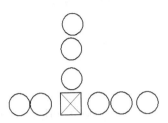

LB   LB   LB
Diagram #2. Fits versus cans/scouts

Drill Set-up

- Equipment: Five trash cans - Align trashcans (scouts) as an offensive line.

- Use other scouts/coaches to finish an offensive formation.

- Walk-/Run-through offensive plays you will encounter.

Coaching Points

- Linebacker alignment

- Linebacker play recognition/ fits/responsibilities

  - Spill or squeeze

  - Fast flow or cutback responsibility

Our next progression is our fits versus scouts and half-line drill. We get two defensive tackles and a Mike linebacker against two guards and a center, fullback, and a tailback. We fit the plays that are pertinent to that group. We work on these drills everyday. They look simple but we do them everyday.

The third aspect of the play for linebackers is tackling. Tackling is hitting up through the man. The key to form tackle is it has to be forward and you must keep the feet moving. We do not want the head, shoulders, or arms to get in front of the feet.

Next, I want to talk about leverage drills. This drill is designed to do is to stay in a proper inside outside position. We *seldom* missed a tackle this past season because we could not get to the play. We *often* missed the tackle because we overran the play.

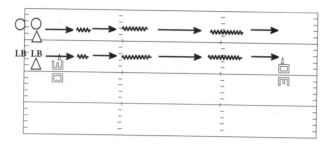

Diagram #3. Leverage drill

Drill Set-up

- Split linebackers into two lines on a straight line, three yards apart. (BC/Tackler)

- Give ballcarriers a two-yard head start. Have them cross the field changing speeds.

- Linebackers move to maintain inside-outside leverage on the ballcarrier. (We keep the lines three yards apart.)

- Linebackers alternate from a run to a shuffle to maintain leverage.

Coaching Points

- Maintain inside-outside leverage on the football.

- Play full speed, but eliminate the cutback.

- Footwork — Never cross over when you have the proper leverage.

We are going all the way across the field on the drill. The ballcarrier is going full speed, to a jog, to a sprint, changing his pace. The linebacker must adjust his speed without over pursuing. If the linebacker over pursues the ball we tell the ballcarrier to cut up field on the linebacker to let him know he over pursued.

Once we have worked on the leverage drill, we are going to the open-field tackling drill. In 2002, Ohio State won the National Championship. If you ask our head coach, Mark Dantonio (who was the defensive coordinator at Ohio State at the time)

what the key was to winning defensive, he will tell you it was these open-field tackle drills.

Linebackers must understand if they want to play every game then must be able to step up and take on an isolation block, and tackle a slot receiver or running back in space. He must be able to do both, otherwise he will only be on the field a short period of the game.

We started doing the open-field tackling drills repeatedly. We try to get scout team running backs if possible. The first drill is the toss-sweep drill (Diagram #4).

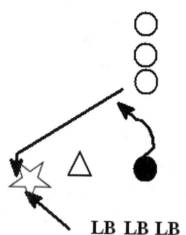

Diagram #4. Open-field tackle drills

Drill Set-up

- If possible, use scout wide receivers and running backs. If they are not available, split the linebackers into ballcarriers and tackler lines.

- Align players on the field based on the drill executed.

- Begin with the ball in the offensive player's hands. We progress from one drill to the other, using the coach to pass the ball.

- Begin with linebackers in an aligned drop; progress to incorporate the pass drop.

- Linebackers must attack the ball full speed with leverage, and eliminate the breakdown.

- 6. Use a two-hand tag *below the waist* if you do not want contact.

Coaching Points

- Ball leverage, eliminate the cutback.

- Close the cushion fast. Do not "breakdown." Take a flat step (shuffle).

- Settle feet when the quarterback settles his feet, "vision and break."

- You must be able to play in space to play today's game of football.

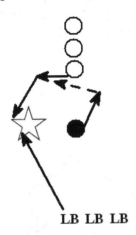

Diagram #5. Swing pass – pre-aligned drop

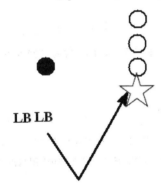

Diagram #6. Now pass (incorporated pass drop)

You cannot go live on these drills everyday. On the other hand, we need to work on open-field tackling everyday. We work on these drills everyday and it does not matter if we are in pads on not. We can tell the players how we want them to tackle. We have them tackle with a two-hand touch, underhand touch below the waist. This is the way we "tag off." The reason we do this is that it teaches the players perfect form for tackling.

We talk about two methods of defeating the block. One is the rip and the other is the jam. On the

rip move, all of the power comes from the same arm and same leg when the linebacker steps. When you are defeating a block you need to take the same side arm and same side leg and rip by the blocker. You should be able to tie a string between your arm and your leg because they are working on the same level. The rip is not a way to avoid the block. You are not trying to avoid contact. The rip technique is a physical move. You need to lean back into the blocker and fight pressure. It is a physical move.

The jam is also a physical move. We do not use it on offensive linemen. We do not play both gaps on the side of the lineman. That is asking too much for the linebacker to do. They understand their gap responsibility and they can take care of their gap.

The drill we use here is the three-on-three versus the offensive line or scouts.

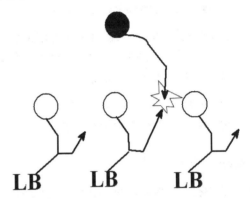

Diagram #7. Inside zone – jam technique

Drill Set-up

- You will need three scout offensive linemen and one scout ballcarrier.

- Align the offensive line on the line of scrimmage, three yards apart from each other. The ballcarrier is at seven yards depth.

- Align three linebackers head up on each offensive lineman, five yards deep.

- Give the offensive line and ballcarrier a direction; the offensive line must zone block in that direction. The ballcarrier must stay on the frontside.

- Each linebacker is responsible for his frontside gap. Work rip or jam techniques.

- Putting an unblocked "cutback" linebacker on each side will keep the ballcarrier on task.

Coaching Points

- This is a competitive drill. Coach the offensive line to make the block.

- Perfect rip/jam techniques should be executed, as well as perfect form tackles.

- This is also a good drill to work key reads, first step, and downhill path.

We do a drill that teaches the linebackers to attack the line of scrimmage. We call the drill Ear Hole. (Diagram #9)

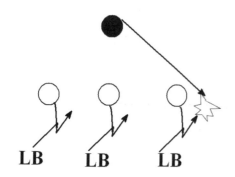

Diagram #8. Outside zone – rip technique

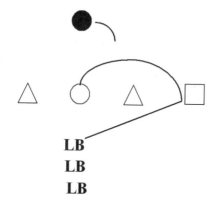

Diagram #9. Ear hole drill

Drill Set-up

- You need one ballcarrier and a line of scout offensive linemen if available.

- Align one offensive lineman on the line of scrimmage, with the ballcarrier at seven yards behind him.

- Place cones on the line of scrimmage four yards outside on the line of scrimmage on each side.

- Align one linebacker head up on the offensive line at five yards depth.

- Give the ball direction. The tailback takes two steps, the offensive line pulls around the cone to block the linebacker.

Coaching Points

- Key read, first step, attack, line of scrimmage downhill.

- Attack your gap of responsibility; knock out (ear hole) the offensive line before he squares his shoulders to turn upfield while maintaining your gap.

- Square back up in the gap.

Our next progression is blitzing. The rest of the lecture will consist of drills related to the passing game. There are some other points I want to cover but blitzing is the last thing I will go over before I show the film.

We want to teach a blitz mentality to our linebackers. We do not design the blitz for linebackers to come free all of the time, and linebackers must understand this. Linebackers come like a bat out of hell on the blitz and they are screaming. If someone is in the hole to block him, he thinks it did not work. Just because there is someone to block the linebacker does not mean the blitz did not work.

We must teach them blitz mentality. We are a zone-blitz team more than a man-blitz team. The zone blitz means we are bringing five people and defending with six on coverage. We are only sending five players on the blitz. Ask linebackers this question: How many offensive players block to protect the quarterback? They have five linemen and one or two running backs to block our five. They may have one or two tight ends stay in and block. They have more players to block than we have blitzing. What would make the linebacker think no one would be blocking him on a blitz? Tell the linebackers this: "The offensive linemen practice the same amount of time as the linebackers. They watch film and know the blitzes we are going to run. Their job is to pick up the blitz. What makes you think you are going to come free on the blitz?"

We may be able to come up with a scheme, get lucky, and get a blitz where we get a linebacker come free on a blitz. However, we want to convince the linebackers there will be someone to block them on the blitz. The intent of the blitz is to get several one-on-one blocks where the defense cannot double-team the linemen. We tell the linebackers there will be a blocker when he blitzes and his job is to beat the blocker on the blitz.

We do blitz a lot, but we work a lot on blitzing. We run the hoops drills. The first drill is the hoops with the circle. We use a hoop. We put the hoop on the ground and work against it on three different aspects of the blitz (Diagram #10).

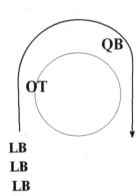

Diagram #10. Hoops drill

Drill Set-up

- You need one large hoop or use a circle drawn on the ground.
- Alternate all defensive line on hoop drill.
  - Run or chase Hoops
  - Versus a tackle pass-set
  - Strip quarterback

Coaching Points

- Lean into corner, stride length.

- Use hands, set-up tackle
- Use proper quarterback strip technique

Diagram #11. Stand-up dummies drill

Drill Set-up

- Get four stand-up dummies
- Place them on a line four yards apart
- Consecutive rush moves
  - All rip or swim
  - Mix rip/swim/spin

Coaching Points

- Master rush moves
- Use hands, play physical
- Close cushion on offensive line

These drills are nothing special. The important thing is to understand the blitz mentality.

Here is the blitz mentality drill. We do not run it all of the time. It is our kamikaze blitz drill on mats. The first drill is against the stand-up dummy (Diagram #12).

Diagram #12. Stand-up dummy

Drill Set-up

- Equipment needed: One crash pad or mats, one stand-up dummy.

- Linebackers are at five yards depth, stand-up dummy placed on line of scrimmage, with the crash pad two yards back.

- Blitz towards the stand-up dummy, jam/run through it, and flip onto the crash pad.

- Move stand-up dummy to far side of crash pad. The dummy is now the quarterback.

- Place a scout player in front of the crash pad. He should cut block three or four reps.

- Linebacker must bull rush the blocker but "launch" to quarterback versus the cut.

Coaching Points

- Teach a relentless blitz mentality.

- Do not slow down or dance around. Close the distance to the quarterback without hesitation.

- Launch yourself towards the quarterback and scramble versus a cut block. You cannot assume the cut.

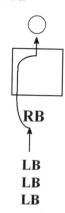

Diagram #13. Versus cut block

The next drill is the ball drills: drop, vision, and break (Diagram #14).

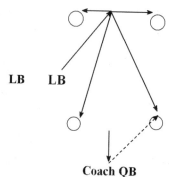

Diagram #14. Ball drills: drop, vision, and break

Drill Set-up

- Use multiple ball drills such as charge, and wave Drills, and other similar drills.

- For drop, vision, and break drills, we form a ten-by-ten box with four coaches and players.

- The first linebacker drops to 10 yards between coaches, then settles, vision and break on the quarterback.

- The quarterback change-ups drop is this. Make the linebacker break on his third step before he gets full depth.

Coaching Points

- Drop technique with vision on the quarterback.

- Seattle when the quarterback settles, "break on his intentions". (Teach the quarterbacks the indicators.)

- Utilize hook and swat techniques.

From the blitz, we go to the matches and re-routes of wide receivers. We use the match drill with cover 4 (Diagram #15).

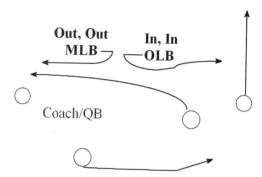

Diagram #15. Match drill – cover 4

Drill Set-up

- You need two to four scouts to be the offensive skilled players.

- Have the scouts run a common rote combination, or one from your opponents.

- Align an outside linebacker and match routes, as your defense requires. You can use the middle linebacker if you want to involve him in the coverage.

Coaching Points

- Read our initial key every snap.
- Coach passing-game assignments and route recognition.
- Emphasize eye control.
- Use proper re-route technique.
- You may add a ball to incorporate vision and break/open-field tackling.

The last drill is the option drill (Diagram #16). You will see this in the film as I am about out of time and I do want to show the tape.

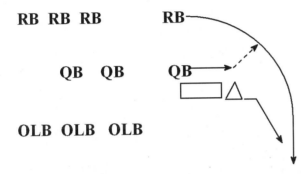

Diagram #16. Option drill

Drill Set-up

- This is a competitive drill. We pit the quarterback and running backs against the outside linebackers and we keep score on the drill.

- Align the quarterback on the hash at 10-yard line, with the tailback behind him. Place a cone for the offensive tackle.
- Outside linebacker assignment is the quarterback. He must react to the pitch.
- Offense scores one point for a running back touchdown. They score two points for a touchdown by the quarterback.
- The defense scores one point for a stop of the running back. They score two points for a stop of the quarterback. The defense receives three points for a fumble recovery.

Coaching Points

- Do your job and make sure to secure the quarterback.
- Slow play so you can react to the pitch, then run a straight line to the goal line.
- You may mix in a periodic edge blitz to teach blitz assignment.

I would be more than happy to spend time with you if you want to visit us at the University of Cincinnati. I am out of time so for questions, I am going two doors down to the Buckeye Room. Come on down and we will stay and as long as you want to talk football. Thank you.

DEFENDING THE SPREAD OFFENSE

Indiana State University

Thanks for the introduction. It is good to be here this morning. The first thing about the eight-man front that I will talk about is the philosophy behind the defense.

First, you must sell the blitz look as much as possible. You must get the players to buy into the defense. No matter what the offense or defense is, you must get the team to buy into what you are trying to accomplish. Every time we line up, we want to sell the blitz look. We want to make it look like we are going to run the blitz on every play. We do this with six or seven players faking the blitz. We want to cause havoc for the offense and especially for the quarterback and his reads.

The second point is that we want to put the game in the quarterback's hands. We want him to make the checks. We do not want the coaches in the box to dictate what is going to happen. Therefore, we want to make sure, when we line up in our eight-man front that we are moving players around showing the blitz. We want to have the ability to run the blitz from any position and any area on the field. We want to give the quarterback problems in checking to another play that he needs to make.

The third point is to create an attacking defense. We do not want to be a reading defense. We want penetration! When the ball is snapped, we are attacking and we are penetrating the line of scrimmage. We want to penetrate into the backfield and make things happen. We have found that players like to get after it on defense and this gives them that opportunity.

We want to get more men at the point of attack than the offense has blockers. In our meetings with the players, we always talk about the "free-hitter."

We want to get as many players to the ball as possible and we want them to be able to make the hits without taking on blockers.

The last point we make in the philosophy is pressure! We like to show it and bring it! We show pressure as much as possible and we are going to bring that pressure at times. We are going to show pressure at times and then we are going to back out of the line. We want to show the pressure and give the offense the illusion we can bring four defenders from each side of he ball. We want to make the quarterback think when he is making his decision on checking to the next play. At each level of play, the quarterback has to do more to control the game. If we can cause problems for the quarterback in making that check to the next play, we feel it is to our advantage.

The fundamentals that we work on everyday include the following. First, is what we call "get offs." In most cases when you think of get offs, you think of the defensive line. We are not only talking about the defensive line getting off, we are also talking about the blitz men. When we have players coming off the edge, we want them in a stance that will allow them not to take a false step. We want them rolling forward on the snap of the ball. This is very important. We work on the get off for each position. We want to get off and attack.

The second point we stress is block destruction. We want to destroy the blocker, get off the block, and go to the football. It is not enough to destroy the man you line up against on defense. You must be able to get off the block and find the football. We work on getting off the block. We practice on how we are going to attack the blocker so we can get off and find the football.

The third point we stress in the fundamentals is communication. First, we need to know where you are going to line up in the defense. The defensive line needs to know where our whip is going to line up on each play. We always give a "whip right" or "whip left" call. We need to know the strength of the defensive call. Our linebackers set the front according to different situations with a "right" or "left" call. The safety gives the "Rip" or "Liz" for the pass call. Therefore, communication is very important in this defense. We want to get them in position but we want to get them in position in an attack mode.

The next point we stress is hustle. Not only do we want the defenders to get off the block, we want them to get to the football. When the play ends in the film, we want to have eleven players in the film frame near the ball. If we do not find eleven players in the frame, we are going to find out why they are not in the frame. Hustle and swarming to the football is a big part of this defense. We want to be an attacking defense and the only way we are going to do that is by swarming to the football.

A big part of our defense is to disguise the looks so the offense cannot get a jump on us. If we are playing man or zone, or if we are blitzing, we want to make the defense all look the same on each play. We want the offense to see that any minute one of our defenders could be coming on a blitz or we could be dropping back. We want everything to look the same as much as possible. It is not always easy to do that but that is what we are trying to do.

We want to show the offense a multiple look on defense. Our base front is our G-front set. It is with four linemen down and the two linebackers with the secondary players. We can also go to a two-deep look. We can go to a two-deep look and move our safeties around to get back to our eight-man front. In addition, we can go to our 46 defense, which most people call the Bear defense. The point I am making is that we can move in and out of the different looks from one defense to the other. We can move in and out of those defensive fronts to try to confuse the quarterback as much as possible.

The last fundamentals we stress are one of the most important aspects of the game. That aspect is tackling. Everyday we use some type of tackling drill. It may be getting off a block and making the tackle, form tackling, or live tackling. At the University of Toledo one day a week during the season, we had a tackling circuit. We worked on different angles in tackling. We worked on getting off the blocks and getting to the ball to make the tackle. If you are going to play good defense, tackling is one of the most important things you can work on. If you can tackle, you will have success.

I want to move on to the three fundamentals when putting together a defense. Three things need to implement when putting together a defense. First is gap responsibilities. When I first talk to the defense, the first thing I talk about is gap responsibility. "Who has this gap, and who has the next gap?" We want to know who is backing up each gap. When you are putting a defense together, the gap responsibility is the starting point. You must decide who has each gap responsibility.

The second point to consider when installing a defense is option responsibility. Who has the dive on the option? Which defender has the quarterback and who has the pitch on the option? When you put the defense in, you must decide which players have these responsibilities. When we install the defense, we make sure we assign the option responsibility to someone on each defensive play we run. This is true when we run a blitz or when we play our base defense.

The third thing we consider when we install the defense is the responsibility for all play-action passes. Whom are we going to assign to cover the play-action pass? If you put all of your eggs in one basket, it is obvious they are going to come back and run the play-action pass on you. Someone needs to be responsible for the receiver running down the field on play-action passes. Again, we make sure we have someone responsible for that play.

If we can take care of these three things when we install a defense, we know the defense is sound.

We want to make sure we cover those points before we every run the defense.

As I said earlier, we are an eight-man-front defense. We call our base defense "G." I want to cover the G perimeter and front alignment rules.

We start with our whip. For some background, let me give you the type of player we want playing this defense. The front four players are the two ends, a tackle, and a nose tackle. The tackle and nose are true defensive tackles. We want strong players that can plug up the middle and players that have good quickness in getting off the ball and the block.

The two defensive ends are oversized linebackers. They may be a step too slow to play linebacker so we move them to defensive end. At the end positions, they are good football players. They are quicker as ends than they are as linebackers. We can get by with the ends that are 6'1" or 6'2" and 225 to 235 pounds. We do not need the big 265-pound defensive ends in this defense. We predicate our defense on a lot of speed. It allows us to use undersized ends and they fit in there perfectly.

Our backer position is a big, strong safety type player. He is one that can run and a player that may not be agile enough to play safety but he can play our backer position.

Our Mike linebacker is more of a plugged type player. He is a player that can plug the hole and get after the ballcarrier at the line of scrimmage. He does a good job in a small space.

Our defensive backs, which include our whip and rover, are keys to our defense. The rover is more like a true safety. He is a player that can come up and make the hit and a man that can play man-to-man defense on the number-two receiver if he has to do so.

The one position that people get confused is our whip position. In the defense we play now, the whip is not an outside linebacker. He is another free safety. He is a player that does many different things. If there were one player that is the key to this defense, it would be the whip. He must be able to run the blitz, he must be able to cover man-to-

man, and he plays a deep third on pass situations. It may be a middle one third or an outside one third. You will see as we continue that he cannot be a true outside linebacker. He is more of a free safety type player. He must be able to fill the alley and he must be able to cover a receiver.

For our corners, we like to have defenders that can play man-to-man defense. They are true cover defenders.

Our free safety is a true alley fill player. He can fill the alley and hit but at the same time he can play pass defense and he can play deep in the coverage.

As we break the defensive huddle, the whip declares himself. He calls out "whip right" or "whip left." When the offense arrives at the line of scrimmage, we take our positions based on the call by the whip.

Whip

Declare yourself with a "whip right" or "whip left" call. If the ball is on the hash mark, he declares to the boundary. If the ball is in the middle of the field, he declares away from the passing strength.

Free Safety

Declare (and align) to the passing strength of the formation with a "Rip" or "Liz" call. Most of the time, he aligns to the "two receiver" side.

Mike

He sets the tackle and nose players with a "right" or "left" call. His call gets the tackle and nose guard in their alignment. It also puts the defensive ends in their alignment. He gives the call with a "right - right" or "left - left" call. He aligns away from the passing strength. If the ball is on the hash mark, he aligns to the boundary. If the ball is in the middle of the field, he aligns away from the passing strength.

Rover

He aligns to the field. If the ball is in the middle of the field, he aligns to the passing strength. He goes to the "rip" or "Liz" call.

Backer

He aligns to the passing strength. He can cover wide receivers and backs out of the backfield on passes. If the ball is on the hash mark, he goes to the field. If he ball is in the middle of the field, he aligns to the passing strength. He is the adjuster. He takes the displaced back on trips or he takes the third man on the strong side. We use this against a one-back set.

Corners

Align right and left. Some people tell them to align to the boundary and to the field. I like the terms right and left. We did that because we do not want to switch those two corners when teams are in their two-minute offense and the field and boundary side changes. I want the on the same side of the field regardless of where the ball is located. We call them right and left corners.

Tackle/Nose

They listen to the "right" and "left" call. One of them will align in a 3 technique and the other man will align in a 2i technique. The outside foot splits the crotch of the offensive guard.

Ends

If the offense has a tight end, we line our end up in a 7 technique. That is an inside shade of the tight end. Some teams call this alignment a 6i. The outside foot splits the crotch of the tight end. If there is no tight end, we align in a tilt 5 technique. We line up two feet outside the offensive tackle tilted in toward the hip of the offensive tackle. We are ready to play from there.

Let me show you the alignments. You can see the end on the split-end side lined up in a tilted alignment (Diagram #1). He does not have to work about containment in this alignment. He is what we call a "bender." If the offensive tackles blocks down inside, the defensive end comes off his butt and bends down to the inside. He should make the tackle on any dive play on that side of the line. That is why we have him tilted inside so he can get off the ball

and get into a bending mode. That is our set up against a pro set.

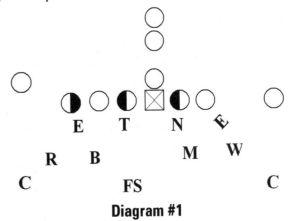

Diagram #1

Let me show you our set up against a Twin Set (Diagram #2). The whip moves into what we call a stack 9 position. The Mike cheats over behind the nose man. The backer cheats over where he is inside the defensive end on his side. That is how we line up against the twin set. We bump our linebackers over on the set.

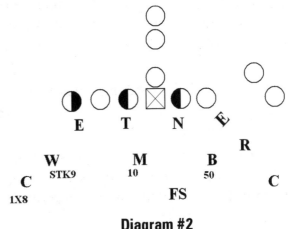

Diagram #2

Let me go through some alignments and keys with each of these players. We are going with a base set. The first thing we do is to set up the front. Here we have a "left" call (Diagram #3). Our tackle lines up in a 3 shade technique. The nose man lines up in a 2i technique. Let me make one point about the tackle and nose man. I let my defensive line coach decide how he wants the tackle and nose man to line up. Some people have them put the hand down that is closest to the ball. Some coaches allow the individual players to decide which hand they want as the down hand.

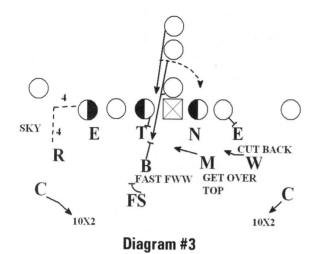

Diagram #3

Our end to the split-end side tilts inside. His feet are outside of the offensive tackle. His aiming point is the outside hip of the tackle. The end on the tight end side is lined up in a 7 technique.

The keys for the ends are a basic triangle. It is "man on," "near back," and "pulling lineman." They want to get off on the snap of the ball and penetrate one or two yards into the backfield and react to the play.

Let me cover the reactions to the ends position. The ends are C-gap players. They have quarterback responsibility depending on blocking schemes. They have containment responsibility on pass plays.

On the backside end if the tackle blocks out on him the end would attack him in the V of the neck. He wants to keep his outside arm free and squeeze the play as much as he can. He has the C gap on that side.

If the offensive tackle blocks down inside, our defensive end comes off the tackle's butt and comes down the line on the bend. He becomes a spill player on the next blocker that comes to him. Some coaches call this technique a "wrong arm" move. We do not wrong arm the play; we spill it. He is underneath the next blocker that comes to him. He wants to make the ball bounce north and south rather than east and west.

Our 7-technique end is keying the tight end to the near back to the pulling linemen. When he attacks, he wants to keep the inside arm free. He controls the C gap. If the tight end comes off the

ball and does not block on the defensive end, he comes off the butt of the offensive tackle to the football. He is looking for his next key on the play.

The two inside players, the nose and the tackle, have a different progression on their keys. This is especially true for the tackle, or the 3 technique. Their keys are man on, to backside lineman, to near back. The reason we do that because of what happens on the trap play. The man the offense traps is the tackle. If the man in front of him pulls, the tackle looks to his next read, which is the near back. If he steps up to take on the near back, he gets earholed from the side. Because of that, we changed his keys. When the offensive man disappears, the next key for the tackle is the backside lineman. Now he can see the backside lineman coming and he can prevent the trap.

If he does not get the trap blocker, now he can look at the nearest back. He takes on the next blocker and he is a spill player. On the spill technique, we try to get underneath the defender but we try to get back upfield on the play after we take on the blocker. We want him to bounce the ball east and west.

On double-team blocks against him, the 3-technique tackle is to try to split the double-team block. As he turns, if he feels he is getting through the double-team, he will continue through the double-team. If he feels he is being moved back or he starts to lose ground, we want him to do what we call "sit on the bar stool." He starts to go down. There is s difference in getting down and starting to go down. We do not want to go to the ground and cause the "pile up" there. What happens now is this. When you start to go down on the roll, the offensive tackle comes off the block and goes to the next level. That leaves the guard to fall on top of the tackle, so we sit on the barstool. As we start to sit down on the bar stool, as we go down if we feel the blocker leaving us, we try to come back up into the gap. If the tackle goes down with us, we keep going down. As we go down, we continue to hold on to the guard. We must have that guard under control and have him locked on us.

The same is true with the nose tackle. He tries to split the double-team blocks. If he cannot split the double-team, he "sits on the barstool." He does not want to give up too early. As a last resort, he wants to create the pile at the line of scrimmage.

The Mike backers lines up four-and-one-half to five yards deep. The Mike is in a 30, or a 3 shade alignment. His key is the lineman. He has to be aware of both linemen. He is looking through the linemen to the I-back tandem. His main responsibility is the B gap. He is aware of what the backs are doing and what those linemen are doing. If we get what we call an open window, with the tackle blocking out and the guard blocking down and the back is coming at the linebacker, he must attack that back. He will see this on the isolation play. They have both backs coming downhill and we want him to attack that look as deep as he can in the backfield. By being back four-and-one-half to five yards deep, he can see what is going on upfront.

The backer is stacked in a 3 technique behind the tackle. His gap responsibility on run toward him is the A gap. He is more of a scrape player. You can see the B gap and the C gap is covered. He is in a position if the window opens in front of he attacks the backs coming downhill.

The other term we use is "window closed." This happens when the offensive tackle blocks down on the line of scrimmage. The defensive end closes down and takes the B gap and the backer scrapes and covers the C gap. This comes into play mostly on options. The tackle takes the dive man and the backer scrapes to the quarterback. If the offense blocks out on the end, the end will take the quarterback on the option and the backer takes the dive play. The linebackers must see through those offensive linemen into the backfield to see the action of the offense.

Our linebackers are Fast Flow player. We do not want to slow them down. The Will linebacker is the cutback player and the Mike linebacker must get over the top on the Isolation play.

Our whip and rover line up as our strong safety would line up. They line up in a four-by-four alignment. They are four yards outside the last man on the line of scrimmage and they are four yards deep. The keys are the end man on the line of scrimmage, the near back, and the pulling linemen. It is the basic triangle key for them. They read their keys and react accordingly.

To the strongside of the formation, the rover has what we call "sky" support. The rover is the primary run support on that side. He keeps the outside arm free and turns everything back inside. He attacks the ball outside to inside.

The whip has easy support on his side of the line. He is forcing everything from the outside to the inside. On run away both the rover and whip are fold players. That is why we can allow the linebackers to be fast flow players. When the linebackers check the inside on the isolation the whip and rover shuffle inside and check the B gap looking for the cutback play.

Next, we look at the corners. In our G-defense, which is our base defense, we call it our cover 1. Cover 1 is a robber coverage. Depending on the formation and the play, we could end up with nine defenders around the football. Our corners will start at eight yards. At the snap of the ball, they back up to ten yards deep and two yards inside the outside receivers. We move them back ten-by-two. They are what we call inverted one-half players. They are playing half the field from an inverted position. It is important not to get the two deep players inside more than two yards inside the wide receivers. The reason we want them inside is to protect against the post route. We emphasize protecting against the post routes. In our cover 2, we have someone outside bumping the wide receiver on his release. On this coverage, we do not have anyone outside to slow those receivers down. They are playing pass first and secondary run support. If he gets a run to his side, he must check the play-action pass first. Then he is the secondary support player. He is the last man in pursuit.

Our free safety lines up over the strongside guard seven to ten yards deep depending on how fast he is and how fast he can read the play. He can become our ninth man against a base set. Our backer takes on the fullback on the Isolation play. If the Mike does not get over to check the play, the free safety is the next man to check the isolation play. On an inside run, he fills where needed. On the outside play, he is an alley player to both sides of the field. That is our G-defense.

Cover 1 is a robber coverage. First, I will talk about the free safety. His reads are as follows. Once he reads pass, his eyes should go to the number-two receiver. In this case, it is the tight end (Diagram #4). If the tight end is on a vertical release at ten yards, the free safety is going to play him man-to-man. He has the tight end all over the field. If the tight end runs a drag route or a flat route, the free safety becomes a robber player.

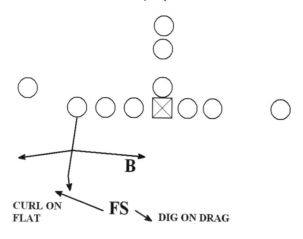

Diagram #4

His first look is to the side where the tight end is dragging. He is looking for the tight end on the dig route. If he does not run the dig route, the free safety looks to the backside for the dig coming from the backside. We allow him to sit in the hole and rob the dig from either side. His first look is always where the number-two receiver is going and then he looks to the backside. When he sees the drag route is not coming in his area, he can look for the play underneath and help where needed.

If the tight end goes outside, he applies the same principle. He looks to the frontside first. If the receiver is running a curl route, the free safety will rob the curl. If the receiver runs a dig route, he will rob the dig route. He will rob any inside route coming inside.

If the number-one receiver stays outside, he stays inside and looks for any crossing route or dig route coming from the backside.

We have talked about the corners. They are responsible for the inverted one-half of the field. If the wide receivers take off straight down the field, the corners cover them man-to-man.

Against the dig route the corner "rolls to the post" area. He does not follow the receiver inside on the dig route. He rolls to the post area to help on the backside.

Our whip and rover are curl to flat players. We say they are robber players underneath the wide receivers (Diagram #5). They will buzz to get underneath those wide receivers. Teams like to run the corner route on us. We buzz to get underneath the outside receivers in what we call "match 1." On the snap of the ball, they take a read step and if they read pass they are opening up and driving to the outside area to get underneath the number one receiver outside.

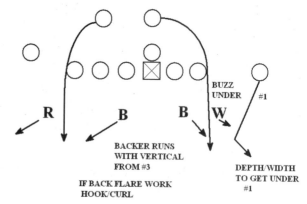

Diagram #5

If the outside receiver runs a deep corner route, the whip is running to get depth to get underneath the outside receiver. If he is running an out route, he is running to get underneath the receiver. Both the rover and the whip are matching number one. They are also responsible for the wheel route. They are keeping their eyes on the quarterback.

The linebackers drop curl-hook. They work off the remaining receiver or the back out of the backfield. They work off the number-three receiver. They drop short on the hook-curl route. If the third receiver runs deep, the backer stays with him on the deep route. This is why the corners do not have to worry about the inside vertical routes. They know someone will be running with the inside receivers.

If the back flares outside, the backer takes his normal drop hook-to-curl drop. It is the same thing for the Mike. He works off number two, which is the back here. If number two goes vertical, the Mike is going to run with him. If the number-two receiver runs to the flat, Mike drops to his hook-to-curl area.

I want to cover the alignment against the twins set. We still set our front to the strength, which is to the tight end. They still have two backs in the backfield (Diagram #6). The backer goes to the passing strength. We give a "bump" call. This tells the whip to move into a stack-9 alignment. The Mike moves over to a 10 alignment. Our backer cheats over to a 40 alignment.

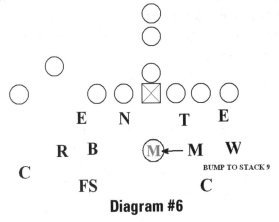

Diagram #6

Our corner on the backside is only eight yards deep. He lines up opposite the whip. If the whip is inside, he lines up outside; if the whip is outside, he lines up inside. He becomes the eighth man in the scheme. We cheat the linebackers over on the bump call and they are reading and reacting as they read their key.

On the backside, we have read support. The read support tells the whip and the corner they are reading the block of the tight end. If the tight end blocks down, the whip will spill the next man to show. The corner plays the force. Let me go back to the option responsibility. If the tight end blocks down on our 7 technique, the whip plays the quarterback, and the corner comes up and plays the

pitch. The backers are scraping looking for the dive to the quarterback to the pitch. This is a good defense to stop the run because we have eight players in the box. The corner can read and become the ninth man in the box on the run against a two-back formation.

Let me show you how we would line up against two tight ends. We take the front and the strength to the two-receiver side (Diagram #7). One important point about the nose and tackle positions is that we do not flip-flop the two positions. They play on one side of the ball or the other. They have to learn to play both techniques. With two tight ends, we have a hot call. Now we want to slide the Mike to the weakside.

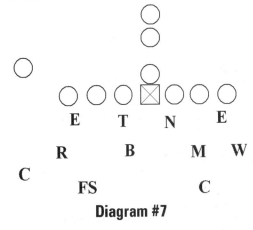

Diagram #7

I want to talk about some of the stunts we run to help our run game. First is our tag stunt (Diagram #8). If we face a team running several trap plays and the tackle is having problems getting underneath the block, we run our Tag stunt. The tackle slants into the A-gap. His keys are the same as before. He reads the guard to the backside lineman. If the guard disappears, he looks for the backside lineman. Now it is easier for him to get underneath the trap block.

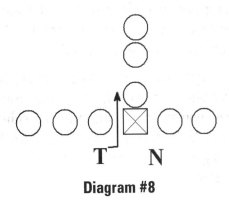

Diagram #8

On the stem, we line up opposite the call. If the linebacker calls "right", the nose and tackle line up left. Just before the snap of the ball, they move over to their normal position. We use the stem when we know the quarterback is checking off to the bubble (Diagram #9). You can have the tackle and nose move on their own or you can have the linebackers move them. We step from one alignment to another to throw the quarterback off if the quarterback is trying to run to the bubble. That is our step stunt.

Diagram #9

Another stunt we run is echo. On stem, we move before the snap of the ball. On echo, we move on the snap of the ball. If we call a "right" call and add the call echo, they line up in a left call. On the snap of the ball, they echo back to their regular position for the "right" call. You can slant to the positions or you can side step to the technique.

If we are getting over split with the tight end, we call spark (Diagram #10). That is a call for the defensive end that allows him to move a 5 technique on the snap of the ball. This allows the end to play the tackle instead of the tight end.

Diagram #10. Spark

If we call evil, we run the backside end inside to the B gap (Diagram #11). We want to protect the B gap. We run this stunt from the boundary. We do not call evil in the middle of the field. He can slant or he can step aside and hit the B gap attacking the football. Evil is good against the cutback play.

One of the best stunts we run is our psycho (Diagram #12). Everyone pinches inside. The rover and whip are the contain players. The linebackers are the

C-gap players. We use this stunt in short-yardage situations. We can play man coverage or we can play zone coverage when we call psycho. We play our zone coverage behind it most of the time.

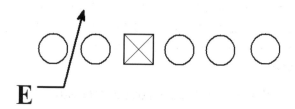

Diagram #11. Evil

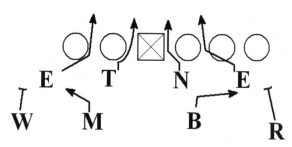

Diagram #12. Psycho

Let me cover a couple of blitzes out of our G-package. The first blitz is our double crash (Diagram #13). We are sending the rover and whip off the edge. With double crash, we are in man coverage. The corners have the number-one man outside. The safeties have the number-two man to the strength of the passing formation. The linebackers have the backs remaining in the backfield. This is a run blitz. We are going to fill up the gaps.

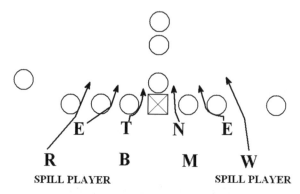

Diagram #13. Double crash

The rover comes up and goes through the C gap. The whip is coming through the C gap on the weakside. What makes this call unique is the fact that the Will and rover are spill players. They must get underneath any blocker that comes to them as they blitz. It does not matter if it is a pulling lineman or a back, he is getting underneath the man. They are bending and spilling everything. The rover must read the tight end as he makes his blitz. If the tight end blocks down, he does not try to get underneath the block. He comes off the tight ends butt to get into the C gap. We do not want him blocked down inside.

If the tight end blocks out on the play, the rover will take on the tight end. He forces the ball to bounce outside on the play.

The linebackers have to play support. If the offense runs an option play, the linebackers become the pitch players. They have to be able to get outside on the option. When we go double crash, the linebackers are in a C-split alignment. They line up wide. They want to get wide so prevent a cut off by the tight end.

If the offense does attempt a pass when we run the double crash the tackles become "hands" players. They come out and they are play a late contain technique. If the quarterback starts to scramble, we have someone that can contain him with our hands players.

The other blitz we run is our double blitz. Now, the end and the whip, and the end and the rover are changing responsibilities (Diagram #14). The end goes upfield and the whip and rover go inside.

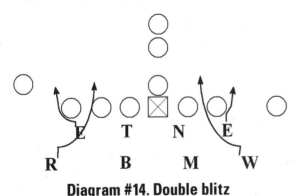

Diagram #14. Double blitz

This is a good change-up for the option. It is a good defense against the bootleg and naked plays.

Our "tuff" defense is our Bear befense (Diagram #15). We try to have two 3 techniques and a nose tackle upfront. We want to cover up those inside

players. We put a linebacker on the tight end. We are playing is man coverage in this look. Most times, we play man-free out of this look.

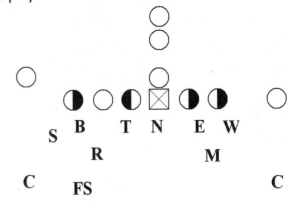

Diagram #15. Bear defense

This is our short-yardage defense. It is a solid run defense because of the gap controls. We move in and out of this defense. We line up in our G-package and shift to the tuff alignment (Diagram #16). When our linebacker calls "move", we move to the tuff alignment. We move away from the whip. The line shifts over and the backer moves up inside on the tight end. The rover moves over to the linebacker's spot.

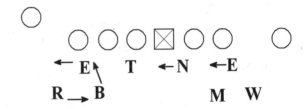

Diagram #16. Move from G to tuff

Now we can move back into our G-alignment. We can move from our G-alignment to our tuff look. We can go from our tuff alignment to our G-look. This gives up an opportunity to dictate to the offense what they can run against our defense.

When we check to our tuff alignment, the first thing most teams do is to check to the option play. We come out, align in our tuff set, and then shift back into our G-alignment. Now we have the offense running the option back into our G-package. If we get motion by any of the backs, the rover takes him.

NEW!

2005
COACH OF THE
YEAR CLINICS
Football Manual

Featuring lectures from several of America's most renowned coaches. Edited by Earl Browning.

$24.95 • 288 pages • 1-58518-932-4

Also available:

1999	2000	2001	2002	2003	2004

1-58518-154-4	1-58518-298-2	1-58518-485-3	1-58518-644-9	1-58518-856-5	1-58518-896-4
271 pp. • $24.95	288 pp. • $24.95	272 pp. • $24.95	288 pp. • $24.95	288 pp. • $24.95	280 pp. • $24.95